alumnus Old

Records and Recollections of St. Cuthbert's College, Ushaw

With Introductory Poem ...

alumnus Old

Records and Recollections of St. Cuthbert's College, Ushaw
With Introductory Poem ...

ISBN/EAN: 9783744764247

Printed in Europe, USA, Canada, Australia, Japan

Cover: Foto ©ninafisch / pixelio.de

More available books at **www.hansebooks.com**

RECORDS AND RECOLLECTIONS

OF

St. Cuthbert's College,

USHAW;

WITH

INTRODUCTORY POEM,

To which are appended copious Illustrative, Historical, and Descriptive Notes.

BY

AN OLD ALUMNUS.

Stet fortuna domus, durando sæcula vincat.

PRESTON:
E. BULLER AND SON, 42, FISHERGATE.
1880.

[All Rights reserved.]

TO THE

PRESIDENT, PROFESSORS, MASTERS, AND
STUDENTS ;

TO THE

ALUMNI AND FRIENDS

OF ST. CUTHBERT'S COLLEGE, USHAW,

THESE "RECORDS AND RECOLLECTIONS" ARE RESPECTFULLY
AND AFFECTIONATELY DEDICATED.

" J'offre ce petit volume : le désire de rendre hommage à ce que j'aime, à ce que j'admire, a fait courir ma plume."

PREFACE.

Seated one winter evening in the quiet retreat of my study—

"My wee bit ingle blinkin' bonnilie,"

and recalling to mind the days of old, the thought occurred to me, as I cast my eyes on two coloured views of Ushaw College, *viz.* south-east, and north-west views, both painted by J. Ramsay, and engraved by C. Turner; and on the portraits respectively of venerated President Gillow, and the renowned historian Dr. Lingard, which adorn my study walls, that it would be an interesting task to record in verse my reminiscences of St. Cuthbert's College, and collect together whatever fragments I was able of the ancient memories and traditions appertaining to it. Such a record would tend to serve a useful purpose in helping to keep these traditions alive, and preventing them from becoming in the lapse of years entirely obliterated. But on account of the multitude of matter, and the wide scope of the subject, I found I had undertaken no easy task, "yea rather a business full of watching and sweat." For not having time, nor skill, nor genius sufficiently Homeric, to write an epic in verse, and to include and group therein the various names of persons, places, things, dates, &c., which would necessarily have to be introduced, I resolved, although, as Byron writes,

"There is a pleasure in poetic pains,
Which poets only know—"

to disengage myself from the trammels of verse, and to continue my narrative in sober, homely prose, adding in an appendix at the end of the Poem a number of historical and descriptive notes relating to Ushaw, to places in the neighbourhood, to notable persons, events, occurrences, memorials of the past, and divers other interesting matters. These notes constitute what may be considered the main portion, and embody the principal details of my little book :—

"*Hæc nostri est farrago libelli.*"

Unable to devote unremitting and continuous attention to the work, it has been composed at irregular periods of time; in intervals of business, "in the aftermath of life," uncertain health, and the infirmities of old age. Hence whatever errors, faults, and omissions it may contain, I beseech my kind Ushaw friends and gentle readers not to censure or criticise them too harshly or severely.

"Let the above be enough in the way of a preface, for it is a foolish thing to make a long prologue, and to be short in the story itself."

January, 1889.

CONTENTS.

INTRODUCTORY POEM..	5
In which divers matters there briefly introduced are more amply and fully treated of in the	

APPENDIX.

ST. CUTHBERT, Patron of the College of Ushaw; brief record of his life and labours...	41
DURHAM—the fair and venerable City	42
ST. GODRIC AND FINCHALE	50
NEVILLE'S CROSS	52
BEAUREPAIRE (OR BEAREPARK)	53
LANGLEY HALL..	54
LANCHESTER and the Roman Station	54
BRANCEPETH CASTLE...	55
ESH OR ASH	55
WATERHOUSES AND FR. ASHMALL	56
NEWHOUSE AND ESH LAUDE...	57
CHURCH OF OUR LADY, QUEEN OF MARTYRS	58
FR. BOSTE, THE MARTYR, one "of the gravest Priests of the North"..	58
USHAW COLLEGE—Historical Records and Memorials............	61
THE FRENCH REVOLUTION	62
DOUAI COLLEGE—its Seizure and Suppression; Dispersion and Imprisonment of its Students......................................	62
CARDINAL ALLEN	64
FOUNDATION AND ESTABLISHMENT OF USHAW..................	67
CROOK HALL—College of; Rev. Thomas Eyre appointed President	70
BISHOP WILLIAM GIBSON..	73
JOHN LINGARD, D.D...	74
NOTES AND EXTRACTS REGARDING USHAW COLLEGE, FROM ORIGINAL LETTERS, &c	82

Rev. Anthony Lund and Ushaw College	89
Subscriptions remitted by him towards Building the College	91
The Exodus from Crook Hall to Ushaw	97
Verses (original) on the Old Ushaw Yew	100
List of Cardinals, Archbishops, and Bishops—Alumni of Ushaw	104
Cardinal Wiseman	106
Cardinal Ferdinand de la Puente	111
Archbishop Errington	112
,, Eyre	115
Bishop Briggs	118
,, Brown	118
,, Sharples	119
,, Hogarth	120
,, Grant	121
,, Turner	123
,, Roskell	124
,, Goss	124
,, Cornthwaite	126
,, Chadwick	127
,, O'Reilly	131
,, Angus Macdonald	139
,, Lacy	142
,, Riddell	143
,, Bewick	149
,, Larkin (Bishop of Toronto)	153
Rev. John Gillow, D.D., President	155
Rev. Thomas Youens, D.D.	166
Right Rev. Monsignor Charles Newsham, D.D.,—Divers improvements and changes effected; important works and undertakings accomplished by him	167
Monsignor Newsham's Jubilee	178
St. Cuthbert's Society	187
Very Rev. Michael Trappes	189
Memoir of the Very Rev. Dr. Gibson, Vice-President	191
Broomehall and Rev. Thomas Carr, *alias* Myles Pinkney	194
Celebration of the College Jubilee	198

DEATH OF DR. NEWSHAM	204
RIGHT REV. MONSIGNOR TATE, D.D.	206
VISIT TO USHAW OF CARDINAL REISACH	208
DR. TATE'S GOLDEN JUBILEE	211
,, ,, Jubilee Memorial Window	213
,, ,, Extracts from Letters	219
,, ,, Edifying Death	231
REV. ANDREW MACARTNEY	232
JOHN CANON WALKER, SENR	233
PROVOST PLATT, D.D.	235
VERSES "In Memoriam"	240
RECOVERY OF DOUAI PLATE	241
VERY REV. FRANCIS WILKINSON, D.D	244
RIGHT REV. MONSIGNOR WRENNALL, D.D.	247
WILLIAM CANON DUNDERDALE	249
VERY REV. JAMES LENNON, D.D.	252
DEATH OF BISHOP BEWICK	256
DEATH OF PROVOST CONSITT	256
RIGHT REV. MONSIGNOR O'CALLAGHAN, D.D., appointed Bishop of Hexham and Newcastle	260
VICE-PRESIDENTS	262
PROVOST COOKSON—Vice-President; Fernyhalgh and "Our Lady's Well"	263
REV. JOHN GILLOW, D.D., Vice-President	266
PROCURATORS	269
GENERAL PREFECTS OF CROOK AND USHAW	272
VERY REV. RICHARD GILLOW —a virtuous and learned Priest, Professor at Ushaw, subsequently Canon of the Diocesan Chapter of Liverpool	277
ATTACHMENT OF USHAW STUDENTS TO THEIR ALMA MATER— "The noble College of St. Cuthbert."	280
ODE TO USHAW	283
VISIT OF CARDINAL MANNING TO USHAW: Address presented to him; the Cardinal's reply	284
SIXTY YEARS AGO	287
GREAT MEN AND DISTINGUISHED ECCLESIASTICS	288
USHAW DESERVING OF A VISIT	290

THE CEMETERY	293
EXHIBITION WEEK	295
USHAW COLLEGE AND THE LONDON UNIVERSITY	296
DEVOTION TO THE CHAIR OF PETER	297
UNDER A PASSING CLOUD	298
RELICS OF JOY	299
CORNSAY AND CORNSAY DAYS	300
PRIESTS FROM LANCASHIRE AND THE FYLDE DISTRICT	303
THE REV. JOHN CARTER	304
THE NEW COLLEGE CHAPEL OF ST. CUTHBERT	305
BISHOP BEWICK APPEALS FOR CONTRIBUTIONS TOWARDS ITS ERECTION	309
SOLEMN OPENING OF	312
FEAST OF THE ENGLISH MARTYRS	318
BISHOP O'CALLAGHAN VISITS USHAW : receives a cordial and affectionate welcome	321
PROVOST WILKINSON : his appointment and consecration as Bishop Auxiliary	322
NORTHUMBERLAND AS DESCRIBED BY FROISSART	325
MINOR INCIDENTS, EVENTS, AND USAGES	326
LONDON UNIVERSITY MATRICULATION EXAMINATIONS : Ushaw again pre-eminently successful	326
CONCLUSION	328
ADIEU	328

ADDENDA.

AN ODE ON PATIENCE, by Dr. Lingard	331
COURSE OF STUDIES AT USHAW	332
"OUR COLLEGE HOME AND HOLIDAYS"	333

USHAW.

Illic "nutriri mihi contigit atque doceri."—

MY harp in silence, Ushaw, long has hung;
    Disordered, dusty, tuneless are its strings;
    But I would fain, before life's sun is set,
And night comes on, when man may no more work,
Once more refurbish and attune its chords,
That, though unskilled and rude my numbers be,
Thy name may mingle with my verse and song.

I loved thee, Ushaw, in my boyhood's days—
Those days (twelve summers had not o'er me passed,
And thou three lustrums had not counted yet,
Since first uprose thy massive, strong-built walls,)
When I, a rustic and unlettered boy,
But docile, with an aptitude to learn,
Within thy schools my studious course pursued;
Toilsome the tasks, but easier soon they grew;
Nor was I left behind those studious youths,
Who with me emulously strove to win
Such honours and rewards, as in those days
Awarded were, nor trivial deemed withal—
The honours of a "good lad's Cornsay Day."
No scholarships, no books, no medals then,
No University degree did crown our toil;
Not e'en an ivy wreath for us was twined.*

---

*Doctarum hederæ præmia frontium.—HOR.

Time on its course rolled on ; those whom of yore
I knew in boyhood—most have passed away ;—
Few, few remain of bygone days to tell,
Or memories and traditions to record,
Belonging to the history of thy past,
And clustering round thee thick as grapes on vine.
Playmates and friends have gone, and I,
As leaf falls after leaf from off the tree,
Shall have my turn to fall. The snows of age
Have drifted round me, and the gloaming shades
Of life's decline, like spectres, haunt my path ;
But though enfeebled by the weight of years,
Already having passed three score and ten—
The solemn epoch of an old man's life—
My heart still to thee—Alma Mater—clings.
I love to speak, in terms of eulogy,
Of what thou wert in the good olden times ;
To hear from others of a younger race
What academic laurels thou hast won
In these more recent days, and how thy sons
Have borne their honours meekly, without boast,
But giving thanks with all humility,
To God and to St. Cuthbert have referred
Whatever meed of merit they obtained.

" Change permeates creation ;" on this earth
Nothing is stable or enduring long :—
And thou, dear Alma Mater, thou hast seen
Mutations various of times and scenes ;
Seen generations come, and others go ;
Kingdoms and empires fall ; the Church alone
Unchanged, and blossoming, in this our land,
Like vernal flowers that uprise from the earth,
When winter's chilling frosts have disappeared.

In Northern clime, and on a tract of land,
Where scarce a trace of cultivation showed ;—
A stony, stubborn soil, whereon there grew

Nor green-leafed shrub, nor stately branching tree,
Save one old, solitary, sable yew
That nobly had withstood, time out of mind,
The tempest's shock, and winter's storms and blasts;—
Where homes of men were sparse and few, and where
A farmstead rarely, or a rustic grange
Appeared in sight on roadside or in field, .
Were dug and laid, with measure broad and deep,
Foundations of a structure that arose,
Like to "the shadow of a mighty rock,
In barren land," and which in lapse of years
Religion would diffuse, and knowledge spread,
And foster piety and zeal in those,
Who would in after-times frequent its schools,
Their thirst to satiate at learning's font.
But hallowed was the ground, and portion formed
Of that which was St. Cuthbert's patrimony—
That holy man, who fed the sheep and lambs
Of Christ, among Northumbria's hills and vales,
And ruled with gentle and paternal sway
"In Lindisfarne, Chief Bishop of the North."
The Lowland peasant, orphan shepherd boy,
The saintly Monk of Melrose, who became,
And was twelve years, Prior of Lindisfarne;
Then next the Bishop of that See—the sixth
From Aidan in succession. From the rude
And rock-encompassed solitude of Farne,
Where he abode, having companions none,
Save the wild fowl and sea birds of that isle,
The Saint was called to rule, as Bishop o'er
Northumbria's dual realms—Bernicia
And Dëira. A worthy Bishop he,
Who vigilantly and with tender care
Guarded his flock from danger and from ill;
Whose jurisdiction o'er a wide and wild
Extent of country ranged. The vales of Tyne,
Tees, Wear, and Eden, unto Humber's shores,
Were subject to him, and the cloud-capp'd heights

Of Skiddaw, and Helvellyn, and Crosfell,
To his authority in reverence bowed.
Egfrid, Northumbria's king, most dearly loved
St. Cuthbert, and 'mong other grants of land
The land of Cartmell he unto him gave,
And all those Britons who did therein dwell.
Where'er his footsteps trod—on heathery moor,
'Mong sheepwalks on hill sides, in woodland glades,—
The people in great numbers round him flocked,
To be instructed, baptized, and confirmed,
To all of whom he spoke sweet words of peace.
And not unfrequently in parables
He spoke ; for parables they asked to hear.

Looming in hazy distance, might be seen
The lofty towers of that majestic fane,
Erected on the wooded banks of Wear,
And justly deemed the glory and the pride
Of Durham, city of the seven hills ;—
" Cathedral huge and vast," wherein enshrined
Saint Cuthbert's body incorrupt reposed,
Receiving reverence and homage due
From those who came to worship at his shrine.
Not far off stood, in ruins, the old walls
Of Beaurepaire. At distance more remote,
Where holy Godric fixed his hermit cell,
Was Finchale, in a lone sequestered dale.
Beyond the neighbouring hill, concealed from view,
In massive grandeur Brancepeth Castle towered,
Where erst the Nevilles dwelt in feudal pride.
To the far west, and down the valley lay
Lanchester, site of ancient Roman camp,
Traces of which may be distinguished yet,
Telling of times when Britain prostrate lay
At the proud feet of Roman conqueror.
Such was the neighbourhood, and such the site
Of the projected College, to be built
At Ushaw, and St. Cuthbert's College named.

Of the new College, and the old yew tree,
Which unto "Ushaw" gave its honour'd name.
Rejoicing on their way the pilgrims went,
Each heart with hope and gladness surcharged.
Not more exuberant and intense the joy
Of those brave heroes, the ten thousand Greeks,
Who fought and conquered on Cunaxa's plain ;
But to retreat compelled, along the banks
Of Tigris they pursued their march, and thence
Amid snows of Armenia, and the crags
Of lofty Caucasus, wherefrom they first
Descried in distance dim, the Euxine Sea ;
And cheering at the sight each other on,
They shouted with glad voice—"The sea, the sea !"

It was a vision of delight, for here
Their life's young days would flow in tranquil stream,
Unruffled by the turmoil of the world ;
Calm and serene their souls, no cloud to break
Their peaceful and perpetual repose.
Thrice blessed lot, thrice glad and happy hearts !
Well might they, upon entering their new home,
Exclaim in all the fulness of their joy,—
"Here is our resting place ; here we will dwell ;
This is the habitation which we choose ;
Here centred are our hopes ; here shall we pass
In studious pursuits, our youthful days,
Amassing wisdom's golden stores, and then
Go forth announcing to an erring world
The message of redemption, peace and love ;
And beautiful the feet of those who preach
Upon the mountains, or in crowded streets,
The gospel's tidings, and all-saving truths."

Peace to this house, to all who dwell therein ;
Peace in its borders, and in all its lands,
From Derness to the Brun.
                The flocks and herds
That range its fields may nothing evil touch ;

In all its confines may perpetual peace,
While sun and moon endure, abound, and crown
With ever blooming olive all its gates.
Ushaw, great and illustrious names are thine;
Not for the feats of arms on battle field,
But for their battles in defence of faith,
And holy Church, and for their zeal for souls,
For which they laboured with incessant toil.
Cardinals, Archbishops, Bishops, and Priests—
Priests learned, self-denying, who proclaimed
The truth to men, and spread the light of faith,
Which in this land had well nigh grown extinct.
The holy and unspotted lives of such
Have earned praise upon earth, and crowns in heaven.
In the hierarchic galaxy of names,
Transcendent in renown and lustre shine—
A constellation glorious and bright,
Set in the firmament of holy Church,—
Wiseman, Puente, Lingard, Newsham, Tate,
Archbishop Eyre, and Angus of the "Isles,"
Goss, mighty Pontiff, and the saintly Grant,
Cornthwaite and Lacy, Yorkshire prelates both,
And Arthur of Northampton. Bernard too,
Right worthy Bishop—worthy mention claims—
Bernard who holds the See of Liverpool,
Whose pastoral authority extends
From Mersey, over Ribble, unto Lune;
Who, that a continuity of priests
Might educated be, at no small cost,
Noble in its proportions and design,
Has built a College, whose foundations are
Among the bleak and stony hills; whereof
His Alma Mater, Ushaw, has supplied
The model and the plan; and if you seek
In after-times a monument of zeal,
Foresight, and labour, on the Bishop's part,
A visit to St. Joseph's College pay.—
Nor from the roll of classic, renowned names

Omitted be the name of Provost Platt,*
That scholar ripe, who to me was endeared
By ties of steadfast friendship, which endured
From boyhood's days unto declining age ;
Nor Youens, Gibson, Gillow, each of whom
Commenced their intellectual toil in thy retreats,
And rank pre-eminently as men of mark.—
Friend of my youth, and of my riper years,
Dear Bishop Chadwick, most devoted son
Of Alma Mater, his much honoured name
Deserves to be enshrined in golden verse,
And by affection tenderly embalmed,
That it may never from remembrance fade.—
That kind, benignant heart has ceased to beat ;
The prelate whom all reverenced and loved ;
Who watched his flock with all a shepherd's care ;
Of whom most justly Ushaw may be proud,
And his departure with deep sorrow mourn,
Has been called home, and here, alas ! his place
On earth, by men is now no longer known.
Bring flowers to deck his grave ; he sleeps hard by
The grave yard cross—God rest his soul in peace !
The venerable yew, of which his muse
In playful numbers sang, shall cease to be,
But as a palm tree, or a cedar tall
His memory shall flourish, and be held
In reverence for ages still unborn.
And who is he—true Northman, who succeeds
Unto St. Cuthbert and St. Wilfrid's See?
Another worthy son of Ushaw,† deemed
Most worthy of the mitre which he wears ;
Long may he wear it, and with health be blessed,
And length of days.   In virtue and in grace
May he abound, and unto pastures fair,

---

*Cognatus mihi erat ; una a pueris parvolis
Sumus educati.—TERENCE ADELPH. III., 4.
Dr. Platt was well versed in the Greek and Latin tongues—"doctus sermones utriusque linguae"—and skilled alike in secular and ecclesiastical learning.
He died February 4th, 1874, at Dodding Green, aged 62 ; and his remains there rest among the bowers he loved so well, among the trees he planted.
†Bishop Bewick.

And sweetly flowing streams conduct his flock,
And fold them on the everlasting hills.

Speed on your course, ye cycles of the years !
Seasons speed on ! may God speed Ushaw too !
Praise to Him be, Who wondrous things has done
In its regard, exalting high its horn.
As from the puny acorn grows the oak,
Deep-rooted, and with branches towering high ;
As from a tiny rill, hid in recess
Of some deep glen, the river takes its rise,
And sweeps along its course unto the sea,
So Ushaw from beginnings small, became,
In lapse of years, a College, whose renown
Grew with its growth ; and unto its retreats
Flocked studious youths from near and distant parts,
Their intellectual culture to pursue.

"I look, and lo ! the former scene is changed :"
Sterile and bleak, as stated, was the soil
Of those broad acres, that a portion used
To form of Esh demesne, and which the lord
Of that old manor, good Sir Edward Smythe
Ceded and sold, that thereon might be built
The College, which, like watch tower on the hill,
Conspicuous stands—a noble monument,
With device on its banner and its shield
Inscribed—" Durando sæcula vincit."
Its cords how are they lengthened, and its stakes
How strengthened mightly on every side !
All round a goodly prospect meets the eye :—
Meadows brimful of clover and of grass,
Pastures with herbage saturate, where graze
Fat kine, sleek heifers, flocks of lambs and sheep ;
Orchards and gardens with rich fruitage stored,
Fields with their golden harvests all aglow,
Woods and plantations that diffuse their shade,
O'er places where sterility once reigned ;
Farm yards and granges with abundance filled :—
Thus good has God to Alma Mater been.

What is the next "departure" that we note,
What further change and progress, in its course,
Does time evolve, as year succeeds to year,
At Ushaw? What does history record
Of the mutations, and improvements made?
Stay, let us pause, and contemplate awhile
The little chapel with its altars three,
Where, when a boy, morn, noon, and eventide,
I knelt and prayed, and heard the daily mass;
No trace of decoration on its walls,
Save painting of the Crucifixion placed
Behind high altar, and which fresco-like
Appeared to those who from a distance gazed:
This humble chapel which no statue graced
Of sculptured Saint, or the Madonna mild,
Was turned to other uses, and transformed
Into a spacious academic hall.
Appointed to the Presidential chair
Was one, whose years in College had been spent
From early youth to manhood's graver age;
A man whose life was hidden and retired,
Devoted much to study and to prayer,
With whom few intercourse had held,
And whom few knew, for rarely with the world
He came in contact, rather from it sought
Escape, as from a chilling north east wind.
Installed as President, with earnest zeal
He undertook its duties, and pursued
Boldly, as a swift runner does, his course.
His vigorous, and far-seeing mind conceived
Great projects :—these he nobly achieved,
And unto eminence St. Cuthbert's raised.
In place of the old chapel, most of all
He wished to raise an edifice—a church,
Faultless in plan, and beauty of design,
In all its parts and details well arranged,
And well proportioned as to form and size,
Where worship might more worthily be paid,

And homage rendered to the King of kings.
At length a church, most exquisitely fair,
Designed by Pugin's genius arose,
With altars, oratories, and screens adorned ;
Windows enriched and glowing with stained glass ;
Statues of patron and of other Saints ;
The Virgin Mother, and the Child divine,
Sculptured in marble pure and white as snow.
The church completed, other buildings next
Successive rose—a library well stored
With many thousand books, encased in shelves
Of cedar wood, in useful bindings all,
And all arrayed with classic skill and taste ;
Infirmary, museum, cloisters, halls,
Rooms set apart for study and for class ;
Refectory enlarged and beautified,
And ambulacra with art treasures dight ;
Extended play grounds, shrubberies, and walks ;
Farmstead, domestic buildings fitted up
With all appliances of modern date.

That fair and goodly structure which you see,
West side St. Cuthbert's, and graft-like appears
United to the old and parent stock,
Is "College of St. Aloysius" named—
Angelic Saint, Patron of virtuous youth.
Withdrawn from fostering, parental care,
Those of more tender years herein are reared,
And tended like young lambs ; then afterwards
Removed and folded with the older flock.
Unto their comfort all things minister ;—
Indulgent masters, lessons easy made,
Of play and study intermixture due ;
Music and sacred song, and prayer withal,
Which draws and elevates their souls to God.
The seminary chapel, where, each day,
These clients of St. Aloysius meet,
To tell their beads, or hear the holy Mass,

Is "neatly edified," enriched as well
With sculpture, painting, and the rainbow dyes
Of windows all ablaze with storied glass ;
Its statues, altars, tabernacles, all
Most beautiful and lovely to behold ;
So is the festal garniture of flowers
And plants, around and near the altars ranged,
In graceful beauty and variety.
Hail ! happy home, who would not be a boy,
Within thy sacred bowers in peace to dwell,
The days of childhood gliding into youth,
Like silver cloud across a summer's sky,
And childhood's prayers ascending unto God,
Like fragrant incense, or the breath of flowers.

Years sped their flight ; ten lustrums now had brought
The fiftieth year, the year of jubilee,
Which Alma Mater and her sons prepared
To celebrate with joyful, solemn feast :—
A glorious occasion, fifty years
Since from Crook Hall the exodus took place,
And the small colony a shelter found,
And home, beneath the aged yew tree's shade.
Unto this great solemnity there flocked
From length and breadth of "merrie England,"
From Scotland, and from Erin's emerald Isle,
Like Israel's tribes unto Jerusalem,
Men young and old, and men of middle age ;
Prelates; and dignitaries of the Church ;
Priests near and far, from village and from town ;
The owners of broad acres ; men in trade ;
And men "of light and leading," who all came,
To testify to Ushaw their regard,
To share its hospitality, and join
In the festivities, and general joy.

Say who is he yclad in purple robes,
Towards whom all eyes and looks respectful turn ;
Who in exalted orbit moves, and shines

Like glorious moon among less glorious stars ?
A Cardinal and Prince of holy Church,
Who Ushaw for his Alma Mater claims,
Whose name and praise are echoed in all lands,
In all the churches ; whose exalted rank
And singular endowments Ushaw may
Justly be proud of, honour, and extol.
He's come to grace the joyous festival ;
To lend a halo to its festive scenes,
And at performance of "The Hidden Gem,"
Which for the jubilee he kindly wrote,
To present be, and graciously preside.

England, my country ! once the Isle of Saints,
Watered with blood of martyrs and their tears,
Whilhom the dowry of sweet Mary named,
The restoration of thy hierarchy,
And exaltation of thy glorious church ;
The efflorescence of its "second spring,"
When "the lopped tree" put forth, the winter past,
Its leaves anew, and green, wide-spreading boughs,
And flowers once more adorned thy wintry land—
For all these boons to Wiseman grateful be.
The impious robbed thee of thy ancient faith ;
Like wild boars from the forest they rushed in,
And trampled down thy vineyard ; all its walls,
Its fences, and enclosures, they laid low,
And to an alien creed thy temples gave ;
Destroyed thy altars, and effaced thy shrines :—
An instrument in the Almighty's hands,
He helped to raise thy prostrate church, and make
Its dry bones live again, and prophesy.
Certes great priest and prelate in his day,
To God most pleasing, and beloved by men ;
The pride of Ushaw, pillar of the church ;
His mind enriched with learning, and endowed
With store of wisdom, as a mine with gold.

The banner of St. Cuthbert waved on high,
And wafted on the summer breeze were heard

The strains of music, and the shouts of joy,
For there were great rejoicings, "great to do"
At Ushaw, on the day of jubilee.
Each portal and each door was opened wide
To welcome and admit the numerous guests;
The entrance in front with wreaths of flowers
And evergreens was most profusely decked;
Over the doorway were inscribed the words,
Bold and conspicuous, "*Salvete vos*,"—
We bid you welcome and we greet you well;
May nothing harmful or vexatious here
Occur to mar your peacefulness and joy;
And may this jubilee, this fiftieth year,
An earnest be of success in the past,
And happy omen for the years to come.
Those entering this house will therefore pray
For its prosperity and good estate,
And in accord, with heart and voice exclaim—
"*Avete vos*"—all hail! and welcome all.
Friends, whom long years and distance had estranged,
Renewing old acquaintance met once more,
And from the depths of memory recalled,
With transports and with joy, the good old times.
I tarry not, nor linger, to describe
The banquet, and the feast, of which the guests
Most heartily and cheerfully partook;
Solemn *Te Deum*, and the grand High Mass;
The veneration of St. Cuthbert's ring,
Unto the College as an heirloom left,
And by the Cardinal on that day worn.
There, howbeit, is one to whom all hearts,
Sympathies and affections gravitate
As to a centre;— main, almost the sole
Remaining link in the extended chain
That bound the present generation to the past;—
With one accord the "Doctor" he was called;
And worthy was he of that honoured name,
For as a beacon, on a lofty hill,

His light, not hidden, was diffused around,
Enlight'ning all who came within his sphere :
Training and guiding them in virtue's way—
He above all pre-eminently deserves
To have his name chief in these records placed.
His praises sung in loftier verse than mine.

The year of jubilee draws to a close ;
The Doctor saw the day, and his glad heart
Rejoiced, but his own day was well nigh spent,
And of his labours and his works the term
Was fast approaching. Now dismiss, O Lord,
In peace, Thy servant. He has run his course ;
The good fight fought, and kept firm to the faith,
Transmitting it to others unimpared—
The heritage of martyrs and of saints.
Precious his death, for he had long before
His life and death to Mary's tender care
Entrusted, and invoked her loving aid ;
Thus dying, with Suarez he might say—
" I did not know it was so sweet to die."

To fill the office vacant by the death
Of the esteemed " old Doctor," had you sought
The northern counties, and eke England through,
A man more excellent, of greater mark,
Could not have been selected, or been found
Than the Right Rev. Prelate, Dr. Tate—
A presbyter of manners and of life
Approved ; a man of culture, and of books ;
Well read in holy Writ, whose sacred words
Of truth and wisdom, in his mind and heart
He kept enshrined, as gems of costly worth,
And jewels rare, in casket are enclosed.
Of manners courteous, dignified, and kind,
His friends a numerous circle round him formed ;
Brimful of classic, and patristic lore,
Amassed with studious diligence and toil,
He valued learning's treasures more than gold :

Conservative of what was great and good,
For ancient ways he tender reverence showed;
Scorned novelties, and all new fangled modes
Of thought and action, plausibly set forth.
Who more devoted in their love and zeal
For holy Church, the mystic spouse of Christ?
Who clung or held more firmly to the rock
Whereon t'is built—that rock—St. Peter's chair,
Abhorring heresy in every form
And phase; all errors and devices strange,
The vain delusions, and conceits of men?
He loved withal the beauty of God's house—
The temple where His glorious presence dwelt;
He loved the Church's hallowed liturgy,
Her ancient rites, feasts, and solemnities,
Her solemn chaunts, her antiphons, and hymns,
And gloried in her psalmody and song.
With what o'erflowing gladness and delight,
At Compline hour, devoutly in the church,
Would he intone, or join in that sweet strain,
Wherein our clement Mother is invoked
To guard us from the tempter's wiles and snares,
And to receive our souls at life's last hour.*
Holy his life, most glorious his death :—
Finding his end draw near, he prayed to be
Conducted into church, and like good priest,
Or pious monk of mediæval times,
When faith abounded, hope entranced men's souls
With visions of a bright and better world,
There with devoutest fervour to receive
The last anointing, and profess his faith
Before God's Altar, while his sorrowing friends,
The students and professors, knelt around.
Sweet Jesu! to his soul give peace and rest.
So, 'tis related of St. Kentigern,

---

*Maria, mater gratiæ,
Dulcis parens clementiæ,
Tu nos ab hoste protege,
Et mortis hora protege.

That in extreme old age, and at approach·
Of death, he round him his disciples called,
And to the keeping then commending them
And care of the most holy Trinity,
And to God's Mother, Mary ever blest,
Devoutly in their presence he received
The last consoling Sacraments of the Church ;
Then calmly rendered up his soul to God.

Long life to him who in St. Cuthbert's now
Holds chief authority. His gentle rule,
Experience and wisdom cannot fail
To win esteem and love, and make his name
'Mongst Presidential worthies to rank high.
The eldest of four brothers, all of whom,
Like fruitful olives in the house of God,
Were taught and trained at Ushaw from their youth,
In godliness, good learning, and withal,
In rev'rence for authority and rule ;
Offspring of parents, who to the faith
Had clung persistently in evil days,
And to their sons and daughters had bequeathed
The same great boon, and precious heritage ;
Of Lancashire descent—that land where flowed
The blood of martyrs in empurpled streams,
And where, with savage butchery employed,
Racks, ropes, and gibbets for the sufferers won
Imperishable and celestial crowns :—
" Time honour'd Lancaster," where ne'er extinct
Has been the lamp of faith ; whence priests,
In numerous succession, have gone forth
To labour in the vineyard, and their flocks
From heresy and error to preserve.
Under his mild, conservative regime,
May learning flourish, and the liberal arts ;*
May faith, and piety, and zeal for souls

---

*Artibus eminent semper, studiisque Minervæ.—VIDA.

Be more and more diffused, and holy Church,
Exalted be, and ever glorified ;
And may each year a race of priests go forth—
Men of unblemished, and unspotted lives,
Whose will is set upon the law of God,
And in whose hearts, inflamed as if with fire,
His love burns and consumes all worldly rust.

To those foundations that, in recent years,
Have been erected, to supply, and train
For their high office good and holy priests,
Sincerely do I wish prosperity,
And pray devoutly for their good estate :—
Not that I love these institutions less,
But Ushaw I love more.
      To it belongs
A history of well nigh four score years,
A hallowed, and a venerable name,
Matured traditions, and renowned prestige ;
Hence for all time, while age succeeds to age,
May Ushaw be with prosperous fortune crowned ;
May God's protection ever on it rest ;
Upon it may His sanctification
Flourish,* that so like to a goodly tree,
Abundant store of fruitage it may yield.
Nor ever favour at St. Cuthbert's find,
Nor countenance receive, the theories,
Specious and unsubstantial, of the school
Of modern philosophy ; and may ne'er
The love of classic lore, which has so long
Successfully distinguished Ushaw's sons,
Give place to the new learning :—and those loved
Old classic authors, with which day and night
We converse held, and which in life's young day,
And e'en in its decline, a solace were,
And of enjoyment a perpetual source—

---

*Super ipsum autem efflorebit sanctificatio mea.—Ps. cxxxi., 18.

Oh! cast them not aside; much less consign,
Unto the limbo of forgotten things,
Those ancient treasures, which the manners rude
Of nations and of peoples have refined
And humanized, in order to adopt
The superficial system of an age,
To change and novelty so greatly prone.
But, Ushaw, thou in the old beaten paths
Steadfast remain, not caring to pursue
The *ignes fatui* of the new lights;
Then shall thy fortune be safe and secure,
And nothing mar or tarnish thy fair fame.

God grant that Alma Mater's sons may ne'er
Degenerate from the high purposes,
Exalted aspirations, lofty thoughts
By which aright our fathers formed their lives,
And conduct ordered.
     Such the motto is
Characterizing the Society,
Composed of old Alumni, and of friends,
And named St. Cuthbert's. Years twenty-five
And more, it founded was and placed
Under the patronage and gracious care
Of blessed Cuthbert, and our Lady dear—
Her "at whose shrine all kings and nations bend,"
And whom as "*Sedes Sapientiæ*,"
It piously and lovingly invokes.
Facing the College entrance you behold
Within a niche, and carved by skilful hand,
An alabaster statue. 'Tis of her
"The Seat of Wisdom," and the Patroness
Of this Society: it there was placed,
And solemnly unveiled to sight, with chaunt
Of litany and hymn, amid the throng
That there assembled had, to celebrate
The silver jubilee of the Society.
Many a youth, I ween, since then has knelt

Before that sacred image, and has prayed
For wisdom and for knowledge from above,
Through Mary—who before God is the hymn
Unspeakable that Him befits in Sion ;—
Mother of knowledge, fear and holy hope,
Whose aid no one has e'er implored in vain.
Albertus Magnus her assistance craved,
And sought her help in order to obtain
That knowledge of divine and human things,
That learning which immortalised his name.
His prayer was heard, and knowledge—heavenly gift—
Was granted to him through our Lady's aid.
Blest the Society which Mary has
For Patroness ; and blessed also those,
For whom St. Cuthbert supplicates and prays.
As tiny rills into great rivers grow,
Inundating the plains through which they wind
Their devious course unto th' absorbent sea ;
As the small acorn sprouting into life
Beneath the forest's withered leaves, becomes
In time a mighty and majestic oak,
So this Society has grown and multiplied.
Its members, few at first, great increment received ;
While numerous members are each year enrolled,
And in its list of patrons may be found
Many illustrious and distinguished names.
Its aims and objects most praiseworthy are :—
Established 'mong the students to promote
A zeal for learning and religion both ;
Among Alumni and 'mong friends to form
A centre, and a bond of union,
That, wheresoever they may meet, or dwell,
Ushaw's fond memory may be recalled,
And cherished by them in all times, and climes.

I here would speak of that Sodality,
Of which our Lady is the Patroness,
And as the " Help of Christians" is invoked :—

O blessed Mother ! our sweet helper be,*
Through this our chequer'd life, and for us pray
To thy dear Son, that we may through thee come
To the fruition of eternal joys.
I well remember, in white marble carved,
The lovely statue near her altar placed ;
In ante-chapel of St. Cuthbert's church
It stood ; lights near it in her honour burned,
And choicest flowers were scattered at her feet—
She, fairest flower of all, flower of the field,
And of the valley peerless lily queen.
Go when you pleased, at morn, or noon, or eve,
One, even more of Mary's clients there,
Before that image kneeling, you would find,
Imploring from her help with suppliant prayer.
O happy youths ! to Mary so endeared,
Who " in the odours of her ointments" run,
Whose love has taken root within your hearts—
Hearts honourable, innocent, and pure,—
No wonder that among you holy zeal
And fervent piety have been diffused,
Since Mary for you prays and intercedes,
And from her Son largess of grace obtains.
It skills not here in numbers to rehearse
All the activities of College life—
Studies and recreation, each in turn
With unremitting earnestness pursued ;
Nor to narrate the hard contested games—
Football and cricket, battledore and cat,—
'Twixt school and school, 'twixt Lancaster and York,
With chivalrous contention nobly played ;
Peregrinations frequent and afar ;
Rambles by rivers, and along brooksides,
Through bosky glades, and glens, and pathless woods,
Chasing the squirrel, searching for birds' nests,
Filling their satchels, in th' autumnal months,

---

*Beata mater, auxiliatrix nostra, ora pro nobis.

With nuts from hazels gathered ripe and brown.
Then when the frosts and snows of winter came,
Congealing rivers, freezing lake and stream,
How all rushed forth in triumph with their skates
To frozen deeps, mill dam, and ice-bound pond,
There to disport and pass the live long day—
Enjoyments and adventures these, whereon,
It is not to my purpose now to dwell :—
In sooth the old proverbial Roman taunt,
" He is no scholar; cannot even swim,"*
Does not apply to Ushaw's studious youths,
Who all have learnt both exercise and health,
No less than learning, to esteem and prize.
A hardy race those students were of yore,
Who, at an early date of Ushaw's history,
Thither repaired their studies to pursue :—
Men from the Fylde and towns of Lancashire,
From York's old city and its verdant plains,
From meads and valleys of Northumberland,
And eke a few from dales of Westmorland :—
A race of labour patient, with few wants ;†
Not to indulgence prone, nor love of ease,
" They scorned delights, and lived laborious days."

What marvel that at Ushaw rural walks,
And rambles were a source of heart-felt joy ?
They told of playdays, leave out, asking down ;
Of festive celebrations,—chief of all—
The annual feast which the good President
Gives to the students, and to friends, and guests,
At Christmas time.   And when the gladsome spring
Brought length'ning days, and radiant summer came,
With all its witchery of leaves and flowers,
What infinite delight to wander forth

---

*" Nec natare, neque literas novit."
†Paticns operis, parvoque assueta juventus. —VIRGIL.

Away into the country, there to view
The site of Danish or of Roman camp,
Some distant hamlet, or old village church,
Or ancient castle tottering to its fall,
Or ruined abbey, venerable pile,
Whose very stones from out the sacred walls,
Indignantly against the spoilers cry.
Much as these rambles unto health conduced
Of body, certes much more to the mind
They elasticity and vigour gave.
The garniture of woodlands and of groves,
The wintry torrent rushing down the hills,
The placid stream meand'ring through the vale;
Ferns, grasses, flowers; the meanest shrub and plant;
The gorse that grows on common and wayside,
Which, when in flower Linnæus first beheld,
He prostrate fell before it on his knees,—
All tend a love of nature to inspire,
To fill and feed the mind with lofty thoughts,
"To lead from joy to joy," unto the source
Of the eternal, universal joy;
And teach man more and more to love and praise
Him who the Sovereign Beauty is of all,
That in this world is beautiful and fair,—
The Beauty ever ancient, always new,
Creation's God and Lord, whom Nature's works
With hymn unceasing magnify and praise.*

When in the cycle of the Church's Year,
The several feasts and festivals came round,
With what devotion and solemnity
Were they observed. The holy time of Lent,
And Passiontide; Easter and Pentecost;
The feast of Corpus Christi, and All Saints;
The glorious Assumption into Heaven
Of Mary, Queen of Angels and of Saints—

---

*The mere sight of a flower would fill St. Ignatius of Loyola with the most devout feelings of love and admiration for the Author of nature.

Each in its turn with piety and prayer,
Processions, sacred chaunts, and canticles,
The joyous Alleluia, or mayhap
The sad and plaintive *Miserere* strain,
Was celebrated.
              But say how describe
The glories of an Ushaw Christmas night,
And all the splendour that around it shone ?
O holy and most solemn night ! night when
The sapphire stars, and vestal moon
Before th' effulgence paled of that sweet Babe,
Who was this night of Virgin Mother born,
And in a manger laid ; whose bed was formed
Of coarsest straw ; a humble cattle shed
The only shelter from the cold of night.
No time for sleep on such a night as this :—
Hark ! Angels singing in the midnight sky,
Announcing tidings of great joy to men.
And shepherds, when they heard th' angelic strain,
And saw the hills on which they watched their flocks,
Bathed in a flood of light, with gladdened hearts,
They hastened to the manger to adore
Their infant Saviour, new-born King and Lord.

A winter's night ; the snow upon the ground
Lies thick and crisp ; a keen frost chills the air ;
The bright clear moon, Sultana of the night,
Surrounded by her sentinels, the stars,
With soft, serene illumination fills
The hills and vales, the mountains and the plains ;
A universal stillness reigns around,
Save where in crowded city and in town,
The noise of riot and intemperance,
And sound of revelry and sin prevail ;
Or where the Christmas minstrels wandering forth,
And village waits, in tuneful strains proclaim,
That on this night our Saviour Christ was born.
And as the shepherds on this sacred night,

Abandoning their flocks upon the hills,
Hastened with hurried steps to Bethlehem,
I also for the nonce would leave the ties
Of hearth and home, the world's absorbing cares,
The bickerings, and strife, and toil of life,
Th' unceasing round of business pursuits ;
And cherishing the memories so dear
Of olden times, in spirit would repair
To Ushaw, and from earth-born cares set free,
My Christmas vigil keep there, and in peace
And prayer once more the holy, joyful feast
Of Christmas spend.
                    Oh ! how delightful are
Thy tabernacles, Lord of hosts, my King,
My God ! God of my strength ! Thy altars are
Exceeding lovely. On this blessed night,
St. Cuthbert's College church shall be the place,
Where, meditating on the mystery
Of the Incarnate Word, I'll seek for rest
And quiet from the turmoil of the world.
For on this holy and auspicious night,
No greater privilege and comfort sweet,
In one's old age, than in this church to kneel,
Adoring the Eternal, by whose word
All things were fashioned, and the world was made ;
While in the silent, circumambient sky,
Nor star nor planet but what uttered praise,
And joined in the grand hymnal unto Him
Who ruled in Sion, and for love of man,
And man's redemption, human nature took,
A babe in David's royal city born.

Into the temple, to the church I go,*
To pay my homage to the new-born Child, —
The Babe of Bethlehem, who on earth to dwell,

---

*Oui, je vais dans le temple adorer l' Eternel. —RACINE— ATHALIE.

Descended from his heavenly Father's throne,
Gently as dew falls on a summer's night.
Beauty and holiness become this house,
And shall become it unto length of days.
God's glory here doth dwell ; His presence here,
In His august and wond'rous Sacrament
Of love, perpetually night and day
Resides, refreshing, comforting all those,
Who to Him come with sad and weary hearts :—
And loving hands have piously combined
To beautify and decorate the church,
For the solemnities of Christmastide ;
Pillar and capital and architrave,
Corbel, and niche, and saints high placed therein,
Roodloft and ante-chapel, lectern, stalls,
Cloisters and oratories, in tasteful guise,
Enwreathed and festooned are with evergreens—
Festoons of laurel, ivy, box, and yew,
Inwoven with the arbutus, and pine,
The fir, and cypress, and the holly green,
Each prickly branch and spray decked and begemm'd
With berries glistening like coral beads ;
Innumerous lights, with brilliant lustre shine,
Throughout the church ; and reredos, altar, shrine,
Chancel and Sanctuary—one might deem
Irradiated were with heavenly light.
And then the mimic Crib we wot not of
In boyhood, more than sixty years ago—
Here let me kneel, adore, and contemplate
The great stupendous mystery that Crib
Brings to the mind, and mirrors to the sight—
Jesus in Bethlehem, born of Virgin maid ;
True God, true Man ; a manger for His crib ;
Beasts of the field—an ox and patient ass—
Stabled in the same stall in which He lay ;
Shepherds in adoration bending down ;
St. Joseph rapt in wonder and in awe ;
The Mother blest, encircling in her arms

With tenderest embrace, her God-born child ;
The while, in her abundance of delights,
She e'en more beautiful and sweet became ;
And nations, for redemption and new life
Through her received, sang praises unto God.

Hark ! peals the organ, and its dulcet notes
Re-echo through the church's lofty roof :
The bell for Matins rings ; into the choir
Priests, choristers, and acolytes, arrayed
In surplice white, in fair procession move ;
And soon float sounds, celestial melodies,
Announcing that the Prince of Peace is born.
Most wonderful the mystery which to-day
Is every where proclaimed through earth and heaven ;
Hence let us praise the Lord with songs of joy—
Venite exultemus Domino—
And falling down Christ this day born adore—
Venite adoremus Dominum ;
Joining th' Angelic choirs, erst seen and heard
By wond'ring shepherds, harping on their harps,
And chanting praises to their new-born King.[*]
Psalms, antiphons, and lections being sung,
Te Deum is intoned, and loud resound
Its strains of jubilation and of joy.
Banner, and cross, and golden vestments gleam,
And clouds of incense odoriferous rise
In spiral wreaths, exhaling all around
Sabean fragrance.
       Then the midnight Mass
Is sung, Angels invisibly around
Assisting. Now the *Gloria* resounds—
Gloria in Excelsis, like the voice
Of many waters, rushing, foaming down
Some rugged crag, or mountain precipice ;
Or noise of mighty wind that unchecked sweeps

---

[*] Natum vidimus, et choros Angelorum collaudantes Dominum.—RESP. AD MAT.

Through pine woods, and the lofty cedars breaks,—
Glory to God in Heaven, and peace on earth
To all men of good will and loving hearts.
O, heavenly hymn by Angels whilom sung !
Come, all ye faithful souls, on this night come
To Bethlehem, and with jubilation join
In singing " Glory be to God on high."
The holy Mass proceeds ; the sacred words
Of consecration are pronounced ; then bends
Each head, each heart, in adoration down ;
Devoutly they adore the hidden God ;
And to His sacred banquet, on this night,
All with profoundest faith approach, and eat
The bread of Angels, corn of the elect,
The hidden manna, which with grace their souls
Replenishes, and their glad youth renews.
The " *Ite Missa est*" the sacred rite
Concludes ; and turning, with uplifted hands
The celebrating Priest his blessing gives.

Invoking next the help and aid of God —
Deus in adjutorium meum—
To sing his praises with becoming strain,
The song of Lauds bursts forth : all works of God,
His creatures all, and all created things ;
Angels and men ; the sun, and moon, and stars ;
The fountains of the deep ; mountain and hill ;
Birds of the air, and beasts that range the fields ;
Dews and hoar frosts ; herb, flower, and all green things ;
Kings, peoples, and all nations of the earth,
Invited are to magnify and praise,
Superexalt and bless the Lord for aye,
Who everlastingly has reigned, with strength
Girt round, with beams of splendour clothed :—
Hence every spirit praise and bless the Lord.*

---

*Omnis spiritus laudet Dominum.—Ps. cl.

Thrice happy youths ! you who within the courts
Of God have stood, and chanted psalm and hymn
With joyful voices, on this sacred night—
Go now and seek repose, and take your rest
In peace, till morn to other duties calls.
May He who never slumbers, never sleeps,
Preserve you as the apple of His eye,
And give to His beloved ones sweet sleep.

It is a work of no small magnitude
To build a church, where God may worshipped be
With sovereign adoration, faith, and love ;—
A temple where through the long tract of time—
Of days and years, within its hallowed walls,
Beauty and holiness together may
Find an abode, and may together dwell.
On the respected President this work,
Bequeathed him by his worthy predecessor,*
Removed, alas ! too soon by death, devolved.
With energetical activity,
Like strong man armed, he undertook the task,
Nor sought repose nor rest, until the work
Auspiciously unto the end was brought.

There may be some who with affection cling
Unto the church, which forty years had stood—
Enhaloed with the cherished memories
Of a past age and race ; whose every stone
Was by them held in reverence and regard :
But as the flock increased, perforce 'twas deemed
An urgent duty to enlarge the fold ;
To amplify its borders, and thereon
To build a more commodious, spacious church,
More stately both in grandeur and design.
So with august solemnity and rite,
The first stone of the edifice was laid

---

*Very Rev. F. Wilkinson, D.D.

By an Archbishop* and attendant priests,
Students and visitors assembling round,
The sacred rite to witness, and to join
Their voices in the psalmody and hymn.
None present but who most devoutly prayed
That this last house might e'en transcend the first
In glory; that tranquillity and peace
Might there eternally established be,
And God for evermore adored and praised.

Ushaw, triumphantly thy banners wave;
Be with the loveliest flowers thy Altars wreathed—
Flowers breathing fragrance, and of brightest hue,
From garden and conservatory culled;
Thy shrines, thy cloisters, and thy halls bedeck
With all the greenery of branch and bough,
Sought in recesses of the wood and grove;—
Ring, joyous bells, sonorous organ peal—
Peal forth with rapturous, exultant strain;
Let sweetest hymn, and psalm, and antiphon
Be heard; and voice of prayer and praise ascend,
Amid hosannas loud, unto the skies.
Let solemn Mass be sung by Prelate robed
In chasuble of gold, and on his brow
Mitre, enriched with jewels and with gems:
Eternal gates be lifted up, and let
The King of glory enter in, and bless
This house, where God will love to dwell with men :—
Holiness unto length of days becomes
God's house, and all should holy be, who come
To offer here their prayers, and pay their vows.
In long processional array, behold
Prelates and priests, and youthful levites,

---

*His Grace the Most Rev. Count Eyre, Archbishop of Glasgow, who was educated at Ushaw; the see of Hexham and Newcastle being then vacant by the death of Bishop Chadwick.

Thronging the sanctuary, and the stalls
Arranged along each side the spacious choir.
Transcendent, glorious, and sublime the sight
That meets the eye which way soe'er it turns :—
The church, like bride for her espousals decked,
In comeliness and beauty is arrayed ;
The garniture of flowers, the blazing lights,
The unextinguished lamp, which, night and day,
In presence of the Sacrament of love,
In which the Eternal Word in silence dwells,
Emits, like some faint star, its flickering gleam;
Incense in clouds ascending, which diffuse
Ambrosial perfume through each arch and screen ;
Vestments of golden texture ;* dazzling tints
From gems of storied glass, through which the sun
With rays effulgent streams, and pours its light—
What sight more calculated to uplift
The soul from this terrene abode to heaven !
The clean oblation that is offered up,
From rising to the setting of the sun,
Upon a thousand altars,—holy Mass—
That great, all-saving sacrifice is sung,
And celebrated with mysterious rite,
And music's thrilling and ecstatic sound :
As when the surging and high-crested waves
Of ocean, roll and chafe against the shore,
So from the pealing organ and the choir
Of many voices, roll th' harmonious waves
Of music, through the spacious length and breadth,
And lofty height, of this most glorious church.

All hailed the festal day ; gladness prevailed
'Mong old Alumni, visitors, and friends,
And present race of students, who had been
Allowed to see this day, and to behold
The sacred dedication of a church,

---
*vestes auroque ostroque rigentes.—Virg.

So elegant in structure and design,
So creditable to the skilful craft
And genius of those by whom 'twas plann'd,
And to completion brought.*
       I too have seen
This day, and have admired this noble church,
And at the solemn opening present been,
When it was dedicated unto Him,
Whose temple is all space, to whom the earth
And all the boundaries thereof belong.
Church bright and glorified! may God protect
And guard thee; may He bless and sanctify
All those who love the beauty of His house,
And in His heavenly courts delight to dwell.†
Most memorable ever too will be
The day of dedication. At same time
Was celebrated with great festive joy,
Welcome and hospitality to all,
The third half jubilee,—full seventy years
And more, since Ushaw, in the "North countrie,"
From its foundations as a college rose,
Whereof, home and abroad, the fame has spread,
As wave on wave by summer breezes stirred,
Diffusive spreads on placid stream and lake.

The aged minstrel now must close his lay,
And in poetic reveries no more
Indulge; but ere his song has ceased,
And echo of it lingers and remains,
Dear Alma Mater! fervently he prays,
That all thy undertakings with success
Be crowned, and for their holiness of life
And manners all thy sons distinguished be:—
From virtue unto virtue may they go,

---

*Dunn and Hansom, architects.
†Plenitudinem ecclesiae tuae, Domine, custodi, et sanctifica eos, qui diligunt decorem domus tuae.

And ever strive faithful and true to prove
To the vocation unto which they're called :—
Then shall they in the multitude of peace
Delighted be, and pleasant all their ways.

Ushaw, farewell! farewell, old College days!
Friends of my youth, farewell! few, few remain :
Where are they now? Gone to that distant bourn,
From whence the traveller no more returns ;
Ushaw, farewell! to thee I owe whate'er
Of intellectual culture I possess ;
Whatever knowledge, human or divine,
Whatever virtues to me appertain,
To thee attributed the merit be.
Ushaw, farewell! my failings and my faults,
The frailties and the errors of my youth—
Be tender to them, and forgive them all.
Ushaw, farewell! when summoned from this world,
And gathered to my fathers, the cold grave
Shall o'er me close, and cover my remains,
Have pity on my soul, have pity, pray,
And piously remembrance of me make,
And offer prayer to God, that He will be
Unto me gracious, and will grant me rest
Eternal, light and peace, with all his Saints.

APPENDIX.

Quæ didicisti, quæque ab adolescentia pulcherrime a sapientissimis viris tradita, memoria et scientia comprehendisti—iis hoc tempore utare.—CIC.

Under this head are comprised numerous and various descriptive notes more fully illustrating the Annals of Ushaw's History, and more amply developing its Records and Traditions than, in the preceding preliminary verses, I was capable of doing.

PRÆNOTANDUM.

In attempting to write the annals, and to detail the reminiscences connected with this college, no one should approach the task without invoking the aid of its patron Saint, and having recourse to him for assistance to do it worthily and truthfully; nor should a memoir, however brief, of the sainted and wonder-working Bishop be omitted in any history of Ushaw, hence I have introduced my Records of that College with the following short sketch of holy and blessed Cuthbert's life.

Several instructive and edifying lives have been written of the blessed and glorious Saint Cuthbert, Bishop, first of Hexham, then of Lindisfarne, Patron of the diocese of Hexham and Newcastle, and of the renowned Northern College of Ushaw.

Sainted Bishop of Lindisfarne, holy anchoret and recluse of Farne,
"Where man till then had never dared to dwell
By dreadful rumours scared ;"
who while a boy didst wander among Northumbrian woods and vales "well loving God and man," and bringing peace and solace unto all, aid me to accomplish the task I have undertaken, and to bring it to an auspicious conclusion, to the greater glory of God, to the honour of thy name, and of the noble College that glories in thy patronage and protection. *Inceptis annue, beate Cuthberte, meis.*

ST. CUTHBERT.

SHAW COLLEGE, to the records and recollections of which the preceding and subsequent pages are devoted, venerates and invokes as its patron the blessed and holy man St. Cuthbert.

To God under his invocation its Collegiate Chapel is dedicated; under his patronage St. Cuthbert's Society has grown and prospered; the Bishopric of Durham was erstwhile his patrimony; and the majestic Cathedral was erected and dedicated to his honour. The unwise and the ungodly may scoff and jeer at the invocation of Saints, but around St. Cuthbert's memory in Durham, even in this deplorable age of ours, a certain indescribable glamour and renown linger. A shepherd boy, he sought no other name; but God had other designs in his regard. He called him to be a good shepherd of the people; a priest, a bishop, and a worker of miracles -"*Fecit enim mirabilia in vita sua.*" With glory and honour He crowned him and placed him over the works of His hands. Nothing for certainty is known either of his place of birth, or the rank of his family. The vision of St. Aidan, first Bishop of Lindisfarne, whom he saw one night while he was tending his master's sheep "*in montibus juxta fluvium Lader*"--in Lauderdale, a valley watered by the river Leader, which flows into the Tweed below Melrose, carried up to heaven by angels, determined his monastic vocation. He entered the Celtic monastery of Mailros, at the age of 15. Mailros, or old Melrose, stood two miles to the east of the present Melrose Abbey, on the south side of the river Tweed. It was established by St. Aidan, about or very soon after the year 635. In 664 on the death of his friend St. Boisil, the Prior, Cuthbert was elected Abbot of Mailros. On March 26th, A.D. 685, he was consecrated at York, Bishop of Lindisfarne, by Archbishop Theodore, assisted by six bishops. His episcopate lasted only two short years. In January, 687, he returned to his rocky solitude of Farne to prepare for death, which occurred March 20th, 687. His friend Herbert, a priest, who lived as an anchorite in an island of Lake Derwentwater, died at the same hour. The chronology of St. Cuthbert's life is briefly as follows :—Born 637; became a Monk at Mailros in 651; Prior at Lindisfarne 676; Bishop 684. He abdicated in 686, and died 687, in the island solitude of Farne, whither he retired after his abdication.

"Never such Bishop walked till then the North,
Nor ever since, nor ever, centuries fled,
So lived in the hearts of men."

Nearly 70 churches in England and Scotland bear St. Cuthbert's name. Most of the places where churches were erected in his honour, were the very spots where the monks in their wanderings had rested with the incorrupt body of their beloved Saint.—See Venerable Bede's historical and prose 'Life of St. Cuthbert,' (Venerable Bede had attained the age of 14, when St. Cuthbert died) ; also Very Rev. Mgr. Eyre's (Archbishop Eyre), "The History of St. Cuthbert ; or an account of his life, decease, and miracles ; of the wanderings with his body at intervals during 124 years ; of the state of his body from his decease until A.D. 1542, and of the various monuments erected to his memory"—a work of considerable interest, much learning, and research.

> Felix locus, felix civitas in qua Cuthberti
> Viget memoria ; felix terra quæ dedit
> Præsulem ; felix ille quem regit populus ;
> Felix ecclesia quæ incorruptum tenet corpus.
>
> *Imitated from an Anthem in the Sarum Office on the Feast of St. Thomas of Canterbury.*
>
> How blest the city, and how blest
> The church which incorrupt possessed
> St. Cuthbert's body ; blest the land
> He ruled with gentle pastoral hand ;
> So great a Bishop has not been,
> Since Cuthbert, in Northumbria seen.

DURHAM.

Durham, a fair and venerable city, is situated on a rocky eminence, the centre of which is occupied by the Cathedral and Castle. It is surrounded on every side, save on the north, by the Wear or Were, (*Vedra*—Ptolemy) (*Wirus*—Bede), "a river of rapid waves," and "quaint meanderings." It rises in the extreme west of the county of Durham, in Weardale, and speeds its course eastward. From Auckland, after receiving the Gaunless, it assumes a north-eastern direction. After reaching Durham, it flows northward, passes Finchale and Chester-le-Street, and falls into the sea near Sunderland. Durham derives its name from its situation, the term being a corruption from the Saxon words Dun, a hill, and Holme, a river island, called *Dunelmum* by the Romans, by the Normans *Duresme*. To the relics of St. Cuthbert and the magnificent Cathedral erected in his honour, and wherein his sacred relics were enshrined, Durham owes whatever celebrity it possesses, even its very existence. "St. Cuthbert—blessed ascetic that he was, who shall count the debt the men of Durham owe him ? Forgotten, as many Catholic things are, the poor of that seven-hilled city in the north have yet an affectionate remembrance of the wonder-working Cuthbert, and his strange wandering relics." St. Cuthbert, who died Wednesday, March 20th, 687, of his age about 50, in the lonely island

of Farne, was buried with due honour by the altar of the Church at
Lindisfarne. In 875, the monks of Lindisfarne, in consequence of the
incursions and ravages of the Danes, fled from their church and island,
carrying with them the sacred and incorrupt body of the Saint. At
intervals during 124 years they journeyed far and wide, over hill and
dale, to keep his body safe from the hands of the fierce Danish heathens.
In the same coffin they had put the head of St. Oswald, and with the
body of blessed Cuthbert, it performed the same long and mysterious
pilgrimage. At length a resting place was found for the Saint's remains
at Durham (Dunholme). When they first brought St. Cuthbert's body
to Durham, it was a barbarous and rude place, with nothing but thorns
and thick woods, where they first built a little church of wands and
branches, wherein they laid his body; whence the said church was
afterwards called Bough Church. Shortly afterwards a church of stone
work was erected by Bishop Aldhun, and in this stone church, called the
"Great Church," the Saint's remains were reverently deposited in the
year 999. There the body remained till 1093. In that year, Bishop
William of St. Carileph, 7th Bishop of Durham, and 24th Bishop in
succession from St. Cuthbert, pulled down the church that Aldhun had
built, and in its stead erected the present august and majestic Anglo-
Norman fane. Bishop Carileph died A.D. 1095, two years after he
had laid the foundation of the new church. Ralph Flambard continued
his predecessor's work. Bishop Hugh Pudsey built the beautiful Lady
Chapel, or, as it is called the "Galilee;" it was re-edified and
embellished in the 15th century by Cardinal Langley. Towards the
end of the 13th century, at the east end of the Cathedral, was
constructed the chapel of the nine Altars. The jewelled shrine of St.
Cuthbert was placed between this chapel and the High Altar; above it
rose the beautiful screen of Portland stone, with its one hundred and
seventy saintly figures. The screen stands in its old place, but the
figures are removed and demolished. The Cathedral, dedicated to the
Blessed Virgin and St. Cuthbert, is 411 feet long, 81 feet wide, and 70
feet high. It has three spacious aisles, one in the middle, and one at
each end. The middle aisle is 170 feet long; eastern aisle 132 feet long;
western aisle, in which was the "Galilee," 100 feet long. The central
tower, re-built in 1859, is 214 feet high. "They dreamed not of a
perishable house, who thus could build." In the old time the priveleges
of Sanctuary attached to the church of Durham. "The abbey church
and all the church yard, and all the circuit thereof, was a Sanctuary for
any man who had committed a great offence, and fled to the church
door, knocking at it, to have it opened." On the 26th September,
1448, King Henry VI. arrived at Durham, on a pilgrimage of devotion
to St. Cuthbert. The Feast of St. Michael, September 29th, fell on
the Sunday, and the King attended Mass, and first and second Vespers,
&c., in the Cathedral. "Blessed be our Lord God," he says in a letter
to his 'Right trusty and well beloved John Somerset,' "we have been
right merry in our pilgrimage. The Church of Durham be as noble in
celebration of divine service, multitude of ministers, and in sumptuous
and glorious buildings, as any in our realm. We were edified by the
people of Durham, inasmuch as our Lord hath rooted in their hearts his
faith and his law, and they be as Catholic a people as ever we came

among, and all good and holy, so that the first commandment is kept right well by them. They love the Lord their God with all their heart : therefore the blessing of God descend upon them all."

The city of Durham is surrounded almost on every side by steep and precipitous hills—"*Montes in circuitu ejus ;*" and from the above description given of it, and of its inhabitants, by Henry VI., one might conclude that at that date at least, 1448, God was in the midst of its people—"*Et Dominus in circuitu populi sui,*" and that they were devoted to godliness and piety. Not only was Durham the city of St. Cuthbert, and of the Cathedral erected in his honour, but it was the city of William of St. Carileph, Ralph Flambard, and Hugh Pudsey, nobly descended and nephew to King Stephen, of Antony Bek, Louis Beaumont Richard de Bury, Thomas Hatfield, Thomas Cardinal Langley, and other illustrious Prince Bishops. "All these have gained glory in their generations, and were praised in their days ; ruling over the people, and by the strength of wisdom *instructing* the people in most holy words. Such as by their skill sought out musical tunes, and published canticles of the Scriptures. Rich men in virtue, studying beautifulness ; living at peace in their houses."—*Ecclus. xliv.*

Hugh Pudsey, Bishop of Durham, restored Durham Castle, which a fire had almost wholly destroyed, re-edified Norham Castle, which had fallen into disrepair, built the beautiful chapel of the Blessed Virgin, called the Galilee, or Lady's Chapel, at the west end of the Cathedral, constructed a magnificent shrine for the Venerable Bede, built Elvet Bridge, founded Sherburn Hospital for lepers, erected a noble church at Darlington, where he instituted a deanery, and many other magnificent edifices, besides undertaking and completing the Boldon Buke, a general survey of all the ancient desmesne lands and possessions in his bishopric, in the form and manner of Doomsday Book.

On the tomb of Louis Beaumont, who lay buried before the High Altar in the church at Durham, were engraven in brass certain divine and celestial sayings of the Holy Scriptures, which he used peculiarly to select for his spiritual consolation.

Richard de Bury, also Bishop of Durham, was sometime Chancellor of Edward III. He wrote an excellent treatise on the love of books, entitled "Philobiblon." The Latin text has recently been re-edited, and a new English translation added. He was celebrated for his love, and encouragement of literature. Besides having libraries in all his palaces, it is related that the floor of his common apartment used to be covered with books, so that it was no easy matter to approach him.

In the Cathedral, besides the incorrupt body of St. Cuthbert, were interred the head of the Beloved of God, St. Oswald, King and Martyr ; the venerated relics of Aidan and Eadbert, Eadfrid and Ethelwold, Bishops of Lindisfarne ; and the bones of Venerable Bede, the saint, the scholar, and historian, which repose in the chapel of the "Galilee," "*magnus ubi sacro marmore Beda cubat.*" His remains are covered with a plain slab of blue marble, on which is inscribed "*Hac sunt in fossa Bedæ Venerabilis ossa.*"

For four centuries and a half the church of Durham had continued to be a great Benedictine monastery, 1083-1540.

From Aldhun, the first Bishop, A.D. 995, to Cuthbert Tunstall, the last Catholic Bishop of Durham, 1530-1559, thirty-six Prelates occupied the see of St. Cuthbert. Tunstall, who lived in most trying and difficult times, was translated from London to Durham in 1530. He was noted for wisdom and piety, and great literary accomplishments; and was an ornament to his native country. He had unhappily been too subservient to the tyrant, Henry VIII. "This subserviency," says Dodd, "was the only blot in Bishop Tunstall's life. He, however, recovered himself in the next reign, when he not only refused to subscribe to the new-fangled scheme of religion which the ministers of Edward VI. were contriving, but sincerely lamented his temporizing and servile condescension in the article of the king's supremacy." Extruded, together with other prelates, from his see, he was committed to the Tower, Dec. 20th, 1551, and in the following year, Oct. 11th, was deprived of the bishopric of Durham. In 1553 the bishopric was dissolved, and annexed with all its rights to the crown. In the reign of Queen Mary, Tunstall, and the rest of the deprived Bishops, were restored to their sees :—

"Gardiner ! uplift the cross once more in Winton ;
Tunstall ! take back thy staff to Durham. Bonner !
Be mitred chief of this proud city again."

In consequence of Elizabeth's heretical innovations, Bishop Tunstall left Durham of his own accord, and though a very old man, travelled to London. Being admitted to the Queen's presence, he addressed her in most weighty and forcible words, and cautioned her against making any innovations in religious matters ; if she did, she need not expect either the divine blessing or his. The venerable Bishop's advice was lost upon the Queen. He was deprived, Sept. 28th, 1559, of his bishopric, and committed to the custody of Parker, at Lambeth Palace, where he died an illustrious Confessor of the Faith, Nov. 18th, 1559, having lived during the reigns of Henry VIII., Edward VI., Mary, and Elizabeth. Observing his latter end approaching, he made a noble profession of his faith, and thus wiped away the stain of schism, which his once temporizing spirit had contracted. He was buried in the church of Lambeth, where he was consecrated Bishop, 40 years before.

The first Bishop, after the deprivation of Tunstall, and under "the new order of things," was James Pilkington, and we blush for the honour of his county, a Lancashire man, born at Rivington, a village underneath Rivington Pike. In Queen Mary's time he had taken refuge at Geneva. Pilkington is said to have been very penurious. The edifices belonging to the see were left in a most ruinous condition ; and the churches were much despoiled and defaced. He portioned two of his daughters with £10,000 each. His two brothers were prebendaries in the Cathedral, and held several benefices in the diocese. Of these Reformation Bishops the "*auri sacra fames*" appears to have been the ruling principle ; spoil, plunder, mammon, and matrimony, their sole gospel. It fared badly now, as elsewhere, with the church at Durham. "The abomination of desolation was in the holy places ; the ways of Sion mourned, because there were none that came to her solemnities. Her adversaries have become her lords ; her enemies are enriched."

"Alieni insurrexerunt adversus eum, et fortes quæsierunt animam ejus ; et non proposuerunt Deum ante conspectum suum."

The "Rising of the North" in 1569, threw a faint gleam of hope athwart the dark atmosphere. It commenced at Durham, and the insurgents took possession of the city and the Cathedral, which, together with all the other churches in the town, were at once restored to Catholic worship. The sympathies of the people were undoubtedly with them ; for "the antient faith lay like lees at the bottom of men's hearts, and, if the vessel was ever so little stirred, came to the top." The North clung to the old religion with a tenacity and constancy that did it honour ; and Durham was the last of our Cathedrals in which the Holy Sacrifice of the Mass was celebrated. For participation in the insurrection, no fewer than sixty-six persons were executed at Durham ; amongst them Thomas Plumptre, Priest. In 1594, Father John Bost, was martyred in the Market Place, Durham ; and six years later, Father Palasor suffered there.

The following is an entry of an execution in the parish register of deaths—St. Oswald's, Durham :—

	"1590			
Duke		Seminaryes	to	were hanged and quartered
Hill	iiij	Papists	hyr	at Dryburne for there
Hogge		Treytors	Majes-	horrible offences the 27th
Holiday		and Rebels	tye	day of May."

Water's Parish Registers in England.

Their only "offence" was their priesthood. Local tradition affirms that Dryburne brook, which flowed near the gallows, was miraculously dried up on the day of their martyrdom.

The population of the city of Durham, according to the census of 1881, was 14,932. The Catholics, who possess two churches, St. Cuthbert's and St. Godric's, the districts of which however extend beyond the city, are 2,700. The former, built in 1827, is at the top of Old Elvet ; the Right Rev. Monsignor Provost Consitt, an alumnus of Ushaw, and at one time a Professor in that College, is the worthy and respected Missionary Rector ; the latter at the top of Framwellgate, was erected in 1864, under the superintendence of Mr. Pugin, in honour of St. Godric. Its situation is a most commanding one, lying immediately underneath the Railway Station, and on an eminence directly opposite to that on which towers the majestic Cathedral. No site in Durham could have been better selected. A superb view is obtained of the city, the castle, and Cathedral, and of the river winding in mazy course beneath. As the Architect observed, "so splendid a spot should have a church equally splendid erected upon it."

At the laying of the foundation stone of this church Mgr. Consitt spoke as follows :—"It is impossible, my brethren, to stand upon this spot and witness this scene before me without being deeply moved. We are surrounded by the memorials of the past glories of our holy faith. The eye, without an effort, can single out amidst the roofs and streets of the picturesque, ancient city at our feet, nearly every one of its old churches, built by Catholic hands, and witnessing by the names they still bear to the worship which was once offered within their walls; and, looking down upon us from its magnificient site, is the venerable Cathedral, with its grey towers standing out in their massive beauty—every stone proclaiming its Catholic origin. There it stands upon its rocky height, as if it grew out of it—venerable with the weight of 800 years—redolent of the sanctity which the presence of the sacred, incorrupt body of its patron, like a sweet perfume, gives to it—bringing back the remembrance of the splendid rites of which a special record has come down to us—of stately processions issuing on the great festivals from its rich Norman porch into the winding streets of the old town, with the banner of St. Cuthbert waving at their head, and censers smoking before the Sacramental-Presence of the Lord of Glory—of the solemn daily mass and the chanting of the midnight office—of the gold and silver lamps before the numerous altars, in token that the "house was watching to God"—of the throng of pilgrims of every rank, and from every land, kneeling round the costly shrine of our glorious father and patron, Cuthbert. And who are we, and why are we come? We are the brothers in the faith, and the rightful heirs, of the Saxon men and women, our ancestors, who in this city worshipped God, and honoured His saints. Here are the young boys, in their white surplices, who in those churches ministered at the altars, now broken down and trodden under foot; here are the priests who daily now, as did their brethren then, lift up in sacrifice the unspotted Victim of Redemption—here are the very monks, still bearing the name and habit of their founder, Benedict, the lineal descendants of the men who, but 300 years ago, in that monastery, walked in the beautiful cloisters, eat in the refectory, slept in the dormitory, and, under the vaulted roof of that Cathedral, guarded the feretory of their patron: sat in the stalls, chanted the divine office, and offered the unbloody sacrifice on the high altar of its exquisite chancel; in its majestic nave preached Catholic truth to generation after generation of the faithful, and after death were laid to rest in the cemetery garth which extends along the southern extremity of its nine altars. Here, in fine—possessing everything but the title of the see, its ancient churches and princely revenues—is the veritable successor of that long line of prelates who, commencing with St. Aidan and ending with Bishop Tunstall, first at Lindisfarne and Hexham, and then at Chester-le-Street and Durham, ruled over the fair north country. We have come to bring back the past—to bridge over the chasm which separates the sixteenth from the nineteenth century."

I care not further to pursue the history of Durham; to trace its fortunes through a succession of twenty-three Bishops, intruded into the see of St. Cuthbert; to narrate the deeds of vandalism, spoliation, and sacrilege which have been enacted, and the efforts made to remove and efface every vestige of the ancient faith. "Truly the enemy hath put out his hand to all her desirable things, and she hath seen the Gentiles enter into her Sanctuary;" pull down and desecrate her altars, despoil her shrines, confiscate her chantries, and convert her sacred vessels to profane and domestic purposes. It may with truth be said that "the very stones of the Sanctuary were scattered in the top of every street;" and that the wild beasts were let loose in the church of Durham.

A sad and gloomy picture of the times is drawn by Butler, a learned and commendable man, and Bishop of Durham, 1750. In his charge to the clergy, after lamenting the general decay of religion, he observes— "The influence of it is more and more wearing out of the minds of men, even of those who do not pretend to enter into speculations on the subject ; but the number of those who do, and who profess themselves unbelievers, increases, and with their numbers their zeal. Zeal—it is natural to ask—for what ? why, truly, *for* nothing, but *against* everything that is good and sacred amongst us."

In one of his recent utterances at a public meeting, Bishop Ryle (Liverpool) stated "that a century ago Christianity had in England scarcely any real existence."

That such a state of things existed in the last and two preceding centuries none can gainsay. Faith, alas ! had become eclipsed ; incredulity was on the increase ; morals had sunk to very low depths ; the eminent good works had lost their meaning ; the evangelical counsels were despised or forgotten. But the hardest and the rudest winter yields to the benign influence of spring ; and to the devastating storm succeeds the peaceful calm. Not unfrequently does it happen that the darkest hour is the one preceding the dawn ; and that on the edge of the black, thunder-charged cloud a silver lining is discernible. Between fifty and sixty years after Bishop Butler had passed away; at the beginning of the present nineteenth century, a streak of light, a hopeful gleam flickered on the horizon, to the west of the city of Durham, "*Exortum est in tenebris lumen rectis.*" The little remnant of Catholics scattered here and there took heart, and were cheered by the erection of a College at Ushaw, on a site four miles west of Durham, of which the great and blessed Cuthbert was the sainted patron, and which in progress of time was destined to achieve a great and signal work in restoring the old faith—the faith of Sts. Aidan, Oswald, Oswin, Cuthbert, Wilfrid, Benedict Biscop, Venerable Bede, and other Saxon Saints ; in diffusing religion and learning ; dispelling the darkness of error and unbelief ; educating learned and holy priests, and sending them forth to cultivate the unfenced, neglected, and down-trodden vineyard ;—thus would Ushaw, as years sped on, become a beacon, a light set upon a hill, irradiating the gloom that had so long overshadowed and darkened the land.

I purpose in a subsequent portion of these notes to revert to St. Cuthbert's College ; and gathering up the fragments of what others, as well as myself, have previously written respecting it, to embody and group them together, in one uninterrupted and continuous narrative, from the foundation of the College, to the present time ; and thereby, to the best of my ability, supply a number of historical and traditional records of venerable *Alma Mater*, which otherwise might have passed away unremembered and unknown, but which to some more skilful and able historian, who, in the future, undertakes to write the history of Ushaw (for I consider its history is yet to be written in fuller and more complete detail) may prove of some small value, and tend to facilitate his labour and undertaking.

Well—Durham, after all, is a quiet and quaint old city, built like Rome on seven hills. It has a grand and noble Cathedral—
" A dim and mighty minster of old time,
A temple shadowy with remembrances
Of the majestic past ;"—
A truly noble monument of the faith of our fathers, whose walls were raised when modern prevailing heresies and misbeliefs in England were unheard of It has ecclesiastical dignitaries who share the *opima spolia*, of which sacrilegious hands dispossessed and plundered the rightful possessors, and converted them to the use and emolument of an alien creed. It is hallowed by the sacred relics of St. Cuthbert ; it has its old churches, its old castle, its old bridges, built six and seven hundred years ago by Flambard and Pudsey ; its old buildings, red roofs, narrow, and winding streets ; and it can boast a long line of lordly and magnificent Prince Bishops, most of whom "have gained glory in their generations, and were praised in their days." It is narrated of one of these Prelates, Antony Bek, that he never took more than one sleep during the night, and would say he was not a man who turned from one side to another in bed. Bek was made Patriarch of Jerusalem by Clement V., and had the sovereignty of the Isle of Man conferred on him by Edward II., so that when he died (March 3rd, 1310,) he was King, Patriarch, Bishop, and Palatine.

We read " that many were the goodly rich jewels and reliquaries appertaining to the church of Durham, some of which would have ransomed a prince. King Richard gave his parliament robe of blue velvet, wrought with great lions of pure gold, a marvellous rich cope. There was another by another prince, such love had the goodly minds of Kings and Queens, and other estates, to God and holy St. Cuthbert in that church."

It is further stated in regard to the ancient church of Durham, "that in the processions, the Prior had a marvellous rich cope of gold, which he was not able to walk upright with, for the weightiness thereof, but one held it up on every side. In the same church, at the east end of the north alley of the quire, betwixt two pillars, opposite one to the other, was the goodly fair porch which was called the anchorage, having in it a marvellous fair rood, with an altar for a monk to say daily mass, being in ancient times inhabited by an anchorite."

It is moreover recorded that at Durham " there did lye on the high altar of the Cathedral an excellent fine book, very richly covered with gold and silver, containing the names of all the benefactors to St. Cuthbert's church, from the first original foundation thereof, the very letters being all gilt. The laying that book on the high altar did show how high they esteemed their founders and benefactors ; and the dayly remembrance they said of them in the time of Mass and divine service did argue not only their gratitude, but also a most charitable affection to the souls of their benefactors as well dead as living." It was called *Liber Vitæ*, the Book of Life, and is at present deposited in the British Museum. Among the names which it contains for the quotidian remembrance, are those of " Beryngton, Blount, Constable, Caley, Charleton, Clyfford, Clyfton, Dalton, Eryngton, Fenwick, Cliffard, Harman, Lawson, Mayre, Myddleton, Ryddyle, Salveyn, Smythe, Stapleton, Taylore, Tempest," &c., &c.

Some twenty years ago, I was staying at Durham, on a visit to my friend, the Very Rev. Provost Platt, D.D., who, at that time, had charge of the congregation of St. Cuthbert's, Old Elvet, and was engaged in the erection of St. Godric's Church, in the progress of which he took considerable interest. St. Bede's Cemetery, situated on the slope of an eminence, outside of Crossgate, on the west of the city, and overlooking the railway, was provided and laid out by him with much taste, for the use of the Catholics of Durham. To him also the little mortuary chapel, so "neatly edified," owed its construction. During my stay I had an opportunity of visiting, in his company, and under his guidance, the chief objects of attraction and interest in the renowned old city. I could not help noticing the dreamy, noiseless quietude that pervaded it, and the hoariness of eld that seemed to rest upon the red-tiled houses, churches, streets, and thoroughfares. But the ground on which we trod was holy, as I great men—"*generatio quærentium Dominum*"—had in days agone threaded its streets and thoroughfares, and left therein their footprints.

ST. GODRIC & FINCHALE.

Who was St. Godric? St. Godric was born of poor, but pious parents, at Walpole, in Norfolk. In his youth he was a pedlar, gaining his livelihood by hawking smallwares about the country. By degrees he became a prosperous merchant, and visited the chief ports of Europe. On one occasion returning from Scotland by sea, he landed at Lindisfarne. He listened to the story of St. Cuthbert, and earnestly longed to emulate the austerities of the holy Bishop. By the direction of St. Cuthbert, he thrice went on a pilgrimage to Rome and Jerusalem. After his last pilgrimage to the Holy Land, casting away, on the banks of the Jordan in which he was about to bathe, his travel-worn shoes, he journeyed barefoot to the north of England, and fixed his abode on the banks of the Wear, not far from the city of Durham. His first hermitage is called by the old writers *Mansiuncula vetus*, or old Finchale. In a short time, about 1107, he took up his abode at Finchale, a secluded and romantic spot on the northern bank of the Wear, about three miles from Durham. Here he lived a hermit 63 years, dying after many austerities and miracles, May 21st, 1170, in the reign of Henry II., a few months before the murder of his illustrious contemporary, St. Thomas of Canterbury, whose martyrdom and future glory he foretold. He has been called by Camden, the Protestant historian, "a man of ancient and christian simplicity, wholly fixed in God." Sometimes to keep himself awake, he would make his meditations standing up to his chin in the river. He would walk into Durham for church functions; and one Christmas night, when the snow lay frozen on the ground, he left traces of his bleeding feet along the road. St. Robert, Abbot of Newminster, near Morpeth, was greatly attached to the holy hermit of Finchale, and used to consult him in all spiritual matters. At the time of Abbot Robert's death, St. Godric saw the soul of his friend ascend to heaven, of which the gates were opened for him. He passed to his rest on the 7th of June, 1159.

In a book of hymns, compiled by the Very Rev. Provost Platt, and called "St. Godric's Hymn Book," are the words of the Hymn a little modernized, which, as well as the music of the Hymn, St. Godric was taught by the Blessed Virgin herself. It was sung by St. Godric in the woods of Finchale more than 700 years ago, and the same Hymn, and the same air, are still sung in St. Cuthbert's, Old Elvet, and in St. Godric's, Framwellgate, Durham. The words of the Hymn are as follow :—

St. Godric's Hymn to the Blessed Virgin.

SANCTA MARIA, O Virgin fair,
Who in thy womb Christ Jesus did bear,
Come shield thy GODRIC from every foe,
And GOD's rich blessings upon him bestow.

SANCTA MARIA, Jesu's sweet Bower,
Fruit-bearing vine, and chaste Lily Flower,
Blot out my sins, my frailty sustain,
That with my Jesus and thee I may reign.

During my sojourn in Durham, I made a pilgrimage to Finchale's ancient Priory. It stands ruined, desolate, and desecrated, in a sequestered glen on the banks of the Wear, here flowing in a tortuous current over its rocky bed, the noise of whose waters is almost the only sound to disturb the stillnes of the hallowed place. The opposite bank of the river is clothed with over-hanging woods, and guarded by steep beetling cliffs. A spot more suitable for contemplation and retirement I wot not of. In this hermitage lived and died the holy Godric, where he built a chapel and dedicated it to St. John the Baptist. He died, his head resting on the step of St. John the Baptist's altar. It is still there—that sacred stone step, all overgrown with grass and brambles. Bishop Flambard, about 1128, granted the reversion of the hermitage, with its woods, and waters, and fisheries to the Prior and Convent of Durham, on condition that after the death of Godric, some brethren of their house should occupy the cell. It was accordingly held by Reginald and Henry, two monks of Durham. Bishop Pudsey, in 1180, ten years after the decease of St. Godric, granted a foundation charter for a cell at Finchale, but it does not appear to have been carried into effect until A.D. 1196. Henry Pudsey transferred to Finchale the possessions previously conceded to "our Lady of the New Place at Baxtanford (*hod*. Baxterford), upon the Brun (Browney)," and placed it under the jurisdiction of Durham. He conferred the dignity of Prior upon Thomas, the sacrist of Durham. At first, the monks were content with the oratory of St. Godric and his successors, but, as their numbers increased, in 1241, forty-five years after their settlement at Finchale, they came to the resolution of rebuilding their church. The remains of the Priory and outbuildings cover a large space of ground. The church formerly consisted of a nave and side aisles, a chancel and a transept. The side aisles were removed in 1436, and the four pointed arches along each side of the nave and choir walled up, and the outer windows inserted beneath each. As originally constructed, the edifice was similar in its arrangements to that at Durham, but on a much smaller scale. At the intersection of the nave and transept are four circular columns, with octagonal capitals. These columns formerly supported a low tower and spire, on pointed arches, of which no portion now exists. The cloisters, refectory, and Prior's lodgings ranged on the south side of the nave. Beneath the refectory was a spacious vault or cellar, still in a state of preservation. Below a large window, on the east side of the north transept, is the supposed site of the shrine and altar of St. Godric, and here, it is said, both the saint, and Henry Pudsey, the founder, are interred. The ruins are mantled with ivy, and in several parts of them, the ash, the elm, the sycamore, and the elder have taken root, and grown into goodly trees—to say nothing of the nettles and thistles which are growing in rank profusion. Stones scattered here and there, names of persons, who have visited the ruins, scratched or carved upon the tottering walls and pillars, the dismantled church, the ruined altar, the desolate apartments where the Prior resided, the flutter of birds among the branching ivy, the sighing of the wind, and the eternal murmuring flow of the winding, woodland Wear,

"*Labitur et labetur in omne volubilis ævum,*"
begot a pensive mood, and rendered each object a melancholy memorial. So having traced on the river side the old foundations of the abbey mill, and drunk at St. Godric's Well, I turned from the contemplation of the ruins, and knowing that "flowers are holy things," I commenced searching for haunts of wild flowers near the river, and found our Lady's bedstraw (*Galium verum*), and the rest arrow (*Ononis arvensis*), in abundance, and among some of the clumps of *debris*, the crane's bill (*Geranium Robertianum*). I also noticed a solitary flower of the yellow goat's beard (*Tragopagon pratense*), springing out of a crevice in the Douglas tower of the Prior's apartments.

Returning to Durham, I took the way that leads past the site of the famous and goodly cross called

NEVILLE'S CROSS,

erected by Ralph, Lord Neville, on the Red Hills, to commemorate the victory gained over the Scots and their King, David Bruce, October 17, 1346. After a desperate engagement which lasted only three hours, the Scottish army was entirely defeated, 15,000 being left dead on the field, and the king, David Bruce, made prisoner. Though fewer in number than the Scots, the English fought most bravely, and St. Cuthbert fought for them. At his shrine the English leaders devoutly knelt before going to battle. They also took with them the sacred Corporal, which St. Cuthbert had used when saying Mass, and which was carried into the field on the point of a spear, by Benedictine Monks, within sight of both armies, and made to serve as a banner. The Monks of Durham watched the battle from the central tower of the Cathedral, and on

receiving a signal of victory, celebrated the triumph with a *Te Deum*, and on each anniversary of the battle, this wide-world hymn of praise, continued for many years, except during the Commonwealth, to be sung on the 17th of October, on the top of the tower ; the practice was discontinued in the year 1811. The site of Neville's Cross is about half a mile from the head of Crossgate, in the city of Durham, on a mound by the side of the road leading from Brancepeth to Durham, near where two roads pass each other, and close to the old turnpike gate. The Cross was defaced and demolished in the year 1589, "by some lewd, contemptuous, wicked persons," probably unmannerly Puritans—
——" out upon thee,
Unmannerly Puritan !"
and now nothing but a stump, most likely portion of a pillar, inserted therein in times of modern date, resting upon solid steps, remains of this once elegant Cross. The shaft was placed upon seven steps, and its height was 3½ yards to the boss. It had eight sides ; in every second side were Lord Neville's arms ; and at every corner of the socket sculptures of the four Evangelists. On the boss were sculptures of our Saviour crucified, the Blessed Virgin, and St. John the Evangelist. The mound, on which the base, or steps of the cross are placed, has recently been raised to a higher elevation, and fenced with iron palisading. A not unwise precaution, which it would have been well to have adopted long years ago. "*Damnosa quid non imminuit dies !*" and more than the effacements of time, the spoliation of ruthless barbarians ! For a fuller description of this elegant Cross, see Davies's "*Ancient Rites and Monuments.*"

BEAUREPAIRE, (Bere, or Bearepark).

About three miles north-west from Durham, and one mile from Ushaw, stand the ruins of the house and chapel of Beaurepaire, the ancient retirement of the Priors of Durham, now "the mere carcase of a sanctuary." The origin of the name will at once appear from the following remarks of Billings :—" Situated on the brow of a short slope, descending to the rivulet's bed, (the Brun, or Browney), and within hearing of its pleasing ripple, it overlooks an alternation of copse-wood, wild and cultivated field, of upland knoll and lowly dell, forming a prospect on which the eye may dwell with pleasure." Little more of the building remains than a small grey moss-clad fragment, in the form of a gable-end, containing a large and beautiful window, surmounted by a cross. Prior Bertram de Middleton (1244-1258) founded Beaurepaire as a place of solace and retreat for himself and his successors. Edward III. passed the night here on his return from Scotland in 1327. In 1346 David Bruce lay encamped near it before the battle of Neville's Cross, and did a great deal af injury to it ; however it was rebuilt, but finally destroyed by the Scottish armies in 1641, and 1644.— *(Fordyce's History of Durham.)* A railway diverging from the Bishop Auckland Branch, near Alden Grange, passes immediately underneath the ruins, along the margin of the Browney, and through Lanchester Valley. The Wallwork Station, near the village of Witton Gilbert, is not far from Ushaw, but being situated at the bottom of a very steep hill, is not found so convenient.

LANGLEY HALL.

Of this Hall not much appears to be known for certain. It is supposed that Henry Lord Scroop, the 11th Lord of Bolton, who died 25th Henry VIII., built the Hall of which the present ruins remain. These ruins, about five miles N. by W. from Durham, stand on the slope of a lofty hill, commanding a beautiful view over the vale of the Brun, or Browney, with Durham Cathedral and its surrounding hills in the distance. Some armorial shields, with bold triple corbels of unique character, still remain. It was formerly protected by a moat, and partly by the Langley Burn, which turns the old water mill below, and descends into a pleasant dell into the Browney.—(*Fordyce's History of Durham; also Hutchinson's.*)

LANCHESTER.

The village of Lanchester is irregularly built in a warm sheltered vale, watered by the Smallhop Burn. It is eight miles north-west from Durham, with a population of about 700 persons. Great part of the village, as well as the church, is composed of the pagan masonry of the adjacent Roman station; so that, as far as the materials of construction are concerned, Lanchester may claim precedence even of Jarrow. The parish church, though stripped of its vast revenues since it ceased to be a collegiate church,* still exhibits many traces of its ancient grandeur. It was originally built during the Norman period, but shortly after destroyed or nearly so; the greater part of the present church being of the early English style, about 1250, with some additions of a later date. The west tower is a square of 20 ft., and is 70 ft. in height. The nave with the aisles is 54 ft. wide, and 45 ft. long, and the chancel is 41 ft. long, and 15 ft. wide. Fragments of Roman sculpture, Saxon sepulchral stones, and ancient tombs have been discovered both in the building and its vicinity. At the dissolution, the revenues of Lanchester college were valued at £49 3s. 4d., but had been valued in Lincoln taxation at £90 13s. 4d. The remains of the Roman station occupy an eminence a little to the west of the present village, and it exhibits one of the most conspicuous remains of a Roman fortress in England. It formed a parallelogram 183 yards in length, and 143 yards in breadth, having Watling Street extending along its eastern side. It has the river Browney on one side, and a rivulet (the Smallhop) on the other, and not far from either the Watling Street passes 'it within a few yards. It has evidently been a station of considerable importance; and numerous monuments, altars, coins, remains of buildings, and other relics, have at various times been found here. The site of the Pretorium is still distinguishable, and also a reservoir near the station, into which the stream was conducted by a channel, or aqueduct, that may be traced winding along the rising ground, to the distance of about two and a half miles north-west: where are five small springs whose waters appear to have been collected

---

*Antony Bek, Bishop of Durham, founded the collegiate church at Lanchester, for a dean and seven prebendaries; also another at Chester-le-Street. These, with four other collegiate churches of the Bishopric, were dissolved in the reign of Edward VI.

into a capacious basin, formed for the purpose, whence they are at first brought towards the station by two channels, which are afterwards united. The date of the foundation of the station, and the derivation of the name is disputed. Some derive it from the camp on the "lan," or "linn," which means a still or quiet stream. That it existed in the early ages of the Roman dominion may be inferred from the large number of coins found here of the higher empire. It afterwards fell into ruins, but as we learn from an existing inscription, was repaired by A. Quirinus, prefect of the first cohort of the Gordian Legion. The 20th legion was occasionally quartered there. The final destruction of Lanchester station is involved in the same obscurity. Its destruction was probably due to fire, soon after the Romans abandoned the island. A century after the Norman conquest we first find a christian Lanchester. —*(See Fordyce's History of Durham.)*

BRANCEPETH CASTLE.

This stately, castellated building is on the banks of the Wear, about four miles south-west of Durham. A great portion of the present edifice is comparatively a modern structure. The old castle which was strongly fortified, and defended by towers and moat, was erected by the ancient family of the Bulmers, from whom at the beginning of the 12th century, by the marriage of the daughter and heiress of Sir Bertram Bulmer, with Geoffrey Neville (*de nova villa*), it passed with other possessions to the powerful and lordly family of the Nevilles, Lords of Raby, and from them in right of succession to the famous Earls of Westmorland. Doughty warriors these Nevilles were. Lord Ralph Neville, and John Lord Neville—father and son—fought at Neville's Cross ; both are interred in the south side of the nave of Durham Cathedral. Ralph Neville, first Earl of Westmorland, led his retainers from Brancepeth, to fight at Agincourt, under Henry V. On the attainder of the Nevilles and Percies, on account of the active part they took in the " Rising of the North ;" for the restoration of the Catholic faith, the castle and lordship of Brancepeth became forfeited to the Crown. Near the castle is the parish church, dedicated to St. Brendan, who was Abbot of Clonfert, in Ireland. It is an ancient edifice, built in the form of a cross, and is chiefly interesting for its being the burial place of the Nevilles—Earls of Westmorland, of which family there are several tombs and monuments.

There is a tradition that the village of Brancepeth, originally called Brawn's path because it led to the boar's den, takes its name from the fact that a furious boar once dwelt in that neighbourhood, and used to range the country round, till being decoyed into "a depe, depe pit," it was destroyed by one Roger Hodge, of Ferry (Hill).

ESH or ASH,

anciently gave name to a resident family, the various branches of which held the estate from the middle of the 13th century, till the reign of Henry VIII., when Anthony Eshe left two only daughters, Elizabeth and Margaret. The latter married William Smythe, of Nunstainton, who being implicated in the Northern Rebellion, forfeited his estates, but his son, George Smythe, succeeded to the property. George's son was John Smythe, who married Margaret, daughter of Sir Bertram Bulmer, Knight.

Esh Hall, the ancient seat of the Smythes, of Acton Burnell, in Shropshire, occupied the centre of the height between the two vales of Brun (Browney river), and Derness (Derness river), which flow into the Wear near the city of Durham. The Derness rises in the neighbourhood of Tow Law, and joins the Browney (rising near Skaylock Hill), about two miles before its junction with the Wear. The Hall (Esh) was a large irregular building; a room in the highest story served for a chapel. It is not known which of the family reared this venerable pile, but two shields on the gateway of the court showed that these, and perhaps other portions of the building, were erected by Sir Edward Smythe, after he had been created first Baronet of the family at the Restoration. He died 1714. A grove of old sycamores used to overshadow the ancient hall, which was vacated by Sir Edward's descendants for their maternal estates at Acton Burnell, in the early part or middle of last century. The hall was then suffered to fall into decay, and was pulled down in 1858. On its site a farm villa has been erected. Hither the Ushaw Professors occasionally repair for a pic-nic, and "*partem solido demere de die*," in leisure and recreation. Most of the land belonging to the Esh Hall estate is occupied and farmed by the College. It is to be regretted that the old hall was not suffered to stand as "*unicum antiquitatis specimen*." In the centre of the village stands Esh Chapel (Protestant) dedicated to St. Michael. The chapelry of Esh is mentioned as appertaining to the first Prebend of Lanchester. Here at the Altar of Mary, on the 10th day of August, 1303, King Edward I. made an offering of seven shillings, on his way from Durham to Hexham, and on the same day, during Mass in his private chapel, he made an offering of three shillings in honour of St. Lawrence, at Lanchester. Edward was making his last march on Scotland. The church or chapel at Esh used to be an unsightly, ill-kept fabric. In recent years it has been repaired and renovated. The Smythe family had the presentation to it.

The old Catholic chapel at Waterhouses was within a mile of the present edifice, at Esh Laude, and was celebrated as the residence of the Rev. Fr. Ferdinand Ashmall, who lived to the patriarchal age of 104 years; and whose memory was much cherished by those who remembered his hospitality and virtues:—

"For that old man of pleasing words had store."

I cannot here refrain from mentioning the travelling costume and equipage of Mr. Ashmall, at once characteristic of the man, and the times in which he lived, when to be known as a Catholic priest might have endangered his safety, or exposed him to insult at least. The old leathern gaiters, drawn considerably above the knee, the left heel alone armed with a spur, the well-worn grey coat, the check cloak, wrapped up, and fixed behind the saddle, and the slouched hat drawn carefully over the flaxen wig. Mounted upon a pony, whose colour age recounted should have been white, but whose rough and soiled coat wore the appearance of no great expense of grooming, and whom the loss of sight rendered at once unfashionable, and unsafe. The salutation of the peasant, as going to his daily toil, of " Weel, I warrant ye are for the fair," and the ready reply of " Aye, aye, I reckon see," has afforded many a joke to his friends.—*(Catholic Magazine, March, 1832, p. 118, copied by Mackenzie, and also by Fordyce.)* He adds that he died on February 5th, 1798, being the last of the family of Ashmall, of Amerston. His Christian name was Ferdinando. Surtees has in his pedigree of the Ashmalls, that Fr. Ashmall was born January 9th, 1695 (Elwick Register), and died at Newhouse, near Eshe, aged 104. The only priests in Durham, of whom there is any mention before Fr. Ashmall, are Edmund Winstanley, died at Mapledurham, December, 18th, 1783. Henry Blunt, *alias* Aspinal, S. J., at Durham Hall, aged 69, on January 9th, 1784. James Johnson, at Pontop, November 9th, 1790.—*(" Clerical Obituary," Catholic Annual Register, 1850.)*

NEWHOUSE, & ESH LAUDE.

There has always been a Catholic priest resident on the Esh estate. The chapel was in the hall, in an upper story. On leaving the hall, to reside at Acton Burnell, the Mission of Newhouse was established by the above named family, who, in peril and persecution, had remained steadfast adherents of the ancient faith. The deed of Newhouse bears date April 15th, 1651, the " Partys to ye deed" being George Smythe, and Edward Smythe, his son. " That one priest of the secular clergy of England may for the comfort of our neighbours have a convenient lodging, with provision for fire, and meat for 1 horse and 2 kine, in the most convenient place for the purpose, with a stipend or annuity of 10 pounds yearly, to be paid unto him. Trustees—Thomas Bellasis, Esq., and Austin Bellson." From 1651 to 1713 the names of priests at Newhouse are not known. 1714, Rev. John Simpson ; he died January 29th, 1736. 1736, Rev. Robert Carnaby succeeded, and died 1740. 1741, Rev. Ferdinand Ashmall, who was the last priest of Newhouse, and died February 15th, 1798, at the patriarchal age of 104. In connection with Newhouse, in Bishop Dicconson's list of Priests are mentioned the following as serving at Newhouse, *viz.*, Mr. John Debord, and Mr. John Couban. These two last named were probably only temporary assistants to Fr. Ashmall. Fr. Ashmall was educated at Lisbon, and was the last of the family of Ashmall, of Amerston. He had, it is recorded, on several occasions to fly, and hide himself in the woods of Waterhouses from " searchers," who had a warrant out to take him, but his neighbours, by whom he was much beloved, and his friends, many of whom were Protestants, always took care to apprise him of any such warrant, and thus he contrived to elude it. He was a most active, kind, and zealous missioner ; a man of family and fortune, and respected by every body :—

" A man he was to all the country dear."

Were it permitted to Fr. Ashmall to revisit the scenes and places of his former missionary life at Newhouse and Waterhouses, what a changed aspect would he not behold.

" *Omnia, proh ! quantum mutantur in annis.*"

He would find the cottage which he inhabited, with its red-tiled roof, its little parlour and kitchen, still standing, and its little garden adjoining, but of his chapel not a stone left upon a stone. On its site, which has been added to the garden, tradition states that for many years nothing would grow, but after Mass was again said at Newhouse, it lost its sterility, and now produces flowers, vegetables, and other green things. Russell's wood, grown more dense and umbrageous, he would find still standing where it used to do; and the small brook (the Murgot, or Priest's beck), on whose banks his cottage and chapel stood, rippling and hurrying on to join the Derness, in the valley hard by. Esh hall, he would learn with regret, was demolished; Flass hall restored and inhabited by a worthy occupant, Major Leadbitter Smith. Instead of the scattered dwellings of rustic men, and the sounds of rustic labour, he would see groups of populous colliery villages, and hear the whir and whistle of the steam engine, on the railway that runs through the Derness valley. But on the neighbouring hill, overlooking the said valley, he would descry a famous, flourishing, well conducted College (Ushaw), surrounded with broad acres abounding in crops, and rich with cultivation. Near the site of his old chapel he would rejoice to find that there had been erected a compact and useful church, dedicated to "Our Lady, Queen of Martyrs", with commodious presbytery attached. With what reverence and respect would he be welcomed and received by the young priest, Rev. Philip C. Fortin, his successor in charge of the Newhouse Mission. By him he would be informed that July 16th, 1871, Mass was said for the first time at Newhouse since the year 1800, in the newly erected school;*that on October 22nd a church was opened; that the Catholic population having increased from 300 to 1,300, this church was necessarily enlarged, re-built, and solemnly re-opened with high mass (coram Episcopo), on St. Patrick's day, March 17th, 1883. The good old priest would be delighted withal to hear of the progress education was making in those parts; that well attended, well taught, well reported schools had been established at Newhouse, Cornsay, and Ushaw Moor. He would be told of, and have explained to him, the occurence of a strike among the colliers at Ushaw Moor, for higher wages; of people in consequence being turned out of doors into the road, and of women and children (mostly Protestants) being sheltered by Fr. Fortin in his iron school, where they were domiciled from Christmas, 1881, till September, 1883; that for having thus "harboured the harbourless," Fr. Fortin was presented with a gold watch, and purse of 50 guineas, by the Durham Miners' Association (4,500 men), "as a mark of appreciation." The old man's heart too would be gladdened on learning that the day of searchers and informers had passed and gone; that like a torrent in the south—"*sicut torrens in Austro*"—the captivity of Catholics had been turned back, and that now each one could sit unmolested under his own vine and fig tree.

With Newhouse and Waterhouses is associated the name of one "of the gravest Priests of the north,—" John Boste, or Boast, who was apprehended September 10th, 1593, at Waterhouses, after celebrating mass in the presence of Lady Margaret Neville, and of other representatives of the Catholic nobility, and gentry in the North of England.

---

*The land for church, presbytery, and schools at Newhouse, which had been commuted, was generously given back by Sir Chas. Fred. Smythe.

Fr. Boste was a Priest of "so much worth," that the spies and pursuivants were most intent upon apprehending him. Being betrayed, and seized by the sacrilegious traitor, Francis Ecclesfield, he was sent to London, and was four times most cruelly racked, besides suffering other tortures and torments during his imprisonment. At length he was sent back into the north, and being sentenced to death, he suffered at Durham, July 24th, 1594, being hanged, and immediately cut down, and butchered alive.

" Pœnas cucurrit fortiter,
Et sustulit viriliter,
Fundensque pro te sanguinem,
Æterna dona possidet."

Fr. Boste was born of highly respectable parents, in the town of Penrith. He was a man "of great courage, learning, and wisdom," according to Bishop Challoner, and being reconciled to the Catholic church, he was received into the College recently translated from Douay to Rheims. I find the following entry in the Douay Diary, August 9th, 1586,—Ex Anglia venit Fr. Boste, oxoniensis in artibus magister; Dec. 15, same year, he was ordained subdeacon; February 21st, 1581, deacon; March 4th, 1581, priest; March 14th, said his first mass; sent to England, April 11th, 1581.

From several letters in the Surtees "Hutton Correspondence," it would appear that poor Lady Margaret Neville, after her capture with Fr. Boast, in order to save her life, renounced her religion, and became a pervert—"Frailty, thy name is woman."

One hundred years after Fr. Boste's martyrdom, Fr. Ferdinand Ashmall was born, and he in aftertime "Said mass att ye Waterhouse," residing there nearly 60 years. He was contemporary with Bishop Challoner, who was three years his senior, and was consecrated Bishop the same year Fr. Ashmall went to Newhouse. During the eighteenth century in which he lived, the following successively were Vicars Apostolic of the northern district :—Bishop James Smith, (first Vicar A'postolic), who died 1711, George Witham, Thomas Dominic Williams, Edward Dicconson, Francis Petre, William Walton, Matthew and William Gibson. He lived eight years after the latter's consecration, December 5th, 1790. Bishop Walmesley, of the western district, died a few months before Fr. Ashmall. He had also for contemporaries, the learned Alban Butler; and those two Lancashire worthies, Anthony Lund, priest at Fernyhalgh, and John Barrow, priest at Claughton, though in years all three were younger. The Rev. James Barnard, who was educated at Lisbon, and became V. G. at London, lived at the same time as Fr. Ashmall. He wrote in defence of Christ's Divinity against Priestley, and was author of a life of the venerable Bishop Challoner. At the period of Fr. Ashmall's birth, Dr. Hawarden, and Hugo Tootell (Dodd, the historian) would be in the prime of manhood.

The Gordon riots occured in 1780 : Fr. Ashmall at the time would read, or have narrated to him the account of them; and he lived long enough to hear of the horrors of the French Revolution; the seizure of Douai College; the expulsion and imprisonment of its students; and what would be most gratifying to him, the subsequent establishment of Crook Hall College.

The following is an extract from a letter written by Fr. Ashmall—unto whom, it is not stated; probably to Rev. Thomas Eyre; his Lordship, no doubt, was Bishop Matthew Gibson :—

"I live in hop's of seeing his Ldsh. (Lordship) and your selfe att my little cottage, which would be no little pleasure to your obt. sert.,
Ferdinando Asbmall.
Newhouse, Nov. 14, 1787."

As stated above, this aged and venerable Priest died Feb. 5th, 1798. He was buried at Esh, in the grave yard of the Protestant chapel,
"Where the rude forefathers of the hamlet sleep."
When Fr. Ashmall died the chapel at Newhouse was in a very ruinous state, actually falling down, but he would never consent to leave it. As Sir Edward Smythe had oftentimes expressed a wish to have a new chapel and house built at a more convenient situation, and with a view of its becoming a fixed incumbency, application was made on the death of Fr. Ashmall by the Very Rev. Thos. Eyre, Vicar-General, and the Rev. Jno. Yates, who had been assistant priest to Fr. Ashmall, for the present site, called then "Salutation Field," at Esh Laude. It is the first point from which a view of Durham Abbey is seen coming from the west; and the hill whence you catch the first view of the Abbey from the east to Durham, is called "Signing Hill" to this day. Sir Edward Smythe gave a ready consent to the Very Rev. Thomas Eyre's application, and it was finally arranged to exchange the Newhouse property (16 acres) for the present premises of about 10½ acres, at Esh Laude, and which on his son coming of age were made over "in perpetuity." The new chapel was commenced in 1798, and opened in 1800. It is dedicated to St. Michael. The house was begun two years later—1802, and finished in 1804, which together with the stables cost only £327 14s. 1d. The same could not now be built for three times that amount. Fr. Yates visited Preston, Liverpool, and other places in Lancashire, at his own expense, to collect money to complete his work. He was a native of Lancashire, and an active, self-denying, and laborious missioner. He died June 1st, 1826, and was buried at Ushaw, having laboured zealously in the vineyard at Newhouse and Esh Laude thirty-three years. The chapel and house at Esh Laude were plain, but substantially built. There was no attempt at any style of architecture. When first erected, like the other chapels built at that period, there was nothing, not even an external cross put up, to indicate it being a place of worship. Rev. W. Fletcher succeeded Fr. Yates, and was at Esh about ten years. Rev. Roger Glassbrook was next in succession : after him came in 1840 Rev. Thomas Witham (Right Rev. Monsignore Witham, Lartington Hall), but in consequence of ill health he resigned the mission in 1841. The Rev. William Thompson (Monsignore Canon Thompson), who had been assisting Mr. Witham, was appointed by Bishop Mostyn to succeed him. Canon Thompson fulfilled the duties of a good and faithful pastor ; was assiduous in well doing, and most zealous for the welfare and spiritual interests of his flock. He built new schools at Esh, on land given by Sir Edward Smythe, and to the education of the children, and the diffusion of knowledge among them, he attended with solicitous care. He enlarged St. Michael's ; added an apse and new altar ; painted and decorated

the church, and improved the mission considerably, from which, in 1881, he retired, after forty years' of missionary labour. The Rev. S. Harris was appointed to succeed him as pastor of Esh Laude. The congregation at Esh Laude number about 950 : the population of Esh village is about 300.

For much of the information respecting the Newhouse and Esh Laude missions, and for the access he afforded me to several interesting documents, I am indebted to the Right Rev. Monsignore Canon Thompson ; also to the Rev. Fr. Fortin, of Newhouse, to both of whom I beg to express my kindest acknowledgments.

Last summer I visited the scene of Fr. Ashmall's missionary life and labours. I stood on the banks of the Murgot brook, and inspected the site which his little chapel had once occupied. I entered and looked round the cottage where he dwelt for so many years. It recalled solemn thoughts and reflections, and the following verses from Spenser's *Faery Queene* were brought to my memory, as being appropriate to the place and the occasion :—

A little lowly hermitage it was,
Downe in a dale, hard by a forest's side,
Far from resort of people, that did pass
In travaill to and froe : a little wyde
There was an holy chapell edifyde,
Wherein the good priest dewly went to say
His holy things each morn and eventide :
Thereby a christall streame did gently play,
Where from a sacred fountaine welled forth alway.

USHAW COLLEGE:

HISTORICAL RECORDS AND MEMORIALS.

INTRODUCTION.

"Movemur enim, nescio quo pacto, locis ipsis, in quibus eorum, quos diligimus aut admiramur, adsunt vestigia."—CIC. DE LEGIBUS, ii., 2.

" Floating anew on the stream of things," I purpose now to resume in sober prose, my " RECORDS AND RECOLLECTIONS" of Ushaw, and to explore at greater length the annals of its history, from its foundation as a College to the present time :—" *Quacumque ingredimur, in aliquam historiam vestigium ponimus.*"

It seemed right that so illustrious a history should not be left to silence, and I shall begin, like the old Roman writers, from the most ancient traditions and narrations that have come down to us, and for which I,

am indebted to various authentic sources and authorities; so that, "*quasi a quodam sancto augustoque fonte omnis manabit oratio.*"— Cic. Tuscul. I have gone forth, in fact, as a gleaner, into other men's fields—
"A lonely gleaner in time-wasted fields;"—
binding into sheaves the scattered ears of corn which have dropped from the hands of the reaper. In many instances, in these gleanings and researches, I have met with only fragmentary details—
"*Non bene junctarum discordia semina rerum;*"—
these I have collected (for fragments of history are not without value), and carefully arranged; and then requisitioned and employed them in the composition of my narrative.

THE FRENCH REVOLUTION.

In the last decade of last century, in the year 1790, the French Revolution, with all its horrors and atrocities, swept over France like a torrent or tornado. Its track was marked with massacres, plunderings, profanations, and sacrileges; with desolation was the land laid desolate; the king, Louis XVI. and his queen were deposed, imprisoned, and beheaded; and "a Church and a nobility swept away in a night:"—
——"*Crudelis ubique*
Luctus, ubique pavor, et plurima mortis imago."
The reign of terror continued and increased with frightful fury. At last the storm which had threatened to involve in the common ruin the English College at Douai, and of which for some time there had been ominous fears and forecasts, burst violently upon it. The crisis came, and with it Douai's doom and downfall:—
"*Venit summa dies et ineluctabile tempus.*"

DOUAI COLLEGE:

ITS SEIZURE AND SUPPRESSION; DISPERSION AND IMPRISONMENT OF ITS STUDENTS.

Douai College, the nursery and home of confessors and martyrs; which for upwards of two hundred years continued to supply the chief portion of the missionary priests in England; whence a noble army of one hundred and sixty martyrs had issued; where many of our Catholic nobility and gentry received their education—Douai College, that venerable *Alma Mater*—
"*Religione patrum multos servata per annos,*"
was seized, confiscated, and suppressed. On the 12th day of October, 1793, about nine o'clock at night, a revolutionary band of armed soldiers surrounded and took possession of the College. Those students, who had not previously made their escape, were removed to the Scotch College, there to be detained close prisoners. On the 16th of October,

the Rev. John Daniel, the last President of the English College at Douai, and the professors and students who remained with him at the College, were imprisoned in the citadel of Dourlens. The prisoners were forty-one in number, four of whom, on the 24th of November, 1793, and eleven others, two on the 14th, and nine on the 15th of January, 1794, effected their escape from the citadel by descending in the night time by a rope let down from the ramparts. All these, after many adventures—
"*Per varios casus, per tot discrimina rerum*,"—
reached in safety their native country. The rest, twenty-six in number, remained in prison till February, 1795, when they were liberated, and on the 2nd of March, in the same year, set foot on their native soil.

"When the English College at Douai," says Digby, "was invaded by the agents of the revolution, by spies, and guards, it might have been presupposed that no one could then venture to retain his cheerfulness. But there was only occasion to show, as a venerable priest observes, 'what college boys can do in the way of generous self-devotion and dauntless enterprise; for every one then was intent upon devising and practising some ingenious plan to rescue various articles of value from the grasp of the plunderers. To carry off a lamp or a sacred vestment some would ascend the funnels of chimneys, and others would descend the external walls by ropes to enter windows of forbidden rooms. Strange as it may appear,' continues the narrator, 'never do I remember a more cheerful flow of spirits than what was manifested the whole time. We sang *God save the King*, and *Dulce Domum*. Such a behaviour astonished every one; friends and enemies wondered alike how we could sing in such circumstances, and sometimes heaved a sigh of concern to tell us we did not know what we had still to expect. Our classical and devotional exercises went on as usual, and continued till the 9th of August, when the message came on Saturday night, which ordered us to leave the college for a prison. The clock had struck eight, and we were waiting for the summons to night prayers. We were soon ready, for we had little to carry away. Some went to take their last farewell of the church, by a short prayer before the altars, which, alas! were soon to be no more.' Thus closed the oldest Seminary of English Catholics, the mother and nurse of so many martyrs, the bulwark of faith, as Baronius calls it, created by God to protect the Catholics of this land from the blasts of heresy. It was overthrown by French atheists in the frenzy of revolutionary zeal; but it was reserved for the statesmen in our age of that people which of all the world boasts to be the most generous, in the cool deliberation of their cabinet, under the cloak of a zeal for God's unpolluted worship, by a judicial sentence pronounced in all the solemn forms of equity, to legalize and consummate its ruin."
—So far Digby, in *Mores Catholici*.

By decision of Lord Gifford, the Douai College funds were alienated to the English Government as being for "superstitious purposes; for on that occasion, taking advantage of a forgotten penal law, it transferred to its treasury the money of which the French monarchy made restitution to the English Catholics for the colleges and funds that the revolution had seized from them, leaving to die of a broken heart the too confiding prelate (Bishop Poynter) whom it had decoyed into an avowal of the pious purposes for which the money was intended."

"We had loved it with fondness like our native home," says one whose early years were spent in the English College at Douai, "and I will affirm that many now living look back with complacency to Douai, and call the happiest period of their life the years of youth spent there in preparatory studies, with companions and friends who were dear to them."

Dr. Robert Witham, who succeeded Dr. Paston as President of Douai, and was a zealous and learned superior, in 1714, re-built the College Church, together with a considerable part of the College itself.

CARDINAL ALLEN.

"Lives of great men all remind us,
We can make our lives sublime,
And departing leave behind us
Footprints on the sands of time."—*Longfellow.*

The venerable English Seminary at Douai, supposed to be the first Ecclesiastical Seminary instituted in strict accordance with the Decrees of the Council of Trent, was founded by William, afterwards Cardinal Allen, who was its first superior, and which proved the chief means by which the Catholic religion was maintained and propagated in England. William Allen was born 1532. His father, John Allen, of Rossall, in the Fylde, Lancashire, was of gentle birth, and related to the principal families in the county. His mother, Jane Lister, of Yorkshire, was a woman of great virtue, and very highly connected. Allen was fifteen when he went up to Oxford. His childhood and youth were cast in troubled times, but he belonged to a family whose attachment to the faith, and freedom from all taint of heresy, were proved by many subsequent trials. Moreover, the part of Lancashire, called the Fylde, in which he was born, (he was born at Rossall Hall), was remarkable for its steadfastness to the faith. In the year 1583, he wrote with evident satisfaction that the Fylde was still wholly Catholic, though some of the common people might now and then go to the Protestant church to escape the pains and penalties of recusancy; that his sister-in-law Elizabeth Allen had three or four masses a day often said in her house (Rossall Hall), and on the anniversary of the death of her husband, George Allen, the Cardinal's eldest brother, twelve masses. Would that Fylde men, and the lords of the Fylde's broad acres, were as in the days of Allen. But

"Old times are changed, old manners gone;"

faith has languished, piety waxed cold ; defections and apostacies, it is to be lamented, have occurred ; ecclesiastical vocations become much less numerous ; the old fashioned Catholics--the "*veteres coloni*" of the Fylde, who had occupied lands and tenements, on which their fathers before them had resided for ages, have had to give place to an alien and heretical population.

In 1554, William Allen took his degree of M.A. He was 26 years old when Elizabeth ascended the throne. In 1561, being forced into exile, he withdrew to the Low Countries, and took up his residence for some time at the University of Louvain. He had not been long there, when, on account of ill health, he was advised to return for a time to his native county of Lancashire. He spent three years in England, from 1562 to 1565, but he was compelled once more, in order to escape the machinations of his enemies, to return into exile. He was shortly afterwards ordained priest at Malines, where he had previously received all the other orders. In 1568, he founded the English College at Douai, which he ever regarded with singular affection, and which, writing to a priest in England a few months before his death, he declared was as dear to him as his own life. In 1573, four of the Douai students were ordained Priests ;—they were the first, and among them was Richard Bristow (Dr. Bristow). In 1574, the first priests were sent from the College to the English mission :—their names were Louis Barlow, Henry Shaw, and Martin Nelson ; and one hundred priests had been sent from it to England by the middle of the year 1580.

Dr. Allen inaugurated Douai College with only six companions, five of them Oxford men. In a short time more than a hundred and fifty exiled Englishmen had been enrolled on the books of the college in order to study, and prepare for the priesthood. In less than five years, ninety-six priests had landed in England.

Bishop Challoner states that Douai counts amongst her Alumni, or such as have been some time her members, one Cardinal, one Archbishop, twelve Bishops, two other Bishops elect, three archpriests, with episcopal faculties, eighty doctors of divinity, seventy writers, many of the most eminent men of divers religious orders, and what is most glorious above all, above one hundred and fifty martyrs, besides innumerable others, who either died in prison for their faith, or, at least, suffered imprisonments, banishments, &c., for the same.

Dr. Allen was created Cardinal by Pope Sixtus V., August 7th, 1587 ; he died at Rome, Oct. 16th, 1594, and was interred in the ancient church attached to the English College, in that city.

" *Multis ille bonis flebilis occidit ;*"

but by none was he more sincerely and deeply lamented than by the widowed, afflicted, and desolate church in England.

Certain vestments and other furniture from his private chapel he bequeathed to the church of Poulton-le-Fylde, in which parish Rossall*

---

*Rossall, the noble mansion of his ancestors, was, in the year 1583, ruthlessly despoiled by the pursuivants ; more than £500 worth of plate was stolen, all the household furniture broken or carried off, and the Cardinal's widowed niece, with her three daughters, Helen, Catherine, and Mary, after being robbed of all they possessed, were forced to cross the sea, in order to escape imprisonment, and most probably torture and death, and seek protection from their illustrious relation at Douai, on whose was situated, and to St. Michael's-on-Wyre, the mother church of the district from the time of the Heptarchy, but meanwhile, till the orthodox faith was restored, and England returned to the unity of the Catholic church, they were to be retained in possession of the English College at Rome. To the same College the Cardinal left his library of books.

So long as the Wyre flows onward to the sea, and the same sea laves the coast of Lancashire, and dashes against the promontory on which Rossall Hall, the home of the Allens, is situated, but which is now occupied as a Protestant school or college—
"*O domus antiqua a quam dispari dominaris domino;*"—
so long as the faith which Allen re-kindled, and which he laboured with such solicitude to maintain and propagate, continues to gain its victories and win souls to Christ; so long as the sufferings and triumphs of the martyrs and priests, who were sent from the College at Douai into England, are remembered and recorded, the memory so long of William Cardinal Allen will be cherished, and the name of that "great-hearted and apostolic man" be held in benediction and honour;
"*Semper honos, nomenque tuum, laudesque manebunt.*"

The following is from an article entitled "Memoirs of Cardinal Allen," which appeared in a recent No. of the *Edinburgh Review*, October, 1883:—"Cardinal Allen's intellectual and literary gifts, the virtues of his private life, his undoubted orthodoxy, his energy and tact, marked him out as foremost among his co-religionists, at a time when they could boast of numbering two-thirds of the population of England. His influence with the laity was unbounded. 'He possesses the hearts of all,' writes Father Parsons. As a Lancashire man of good family, a Fellow of Oriel, Master of St. Mary's Hall, and Canon of York, Allen was thoroughly English in his early education, while his handsome features, dignified presence, and courteous manners, were only the least of the many qualities which fitted him to become the 'Cardinal of England.'"

We live in more halcyon and sunny days than Cardinal Allen did; and though well nigh three hundred years have elapsed since his death, who is there among Catholics who does not cherish and venerate the memory of this great man? A Lancashire man, an exile for conscience sake from country and friends—*egrediebatur de terra sua et de cognatione sua*,—the founder of a College, through means of which the faith was rehabilitated and preserved, and a succession of native priests kept up in England, despite the severe enactments, fines, imprisonment, perils from false brethren, and even death itself, to which Catholics were subjected—Cardinal Allen, this Prince of the Church, was unquestionably in his age and generation the "*grande decus columenque rerum*," the pillar and support in England of our holy faith, against which heretics raged, and a cruel queen and wicked counsellors meditated vain things. "*Benedictus Dominus, qui non dedit nos in captionem dentibus eorum.*" "All the phases of Cardinal Allen's life exhibit, under various forms, that burning zeal for God's glory and the

account they had endured so much. The ruffians who plundered Rossall, not being a' le to lay hand. on the Cardinal in person, wreaked their vengeance on his picture, which they besmeared with mud, and stabbed and hacked with their knives and s* ord. NORTHERN CATHOLIC CALENDAR, 1873.

salvation of souls, which never permitted him to rest. And when at length the hour was come for him to rest from his labours, and he lay dying, 'his greatest pain,' he said, 'was to see that, whereas God had given him grace to persuade so many to suffer prison, persecution, and martyrdom in England, his sins had merited for him to end his life on that bed.'"—*Historical Introduction to Letters and Memorials of William, Cardinal Allen.*

FOUNDATION AND ESTABLISHMENT OF USHAW.

"We have wandered; let us regain our road." The next necessary and important step was to provide a domicile, a "*domum refugii*" for those scattered ecclesiastical students from Douai, against whom the college had been closed, and who, being compelled to leave France, had arrived in England. Some, as before stated, had escaped, and encountered, in their flight, many perils and adventures; others at a later period were liberated from prison on the fall of Robespierre, and reached England on the 2nd of March, 1795. These latter were the Rev. John Daniel, the last President at Douai College, and 25 professors and students.

When the party who had escaped from prison in the January of 1794, arrived in London, several of them called upon Bishop Douglass, Vicar Apostolic of the London District. The Bishop being unable to make any arrangement for them, they proceeded on their journey to their friends, most of whom resided in the Northern Vicariate. Those who wished to pursue their studies for the priesthood were directed by Bishop Gibson to go to the school conducted by the Rev. Arthur Storey, at Tudhoe, near Durham. This took place in the beginning of March, 1794. In reference to the establishment at Tudhoe, I have discovered among an old collection of papers the following document:—

"The unhappy events which have taken place in a neighbouring country having deprived the English Catholics of the greater part of those places of education, in which hitherto the succession of their clergy has been preserved, and to which also they have been accustomed to send their children for instruction, we, the undersigned Apostolic Vicars, have taken into our most serious consideration the dreadful consequences of such a failure to the rising generation; and we feel it to be our duty, most earnestly, to exhort and solicit the body at large to concur with us in supplying the said deficiency, by setting on foot a proper place of education in this kingdom from which the ecclesiastical Ministry may be supplied, and in which the Catholic youth in general may receive a solid, pious, and learned education.

An establishment for that purpose w... commenced immediately, at Tudhoe, in the county of Dur... cheapness of fuel and provisions, healthiness of climate, ... considerations, has been deemed an eligible situation for su... ...

The plan of studies wi'l be th... ...ch was pursued in the English Colleg. at D... ...only will be admitted as shall appear from cir...

To provide and furnish such a school must be attended with a considerable expense, far beyond our resources, without the assistance of the zealous and the charitable. We, therefore, earnestly exhort all Catholics, whom Providence has blessed with the means, to concur with us in this plan for the support of our holy religion. And as the greatest part of those foundations, on which a considerable number of the clergy have hitherto been gratuitously maintained during their studies, is now lost in the general wreck of religious property in France, we are under the necessity of soliciting the zealous and opulent members of our body to remedy that evil, either by new foundations, or by annual subscriptions for the important purpose.

Contributions to the commencement, or to the subsequent support of this establishment, will be gratefully received at Messrs. Wright and Co., bankers, Covent-garden, London ; at Sir John Lawson and Co., bankers, Richmond, Yorkshire ; and by the undersigned Apostolical Vicars.

Right Rev. CHARLES WALMESLEY, Bath,
Right Rev. WILLIAM GIBSON, York,
Right Rev. JOHN DOUGLASS, London.

London, June 20th, 1794."

The eminent naturalist, Charles Waterton, of Waterton Hall, was a student at Tudhoe at this time. Tudhoe was a secular school, about five miles south-east of the city of Durham.

The first to arrive at Tudhoe, on the 10th March, was Mr. (afterwards the Rev.) Thomas Cock ; he was soon after joined by others, among whom was the late Dr. Lingard, who, hearing that some of his former pupils at Douai College had escaped from prison, and assembled at Tudhoe school, requested Lord Stourton, by whom he had been engaged as tutor to his son, to allow him to join them. Lord Stourton acceded to his request, and Doctor Lingard was their teacher at Tudhoe till his removal with them to Pontop Hall, and afterwards to Crook Hall.

Pontop Hall, near Lanchester, in the county of Durham, was the mission house of the Rev. Thomas Eyre, and an old mansion belonging to the Swinburne family. Crook Hall was an unoccupied mansion, the property of Mr. Baker, of Elemore, near Durham, and about two miles distant from the mission house at Pontop.

In the beginning of September, 1794, Bishop Gibson, who was greatly assisted by Mr. Silvertop, of Minsteracres, in the undertaking, took a lease of Crook Hall for the purpose of a temporary college, while he matured his plans for erecting a building on a scale proportionate to the requirements of the Northern Vicariate.

The students at Tudhoe, under Dr. Lingard, were directed to repair to Pontop Hall, where they arrived on the 9th of September, 1794. Here they were joined by Messrs. Bradley and Lupton. By the 15th of October, 1794, the preparations made at Crook Hall were sufficiently advanced to allow the colony to take up its residence within its walls. Possession was taken of it, and, from that day, the establishment, which was afterwards removed to Ushaw, dates its foundation.

The Rev. Thomas Eyre became President of the college *pro tempore,*— the Rev. John Daniel being still detained in France.

Mr. Daniel, having been liberated from prison, reached Crook Hall on the 29th of June, 1795, resumed the office of President, and was formally installed by the Right Rev. William Gibson. Shortly after this, Mr. Daniel resigned the Presidentship; by this act transmitting the succession of the Presidency from Douai to the new College, which had been founded exclusively by members of Douai College, that mother of missionaries and of martyrs. He was succeeded by the Rev. Thomas Eyre, and the Rev. John Lingard was appointed Vice-President, and Prefect of Studies. Mr. John Bell, author of " Wanderings of the Human Mind," who had been engaged as tutor in the Silvertop family, and at a later period had charge of the mission at Samlesbury, near Preston, upwards of 18 years, where he built the present house and chapel, was appointed General Prefect.

Before the end of the year, the Northern ecclesiastical students, who were pursuing their studies at Old Hall Green, were sent for by Bishop Gibson, to join their brethren at Crook Hall. They were six in number, viz., Charles Saul, Edward Monk, Richard Thompson, (afterwards priest at Weld Bank, and V.G.), Thomas Gillow, (subsequently missioner at North Shields), and Thomas Penswick, who became Bishop of Europum, and Vicar Apostolic of the Northern District. George Leo Haydock, the learned and noted Biblical Annotator, who died at Penrith, Nov. 29th, 1849, in the 76th year of his age, to which mission he was appointed November 22nd, 1839, arrived in the following year, January 17th, 1796, with his brother, Thomas Haydock, and Robert Gradwell. They travelled in a post chaise from Lancashire. Of the professors and students who came to England with the Rev. John Daniel, the President of Douai College, the following proceeded to Crook Hall :—Joseph Swinburne, Matthew Forster, Thomas Berry, John Penswick, and Robert Gradwell. John Penswick, brother of Bishop Penswick, was the last survivor of the Douai priests. He was born 1778, and died October 30th, 1864, at the venerable age of 86, at Garswood, where he resided as domestic chaplain to Sir Robert, now Lord Gerard of Brynn. Up to March, 1849, he had charge of the mission at Birchley, to which he was appointed in January, 1804. He built the church there (St. Mary's), at a cost of £2000, the opening of which took place May 12th, 1828. The Rev. Austin Powell, educated at St. Edward's, Ushaw, and Rome, has been since the year 1872, the zealous and much respected pastor of the Birchley congregation.

Robert Gradwell was ordained priest December 4th, 1802, at Crook Hall. He was born at Clifton, in the Fylde, January 26th, 1777. On leaving Crook, he went to Claughton, as assistant to the Rev. John Barrow, at whose death, February 11th, 1811, he succeeded him on that mission. He remained at Claughton till September 15th, 1817, when he proceeded to Rome, to become Rector of the English College. It was on the recommendation of Dr. Lingard, with whom he was on the most intimate terms, that the Vicars Apostolic named him to Cardinal Consalvi, as well fitted for the post. The Rev. H. Gradwell, educated at Crook Hall and Ushaw, succeeded him at

Claughton, where he said his first Mass, September 14th, 1817. He was then just 24 years old. Mr. Gradwell was Rural Dean, and Canon of the Cathedral Chapter of Liverpool ; this dignity he resigned previous to his death, which took place in May, 1860. His successor and nephew, the Rev. Robert Gradwell, was born in Preston, October 27th, 1825. He was educated at St. Cuthbert's, Ushaw, arriving there August 12th, 1837. He was ordained priest December 20th, 1849, remaining in the college as professor for nearly one year. Failing health compelled him to leave, December 7th, 1850. From June, 1852, to June, 1856, he served at St. Augustine's, Preston ; and since 1860, he has been in charge of Claughton, but on account of infirm health, he has had for some years an assistant, not having been able to perform regular missionary duty. Since Mr. Gradwell went to Claughton numerous improvements and additions have been made to the church, presbytery, and cemetery ; and Monsignor Gradwell, who received from his Holiness, Leo XIII., that mark of honour, unable any longer to minister to his flock, has turned his attention to literature. May God spare him to proceed with his literary labours and historical researches. The Rev. George Gradwell, brother of Monsignor Gradwell, was born in Preston, in the year 1827. He died at Torquay, November 22nd, 1855, being then only 28 years old. He was ordained in 1851, so that he had been more than three years a priest at his death. He was ordained at Ushaw, having gone through his whole course there.

The English College at Rome was re-opened under Dr. Gradwell with much success, "after it had been desolate and uninhabited during almost the period of a generation." The late Cardinal Wiseman, with five other youths, were the first students sent to colonise the restored English College. Under his rule the students were happy and contented, and eminently successful in their studies. Dr. Gradwell was also agent in Rome of the English Vicars Apostolic. On June 24th, 1828, he was consecrated Bishop of Lydda, and Coadjutor to Bishop Bramston. He died March 15th, 1836, aged 56 years, and was buried at Moorfields, London.

The Haydocks of Cottam Hall, near Preston, were an old, respectable Lancashire Catholic family, well-to-do, and flourishing. They were lords of the manor of Cottam, which, with some parts of Ashton, they had held from the earliest times. Some of 'them married relations of Cardinal Allen ; several became priests, and of those some suffered martyrdom; but, in consequence of heavy fines, and oppressive exactions, estate after estate passed away from them, and their worldly substance and possessions became at length considerably diminished. "*Beati pauperes*"—those especially who have become poor for conscience sake, have kept the faith, and lived according to God.

The Rev. Geo. Leo Haydock states in one of his MSS., that his father was offered Crow Trees, a neat residence and estate in Woodplumpton, then worth £300 a year, to become a Protestant, but in vain.

Mr. Eyre, the President of the new College at Crook, had received his education at Douai, and had filled several important offices in that college. He was, therefore, perfectly acquainted with the rules and constitution, and the whole order and discipline of the venerable parent house ; and proceeded to model the establishment at Crook Hall, precisely after the type of his former Alma Mater. At Douai, the students in divinity had annually to write the dictates, which the respective professors thought proper to deliver, or which had been formerly drawn up by Hawarden, Alban Butler, &c. At Crook, the President, Rev. Thomas Eyre, conservative of old customs, and rigidly adhering to central principles, insisted on the *Douai Dictates*, not sanctioning, as class books for the students, either Collet, Bailly, or Dens. Hence those at Crook, who could not procure copies, were forced to spend much time in private, to write them. The name of Thomas Eyre occurs in the Douai Diary as having, on the 11th of March, 1768, taken the college oath, in the 20th year of his age, in presence of Anthony Lund and James Nicolas, Professors of Philosophy. In the same Diary he is mentioned as being General Prefect in 1774. Thomas Eyre, conjointly with John Milner and Thomas Smith, was in 1799 proposed as successor to Bishop Berington, of the Midland District. Dr. Milner was appointed. Mr. Eyre was great uncle to the Most Rev. Monsignor Count Eyre, Archbishop of Glasgow, to his elder brother, the Very Rev. Monsignor Vincent Eyre, who died at St. Mary's, Hampstead, on the Feast of St. Vincent, Jan. 22nd, 1871, at the age of about 56 years, and to the Very Rev. Fr. William Eyre, S.J., Rector of Stonyhurst College. The two first named brothers completed their course of studies at Ushaw. Fr. William Eyre received the early portion of his education at that college. Archbishop Eyre was ordained priest in Rome in 1842, and was appointed one of his Chamberlains by Pope Gregory XVI.

Crook Hall, under the Presidency of Mr. Eyre grew and prospered ; and during the fifteen years of its existence as a seminary, sent forth twenty-five priests to labour on the English Mission. Bleak, cheerless, and desolate was the country in which Crook Hall was situated ; and many were the difficulties and privations which the first students who resorted thither had to endure. God, however, who tempers the wind to the shorn lamb, enabled them patiently to bear, and courageously to surmount their difficulties. In a parody of one of the Odes of Horace (II. 6), Dr. Lingard, during his residence at Crook, has graphically described the amenities of that region. The Sapphics composed by him, and commencing
Crook Duacensi positum colono,
Sit meæ sedes utinam senectæ,
were well known to the past generation of Ushaw students—unto many of whom the Latin and Greek classics were familiar as household words. How it would delight me to know that among the "*Studiosa caterva juvenum*" of the present age and generation, the same familiarity with classical literature was kept up, and encouraged :—
——" *Vos exemplaria Græca,*
Nocturna versate manu, versate diurna."

During the occupation of Crook Hall as an ecclesiastical seminary, it was in contemplation to establish a united college for the Catholics of all England, at Thorpe Arch, near Wetherby, in Yorkshire. This project however was abandoned. The Rev. John Daniel, the last President of Douai College, accompanied Bishop Gibson to Crook

Hall, and was by his Lordship, as before stated, installed as President, in place of the Rev. Thomas Eyre, who resigned in his favour. Shortly afterwards, however, Mr. Eyre resumed the office of President. The object of his resignation was purely an amicable arrangement to enable Mr. Daniel to make his claim upon the French government for the sequestrated property of Douai College, under the title of President of that College.

It was a work of vast magnitude to found the state and city of Rome—
" *Tantæ molis erat Romanam condere gentem ;*"
to make Rome the glory and beauty of the world, and with a wall to encompass the seven hills on which it was built—
" *Scilicet rerum facta est pulcherrima Roma,*
Septemque una sibi muro circumdedit arces ;"
to levy and arm her legions, to place at their head—either to conquer or die—kings, consuls, dictators, and emperors—
——" *Decios, Marios, magnosque Camillos,*
Scipiadas duros bello, et te, maxime Cæsar."
Nor was the undertaking, in its way and measure, of less magnitude and moment, to found and establish a college, wherein to train and rear a chosen generation, a kingly priesthood, who would go forth, not armed with shaft and sword, with spear and battleaxe, to fight against principalities and powers, against kings and rulers of peoples, but having their loins girt about with truth, and their feet shod with the preparation of the gospel of peace—" peace with honour"—whithersoever they directed their steps; in all things taking the shield of faith, the helmet of salvation, and the sword of the spirit—the Word of God. These were the arms and accoutrements they would have to use in their warfare against sin, in their conflict with vice, in their strife against the corruption of the age, in their mission, as "ambassadors from Heaven's court sent," to negotiate among men peace, charity, and good will; adopting and employing, with God's help, all the humble means in their power to restore to their beloved, but benighted country that precious gift of faith, which, in an evil hour, had been wrested from it, and to re-enkindle the beacon of religion in those Cimmerian valleys in which it had been extinguished. This would be their mission, their embassy; this the warfare in which they would have to engage, and in which faith, the victory that overcometh the world, would enable them to push forward their conquests, to stem the progress of heresy, and to reduce the stiff-necked and rebellious to obedience.

A vast and important undertaking, as I have stated, it was to found the noble college of Ushaw;
" Long worked the head, and toiled the hand,
Ere stood the walls as now they stand;"
but the work was accomplished, and this great seminary for the reception of ecclesiastical students for the six Northern Counties, Cheshire, and the Isle of Man, was by the wisdom, perseverance, zeal, and determination of William, Bishop of Acanthus, and Vicar Apostolic of the Northern District, built and completed—" *Wisdom hath built herself a house, she hath hewn her out seven pillars.*"

Overleaping the boundary line between the 18th and 19th century, I reach an important epoch, which brings me to the more immediate subject of my narrative, *viz.*, the erection, occupation, and establishment of the above named college. The previous details have been, as it were, preliminary only, and introductory. It is meet and right however, that at the outset I should give a brief memoir of Bishop William Gibson, by whom the new college was projected and founded.

BISHOP WILLIAM GIBSON.

William Gibson, Bishop of Acanthus (*Macedonia—part. infid.*), and Vicar Apostolic of the Northern District, was born February 2nd, 1738, at Stonecroft, in Northumberland, not far from Hexham—*Hagulsted*, Anglo-Saxon *Hellighedsted*—"a place of holiness." It was at Hexham that St. Wilfrid, its Bishop, thorough going Ultramontane, built the noble minster, which was said by those who had travelled to Rome, to be the goodliest church on this side of the Alps. Queen Ethelreda, daughter of Ina, King of the East Angles, gave Hexham to St. Wilfrid, who, about the year 674, built here the above named church. In 680 Hexham became an episcopal see, in which there was a succession of twelve Bishops, until A.D. 821 it was annexed to the See of Durham. Sts. Acca, Eata, "*coram Deo et hominibus magnificus*," John, surnamed of Beverley, were Bishops of Hexham; and of Hexham St. Aelred, Abbot of Rievaulx, was a native. It was not far from Hexham that King Oswald, in 635, entrenched himself on the banks of the brook Denisesburn, at no great distance from the Roman Wall, where he erected a rude, wonder-working cross of wood, and under its shadow, he routed the army of the usurper Ceadwalla. The field where the battle was fought was called Hefenfelth, or Heaven Field. The place is the present St. Oswald's chapel or Haliden. Denisesburn is at present called Erringburn. Hefenfelth, according to Bede, was "*juxta murum ad Aquilonem*," and is supposed by some to be the same as Hallington, in old writings Haledown, that is, Holy Hill.

From Stonecroft, among the dales of Tyne, William Gibson was sent to Douai College; was there educated, and became President, which office he filled nearly ten years, vacating it June 12th, 1790. According to the Douai Diary, he took, at the age of 18, the college oath, November 3rd, 1755, together with Anthony Lund (priest afterwards at Fernyhalgh), in presence of Revs. William Wilkinson, and Robert Banister, professors of philosophy. He was brother to Matthew Gibson, Bishop of Comana, Cappadocia, V.A. of the Northern District, whom he succeeded as Bishop of Acanthus, being consecrated December 5th, 1790, in the chapel of Lulworth Castle. Dr. Milner preached on the occasion. He resided generally at York; but sometimes at Durham with the resident priest, the Rev. Thomas Smith, whom, in 1810, he chose for his Coadjutor, and to whom, Bishop Gibson having become enfeebled in mind and body, his powers were transferred by the Pope, in 1819. The Bishop died at Ushaw, June 2nd, 1821, at the age of 84, and in the 31st year of his episcopate. He was interred in the college cemetery. The following inscription marks his place of sepulture:—

Illmus. et Revmus. Dnus. GULIELM. GIBSON,
Episcopus Acanthensis,
In Districtu Septent. Vic. Apost., 1790-1821,
Collegii Ang. Duacen.,
Hic apud Ushaw Redivivi,
Fundator Strenuus,
Ob. 2 Junii, 1821,
Æt. 84.
Pater venerande, vivas cum Jesu.

He has the character of having been an excellent Bishop, and a strenuous advocate for ecclesiastical discipline, and maintenance of authority. He was singularly averse to those who were plotting for the introduction of novelties and innovations in religious matters; was exceedingly zealous for the erection of new churches and schools within his district, and his erection of St. Cuthbert's College, Ushaw, in most precarious times, of itself should entitle him to the grateful remembrance of posterity.

Bishop Gibson translated from the French of M. de Mahis, a work entitled "The Truth of the Catholic religion proved from the Holy Scriptures." The copy of this translation, an 8vo. volume, was printed by Edward Walker, at Newcastle, 1799.

I hasten on—"*veterum volvens monumenta virorum;*—great names, great intelligences crowd and gather round me. To Allen, Gibson, and Eyre, a prominence and place have been given in my narrative. But my history would be most incomplete and defective, unless I introduced in special connection with Ushaw, and included in its records and memorials, the name of the renowned and unimpeachable historian,

JOHN LINGARD, D.D.

"*Cura tibi Historia est; per te quoque mortua vivunt.*"

A priest of much eminence and excellence was the celebrated John Lingard, D.D. In his day and generation he served God faithfully, was beloved and esteemed by men :—
"He waxed in high report and fame of men ;"
and for the little flock of which he had charge, he evinced a truly pastoral solicitude. An accomplished scholar, an eminent theologian, a distinguished controversialist, and champion of the Church, a learned antiquarian, an able writer, and eloquent historian; in fine, one of the greatest, foremost, and most impartial of our country's annalists was Lingard, of whom it may truly be said—"*Cui quando ullum invenies parem?*"

The family of Lingard had been immemorially established at Claxby, a secluded village in Lincolnshire. His maternal grandfather was a respectable farmer of the name of Rennell, a staunch, and steadfast Catholic, who, with deep sorrow of heart, witnessed the wreck of faith, and the decay of ancient manners; and who lived in days when persecution penetrated even, and sought for recusants among the fens and watery wastes of Lincolnshire. Farmer Rennell, being known for his attachment to the old religion, was marked out for vengeance by the pursuivants. He was brought to trial, sentenced to two years' imprisonment, and condemned to pay a heavy fine, in consequence of which, combined with other misfortunes, his family was brought to ruin, their ancestral home broken up, his children driven therefrom, and forced to depend upon the charity of friends, or on their own industry.

It was on the 5th of February, 1771, that John Lingard was born, in the ancient city of Winchester. Being a youth of great promise and piety, he was at an early age recommended to the notice of Bishop Challoner, by whose successor, Bishop James Talbot, he was sent to the English College, at Douai, to pursue his studies for the ecclesiastical state. He entered Douai College September 30th, 1782, where his course of studies was marked with brilliant and singular success. In October, 1792, he entered the school of Theology. Douai College being forcibly seized by the revolutionary rabble, among those who were prudent enough to provide for their safety, was young Lingard, who, seeing the danger that threatened them, resolved, if possible, to elude it. He succeeded in his attempt, and on the 21st of February, 1793, he escaped from Douai, in company with William (afterwards Lord Stourton), and two brothers, named Oliveira. By Lord Stourton, father of the above, Lingard was at once invited to his residence, and appointed tutor to his son, with whom he had made his escape from Douai. During the next twelve months he continued to superintend the studies of Lord Stourton's son, but in the course of the summer, 1794, he joined the small colony of refugee Douai students, who had arrived in England, and found a domicile at Tudhoe, near Durham. In the spring of 1795, April 18th, Lingard was ordained priest, by Bishop Gibson, at York, going thither from Crook Hall. From Tudhoe, by transition slight and easy, I pass to the colleges of Crook Hall and Ushaw, with which establishments Lingard became so closely and intimately connected, that he may be regarded almost as the foster-father of St. Cuthbert's, Ushaw, whither the College of Crook Hall was eventually transferred. I would say, therefore, that for the first seventeen years that Crook and Ushaw existed—rekindling the torch of learning so rudely extinguished in France by the French Revolution—Dr. Lingard, though not in name, was really the great architect, who fashioned and moulded *Aug. Duacen. Redivivum.* The fact that he does not appear as head serves only to enhance his merit, for it shows the spirit in which he worked—he did much, and was content that another should receive the glory of it—and not only this, but it serves to trace to its source that spirit infused by some agency into the college, which Cardinal Wiseman has embodied in the words, "Deeds, not words, mark Ushaw's sons."

It might seem that in attributing so much to Dr. Lingard, the effect was as it were to divorce St. Cuthbert's from Douai, whereas Dr. Lingard himself speaks of Crook, and therefore of Ushaw, as the substitute and filiation of Douai ; and moreover he most unmistakeably links Crook and Douai together, where, to quote his very words, he speaks of "our having kept up the Douai rules." But as "the letter killeth, and the spirit quickeneth," so here it required a master hand to give life to those rules, and make them flourish, in a new soil : indeed there was so much that was new in St. Cuthbert's, that whilst there belonged to Crook all the glory of the noblest ancestry—going back through a long line of martyrs to Cardinal Allen, who studied at Oxford—and the privilege of hearing the same rules under which this line of martyrs was trained, there also is due to some one the credit of what may be considered almost a new creation.

In October, 1794, Crook Hall was entered, and Dr. Lingard was made Vice-President from the commencement. It is interesting to note, that up to the end of that year, Mr. Eyre, and the great historian who was to be, had under their charge none but Douai men—nay more, men who had to a man effected their escape from Douai at the peril of their lives.

Dr. Lingard was Prefect of Studies all the time the community was at Crook Hall, *viz.*, for fourteen years. Besides this, he taught philosophy—moral or natural, as occasion required, and we may well understand how literally true it was of his versatile genius that "*nihil tetigit quod non ornaverit.*"

We have a slight insight into the thoroughness with which he trained the students : he wrote his "Antiquities of the Anglo-Saxon Church" in the form of lectures, for a sort of Archæological Society among the Divines ; and tradition presents us with a lively picture in connection with these lectures.

Dr. Lingard is represented to us at Crook seated before the fire, with the Divines about him ; he is reading part of what he had written on the Anglo-Saxon Church. We can picture him before us with that easy familiarity and playfulness of character, which always distinguished him, making every one at home ; and one may understand the effect his lectures had on his hearers. They were delighted, of course, with the lectures themselves, but they were charmed beyond measure with the exquisite manner in which he read them—a charm, which in later years drew so many to Hornby on a Sunday afternoon, to hear him read the prayers and hymns. They urged him strongly to publish what he had written, and thus the earliest students of Ushaw had the glory, not only of being the first to hear from his own lips the earliest efforts of his genius, but also of having helped to draw him from his "illustrious obscurity," and bring him before the notice of the public. The students of St. Cuthbert's, inheriting the love and reverence of the earliest students, used, before Crook Hall was partly pulled down, to take a pride in seeing what was familiarly known as Dr. Lingard's room at Crook.

For fourteen years Crook remained the temporary college, and by the end of that time the numbers had swelled to 52 ; then Ushaw became the settled abode. As the relics of their great patron, St. Cuthbert, found many a resting place before they were enshrined amidst the seven hills, so the living society, which rejoices in having him for its patron, was moved from Tudhoe to Pontop, from Pontop to Crook, before it found a home at Ushaw, almost under the shadow, and within view of the magnificent cathedral built over St. Cuthbert's relics. It is true that St. Cuthbert's College did not really begin till Crook was opened, but still the nucleus of what afterwards became a college, with Dr. Lingard at their head, was at Tudhoe and Pontop.

Whilst at Ushaw, Dr. Lingard had begun to prepare for his history, and a little tradition brings this before us. He was a great friend of Fr. Bradley's, the General Prefect, and supplied his place at times in the refectory. It is related, that on these occasions—at breakfast, no doubt, when the students were allowed to talk—he would at times go up to the reader's desk, which stood in the centre of the refectory, and commit to writing some thought which had struck him in connection with his history; some of those intuitions doubtless, by which his historical sagacity seemed to anticipate what records, then hidden, have since brought to light. His mind was already full of that literary work, which might be regarded as his vocation, and he was waiting earnestly for the time when he might have full leisure to prosecute it.

In 1810 Mr. Eyre died, and Dr. Lingard governed the college as Vice-President, at the same time teaching theology. The following year a new President was appointed, and Dr. Lingard having exerted his genius to infuse something of his own vigorous life into the college he loved so much, could now leave it to itself, and retire (Sept. 3rd, 1811,) to that seclusion where he earned to the full, by his writings, those words of praise addressed to him by Cardinal Wiseman, a few months before his (Dr. Lingard's) death :—" Be assured of my affectionate gratitude . . . . . for the great, important, and noble services which you have rendered to religion through life, and which have contributed so much to overthrow error, and give a solid historical basis to all subsequent controversy with Protestantism."—(May 5th, 1851, Cardinal Wiseman to Dr. Lingard.)

Dr. Lingard had acted as Vice-President for seventeen years, had directed the studies all that time, had taught moral and natural philosophy, had even been Procurator for one year at Ushaw; and finally, had governed the college for a short time, and taught theology.

If, at the starting of a college, any ordinary person had been the President's right-hand man, and had done so much for so many years, a great share of the glory of the work done must be due to him; but when a great mind is in question, who a little later charmed some of the greatest minds in the land, must we not grant that he really was—whatever he was in name—the foster-father of this college; that it was he who carried it, not only safely, but triumphantly through the throes of its early life, and that much which we admire about the college bears the impress of his mind, and is his work?

At Hornby, Dr. Lingard was the influential patron and adviser, and generous benefactor of Ushaw. He had deeply at heart the advancement and honour of the college—his letters prove this; any present Ushaw received seemed to please him, as if he had received it himself. He gave a stained-glass window to St. Cuthbert's Church; he promised his portrait (by Lonsdale) at his death, and all papers in his possessions that were cared for—these were to go to Ushaw ; and last of all, to cherish to the end his first and enduring love, he would be buried under the shadow of those walls he was one of the first to look upon and inhabit. He wished to find a place amongst his children, because in heart and affection he had always been amongst them, though separated in bodily presence for so many years. By this wish of his to be buried at Ushaw, he was leaving to that college a most valuable legacy. The standard of excellence—the very highest and the most unassuming—which he has realised, and as it were, held up before the students of Ushaw, must stimulate the efforts of many a generation, who, coming in twos and threes to the college cemetery, and looking on his simple epitaph, will admire the genius and love of obscurity of that truly great man, and be led to aim at something higher, and to have a nobler purpose in life. Whilst living, Dr. Lingard wished to have placed before the students, the words of Alcuin :—" *Recordamini quam nobiles habuistis patres, neque sitis tantorum progenitorum degeneres filii ;*" in death, the voiceless epitaph of him, her greatest father, silently compels the sons of Ushaw to make the same exhortation to themselves.

Dr. Lingard, having devoutly received the Sacraments of the Church, died at Hornby, on the 17th of July, 1851, in the eight-first year of his age, and the forty-first of his residence at Hornby. By his own desire, his body was conveyed to Ushaw, where it was interred, with those of Bishops and Presidents, &c., in the cloister of the college cemetery. The tablet, marking the place of his interment, bears the following inscription :—

R. D. JOANNES LINGARD, C.L.D., S.T.D.,

In hoc Collegio S. Theol. Prof., Præf. Stud., Vice-Præses.,

Scriptis suis Theol. et Historicis, Fid. Cathol. Defensoe præclarus.

A. S. P. Pio VII.

Laurea triplici ornatus,

A.D. 1821.

Obiit apud Hornby, prope Lancast. Julii 17, 1851.

Ætat. 81.

Rogatu suo hic requiescit.

After President Eyre's death, Lingard remained at Ushaw as a convictor, and in 1811 retired from the college to take charge of the secluded mission of Hornby, near Lancaster, which place he reached Sept. 11th, 1811. Here, venerable and learned priest of God, in this seclusion pursue your ecclesiastical and historic studies ; defend by your writings our holy faith against the attacks and misrepresentations of its enemies ; enjoy the innocent pleasures, the learned leisure and repose of your rustic retirement ;

" *Innocuas delicias doctamque quietem ;*"

arrange in order, and cultivate your flowers ; graft your fruit trees ; plant your oaks, raised from the acorn you brought from lake Trasimene, like to whose wide-spreading branches your fame will grow, and extend even to the limits of the civilized world.

*" Fortunate senex, hic inter flumina nota,
Et fontes sacros, frigus captabis opacum."*

In the spring of the above year, Dr. Lingard had been urged by Bishop Moylan to accept the presidency of Maynooth. But he declined the offer; and at a later period a similar offer from Dr. Poynter, in reference to Old Hall Green. Lingard published "The History and Antiquities of the Anglo-Saxon Church," in two vols., in 1806. It was published at Newcastle-on-Tyne, during his residence at Crook Hall. Four years later, when at Ushaw, a second edition was issued from the Newcastle press. In 1844 he enlarged and re-cast the entire work; it was published by Dolman, in two vols., 8vo. In the early part of May, 1819, the first three volumes of Lingard's great work, the "History of England," were published, bringing the history down to the reign of Henry VII. In the year 1823, the reigns of Henry VIII., and his son, Edward VI., appeard in a fourth volume; those of Mary and Elizabeth, James and the two Charleses, followed at intervals; and in the spring of 1830, the eight and concluding volume brought the history down to the Revolution, 1688. Thrice he diligently revised the whole work, in three successive and severally improved editions. Dr. Lingard, in a letter to Rev. R. Thompson, of Weld Bank, without date, but post-marked May 7th, 1819, speaking of his History of England, says, "I first offered the MSS. to two Catholic booksellers, who gave me no adequate encouragement, and then offered it in exactly the same state to Mawman, who entered into a contract with me without a word being said as to a single alteration, or a remark being made as to my principles as a Catholic. I have not the presumption to expect that I can drive Hume out of the field, but if mine become popular, fewer individuals will read his, and of course fewer will imbibe the prejudices, which so many now imbibe from him." At the close of the year 1849, having finished the revision of the last edition of his great work—"the most complete, the most unbiased, and therefore the most perfect of all the histories of this country that have ever yet appeared;"—having cleansed and purified the Augean stable of English history, he took leave of the public, and bade a final adieu to those studies with which he had been so long familiar.

"We know no general History of England that we would sooner recommend," says the *Edinburgh Review*; and the *Westminster Review* classes Lingard "among the most distinguished writers who have investigated the annals of this country." A man of research and antiquarian learning, he imparted life and vitality to history, and caused its dry bones to live. He discarded the myths, chimeras, and fancies, by which it had become disfigured, relegating them to the weird region of romance and improbabilities; and by adhering strictly to the truth, securing its appreciation and transmission. Hence, on every page of his history is the light of truth mirrored, and the circuit of rapid-gliding years, the revolution of ages, the onward march and procession of times and events, are described with faithful and trustworthy testimony. *"Historia est testis temporum, lux veritatis, vitæ memoria, magistra vitæ, nuntia vetustatis . . . . Quis nescit primam esse historiæ legem, ne quid falsi dicere audeat; deinde ne quid veri non audeat ?"*—Cic. Orat.

Not only as an impartial historian, annalist, and able writer, was Lingard pre-eminent, but in the arena of controversy he was renowned and famous. He scented, like the war horse, the battle from afar, and buckled on his armour for the cause of God, and holy Church. How mighty and puissant an opponent he was, let Shute, Bishop of Durham, who delivered to the clergy of the diocese, and afterwards published, a charge breathing animosity and discord, and replete with misrepresentation and prejudice, testify. The charge, a regular no-popery warhoop, was not suffered to remain unanswered. Lingard met the Prince Palatine Bishop in the field of controversy, and gained in the conflict a signal victory. In an appendix to the Durham controversy, Lingard makes the following terse and facetious remarks regarding the numerous array of episcopal auxiliaries who had entered the lists against him :—" We learn from the mythology of the ancients that Jason had no sooner sown the teeth of the dragon, than each tooth grew up into a warrior. In like manner the Right Rev. Prelate preached his charge, and from each paragraph seems to have started a champion. Already have I had to encounter Elija Index, and the Durham clergyman, and Mr. Faber, and Mr. Le Mesurier, and the Bishop of Durham ;

———*Stiphelumque, Bromumque,*
Antimachumque, Helimumque, securiferumque Pyracmon ;"

but the hostile darts of this phalanx of adversaries fell powerless and innocuous against the shield of our modern Ajax—" *Clypei dominus septemplicis Ajax.*" They were put to flight, routed, and dispersed :—

" *Turbati fugiunt Rutuli ; fugit acer Atinas ;*
Disjectique duces, desolatique manipli
Tuta petunt."

Among Lingard's other literary productions, may be classed magazine articles, various letters on controverted and other subjects, "Lections and Prayers proper for the English Saints," which he selected and arranged at the request of Bishop Milner, in 1823, and the sanction of which was obtained at Rome by Bishop Poynter. He was also author of " Remarks on the ' St. Cuthbert' of Rev. James Raine ;" "Translation of the four Gospels ;" "Catechetical Instructions ;" "Manual of Prayers for Sundays and Holidays," in which his beautiful translation of the " *Ave Maris Stella*" appeared—" Hail ! Queen of Heaven, the ocean star," &c.

In the spring of 1817, Dr. Lingard, with a party of friends, went on a tour to Rome and the Southern States of Italy. They arrived in Rome on the evening of the 25th of May. While there, he successfully negotiated some business of importance with which he had been entrusted by Dr. Poynter ; among other matters, the restoration of the English College to the government of the Secular Clergy. In Rome it was generally understood that Lingard had been reserved in *petto* by Leo XII., for the dignity of a Cardinal.

Dr. Lingard was a man of simple, modest, and retiring habits ; kind and benovelent, who
" Did good by stealth, and blushed to call it fame."

The interests of religion were the lode-star of all his views and intentions ; and the savings of his literary labours were devoted not only to the establishment of burses for the education of ecclesiastical students at Ushaw, but to other charitable and religious purposes.

The little rustic chapel at Hornby was built by Dr. Lingard out of the proceeds of Vol. iv. of his History of England, containing the reign of Henry VIII., and he used jestingly to call it Henry the Eighth's Chapel.

Cardinal Wiseman, in his "Recollections of the last four Popes," published by *Hurst & Blackett*, pays the following graceful tribute to the memory of Dr. Lingard :—"An acquaintance begun with him under the disadvantage of ill-proportioned ages,—when the one was a man and the other a child,—had led me to love and respect him ; early enough to leave many years after in which to test the first impressions of simpler emotions, and find them correctly directed, and most soundly based. Mr. Lingard was vice-president of the college which I entered at eight years of age, and I have retained upon my memory the vivid recollection of specific acts of thoughtful and delicate kindness, which showed a tender heart mindful of its duties, amidst the many harassing occupations just devolved on him through the death of the president, and his own literary engagements ; for he was re-conducting his first great work through the press. But though he went from college soon after, and I later left the country, and saw him not again for fifteen years, yet there grew up an understanding first, and by degrees a correspondence and an intimacy between us, which continued to the close of his life. Personally, there was much kind encouragement in pursuits, and in views of public conduct ; then—what is a more valuable evidence of regard—the mooting occasional points of difference for discussion, and from time to time "notes and queries" for information to be obtained, often formed the peculiar links of epistolary communication between us. Then, no one could approach him and not be charmed by the prevalent temperament of his mind. A buoyancy, a playfulness, and a simplicity of manner and conversation ; an exquisite vein of satirical and critical humour, incapable of causing pain to any reasonable mind ; a bending and pliant genius, which could adapt itself to every society, so as to become its idol, made him as much at home with the bar of the Northern Circuit, in the days of Brougham and Scarlett,[*] as with the young collegian who called to consult him at Hornby on some passage of Scripture, or a classic. But a soundness of judgment, and a high tone of feeling, united to solid and varied learning, strong faith, and sincere piety, supplied the deep concrete foundation on which rested those more elegant and airy external graces. Such was Lingard to all who knew him, sure to be loved, if only known."

N.B.—Page 78, *for* Joannes Lingard, C.L.D. ; *read* Joannes Lingard, LL.D.

---

[*] The bar presented him, by subscription, with his own portrait.

NOTES AND EXTRACTS REGARDING USHAW COLLEGE,

FROM ORIGINAL LETTERS, &c.

April 5th, 1796. A letter of this date, written by Rev. Thos. Eyre, shews that he was then acting as President of Crook Hall, the numbers of the community being fourteen.

Oct. 4th, 1802, Copy of Agreement to purchase Hazlewood Hall, Yorkshire, for a College for the Northern District, with chapel, barns, stables, gardens, &c. ; with surrounding land staked out, 58 acres or thereabouts. Sir Walter Vavasour to deliver possession 22nd Nov. next. Manorial rights reserved. Purchase money, £12,000. Signed by Walter Vavasour, Wm. Gibson, Jno. Gillow, Thomas Eyre, Jas. Melling, Wm. Croskell.

The negociations were brought to an end by the death of Sir Walter Vavasour, about the 2nd of Nov., 1802.

Letter from Rev. J. Lingard, dated Crook, Dec. 26th, 1802, says, "Crook is very full—obliged to put beds in the Philosophers' school. Dr. Lingard thinks it would be desirable to hire a larger place, such as Greencroft, about three miles off."

Jan. 3rd, 1803. Rev. J. Lingard to Rev. John Orrell, written from Crook Hall, where he was then Procurator, says "that the Bishop is going to begin to build next week."·

From Rev. Thomas Eyre to Rev. John Rigby, D.D., Lancaster.

Crook Hall, Gateshead,
July 24th, 1804.

Dear Sir,

As you must have heard that the building of the intended College at Ushaw is begun, you probably may be anxious to know in what manner we are proceeding in this important undertaking. As soon as the Bishop returned from Lancashire, he expressed his determination in pursuance, as he said, of the advice of our Brethren in that county, to commence the building immediately ;—and the Brethren in this Vicariat, without hesitation, and with only one dissentient voice, agreed to furnish from the general fund £500 towards the execution of the design. In this measure they were actuated by the same motives as the Brethren who assembled at Fernyhalgh, the 10th of July, 1798. "They conceived like them that they were bound in conscience to endeavour to preserve, by all possible means, the succession of Catholic pastors ; that they ought to divest themselves of all low prejudices and unmeaning objections to the prosecution of this noble and heavenly object: and that in order to show they were in earnest, it was necessary to lead the way by a liberal contribution from their general fund."

By the help of this donation and sundry other sums in the Bishop's hands, the foundations of two parts of the intended building (capable, when complete, of accommodating about 60 persons,) have been laid, and the walls have been raised in some parts several feet above the ground. All the timber necessary has been purchased at a low price, by favour of a Catholic merchant at Newcastle, in which a saving of at least £200 has been made. But in order to complete the undertaking, further donations will be necessary ; nor can I persuade myself that the Brethren in Lancashire will be unwilling to concur with us in so desirable an object. Indeed, when I call to mind the meeting at Fernyhalgh of our most respectable Brethren, and recollect the zeal which you and so many others manifested on that occasion, I flatter myself that you will still exert yourselves in the prosecution of what you then deemed necessary to the preservation of this mission. I humbly presume that no change of circumstances has since taken place of such material consequence, as to compel you to deviate from the resolutions into which you then entered. The necessities of the mission have increased in a tenfold proportion ; and the only change (a change I frankly own I regret) from the plan then proposed, is, that the committee does no longer act. Still, I hope that the building may yet be conducted in a proper manner. The plan has been submitted to the inspection of several of us, as well as of professional men : the improvements suggested have been adopted, and the whole is accurately drawn out, that no mistakes of any consequence can well be made. The prices of every article of workmanship are agreed upon, so that no extravagance on the part of the Bishop is to be feared. You already know the land, whereon we are endeavouring to build, is properly secured against the risk of any accident within human probability. There is every reason to hope, that in due course of time, the whole of this concern will be settled to the satisfaction of all our Brethren. Can any of our Brethren object to subscribing something very handsome from their general fund, that has but once heard the solemn decision of those assembled at Fernyhalgh, July 10th, 1798—that there is a power lodged in the Brethren to dispose of any part of the general fund, for pious uses, in certain cases, the most urgent of all, which is the introduction and preservation of the Catholic religion ; that all are bound in conscience to use every possible means to keep up the succession of our pastors ; and that no means can be so effectual to this end as the immediate establishment of a college, that will educate such a number, as may afford a sufficient choice of proper candidates for the church, as well as a supply of able and suitable masters. If you were to condescend to bring forward this business at your next meeting, it would in all probability ensure it success, and you would render essential services to religion.

               I am, dear Sir,
                       Your very obedient humble Servant,
                             THOMAS EYRE.

    The Rev. Thomas Eyre, President of Crook Hall, in a letter from that College, August 20th, 1804, writes to Rev. Dr. Rigby, of Lancaster, as follows :—" You seem to suppose this house possessed of a splendid allowance for our professors. What will you think when you hear that all our masters' pensions, when summed up together, will not amount to your servant's wages for three months. With this ample provision, each master fills up the place of two or three offices at Douai. In poverty we can vie with any college in Europe, and in disinterestedness with any professors, even in the golden days of *Alma Mater*. The bare maintenance of our professors is with difficulty squeezed out of the rigid economy of this house...... The possibility of our being dispossessed of this mansion, of which we are only tenants at will, either by its being sold, or otherwise ; the daily prejudice to a regular supply for the mission, as well as to ourselves in point of economy, occasioned by our being limited to so small a number ; besides the grounds we have to hope that our number might and would increase, if we had more spacious accommodation :—these thoughts frequently revolved in my mind tended to excite something like impatience to obtain more extensive premises. Hence I could not but rejoice last summer to hear that our Brethren, on your side the hills, proposed raising a sum out of your general fund. . . . Our Brethren here were solicited to subscribe, and they agreed to do so."

In October, 1804, the Rev. Thomas Smith, Missioner at Durham, and afterwards Coadjutor to Bishop William Gibson, states as follows regarding the progress made in building the College at Ushaw :—" All things considered, I think the building has got pretty well forward. The workmen are now setting the roof upon the east wing, which contains on the ground floor a range of schools and an ambulacrum. On the upper story, a dormitory about 120 ft. long by 28 ft. wide, with a prefect's room. The north front containing a chapel the whole height of the building, kitchen, &c., and refectory, with cellars below, and rooms above,* must be left for this season, about 6 ft. above the ground ; but as the timber, slate, &c., are all ready, it may be got up early next summer, as may also the west wing, if money be not wanting."

The said Rev. Thomas Smith, of Old Elvet, Durham, " Acknowledges (October 29th, 1804,) to have received of the Rev. Dr. John Rigby, Treasurer to the Old Secular Clergy Fund for the counties of Lancaster, Westmorland, Cumberland, and Cheshire, the sum of £500, for the immediate purpose of carrying on the college now building at Ushaw." The above sum was advanced, as stated in the acknowledgment, " On the express condition, that in case the General Fund of the said Old Secular Clergy should at any time be found inadequate to the support of the indigent Brethren, the legal interest of the said sum of £500 shall be paid on demand, to the Treasurer of their General Meeting, for the time being."

The grant of this money was objected to on the part of some of the members of the Fund. The matter, however, was at length amicably settled, and the sum above named advanced.

The Rev. John Rigby, D.D., priest, was born at Pemberton, near Wigan. After going through his studies, first at Douai, and then in the schools of the Paris University, he was ordained priest in that city, and was made Doctor of the Sorbonne in 1784. He was an accomplished scholar, and had for many years charge of the mission at Lancaster, where he departed this life, in the sixty-third year of his age, on the 10th June, 1819. He was treasurer of the Lancashire Infirm Secular Clergy Fund, of which he became a member in 1784, from 1796 to the time of his death.

---

*The old little dormitory, of which no vestige now remains.

May 26th, 1805. Rev. J. Lingard, writing from Crook Hall to Rev. John Orrell, says "that Mr. Storey's School (Tudhoe), is broken up. Some of the boys are come here, so that we are 51 in number."

Letter from Rev. J. Lingard, dated Crook Hall, July 12th, 1805. Was then Procurator.

Aug. 10th, 1805. Rev. J. Lingard to Rev. John Orrell. "With respect to Ushaw, the north wing is very nearly ready to receive the roof; the south front is raised above the first joisting. The expense each week is about £50. Few gentlemen have yet given any thing. Last week Mr. Croskell sent £200, raised in Yorkshire, and says that he will be able to send £400 more before the close of the month. Mr. Gillow promises £150 more from York, (he had previously sent £200,) and says that an old lady has left in her will £400 to the building. Yet if we consider that £1200 worth of timber is wanting to complete the front and north wing, I sometimes fear we shall be at a stand. Another £50 is come from Liverpool. It was sent by Mr. Macdonald."

Oct. 15th, 1805. Rev. Thos. Eyre to Rev. John Orrell, says, "within the last six weeks we were within an ace of having Dr. Lingard wrested from us. He was to go to London, to which diocese it appears that he originally belonged, but Bishop Douglass was persuaded to let him remain with us."

Feb. 10th, 1806. Rev. J. Lingard to Rev. John Orrell, written from Crook Hall about money matters.

Aug. 4th, 1806. The same to the same says "that the three wings at Ushaw are covered in, and some of the rooms plastered."

Letter from Rev. J. Lingard, Crook Hall (no date), to Rev. John Orrell, speaks of Ushaw as progressing, and as having cost £9000, not as much as was expected.

Letter from Rev. J. Lingard, dated Crook Hall, April 9th, 1807, speaks of his works as attacked by Dr. Milner, and defends himself. Expects to enter Ushaw in Sept.

May 20th, 1807. The same to the same says "that when we enter Ushaw, we shall transfer 45 from Crook, 18 from Tudhoe, and 10 others; making above 70.

Nov. 5th, 1807. The same to the same says "he is glad to have the merit of discovering his merit; he would sooner have discovered it than the comet."

Ushaw College was entered in the summer (July 19th), 1808, and after the students had occupied it a few months, a fever broke out amongst them, which had very fatal results. The following two letters from the President, Rev. T. Eyre, and Rev. J. Lingard, Procurator, addressed to Rev. John Orrell, whose nephew was one of the victims, gives a graphic picture of the visitation. It will be seen that Dr. Hogarth, the first Bishop of Hexham, was at death's door at this crisis.

Rev. Thos. Eyre to Rev. John Orrell (no date), Ushaw, Durham, Friday night, 10 o'clock. "Dr. Cox, who arrived after I had sealed my last letter, confirmed the Apothecary's report that Master Joseph's symptoms became sensibly more favourable. He took Friday for Saturday, said he must be up to-morrow time enough for High Mass, but hoped he should not have to stand acolyth. His thoughts begin to be more collected and regular. He seems likely to be pretty much composed for rest, so that I hope our housekeeper will be at liberty to obtain a little sleep to-night, as she has been by Master Joseph's bed side for five nights successively. 11½ o'clock. As it is again my turn to sit up in the prefect of the dormitory's room, where I have watched, four different nights, two persons, viz., Mr. William Hoggart, and William Turvile, who have both of them been at death's door a very little time since, but I hope are now mending fast, I have been frequently interrupted by the performance of sundry offices about my patients. I am sorry to hear from the housekeeper, who talks of not going to bed to-night at all, that Master Joseph is not quite so well, has more fever on him, &c. Half hour past midnight. I am just returned from taking a cup of tea with my fellow watcher, who is in another apartment. He tells me all goes well in his watch-rooms, where, among the rest, is Thos. Pinnington. His fever seems to have attacked more the nerves than the sanguiferous system. I greatly fear it will be a good while before he gets rid of his complaint. I can scarcely say whether the number of our invalids be diminished or not. Indeed we have now only fifteen confined to their beds, but there are five or six more that feel very squeamish and indisposed. Hence the sick exceed the number of those in health at present, for you must know that near 20 had become panic-struck, and scampered away as if death had been at their heels. We cannot muster a dozen fit to sit up. One o'clock p.m.. The Apothecary has just brought our letters, amongst them yours. He finds Master Joseph much better, &c."

Ushaw, Mar. 5th, 1809. Rev. John Lingard to Rev. J. Orrell. "We are at last freed, or nearly freed from the dreadful visitation which you mention. Including servants, 57 persons have been ill of the fever, some slightly, others, the greater part, more severely. Five have died, one in rhetoric, one in poetry, and three in the lower classes. None of the priests have had it. Of the eight divines, five were attacked, of four philosophers, three, of four rhetoricians none escaped, of eight poets only two. Pinnington grew melancholy, and at last fell into a fever of a different nature, a violent nervous fever, of which he is now recovering. Crook is very low spirited, and desirous of returning home. We have now only four who are confined up stairs, and these are in a very favourable way. Here you have the extent of our misfortune, great part of which, were it possible, it would be prudent to conceal, But I dare say the whole, and much more than the whole will be rumoured all over the nation. At Stonyhurst they have had the goodness to have had public prayers for us. This was certainly very kind and charitable; but the story will be told with many exaggerations in every letter."

The name of John Orrell (of the family of the Orrells of Blackbrook) appears in the Douai Diary as having, in 1764, at the age of 19, and in the class of rhetoric, taken the college oath, at the same time as John Barrow (missioner subsequently at Claughton), who had then had three years theology, and was aged 29 years. John Orrell was afterwards Professor at Douai, and is last spoken of there as General Prefect, 1772-3. In 1778, from September 27th, he was priest at Blackbrook, where he deceased, January 28th, 1810, aged 65 years, and was interred at Windleshaw. Rev. John Orrell was uncle to Rev. Philip Orrell, who died at Ushaw, October 13th, 1866, and was there buried.

Letter from Bishop Wm. Gibson, dated June 23rd, 1809, to Rev. Mr. Crathorne, Garswood, says of Ushaw, "I do not believe there is a better built house, or better secured any where." He adds, "the objection about dampness is looked on as little by intelligent men. It had been built about four years before they came, and had been entered upon by them about six months before any one was ill. The illness that was there was general as in many other places."

Letter of Dr. Gillow, President of Ushaw, to Rev. R. Thompson, V.G., Weld Bank (without date), saying that Bishop Gibson had agreed to surrender the farm to him on receiving £100 a year for life, which was agreed to.

In an historical sketch of the mission of Claughton-on-Brock, which appears in *The Liverpool Catholic Almanac, 1885*, Monsignor Gradwell writes as follows concerning that practical Lancashire man, born at Westby in the Fylde, the redoubtable and intrepid priest, John Barrow, the "old Tar of Claughton," and resident missioner there from 1766 to 1811. It is to the share Mr. Barrow had in establishing the great Northern College of Ushaw that Mgr. Gradwell more especially refers in the subjoined extract, and it is on this account that we cite it :—"Mr. Barrow beheld with dismay the breaking up of the colleges in foreign lands, from which, during ages of persecution, the never failing supply of priests for the English mission had been derived, and he was one of the first amongst the clergy to agitate for a remedy. To erect a college in England was the obvious expedient ; but though all might agree in this, they agreed in nothing else. The first proposal was to found a college for the whole of England at Old Hall Green, and to combine the resources of all English Catholics in one grand establishment, but the Catholics of the great Northern Vicariate, then including the six Northern Counties, besides Cheshire and the Isle of Man, soon resolved on having a College of their own. The selection of a suitable site presented serious difficulties, and involved great delay. At one time a contract for the sale of Hazlewood Castle, the residence of the Vavasours, between the then Baronet, Sir Edward, and Dr. William Gibson, the Bishop, was actually signed, but the death of the Baronet prevented this scheme from being realized. A property at Gainford-on-the-Tees, belonging to the Withams, was then suggested ; finally it was decided to purchase from Sir Edward Smythe a portion of Ushaw Moor, and there erect the necessary buildings ; unfortunately Sir Edward was not a free vendor, as by his marriage settlements, though he could exchange, he was not able to sell. He was willing however to let the Bishop have the land, provided he could secure to him in exchange an adequate property in his own county of Shropshire, he being in too infirm health himself to attend to necessary business. This was a new source of delay, and. here Mr. Barrow came to the rescue. He entered into a correspondence with Sir Edward, and undertook to purchase a property to effect the exchange. In consequence of Sir Edward's increasing infirmity, Lady Smythe had to write the letters for him, but in spite of every difficulty, the energy of Mr. Barrow triumphed, the desirable property was purchased for the Baronet, and Ushaw Moor was conveyed to the Bishop. In this way Mr. Barrow did a real service, just in the nick of time. He ever afterwards regarded Ushaw with an especial affection, and in one of the many wills he made before his death, but which he left unwitnessed, he bequeathed a sum of money to Dr. Lingard, to enable him to finish his history of England, and another sum to his favourite college. When the college was opened, in July, 1808, he could not rest till he had seen it, and though 73 years of age, he mounted his horse and made his way over the hills of Westmorland and Yorkshire to Durham. The Rev. Henry Gradwell, then at the college, remembered him saying Mass at the side altar on the left, in the old chapel, now the College Hall. The appearance of the old man made a deep impression on the mind of his destined successor. Large boned, strongly built, and square shoulders, slightly above the middle height; he wore buckled shoes, worsted stockings, knee breeches, a deep waistcoat whose lappels came well down the thigh, a square cut coat, and above all, a red wig. This remarkable figure hobbled up to the altar, for he was very lame. He had to rest at the altar, and his first act was to pull off his wig, and deposit it on the altar. He then vested, and replacing his wig on his bald pate, proceeded to say Mass. One other proof of his love for the new college is found in his gift to it of the Claughton organ."

The last surviving Crook Hall student, Rev. T. Danson (Douthwaite) in a letter regarding the foundation of Ushaw, furnishes this information :—"I am the only survivor of those who quitted, one July day, the old house, Crook Hall, to tramp it down to Lanchester, and onward across the Rubicon—the Browney,—without a bridge for a help, and up Esh Hill; and so, thoughtless as little boys going to play, into a new house, which, if we had had wit enough, we might have called the palace of the winds—anything but a school.

"There is only one left who was an alumnus of Crook Hall, but he was not there that day, i.e. Rev. T. A. Slater.*

"The real active and only founder of Ushaw College amid a world of difficulties was Bishop William Gibson, and it was thus: Mr. Holdforth, who was then agent for the Acton Burnall estate and Esh, happened to be at Esh Laude with Rev. Mr. Yates, and one or two others, conversing of a school plan, when Mr. Holdforth said 'why not take the outside farm here of Ushaw Moor?' The Bishop, who was

---

*The Very Rev. Thomas Augustine Slater, of Hutton House, died Dec. 26th, 1884, and was buried on the 29th, at Ushaw. In 1807, at ten years of age, he went to Crook Hall, and the following year entered the new College at Ushaw; he was the Patriarch of the Diocese of Hexham and Newcastle, having attained his 89th year.

present, consented, and at that moment Ushaw was founded, about the middle of 1803. Bishop Gibson had closed a bargain for Hazlewood Hall with Sir Walter Vavasour, who had no heirs. The lease was amicably given up, and Bishop Gibson was left the sole founder of Ushaw, where he resided, hampered with much infirmity, till 1821. To him and to no one else is due and ought to be erected the grandest monument that was ever raised to a founder."

REV. ANTHONY LUND AND USHAW COLLEGE.

Four miles north-east of Preston is situated the secluded and time-honoured mission of our Lady of Fernyhalgh, a pleasant country spot almost "unknown to public view," but hallowed by many pious associations, and noted as the place where, amid ferns and moss, there flows a perpetual spring of gushing water, known as "Our Lady's Well" at Fernyhalgh. In olden times this well was accounted sacred, on account of the supposed healing quality of its waters, and the traditionary legend connected with it. It was to Fernyhalgh that, as tradition says, a wealthy merchant was miraculously directed to repair, and in the precincts of this well, above which he would find a crab tree growing, to build a a chapel in honour of the Blessed Virgin ;—in fulfilment of a vow made by him, when, overtaken by a storm on the Irish Sea, he was in peril of shipwreck and of drowning. Hence Fernyhalgh became a place of pilgrimage, and "Our Lady's Well," in the eyes of devout Catholics, was invested with a glamour of healing and sanctity. In this peaceful retreat of Fernyhalgh lived and laboured with exemplary zeal and piety, the Rev. Anthony Lund, "a meet shepherd of the people," the model of a good old priest, whose heart was set on the law of his God —"*lex Dei ejus in corde ipsius ;*"—who knew well that he was ordained both to pray and to work, and had implicit faith in the maxim— "*Laborare est orare.*" Anthony Lund was born at Barton Park, a farm in the township of Barton, near Preston. His mother was a Protestant ; his father a stout Christian, and a staunch Catholic. How, by what agency, special grace and favour, Anthony, a rustic, chubby-faced boy, was transplanted, in the middle of the 18th century, from the fields and meadows of Barton, and from the banks of Barton brook, along which, no doubt, in his boyhood he had often wandered, to the venerable ecclesiastical seminary of Douai, no ancient record reciteth :— but "*justum deduxit Dominus per vias rectas,*"—for

"There is a Providence that shapes our ends,
Rough-hew them how we will ;"

and, doubtless, through that kind Providence, Anthony was sent to the college at Douai, studied at Douai, was ordained priest at Douai, was professor of philosophy and theology at Douai. In the Douai Diary, Anthony Lund, son of John and Ann Benson, is recorded as having, at the age of 20, in his first year of philosophy (logicus), taken the college oath at the same time as William Gibson, aged 18, afterwards Bishop of Acanthus, and founder of the College at Ushaw. In 1765 his name appears as professor of philosophy ; and in 1770, ol theology. In 1773 he succeeded the Rev. Robert Banister* on the mission at Fernyhalgh, only a few miles distant from, and almost within sight of, his birth place, at Barton. For 38 years he resided at Fernyhalgh, and died there, September 21st, 1811, of his age 77 years, of his priesthood 51 years. His remains are interred in the centre aisle of the chapel, near the entrance to the Sanctuary. A blue slab stone covers them. The inscription upon it, written by Dr. Lingard, is in Latin, and reads thus :—

"Hic jacet R. D. Antonius Lund, Sacerdos et Alumnus Col. Angl. Duaci, ibidem S. T. Professor, postmodum Missionarius in Patria, et fidelis hujusce Congregationis Pastor apud Fernyhalgh, annis 38. Hanc B. V. M. sacram ædificavit Ecclesiam suo maxime patrimonio et dotavit ; qui illustrissimus Acanthensis Episcopi Vicarius Generalis, sui contemptor, suorum observantissimus et omnium humillimus, pie obiit die 21 mensis Septembris, A. D. 1811, annis natus, 77, Sacerdos, 61, Missionarius, 38. Requiescat in Pace."

The Philosophical theses of the Rev. Anthony Lund are carefully preserved in the archives of Fernyhalgh, and the names of those Douai students, who defended the several propositions, which the theses contained, are thereunto appended, and their memory thus perpetuated. The names are as follow :—

PHILOSOPHIA UNIVERSALIS.
Præside Rev. Dom. Antonio Lund,
Philosophiæ Professore,
Tueri conabuntur in aula Collegii Anglorum Duaci.

Carolus Belasyse, die 20 Junii, 1768.
Robertus Swarbrick, eodem die.
Thomas Eyre, die 22 Junii, 1768.
Gregorius Stapleton, eodem die.
Gulielmus Shaw, die 23 Junii, 1768.
Rudolphus Southworth, eodem die.

PHILOSOPHIA RATIONALIS.
Gulielmus Mumford,   ) die 1 Junii,
Thomas Eyre,   )   1767.
Robertus Swarbrick,   ) die 2 Junii,
Gregorius Stapleton,)   1767.
Rudolphus Southworth,) eodem
Gulielmus Shaw,   )   die.

PHILOSOPHIA NATURALIS.
Joannes Daniel,   ) die 30 Aprilis,
Joannes Orrell,   )   1766.
Gulielmus Tancred,) eodem
Joannes Perry,   )   die.

---

*The Rev. R. Banister was born at Hesketh Bank, November 1st, 1725 ; and was first taught at Dame Alice's School, at Ladywell. When Mr. Banister was sent to Douai, he made, it is said, the journey as far as London on a donkey. He arrived at Douai October 15th, 1741. I wonder what other priest besides Father Banister Hesketh Bank and North Meols can boast of. They abound in shrimps, donkeys, and dissent ; but as to the central principles of Catholic truth, they, and the whole of the district extending nearly to Preston, are as far removed from them as the poles asunder. Sadly does that ULTIMA THULE of West Lancashire require missionaries (for it is a spiritual desert) to evangelize and instruct them. The railway communication recently established in those parts may possibly produce a more hopeful state of things.

The Rev. Anthony Lund is described as "a grand old priest in his day." He used to walk to Preston every week, and bring back with him, in a wallet, his week's provisions. He had a peculiar craft and aptitude for making bee hives, and when he had any leisure time, he used to employ it in that occupation. He built the present chapel at Fernyhalgh out of his own resources, and in great part endowed it. He was Vicar-General of Bishop William Gibson for that part of Lancashire, and was a priest who won the esteem and affection of all his neighbours. "He seldom"—to borrow the words of the author of the 'Imitation of Christ'—"went abroad; he lived very retired; his diet was spare; he laboured much; rose early; spent much time in prayer, and kept himself in all kind of discipline."

The Rev. Anthony Lund left all his own books, Bishop Petre's, and those of others to Fernyhalgh chapel; also all things appertaining to the use of a chapel, such as chalices, vestments, candlesticks, &c. He ordered the sum of twenty pounds to be be given to the Catholic Secular Chapter in London; and twenty pounds to the Lancashire Infirm Secular Clergy Fund. He established burses at Ushaw for one or more students—particularly Lancashire students—for the Northern Mission of England, for each student forty pounds per annum to be allowed. And when any student, educated on his fund or funds, should have finished his studies, or gives up, another had to be nominated by the Lancashire Grand Vicar, with the approbation of the Bishop,—choice to be made of the most promising boys, in preference to affection, interest, or relationship. "Let this," he adds, "continue as long as my property shall fructify." He moreover directed that when any student or students, educated on his fund or funds, should be made Priest and sent on the mission, ten guineas should be given him as a viaticum. Most kind and considerate on the part of this good old Fernyhalgh priest, of whom it may most truly be said, "*opera ejus sequuntur eum.*"

How, it may be asked, do all these details respecting Father Anthony Lund apply to, or what connection have they with "Records and Recollections of Ushaw?" This point will be sufficiently and satisfactorily demonstrated by the subjoined facts and figures. The Rev. Anthony Lund, as Vicar-General of the Bishop of Acanthus, took special interest in the foundation of the college at Ushaw. He contributed liberally towards that object himself; encouraged and exhorted others to do the same; received the benefactions of friends, and the collections from various missions in Lancashire, which moneys, as will be found stated, he accounted for with great exactitude, and duly transmitted to the Bishop.

SUBSCRIPTIONS AND CONTRIBUTIONS TOWARDS BUILDING A NEW COLLEGE AT USHAW, REMITTED, AT VARIOUS TIMES, TO BISHOP GIBSON, BY REV. ANTONY LUND.

1803.		£	s.	d.
Sep. 2nd, Rev. James Finch		5	5	0
Oct. 28th, Rev. Antony Lund		100	0	0
Fernyhalgh Congregation		68	5	0
,, ,,		2	7	0

Fernyhalgh Congregation..............................	0	3	0
,, ,, ...	7	13	6
From Bank...	2	12	1
Nov. 22nd, Rev. John Lund and Cottam Congregation......	37	10	0

1803.
Oct. 28th, Paid in hand to Rt. Rev. William Gibson......... 100 0 0

1804.
May 11th, I sent to the Bishop a Preston Bank Note value. 73 12 0
May 29th, I sent two Bank of England Notes, one value
    £30, the other value £25........................ 55 0 0
June 16th, I sent a Preston Bank Note value.................. 110 0 0
June 30th, I sent a Preston Bank Note value.................. 144 6 7

1803.
Dec. 12th, Rev. Jas. Maudsley & Newhouse Congregation. 34 6 6

1804.
Jan. 17th, Rev. Richard Edmondson and Alstone Congre-
    gation..... .... 39 4 6
Feb. 8th, Rev. William Fisher & Ribchester Congregation. 7 3 0
Apr. 30th, Rev. Thos. Caton and Townley Congregation... 23 10 6
May 15th, Rev. Robt. Blacoe and Preston Congregation.... 60 0 0
July 17th, Preston Congregation 22 3 0
Aug. 28th, Preston, Mr. Chadwick 10 0 0
Oct. 15th, Preston Congregation................................ 16 14 0
Feb. 25th,   ,, ... 7 5 0
May 25th, Miss Ann Heatley....................................... 100 0 0
May 10th, Rev. James Dennet and Aughton Congregation. 2 0 0
Aug. 28th,   ,,   ,,   4 0 0

1805.
Mar. 16th, Rev. Rd. Thompson and Chorley Congregation. 56 14 2
Apr. 1st, Rev. James Dennet and Aughton Congregation... 10 0 0
May 10th, Rev. James Wagstaffe.................................. 3 0 0
Aug. 28th, Rev. Rd. Thompson and Chorley Congregation. 49 3 0
Sep. 1st, Rev. Rob. Swarbrick and Euxton Congregation... 19 12 6
    Mr. Emet, Gillmoss 1 0 0

1804.
Aug. 31st, I sent to Bishop Gibson a Preston Bank Note
    value 82 6 0
Dec. 3rd, I sent to Bishop Gibson a Preston Bank Note
    value 39 10 6
Dec. 8th, I sent a Preston Bank Note, with Mr. Heatley's
    money, value.. 100 0 0
Dec. 3rd, I paid on the Bishop's account to his niece at
    Preston 3 3 0

1805.
Feb. 16th, I sent a Preston Bank Note value................... 98 3 6
Mar. 28th, I sent a Preston Bank Note value......... .... 70 0 6
June 6th, I sent a Preston Bank Note value......... .... 57 19 0

1804.
Nov. 29th, Mr. William Heatley.................................... 100 0 0
Dec. 11th, Mr. Martin and Gousnargh Congregation......... 10 15 0
Dec. 11th, Mr. Wearing and Lower Hall Congregation...... 5 18 0

Dec. 11th, Mr. Tate and Lee House Congregation	1	8	0
Dec. 13th, Mr. Jos. Higginson and Ince Congregation	9	9	0
,, ,, ,,	0	2	0
1805.			
Feb. 13th, Mr. Dawson and Lytham Congregation	63	0	0
Mar. 16th, Rev. Mr. Berry and Culcheth Congregation	5	13	7
Mar. 16th, Rev. Mr. Shaw, of Leigh	7	12	2
Apr. 24th, Mr. La Lande and Wrightington Congregation	8	0	0
Apr. 25th, Mr. Irving and Mowbrick Congregation	42	14	0
June 1st, Mr. Johnson and Lydigate Congregation	7	0	0
June 4th, Mr. Parkinson and Eccleston Congregation	37	18	6
July 16th, Mr. Butler and Westby Congregation	23	3	6
Aug. 27th, Yealand Congregation	2	9	6
Aug. 31st, Rev. Mr. Talbot and Ormskirk Congregation	38	2	6
Sep. 9th, Mr. Lauronson and Scorton Congregation	13	6	1
Oct. 6th, Rev. Jo. Adkinson and Brownedge Congregation	16	3	0
Nov. 28th, Rev. Jas. Pope and Brindle Congregation	36	13	0
1805.			
June 28th, I sent a Preston Bank Note value	54	18	6
Aug. 14th, I sent two Derby Bank Notes value each £10	20	0	0
Sep. 12th, I sent a Preston Bank Note value	57	4	0
Nov. 5th, Paid by Bishop's orders to his niece, Dame Magdalen, to be charged for Ushaw	3	3	0
Nov. 29th, I sent a Preston Bank Note value	13	2	0
At same time a draft on London	36	13	0
1806.			
Apr., I sent him	0	2	0
July 23rd, I sent to Bishop	1	1	0
Rev. Mr. Grimbeldeston, near Warrington	1	1	0

Total amount remitted, £1260 4s. 7d.

OTHER SUBSCRIPTIONS AND COLLECTIONS IN LANCASHIRE, 1804,
FOR BUILDING COLLEGE AT USHAW.

	£	s.	d.	
Rev. Jno. Penswick, Birchley	30	0	0	or more.
Rev. J. Crathorne, Garswood	20	0	0	or more.
Rev. Jno. Shuttleworth, Brinn	20	0	0	or more.
Rev. Jos. Barrow, Lowhouse	17	14	0	
Rev. Jno. Orrell, Blackbrooke	7	17	0½	

Before proceeding with my account of the establishment of Ushaw, I will for the nonce interrupt the narrative and retrace my steps, to add a few more particulars respecting Crook Hall.

Crook Hall, called "Croke Hugh" in the records of Bishop Langley, is in the parish of Lanchester, and nine miles from the college of Ushaw. Between fifty and sixty years ago, I visited it with some college companions, walking all the way thither on a "Cornsay day." The reminiscences of Crook and its days of old were there. In other respects there was nothing to attract notice except a deserted mansion, empty rooms, and tenantless apartments. Since then, the district having become the centre of a multitudinous collier and industrial population, the *domus antiqua* of Crook, wherein learning and religion, in times gone by, went hand in hand, has been converted into a number of workmen's cottages. How fallen from its high estate! How melancholy its present memorials! Here it was that President Eyre, after a missionary life of twenty years, was placed over the little colony of Douai students; here Lingard taught and wrote; here studious youths were trained and fitted for the work of the ministry; here Bishop Gibson, in December, 1794, ordained his first priests—John Bell and Robert Blacoe—Douai alumni both. To Crook Hall belongs the honour of being the first ecclesiastical college established in England since the Reformation, and of being the eldest daughter of its venerable parent Douai. It became also a light of religion, and a centre of civilization in that wild and desolate part of the country.

Among other places, before a settlement was effected at Crook, Flass Hall, situated in the Derness Valley, about a mile south-west from the site of St. Cuthbert's College, was, among other places, thought of as a suitable house, and eligible locality for the reception of the Douai exiled students, and Bishop Gibson had a satisfactory lease offered of it. It was finally however decided to occupy Crook Hall as a residence, and collegiate establishment.

Below are the names of those students, who, until a more convenient and suitable abode could be found for them, were, in 1794, domiciled at Pontop Hall.

Post graves et diuturnos dolores, omnibus præter magnam in Deo fiduciam deperditis, ad sacros ignes refovendos; tanquam in locum quietis et tranquilitatis plenum, ad Pontop Hall, dum sedes quæreretur, (non admodum longe a Pontop et Brooms in comitatu Dunelmensi) convolarunt:—

Anno 1794.

Mag.	Joa. Lingard,	venit	Sept. 9,	ætat.	24.
,,	Joa. Rickaby,	,,	Sept. 9,	,,	28.
,,	Thoas. Lupton,	,,	Sept. 22,	,,	19.
,,	Joa. Bradley,	,,	Sept. 22,	,,	21.
,,	Thoas. Dawson,	,,	Oct. 9,	,,	18.
,,	Thoas. Story,	,,	Oct. 9,	,,	19.
,,	Thoas. Cock,	,,	Oct. 9,	,,	21.

I append a list of the superiors, and of the several students who were resident at Crook during its existence and occupation as a college, previous to its removal, under happy auspices, to the new college of St. Cuthbert, Ushaw. They number 124.

Thoas. Eyre.
Joa. Bell.
Jac. Newsham.
Thoas. Gillow.
Ric. Thompson.
Joa. Rickaby.

Joa. Lingard.
Nic. Gilbert.
Car. Saul.
Thoas. Penswick.
Ed. Monk.
Jos. Swinburne.

Thoas. Lupton.
Thoas. Dawson.
Thoas. Cock.
Joa. Penswick.
Georg. Barrett.
Hen. Silvertop.
Gul. Swinburne.
Gul. Hall.
Thoas. Berry.
Georg. Haydock.
Jos. Swinburne.
Georg. Eastwood.
Joa. Orrell.
Rob. Hogarth.
Car. Eyre.
Jos. Robson.
Thoas. Stoner.
Dav. Livingston.
Car. Horsman.
Nic. Cunningham.
Ric. Albot.
Georg. Brown.
Edw. Haggerston.
Jac. Platt.
Alfr. Cowley.
Thoas. Dale.
Jac. Wrennall.
Matt. Priestman.
Gul. Caley.
Brian Marsh.
Gul. Sanderson.
T. B. Pros. Ben. Gillette.
Joa. Ashhurst.
Gul. Clifton.
Sam. Jones.
Georg. Corless.
Car. Jones.
Thomas Youens.
Gul. Stoker.
Georg. Howe.
Joa. Briggs.
Jos. Rogerson.
Cuth. Simpson.
Jos. Curr.
Joa. Campbell.
Joa. Gorst.
Georg. Best.
Joa. Kirk.
Mic. Trappes.
Jasper Gibson.
Fras. Turvile.
Thoas. Enhis.

Joa. Bradley.
Jos. Marshal.
Thoas. Story.
Matt. Forster.
Bas. Barrett.
Car. Silvertop.
Joa. Goss.
Car. Orrell.
Thoas. Haydock.
Rob. Gradwell.
Ric. Blundel.
Gul. Harris.
Thoas. Smith.
Gul. Hogarth.
Thoas. Eyre.
Matt. Gibson.
Thoas. Leigh.
Jac. Fairbairn.
Gul. Swinburne.
Jac. Brown.
Thoas. Lupton.
Joa. Eyre.
Rad. Platt.
Thoas. Pinnington.
Joa. Dale.
Georg. Liddall.
Matt. Newsham.
Gul. Leadbitter.
Car. Agar.
Joa. Clifton.
Gul. Smith.
Car. Newsham.
Joa. Young.
Jac. Albot.
Hen. Gradwell.
Joa. Anderton.
Joa. Jones.
Edv. Jameson.
Hen. Leigh.
Gul. Brigham.
Gul. Eyre.
Thoas. Hodgson.
Thoas. Firlo.
Hugh Dick.
Jac. Crook.
Jos. Corless.
Georg. Storey.
Georg. Todd.
Thoas. Aug. Slater.
Gul. Selby.
Georg. Wilson.
Car. Lupton.

Jac. Leigh.	Gul. Turvile.
Georg. Sedgwick.	Hen. Maxwell Macdonogh.
Joa. Hall.	Car. Middlehurst.
Thoas. Douthwaite.	Joa. Gul. Douthwaite.

"OUR GLORIOUS COLLEGE OF USHAW."

" I think we may now glide on cheerfully, and hope ' o'er better waves to speed.' "

From the illustrious seminary of Douai, like a phœnix from its ashes, sprung its no less renowned representative, St. Cuthbert's College, Ushaw. If I cannot go so far as the Right Rev. Bishop of Hexham and Newcastle in characterising *Alma Mater* as
"*Matre pulchra filia pulchrior,*"
I can at any rate designate her as *stirpis filia nobilis,* and style her, as Bishop Bewick does in Pastoral IV., " Our glorious College of Ushaw ;" "our joy and our crown." It is undoubtedly a temple of religion, virtue, and learning, "venerable (as Pindar expresses it) with noble thoughts ;" historic memories, old and sage traditions. Built by the oblations of clergy, gentry, nobility, and people, its history spreads itself over three quarters of a century. Bishop Bewick, in a previous pastoral (Pastoral I.) writes as follows :—" For the education and training of our young clergy through twelve years of collegiate life, it is the glory of our Diocese, that it possesses one of the largest, grandest, and most efficient colleges in the land. Ushaw College holds highest rank in competitive examinations, and contributes yearly an admirable contingent to the ranks of the clergy in the six Northern Dioceses of England."

The erection of the College at Ushaw was commenced in 1804, and on July 19th, 1808, the President and the students from Crook Hall took possession of their new habitation. The building however was not wholly finished until 1819, but Bishop Gibson, who died in June, 1821, lived to witness its completion.

It was an arduous and anxious undertaking on the part of the aged Bishop, with, as is said, only £5 in his pocket to commence the building, but by unwearied zeal and perseverance he encountered and overcame all obstacles, and brought the work to a successful and auspicious termination.

" By wisdom the house shall be built, and by prudence it shall be strengthened. By instruction the storerooms shall be filled with all precious and most beautiful wealth."

"Turn my face towards Assisi," said St. Francis to the bearers who carried him in his last sickness, and then he blessed the place. How appropriately might not the good Bishop, on beholding the completion of his great work, have, in the same words of benediction as uttered by

St. Francis, blessed the college which he had founded :—" *Benedicaris a Domino, quia per te multæ animæ salvabuntur, et multi in te servi Altissimi habitabunt, et ex te multi eligentur ad regnum æternum.*"

They laboured not in vain—those who founded this noble college : God blessed the work, and prospered the cause, and the purpose for which it was instituted, *viz.*, to promote His honour and glory, the advancement of religion, and the exaltation of holy Church.

THE EXODUS FROM CROOK HALL TO USHAW.

In the year 1808, on a beautiful morning in July, the Feast of St. Vincent of Paul, when summer reigned in the heyday of its brightness and splendour, when the new-mown meads echoed with the song of the haymaker, and the wild roses and honeysuckles that festooned the hedges filled the air with fragrance, a small band of studious youths were seen wending their way through the ancient village of Lanchester, and, having traversed the long sweep of the valley that lay before them, overlooking which, hoary with time, prostrate and dismantled, appeared the ruins of Langley Hall, they ascended, with slow and travel-stained steps, the steep hill, the *Mons Sacer*, on which the new college of St Cuthbert, Ushaw, had been erected, and of which they were about to take possession. These youths, with no other equipments than a few books, cat-stick or battledore, which it may be supposed they carried with them, were the Crook Hall students, descendants of those flowers of Martyrs who had been nursed at Douai College, and some of them survivors even of the wreck and spoliation of that venerable establishment. They arrive at Hill Top, and cast a " longing, lingering look behind" towards Crook ; then hurry on, past the old yew tree, reach the college door, and having besought a blessing on the new habitation, and implored the protection of Our Lady and St. Cuthbert, enter with joyful hearts and hopes their future home and abode. Empty, blank, and desolate did each school-room, apartment, and passage appear ; bleak, wild, and barren was the aspect of the surrounding country ; and, as they gazed from the top windows of the front wing, few waving fields, few verdant pastures, few habitations of men met their eyes. Durham, the city of Ralph Flambard and Hugh de Pudsey, drowsy with the sleep of centuries, loomed in the distance ; and the sight of its cathedral, towering in the sky, exercised a gladdening influence upon them, inasmuch as it brought to their minds the times of their holy patron, St. Cuthbert, awakened the memory of his miracles and sanctity, and imparted fresh interest to the graphic account which their own Lingard, in his History of the Anglo-Saxon Church, had penned, of the opening of the Saint's tomb, and the discovery of his body by the monks of Durham. Not one of them but had read and pondered over that learned historian's narrative in class room or study-place. Some of them even had had the honour of being entrusted to take to the printer the proof sheets of that interesting work. Lingard himself shortly follows them from Crook ; he perhaps may have been among them when they were reconnoitring their new quarters, and surveying the country around them. He was their vice-president at Crook Hall ; he continued to hold the same office at Ushaw.

It was not before August 2nd that Mr. Eyre, the President, left Crook, with a few remaining students. After carefully locking the doors of the several apartments, he bade farewell to the deserted mansion, and took his departure to Ushaw.

The Ushaw Diary supplies me with the following notes, and undermentioned names of Superiors and Students who from Crook proceeded to Ushaw.

Prima alumnorum cohors, suis apud Crook Hall sedibus relictis, Collegium apud Ushaw intravit, feria 3tia, in Festo Sancti Vincentii a Paulo, die 19 Julii, 1808.

Feria 6ta, die 29 ejusdem mensis, capella benedicta est a Reverendissimo in Xto. Patre, Duo. Gulielmo Gibson, Episcopo Acanthensi, ac hujus districtus Septentrionalis Vicario Apostolico.

Feria 3tia, die 2 Augusti, has sedes (Ushaw) solus ingressus est Revdus. Dns. Thomas Eyre, primus hujus Collegii Præses, magnis suorum in ambulacro meridionali ordine instructorum clamoribus sublatis, et tintinnabulo sonante.

Die 2 Augusti, A.D. 1808, Collegio ab domicilio vulgo Crook Hall translato ad novas sedes in pago Ushaviensi, auspiciis faustis redintegratæ res sunt faventique summo Deo confirmatæ.

EX CROOK HALL PROFECTI SUNT.

SENIORES.

Rev. Dns. Tho. Eyre.   Rev. Dns. Joa. Lingard,
,, Joa. Bradley.   ,, Rob. Gradwell.
,, Ric. Albot.

THEOLOGI.

Dns. Rob. Hoggart.   Dns. Gul. Hoggart.
,, J. B. Marsh.   ,, Radul. Platt.
,, Jac. Platt.   ,, Geo. Brown.

PHYSICI.

Thos. Stoner.   Jac. Albot.
Mat. Newsham.   Thos. Pinnington.
Jac. Wrennall.

RHETORES.

Mat. Priestman.   Joa. Briggs.
Car. Newsham.

POETÆ.

Tho. Youens.   Tho. Hodgson.
Geo. Corless.   Hen. Gradwell.
Tho. Field.   Joa. Anderton.
Joa. Ashhurst.   Jos. Rogerson.

IN GRAMMATICA.

Jos. Curr.   Jac. Crook.
Gul. Eyre.   Joa. Kirk.
Fras. Turvile.

In I. Classe Rud.

Gasp. Gibson.
Joa. Gorst.
Joa. Campbell.
Gul. Smith.

Geo. Storey.
Car. Middlehurst.
Hugo Dick.
Geo. Howe.

In II. Classe Rud.

Gul. Selby.
Mic. Trappes.
Tho. Slater.

Geo. Best.
Joa. Hall.
Car. Lupton.

In III. Classe Rud.

Tho. Ennis.
Jac. Leigh.
Joa. Douthwaite.

Gul. Turvile.
Tho. Douthwaite.
Geo. Sedgwick.

Ad Collegium apud Ushaw postea venerunt.

Jac. Orrell.
Jac. Tatlock.
Is. Waberton.
Joa. Larkin.
Joa. Smelter.
Gul. Giles.
Hen. Turvile.
Jos. Brown.
Tho. Swinburne.
Jos. Sloane.
Tho. Billington.
Sam. Spooner.
Joa. Caton.
Jac. Ashton.

Jos. Orrell.
Joa. Waberton.
Car. Fox Larkin.
Gul. Cock.
Gul. Smelter.
Angus. Macdonald.
Mic. Ellis.
Gul. Brockholes.
Gul. Birdsall.
Tho. Hearne.
Tho. Strickland.
Gul. White.
Tho. Ashhurst.
Tho. Gibson.

Year followed year; the college went on improving in numbers, means, and resources; and while cultivating the wild places of mind, the uncultured and sterile lands around became cultivated also, and corn, and green crops, and herbage were taught to grow where the briar, the whin, and the bramble had previously sprung up and flourished.

The college was erected under the shadow of an aged yew tree, and from the yew tree it acquired "a local habitation and a name;"*

"For it had been an ancient tree,
Sacred with many a mystery."

It is a common opinion that of all European trees the yew attains to the greatest age—even to the longevity of centuries. But alas! the Ushaw yew is now a wreck, a ruin of its former self; time and tempest have dismantled its boughs and hollowed its trunk; and it has well nigh outlived its popularity. Still around the old tree there verdantly entwine innumerable historic and traditional memorials; and both in prose and

---

*Derived from YEW and SHAW (SCURVA—Saxon—a shadow)—a little hanging wood—a wood that encompasses a close. Johuson derives it from SHUA—Saxon; SCHAWK—Dutche.

in verse has the venerable yew been celebrated and sung. In the year 1880, not long before his lamented death, a poem, entitled " Verses on the old Yew Tree, by an affectionate son of Alma Mater, and dedicated to the Right Rev. the President, W. Wrennall, D.D.," were composed by the Right Rev. Bishop Chadwick. To the writer of this narrative a copy of these verses on " the old companion of their early days," was presented by his old friend and schoolfellow, the Bishop of Hexham and Newcastle. Other bards, other *vates sacri*, have sung of this goodly tree, the aged Ushaw yew. An iron palisade at present encircles and guards it; and even in its decrepitude does this ancient senator of the woods struggle to put forth a few sparse sprays and offshoots.

>Say, who can tell when first in lap of earth
>The seed was cast, from which this Yew had birth?
>It was a sapling, fragile, lithe, and young,
>When Druids dwelt the woods and groves among :—
>Ere Cæsar came, and with invading host
>Landed upon the cliffs of Albion's coast ;
>Ere from his native mountains and his plains,
>Caractacus was dragged to Rome in chains ;
>Before the Saxon marched with conquering horde,
>And devastation spread with fire and sword ;
>Before St. Augustine to the fair-haired race
>Proclaimed the Gospel, source of truth and grace,
>The Yew had grown a spreading, branching tree,
>Stately, umbrageous, and most fair to see.
>It yielded covert to the roaming herd
>Of cattle from the hills ; to beast and bird.—
>The pilgrim, seeking refuge from the storm,
>Beneath its branches felt secure from harm :
>For tempest's fury, and red lightning's glare,
>Were ever wont that sheltering tree to spare.

Carrington has the following lines on the yew tree, in a poem entitled "My Native Village :"

>Tree of the days of old—time-honour'd yew !
>Pride of my boyhood—manhood—age, adieu !
>Broad was thy shadow, mighty one, but now
>Sits desolation on thy leafless bough !
>That huge and far-fam'd trunk, scoop'd out by age,
>Will break, full soon, beneath the tempest's rage :
>Few are the leaves lone sprinkled o'er thy breast,

There's bleakness, blackness, on thy shiver'd crest !
When Spring shall vivify again the earth,
And yon blest vale shall ring with woodland mirth,
Morning, noon, eve,—no bird with wanton glee
Shall pour anew his poetry from thee ;
For thou hast lost thy greenness, and he loves
The verdure and companionship of groves :
Nor shall returning Spring, o'er storms and strife
Victorious, e'er recall thee into life !
Yet stand thou there—majestic to the last,
And stoop with grandeur to the conquering blast.
Aye, stand thou there—for great in thy decay,
Thou wondrous remnant of a far-gone day,
Thy name, thy might, shall wake in rural song,
Bless'd by the old—respected by the young.

 St. Cuthbert's College, Ushaw, is situated about four miles west of Durham, upon an eminence overlooking on the north the beautiful valley containing the village of Witton Gilbert, the woods, the ruins of Beaurepaire, and watered by the stream of the Browney, anon "tripping o'er its bed of pebbly sands," at other times " wrestling with the stones" that obstruct its flow. It commands, from the elevated site on which it stands, an extensive and diversified prospect. Hill and valley, rock and river, woodlands and meadows, corn fields and pastures, mansions and farmsteads, villages and hamlets—haunts of toiling men, Durham and its venerable cathedral, the Hambleton and Cleveland hills —all these are conspicuous objects in the landscape, and lend "enchantment to the view." The college is a large quadrangular building of stone, 180 feet from east to west, and 230 feet from north to south ; round the large court, which the college buildings enclose, run spacious ambulacra, the front ambulacrum or corridor being 160 feet long by 13½ feet wide. If the passage from it to the study place and library be added, the measurement may be computed at 224 feet.

 As time went on, St. Cuthbert's College progressed, not only in material resources,—in the augmentation of its possessions, the extension of its borders, and its lands and landmarks ; in the erection of new buildings, and the enlargement and ornamentation of portions of the original edifice, but in much greater measure and proportion did religion, piety, virtue, and learning flourish, intellectual progress and culture even outstripping the material—internal and external—improvements from time to time effected at the college :—
  " *Crescit occulto velut arbor œvo—*"
Like a tree, in the hidden recesses of a forest, its stature increased, its roots extended, its branches spread out and formed a goodly shade.

 A copy is said to have been made on parchment of the Iliad of Homer, and enclosed in a nutshell ; but it would require more ample pages than a miniature sheet of parchment to give a summary even of the traditions and "chronicles of eld" that Ushaw could furnish; to enumerate the succession of events, the routine of duties, and amusements; and to recount the various phases, mutations, and vicissitudes of college life. Time and space would fail were I to attempt to supply a record of all the pleasant memories, the cherished associations, the life-long friendships, the kindred pursuits, the studious rivalry, the hours of peace and prayer, as well as of the games, the sports, the play-day delights, so familiar to each one whose education commenced and finished at St. Cuthbert's College.

Upwards of three quarters of a century—a jubilee and half a jubilee —have elapsed since St. Cuthbert's College was opened, and in its regard God has been most gracious ;—"*magnificavit Dominus facere cum eis*"—with all who have had the interests and development of Ushaw at heart, and have been concerned for its good estate and welfare. Its career unquestionably has been of marked advantage to religion and of benefit to the church. But the founders of Ushaw and its early occupants, as well as those who had occupied Crook Hall, were not long in discovering that their lines had not fallen in the most pleasant places, and that they had not entered a land flowing with milk and honey—a land where, to quote a verse from Ovid :—

"*Flumina jam lactis, jam flumina nectaris ibant.*"

They had to fare frugally, sparingly, economically; no luxuries in meat and drink ; no superfluities in dress and furniture. To the house which they had entered they might appropriately apply the words of Horace—

"*Non ebur, neque aureum*
Mea renidet in domo lacunar;
Non trabes Hymettiæ
Premunt columnas ultima excisas,
Africa."———

In fact, they had as much as they could well do to make ends meet ; hence every thing was on a plain, simple, unpretentious, inexpensive scale —from salt-cellar to pewter plate—

"*Vivitur parvo bene, cui paternum*
Splendet in mensa tenui salinum ;"

from knife, fork, bread basket, beer can, and drinking utensils. No gas *then ;* nothing but oil lamps, and tallow candles, to a certain number of which latter the students were restricted, one mould candle being calculated to last eight hours of study. For further use a special supply had to be purchased. Some of the students in the higher schools would furnish themselves with a small lamp, and

"*Dum parvus lychnus modicum consumat olivi,*"

comfortably sit down in their rooms, and study by its pale light. *Then* you had to buy your own soap, clean your own shoes, find your own blacking, and use your own blacking brushes, if you wished to appear tidy and respectable on a Sunday or festival. However early Easter fell, and however cold and churlish the season, all fires commenced in October had to be put out at Easter. It is related that a student complained to the old President, Dr. Gillow, how cold he was, and that there was no fire in the school at which he could warm himself. "Go, child, to my room," said the President in answer, "and warm yourself at *my* fire." The fact is the President's room was as fireless and cold as any other place in the college. The dress of the students was not distinguished by much regard to fashion, being more quaint and peculiar than fashionable. "Trousers made of corduroy," blue coats with brass buttons, hats of all shapes and sizes, white cravats, &c., were the generally recognised articles of their attire. Those were primitive and exceptional times—times to try men's souls and ecclesiastical vocations—times to prepare aspirants to the priesthood for the battle of life, and fit them, when sent into the vineyard of the Lord, to endure the hardships of labour, privation, and poverty— "*duram et angustam pauperiem pati ;*" but "*les temps sont changés ;*" better and more hopeful days were dawning—

——"*Non, si male nunc, et olim
  Sic erit ;*"
——"the darkest day,
Live till to-morrow, will have passed away ;"

the sunshine of a brighter future would ere long gild the horizon of Ushaw ; and the privations and discomforts now endured would, as time sped on, be succeeded by a better and happier state of things ; so that those who had sowed in tears would live to reap in joy. "*Euntes ibant et flebant mittentes semina sua ; venientes autem venient cum exultatione, portantes manipulos suos.*" How beautiful and impressive, in allusion to the early history and future development of Ushaw, are the words spoken by His Eminence Cardinal Wiseman, on occasion of Dr. Newsham, the then President's, "grand jubilee." To this event I shall subsequently revert, and introduce an account of it. These are the great Cardinal's words :—"Thy fathers, who cast their seed in tears—thy fathers, who nursed thee in thy infancy—the Gibsons, the Eyres, the Lingards— they are gone to their repose and their reward. But, "*pro patribus tuis nati sunt tibi filii ;*" for though thy fathers have departed, children have sprung up from thee full of devotion, full of affection—children who, if they did not love thee, would not have been here on this festive occasion in such multitudes. "*Pro patribus nati sunt tibi filii ; constitues eos principes super omnem terram.*" Over the whole of this northern land, thou seest thy children appointed to rule over the spiritual welfare of God's people. "*Memores erunt nominis tui, in omni generatione et generationem.*" They will not neglect the duty which they owe thee, nor forget the love thou hast shown to them."

The good time came at last : the clouds of adversity rolled away ; and the winter of discontent gave place to the joyfulness and sunshine of spring, with the promise of an abundant harvest :—"*Etenim Dominus dabit benignitatem, et terra nostra dabit fructum suum.*" Since the college was established and opened, its career has been of marked advantage to religion, and benefit to the church "over the whole of this northern land." In 1809, the year after it was opened, its numbers were 99 ; in the present year, 1885, the students, clerical and lay, number about 300. Well nigh four score years have glided away, and during that period the beneficial advantages to religion, emanating from St. Cuthbert's college, will at once be apparent from the consideration that it has been truly a joyful mother of children—"*Matrem filiorum lætantem,*" having sent into the vineyard between seven and eight hundred priests. True, like their Douai precursors, they did not go forth to the martyrdom of blood, to be racked and tortured, to be hanged, butchered and embowelled; but another species of martyrdom awaited them—the martyrdom of fatigue, fever, cholera, and pestilence; the martyrdom and agony of heart, solicitude of mind, weariness of limb and brain. Priests of the Most High! go on your way from the tranquil bosom of *Alma Mater*, rejoicing. A vast work is before you. Go forth—you need not sigh, like the Conqueror of Macedon, for more worlds to conquer. All around you are worlds of wretchedness, depravity, and crime. Irreligion, insubordination and ignorance, uplift their hydra heads; pride, lust, avarice and ambition, stalk abroad like demons at noonday; hard-heartedness, fraud and oppression, are monsters gnawing the entrails of society. These, priests of the Most High! are worlds for you to conquer. Go forth, then, and may success crown your mission. Uplift the standard of the cross on hill side and mountain summit. Light up the beacon of faith and devotion to Mary in the rural abodes of our peasant population; penetrate the thickly crowded cities, the busy towns—the marts of trade, where sin-bloated faces meet you in the street; where profane oaths and curses, "spilt from lips that once were sweet, and sealed for heaven by a mother's kiss," assail your ears; where you mix with men whose hearts of human flesh have grown stony as trodden ways,

"Beneath the petrifying touch of gold;"

where you see no trace of God, no reverence of his law, no love of sweet Mary. All on the contrary is a wilderness of sin, where abyss calleth on abyss, and the cataracts of the waters of iniquity whirl and eddy with frightful tumult, plunging from depth to lower depth still. These, priests and pastors of the people, sons of dearly cherished Ushaw—these are the worlds that you have to conquer. Go forth to the battle and gird on your armour manfully. But despite the difficulties attending your conquests, despite the fiery serpents, cursing prophets, and armed giants opposing your progress, a renowned victory—faith conquering the world—awaits you; and holy church and your beloved College of St. Cuthbert encourage you to set out and proceed prosperously and reign :—"*intende prospere, procede, et regna.*"

From the same College have issued, since the date of its foundation, fifteen Bishops, two Archbishops, and two Cardinals,—men of light and leading, bright luminaries in the firmament of the Church— "*Magnanimi heroes nati melioribus annis.*"

Subjoined is a list of them, each and all of whom confer honour on Ushaw, their *Alma Mater*, and whom Ushaw regards with profound affection and reverence :—

CARDINALS.

His Eminence, Nicholas, Cardinal Wiseman, Archbishop of Westminster.
His Eminence, Ferdinand, Cardinal De la Puente, Archbishop of Burgos, in Spain.

ARCHBISHOPS.

His Grace, the Most Rev. George Errington, Archbishop of Trebizond.
His Grace, the Most Rev. Charles Count Eyre, Archbishop of Glasgow.

BISHOPS.

His Lordship, the Right Rev John Briggs, Bishop of Beverley.
,, ,, George Brown, Bishop of Liverpool.
,, ,, James Sharples, Coadjutor Bishop of Liverpool.
,, ,, William Turner, Bishop of Salford.
,, ,, William Hogarth, Bishop of Hexham and Newcastle.
,, ,, Richard Roskell, Bishop of Nottingham.
,, ,, Alexander Goss, Bishop of Liverpool.
,, ,, Thomas Grant, Bishop of Southwark.
,, ,, Robert Cornthwaite, Bishop of Leeds.
,, ,, James Chadwick, Bishop of Hexham and Newcastle.
,, ,, Bernard O'Reilly, Bishop of Liverpool.
,, ,, Richard Lacy, Bishop of Middlesbrough.
,, ,, Arthur G. Riddell, Bishop of Northampton.
,, ,, Angus Macdonald, Bishop of Argyll and the Isles.
,, ,, John William Bewick, Bishop of Hexham and Newcastle.

To the above may be added, though educated at Crook, the names of Thomas Penswick, Bishop of Europum and Vicar Apostolic of the Northern District, and of Robert Gradwell, Bishop of Lydda and Coadjutor Vicar Apostolic of the London district.

What a cloud of witnesses to the prestige and renown of Ushaw is presented to us in the catalogue of provosts, canons, doctors, theologians, dignitaries of the Church, and other worthies and celebrities— "men eminent in the senate, on the bench, at the bar, in the army, in literature, in medicine, in architecture, and in other branches of art and science, and in other spheres of life." *Alumni* of Ushaw all these, who, through the various chances and changes of life, have clung to it with affectionate remembrance and unabated attachment.

It is meet that a record should be kept of the lives of these good and holy Bishops above enumerated. Most of them have passed away —gone

"Into the land of the great departed,
Into the silent land."

But though dead, each could testify—"*defunctus adhuc loquitur*," that to the education received at Ushaw might be attributed whatever prestige and position—God be glorified—attached to him as a bishop and pastor of God's Church. The memoirs which follow, though brief, will not, I trust, prove uninteresting.

> Let us now praise men of renown, and our fathers in their generation. For these were men of mercy, whose godly deeds have not failed. Let the people show forth their wisdom, and the Church declare their praise.—ECCLUS.

CARDINAL WISEMAN.

> "A man mighty in word and deed both before God and man, eminent both for his learning and his life."

"A great man," says the author of Coningsby, "is one that affects the mind of his generation, whether he be a monk in his cloister, or a monarch on the field or in his cabinet." That Cardinal Wiseman was a great man, a great Prelate and Prince of the Church, leaving an impress on his age and generation, and influencing the fortunes of the renascent Church in England, cannot be called in question.

Nicholas Wiseman was born August 2nd, 1802, at Seville, in Spain, that land where Jesus is loved, and Mary is honoured; and where the mysteries of religion interpenetrate and entwine themselves round the daily lives of the people. His pious mother laid him as an infant upon the altar of the Blessed Mother of God, in the cathedral of that city. After her husband's death, early in January, 1805, Mrs. Wiseman* left Spain with her children, and on the 23rd of March, 1809, placed her two boys, James and Nicholas, at St. Cuthbert's College, Ushaw. After studying nine years at Ushaw, Nicholas went, at the age of sixteen, to pursue his studies at the newly-restored English College, Rome, where he dwelt and studied for twenty years. His career here as a student was marked with most brilliant and signal success. He was ordained priest March 19th, 1825, having been created Doctor in Divinity in 1824. In 1827 he was named by Pope Leo XII. Professor of Oriental languages, in the Roman University; in that year he published his "Horæ Syriacæ," chiefly drawn from Oriental manuscripts in the Vatican. His first great work was the "Connection of Science and Revealed Religion." In November, 1827, he was made Vice-Rector, and in 1828, Rector of the English College, which office he filled until 1840: in that year he was appointed Bishop of Melipotamus, and Coadjutor to Bishop Walsh, in the Central District. On the death of Bishop Griffiths, Dr. Wiseman, in 1847, was appointed Pro-Vicar Apostolic of the London District. In July, 1848, Bishop Walsh being translated to the London District, Bishop Wiseman here also became his Coadjutor. The former dying in 1849, the Bishop of Melipotamus succeeded him in the London District; and in 1850, on the re-establishment of the Hierarchy, he became the first Archbishop of Westminster, and Cardinal Priest of the Holy Roman Church.

---

*The family name of Mrs. Wiseman, mother of the Cardinal, was Strange; her name, Xaviera Strange, daughter of Peter Strange, Esq., of Aylwardstown Castle, in the barony of Ida, county Kilkenny. This has been an ancestral residence in the family for centuries, and was the birth-place and home of Xaviera Strange and of her immediate ancestors, during the past two hundred years.

Abler pens than mine, and men of greater note and ability, have written the life and recorded the claims of Cardinal Wiseman to the honour, respect, and esteem of posterity—"*Laus ejus in ecclesia sanctorum;*—even to the uttermost ends of the earth—
"From Greenland's icy mountains,
To India's coral strand,"
has the sound of his words, his name, and his fame gone forth, and the ascendancy of his genius and learning been everywhere recognised.

The Cardinal's first pastoral as Archbishop of Westminster and Metropolitan of England, under the restored hierarchy, was issued on 7th October, 1850, and dated from Rome, "*Extra Portam Flaminiam.*" The ferment caused by it through the length and breadth of Protestant England was perfectly indescribable. But His Eminence proved equal to the emergency. He defied the thunderbolts of bigotry; and turned back the rushing waves of intolerance which chafed and surged around him; and though the tempest threatened to overwhelm him, and "no popery" was written on every door and window shutter, at every street end and corner, and was set as a copy by nearly every Protestant village schoolmaster; then, "*Cum exurgerent homines in nos, et forte vivos deglutissent nos,*" he stood unmoved like a rock among the breakers of a wintry sea, God being his refuge and his strength, in the troubles which surrounded him—*Deus noster refugium et virtus in tribulationibus quæ invenerunt nos nimis.*" He issued his "Appeal to the Reason and Good Feeling of Englishmen", which had the effect of allaying the storm, and mitigating the infuriate frenzy—" the whirlwind of passion," which had seized on our Protestant fellow countrymen. Thereby "*obstructum est os loquentium iniqua*—the mouth was stopped of them that speak wicked things." Truly, and with just cause, might the Cardinal, in words of Virgil, and in allusion to the tempest that raged around him, have exclaimed—
"*Omnia ventorum concurrere prælia vidi.*"

His Eminence was unquestionably one of the brightest ornaments of the Church,—"*ecclesiæ sanctæ lumen,*" and the glory of our country. He was a boy at Ushaw, remembered and spoke with delight of his College days at Ushaw,—"*juvat meminisse beati temporis,*"—and for Ushaw he entertained the most affectionate regard. As the home of his boyhood and youth, and of his early recollections, he was most sincerely attached to *Alma Mater.* Not more closely does the ivy adhere to the oak or elm, than did Cardinal Wiseman to Ushaw—
"*Arctius atque hederâ procera astringitur ilex.*"

"I can say," observed the Cardinal on a festive occasion at Ushaw, "for my own part, that I have never felt the sentiments which I entertained, while I was a student at this College, diminished by length of absence, or by distance of place. I believe that I never on any occasion made a journey from Rome to England, that I never did fail to travel down to this College in order to prove my attachment to it; and I am not conscious, on any occasion that has presented itself to me of being of any service to the house, which I have not considered a duty as well as a sincere pleasure:"—
"Where'er I roam whatever realms to see,
My heart untravell'd fondly turns to thee."

Nor can it be doubted that in his last sickness, and at the approach of death, his loving heart would turn to Ushaw, whence he knew prayers and suffrages would ascend for him :—

———" *et dulces moriens reminiscitur Argos.*"

From a record in the Cardinal's hand-writing, unto which my attention has been directed, and which will be found below, one would be led to infer that, at one time at least, having been in boyhood nursed in the bosom of *Alma Mater*, he intended at his death reposing in her lap, in the peaceful, green "God's Acre," attached to the college :— *Ubi a tenerrimis annis vitæ sacerdotalis fundamenta jaciebat, hic veluti in Almæ Matris sinu locum sepulturæ sibi elegit N. S. R. E. Card. W., Domo Hispali: primo quidem in hoc Collegio S. Cuth. ; deinde Romæ in Ven. S. Thomæ Ædibus educatus, harum Pro-Rector, et deinceps Rector fuit ; in Universitate Romana Hebraicas disciplinas plures annos tradidit ; mox Epus. Melipotam. et Vicarii Apostolici in mediterranea Angliæ regione Coadjutor renunciatus, per octo annos Collegii Oscottiani Rectoratum gessit ; inde Londinum a S. Sede deputatus, Archiepiscop. Westmonast. primus est constitutus, eoque in munere ævum consumpsit ; nonnulla etiam scripta post se relinquens, quibus est ista brevis sui memoria connumeranda. Natus die 2 Aug., A. MDCCCII., obiit—*

The following address was forwarded from St. Cuthbert's College to His Eminence, on his elevation to the dignity of Cardinal and Metropolitan of this country :—

TO HIS EMINENCE CARDINAL WISEMAN,

Archbishop of Westminster, &c.

MAY IT PLEASE YOUR EMINENCE,

Amidst the universal joy of the Catholics of England at the return of your Eminence amongst us, we, the Superiors and Students of St. Cuthbert's College, are anxious to express how fully we share in this joy, and to offer to your Eminence our respectful congratulations on your elevation to the dignity of Cardinal and Metropolitan of this country.

The absence of our President has prevented us from addressing your Eminence earlier, but now that it has pleased the Holy See to place us in a particular manner under your Eminence's protection, and thus to connect your Eminence by a new tie with the College of St. Cuthbert, we can no longer delay to express those feelings of respect and esteem which we entertain towards your Eminence.

We have long regarded with admiration the virtues and talents with which your Eminence has adorned and defended the Church in this country, and have felt a pride in remembering that it was in St. Cuthbert's College that your Eminence passed your youth. The warm interest which your Eminence has always taken in this College, and the many marks of attachment which we have so frequently received from you, have endeared your Eminence more and more to our hearts, and make us rejoice still more at this closer connection which now unites you to St. Cuthbert's College.

We have, with the rest of the Catholics of England, welcomed with gratitude the restoration of the Hierarchy in this country, and rejoiced to see one whom we so deeply reverence placed at its head. And though it has been with feelings of sorrow that we have witnessed the outbreak of clamour and abuse from the enemies of our faith to which your Eminence has been so prominently exposed, yet it has been without fear, for we know that God who ever dwells with His Church will not fail to protect her, and make her come forth still more glorious from all her trials.

Signed on behalf of the Community,

BY THE PROFESSORS.

To this Address the Cardinal returned the following reply :—

TO THE SUPERIORS AND STUDENTS OF ST. CUTHBERT'S COLLEGE.

MY DEAR FRIENDS IN CHRIST,

There is scarcely a place on earth, from which expressions of interest and affection could come more welcome to me, than those which, in your address, have greeted me from St. Cuthbert's College. Almost from the earliest dawn of reason till the present hour my connection with it has been unceasing, and, in its comfort to me, unvarying. There was the groundwork of my education, and of my future happiness, laid ; there not only the foundation of sound knowledge was tasted by me, but the sources of spiritual and better wisdom were first approached. And there it is more than probable that I should have completed my course of ecclesiastical studies, had not the splendid temptation of Rome opened itself before me, and an ardent desire, even previously conceived, of studying amidst its sacred monuments, made me join the first colony that went to people the empty halls of our ancient Roman College.

But no distance of time or place could even weaken an affection, still less dissolve a tie, so early formed. I have watched with undiminished interest the growth of stately buildings round the original, and in my time unfinished, pile of St. Cuthbert's College. I have followed, with the lively interest of a faithful son, the varied improvements which have been engrafted on the old solid and vigorous stock of its constitutions. This unbroken connection between that noble foundation and myself, kept alive by reciprocal offices of friendship, has been greatly strengthened by the continuation there, as its worthy president, of the honoured Monsignore Newsham, with whom, more than with any other person, I had the pleasure of being connected, as his pupil, through my whole education. His absence in Rome at the present moment enables me thus to record my sentiments of gratitude and attachment to him.

You will have heard that a new and temporary connection between us has been established, owing to the necessity of fresh arrangements, springing from our altered ecclesiastical organization. That the duty imposed upon me was neither asked nor desired by me, you will easily believe, especially when it is superadded to what already is oppressive ; that it is one of the most friendly and favourable character as it regards St. Cuthbert's, my acceptance will prove. I need not further assure you, how false have been the statements put forth by some secret enemy, that some advantage or power has been gained by me through this appointment. I am confident that its result will be the strengthening of past union between us, and increasing mutual confidence and attachment.

Thanking you sincerely for this expression of your kind wishes, and earnestly entreating your prayers,

I am, ever,

Your affectionate Servant and Friend in Christ,

N. CARD. WISEMAN.

The Cardinal's career was now soon to draw to a close. The time was approaching when he was to be set free from his earthly tabernacle, and his desire fulfilled of being dissolved and being with Christ— "*Cupio dissolvi*," he frequently repeated in his last illness, "*et esse cum Christo.*" He had gone forth to his work in the morning ; the evening had now come when he would have to rest from his labours. From 1840 to 1860 his life was one of untiring and incessant activity. God employed him as a special instrument, and raised him up for a great purpose, *viz.*, to extend the dominion of His Church in this country, to rebuild its ruined walls, restore its desolate altars, and fill up the rents and fissures of our houses and sanctuaries. Cardinal Allen, by resolute patience, energy, and activity, defended and preserved the ancient faith of our fathers, which the rude assaults of heresy threatened totally to extirpate. Cardinal Wiseman re-invigorated, and in part, at least, restored to its pristine influence and prestige that same faith which three centuries of grinding persecution had well nigh effaced and extinguished :—" *Dominus memor fuit nostri, et benedixit nobis.*" The small spark, that had lain hidden under cold and desolate embers, he helped to fan into an ardent flame, encouraging popular devotions, countenancing the establishment of pious confraternities and associations, promoting works of usefulness, charity, and piety, receiving converts into the fold, attacking false doctrine and heretical delusions, in whatever stronghold he found them. The hearts and affections of his Protestant fellow-countrymen, at one time so estranged and antagonistic, began to warm towards him ; and him, whom they not long ago looked upon as an enemy, they now regarded as a friend ; entertaining so high an opinion of his literary attainments that his society became esteemed and courted, and he was solicited to give public lectures on various occasions. His last intellectual work was preparing to give a lecture on Shakespeare, at the Royal Institution, having sometime before been invited to do so. This lecture he dictated during his illness, but he did not live to deliver it. His sickness and sufferings increased daily, and the sorrows of death began to encompass him. But "*omnia pro Christo ;*" he suffered all for the sake of his loving Saviour ; he suffered with courage, resignation, and patience ; and though he desired to be dissolved and to be with Christ, "not my will but Thine be done," would he add, " my dearest Jesus ;" hence he died in perfect obedience to the will of God, and in conformity with our Blessed Lord. "The Last Illness" of His Eminence, by Canon Morris, gives a beautiful account of "the grand and holy ending" of the Cardinal's useful life. We there learn that he died "calmly and peaceably, in the midst of prayers and sacrifices," wishing "only to go home as soon as it pleased God." "Never," as he declared in his last illness, "have I cared for anything but the Church ; my sole delight has been in everything connected with her. As people in the world would go to a ball for their recreation, so I have enjoyed a great function." At length his earthly pilgrimage being ended, he was summoned to receive the reward of his labours. "He had fought a good fight, he had finished his course, he had kept the faith," and on the 15th of February, 1865, he died the death of the just ; on the 25th of the same month he was interred in Kensal Green cemetery, on the outskirts of London, followed to the grave by an immense concourse of friends and mourners. Throughout England, and wherever the Cardinal's name was known, and his renown had reached, his death was deeply lamented. For a great High Priest, a Shepherd of the people ; described by the Sovereign Pontiff, Pius IX., in the year 1863, as "the man of divine Providence for England," had been gathered to his fathers, and his place would be known no more. " *Vivit tamen semperque vivet,*" for the memory of him and of his great works will be spread abroad, like a sweet perfume, and transmitted unto future ages.

What Tacitus has written regarding Agricola, may not inappropriately be said of Cardinal Wiseman :—" *Quidquid ex Agricola amavimus, quidquid mirati sumus, manet mansurumque est in animis hominum, in æternitate temporum, fama rerum. Nam multos veterum velut inglorios et ignobiles oblivio obruet ; Agricola posteritati narratus et traditus, superstes erit.*"

In the sermon preached at his solemn requiem, Dr. Manning thus summarises the bequests the Cardinal has left us—the love of Rome, the love of sinners, the supremacy of faith, the purity of Catholic education.

Cardinal Wiseman's writings were numerous, and embraced a variety of subjects. Perhaps "the most beautiful creation of his mind" was "Fabiola, a Tale of the Catacombs," read wherever the English tongue is spoken, and translated into various other languages. For his "Lectures on the Principal Doctrines and Practices of the Catholic Church," delivered in London during the Lent of 1836, the Catholics of London presented him, prior to his departure for Rome, with a gold medal, appended to a costly enamelled gold chain. Round the medal was inscribed—"*Nicolao Wiseman, avita religione forti suavique eloquio vindicata, Catholici Londinenses, mdcccxxxvi.*" The Pope having requested to see this medal and chain, was pleased to place it on Dr. Wiseman's neck, with many expressions of kindness.

In an article in the *Manchester Guardian*, in which allusion is made to His Eminence, the writer thus speaks of him :—"Cardinal Wiseman was one of the most notable and influential men of his time. The movements he promoted have taken directions sometimes little expected, and the passions he aroused have to a great extent died away. But when we count over the names of those who have helped to make the social and religious world of to-day what it is, among the names, if not of the first rank, yet certainly of the second, must be placed that of Nicholas Wiseman."

CARDINAL FERDINAND DE LA PUENTE

was born at Cadiz, 28th August, 1808. From Cadiz, in 1822, or in the year following, he came as a student to St. Cuthbert's College. He was a most pious and studious youth, of tall and slender form, kind and affable in his manners and deportment. On coming to Ushaw, he was unable to speak a word of English, but by dint of assiduous application and study, he soon became proficient in speaking and writing that language. It required however a longer time to get inured, if he ever did so, to the cold and frosty weather of an English winter. He tried hard, when the ice on the college pond would bear, to learn to skate, but his weak ankles always gave way under the process. Being of a modest, quiet, retiring disposition, and unused to the manly games of an English playground, he was seldom or never seen in the palæstra of the cat ring or football field ; but was oftener found in the racket court, or enjoying a quiet game at handball. In his studies however, he greatly excelled, and was never far off the top of his class. Having at Ushaw completed his Humanities, he returned to his native country, and after finishing there his course of Philosophy and Theology, he was raised to the priesthood. On the 27th October, 1857, he was appointed Archbishop of Burgos ; was created a Cardinal, September 27th, 1861 ; and died March 10th, 1867. The writer, when a student at Ushaw, had the honour of having, when in the class of High Figures, the subject of this memoir for his pedagogue ; hence he cherishes most sincere respect for his memory.

A very fine engraved portrait of the Cardinal hangs in the refectory ambulacrum, at Ushaw, close to the door of the Professors' parlour. At the foot of the engraving, in his Eminence's own handwriting, is inscribed,—

"To my dear Alma Mater, St. Cuthbert's College,
F., CARD. DE LA PUENTE,
Archbishop of Burgos."

In the back ground of the picture is a view of the Cathedral of Burgos. The Archbishop is represented seated, clad in episcopal attire. The retrospect of between 50 and 60 years is a long period, but we distinctly remember, even so long back, that Ferdinand De la Puente was tall and thin, had sleek, dark hair, pale and delicate looking features; lips rather thick and protruding.

ARCHBISHOP ERRINGTON.

Truly a worthy Archbishop—"*justum et tenacem propositi virum ;*" distinguished alike for piety and learning; whose very features bear the impress of asceticism and mortification. Archbishop Errington is evidently one of the old school, who has inured himself to a life of much endurance, and whom a crust of bread would readily satisfy. Indeed, on one occasion I met him in the ambulacra at Ushaw, eating a hard crust of bread, with apparently no small relish, as if he never eat except when he was really hungry. So humble, gracious, and courteous withal, so plain in attire, so grave in deportment, you would, on beholding him, suppose he was some old monk from the cloisters of Citeaux or Cluni. This good Archbishop, at present residing at Prior Park, and there teaching theology, was educated at Ushaw, and for his *Alma Mater* entertains a regard and affection, fresh and unfading as an evergreen shrub in the winter season. It was in the year 1814, the day after the feast of the Assumption, that George Errington was sent to St. Cuthbert's College. He was born at Clints, near Richmond, Yorkshire, in the month of September, 1804, and can legitimately boast of having an old and honourable Catholic ancestry :—

"*Nobilis antiquo veniens de germine patrum,
Sed magis in Christo nobilior merito.*"

In 1821 he left Ushaw to pursue his studies at the English College, Rome, which he did with great honour and distinction. On December 22nd, 1827, he was ordained priest, and created in the same year Doctor in Divinity. In 1832 he was made Vice-Rector of the English College, Dr. Wiseman being Rector. On his return to England from Rome we find Archbishop Errington at St. Mary's College, Oscott, where, for some time, he had the direction of the studies. Subsequently, he was attached to the Church of St. Nicholas, Copperas Hill, Liverpool, and also to that of St. John, Salford, which latter church was opened by him in 1848. From this church he was promoted to the see of Plymouth, being consecrated in St. John's, Salford, by Archbishop Wiseman. In 1855 he was made Coadjutor to Cardinal Wiseman, Archbishop of Westminster, with the title of Archbishop of Trebizond. His connection with the Arch-diocese of Westminster ceased in 1862. He attended the Vatican Council as Archbishop of Trebizond. His Grace is a man of considerable literary attainments, a profound theologian, well versed in Canon Law, and imbued with a great love and knowledge of the Holy Scriptures. During the "Papal Aggression" mania, a course of Sunday evening lectures were given by the Archbishop, in St. John's Cathedral, Salford, on the subject of the Hierarchy. These were subsequently published, and being extensively read, contributed to throw oil on the troubled waters.

To George Errington, Esq., formerly M.P. for Longford, whose frequent journeys to Rome, and residence there, have attracted so much attention, and their purpose and motive been so much canvassed, Archbishop Errington is uncle.

The above biographical notice of the good Archbishop was written and printed some months before the intelligence of his lamented death was announced. He had been on a visit to his friends in Ireland, cold and bleak and wintry as the weather was, and on his journey homewards, after spending two or three days at Southport with his old and much esteemed friend, Right Rev. Mgr. Fisher, D.D., he left Southport on Thursday, January 14th, to return to Prior Park. Here, soon after his return, he began to suffer from a chill; bronchitis set in, under which, having piously received the sacraments of the church, he sank rapidly, and tranquilly expired on Tuesday evening, January 19th, in the 82nd year of his age. On the following Tuesday, after a solemn Requiem Mass, at which Bishop Clifford assisted on his throne, and by whom the funeral sermon was preached, he was buried in peace, his place of sepulture being in the cloister immediately outside the principal entrance to the church. The deceased Prelate "entered the grave in abundance, as a heap of wheat is brought in and garnered in its season."—Pray God grant him eternal rest and endless light.

> "*Rest* for the busy hand and brain,
> Rest for the weary, toil-stained feet;
> For the poor heart that rest complete
> It ever sought on earth in vain.
>
> And *light* God's primal gift of old—
> All life's strange problems now explained,
> All knowledge without toil attained,
> All mysteries as a scroll unrolled."

Though "it is sad to see such men pass away—to see break within our hands the chain of the generous and ancient traditions," *non recedet memoria ejus, et nomen ejus requiretur a generatione in generationem: et laudem ejus enuntiabit ecclesia.*—Eccl. 39. Archbishop Errington was the last solitary link, save one, *viz.*, Rev. Thomas Danson, one of St. Cuthbert's earliest students, in the chain that united the old by-gone generation of Ushaw students with those of the present generation—those who within recent years have pursued, or at present pursue, their studies in the academic bowers of St. Cuthbert's.

The further details of the Archbishop's life and death, here subjoined, I have extracted from the substance of the discourse delivered by Bishop Clifford at the funeral, from the text—"*Fear not the verdict of death.*"

"The Hierarchy having been established in England in September, 1850, by Pope Pius IX., Dr. Errington was appointed Bishop of Plymouth, whilst his great friend, Dr. Turner, was named Bishop of Salford. They both received episcopal consecration from Cardinal Wiseman, in the cathedral church of Salford, on the 25th of July, 1851, and Bishop Errington started shortly after for Plymouth, where he took possession of his See, on the 6th of August of that same year. It was then that Bishop Clifford became his secretary and Vicar-general, and thence dates that warm and intimate friendship that continued undiminished between them during thirty-four years, to the Archbishop's death. The Bishop here spoke of the spirit of abnegation, poverty, and devotedness to duty which marked Dr. Errington's life at Plymouth, and gave several interesting instances of his humility and the hardships he underwent. He laid the foundation on which the zeal of his successor has been able to raise that goodly superstructure, which those who have visited Plymouth admire at the present day. The part which Dr. Errington took in the first and second Provincial Councils of Westminster, as also his inauguration of the first Diocesan Synod at Ugbrooke, the seat of Lord Clifford, were next alluded to. In the year 1855, Dr. Errington was raised to the rank of Archbishop of Trebizond by Pope Pius IX., and appointed Coadjutor to Cardinal Wiseman at Westminster. Bishop Clifford, having referred to Dr. Errington's labours in this new sphere of action, and having alluded to the circumstance of his having been chosen by Pope Pius IX. to assist the Pontiff in conferring episcopal consecration on himself, on the 15th February, 1857, touched briefly on the subsequent difficulties which arose between Cardinal Wiseman and Dr. Errington. We have nothing here to do with the matter in dispute. It suffices for us to know that Pope Pius IX., who adjudicated the question, decided that it was expedient that Dr. Errington should cease to be Coadjutor to Cardinal Wiseman. This decision sufficed for Dr. Errington; henceforth he ceased to be officially connected with the Hierarchy in England, and retired into private life. On two subsequent occasions the same Pontiff made him the offer of two important archiepiscopal Sees; but having now reached an advanced period of life, and not feeling equal to enter upon fresh fields of labour, he preferred, and obtained the Pope's consent, to remain in retirement. But though we are not here concerned with the nature of his differences with the Cardinal, the humility and patience with which he bore his trial deserve our highest praise, as they ever commanded the admiration of those who knew him. Never was he known to show resentment, or heard to utter an unkind word regarding anybody connected with those disputes. But though retired from public life he could not exist without work, and so, at the invitation of his friend Dr. Goss, Bishop of Liverpool, he took charge of the missions in the Isle of Man, and there laboured for some years as a missionary priest. In 1869-70 he assisted with the other Archbishops and Bishops of the Catholic world at the Vatican Council. Dr. Errington had now reached his sixty-seventh year, and was anxious to find some occupation better suited to his strength than the hard work of a missionary priest. As he was journeying home from Rome with Bishop Clifford, after the Council, the Bishop proposed to him that he should come and reside at Prior Park College, and undertake the tuition of the young theological students preparing for the priesthood. He was pleased with the offer, and at the close of the year 1870, he took up his abode in the college, where he remained during fourteen peaceful and happy years till the day of his death. The Bishop then spoke of the edifying life led by the Archbishop at the college, and especially of his great humility, and his scrupulous exactitude and punctuality in the observance of the regulations of college life, and in the discharge of his self-imposed duties. Up to the very end, even on the morning of the day in which he breathed his last, he busied himself about the work of his pupils. Having dilated on his many virtues, and having made reference to the devotion with which he received the last sacraments and disposed himself for death, Bishop Clifford continued :—He was a man of high principles, he was indefatigable in action, he knew not what it was to be idle, he had a stern sense of duty, and was scrupulously exact in all that regarded it. He had an iron will, and the vigour with which he applied it weighed heavily at times on those who worked with him ; but he was supremely just, and no one of his subordinates ever complained of having received from him an unjust or unfair command. When hard or unpleasant work had to be undertaken, he was foremost in claiming his share. With all this he had a kind heart, and was ever ready to assist both by words and by deeds those that were in distress. He was most true and sincere in his friendships, and no man ever had friends more numerous and more attached to him. He had a particular gift of interesting and gaining the affection of children. He was a man of high intellect, and was well versed in ecclesiastical learning, and also in various branches of science. But he was most humble and unassuming in his manner, most patient under adversity and trials. He was most profoundly religious, exact in prayer and his religious duties, faithful in offering the Holy Sacrifice daily. Every day he read and meditated on the Holy Scriptures, and he loved to talk on, and discuss, religious subjects. As he lived, so he died ; he was engaged in his work to the very last. Shall he, then, fear the sentence of death? What is the verdict that those remaining behind shall put upon him? Truly he deserves the name so frequently bestowed upon him in life, of the good Archbishop."

Though the days of the Archbishop were prolonged to a ripe and venerable old age, still might he with truth exclaim—"*Behold thou hast made my days as a handbreadth, and my age is as nothing before thee ; verily every man at his best is altogether vanity.*"

ARCHBISHOP EYRE.

The Eyres are an ancient and respectable family, serving God after the old Catholic manner. Five generations of them—"*avi numerantur avorum,*" have been brought under my notice. I trace them from Nathaniel Eyre, who was born January 25th, 1713, and died June, 1782. Nathaniel had four sons, three of whom—"*fortes creantur fortibus et bonis*"—became priests, viz., Edward, born 1745, died at Hathersage, Nov. 15th, 1834 ; John, D.D. died at the Farm, near Sheffield, Feb. 19th, 1790; and Thomas, President of Crook Hall & Ushaw, born 1748, died May 7th. 1810. Vincent Eyre, of Highfield & Newbolt, Co. Derby, Nathaniel Eyre's eldest son, had issue four sons, all educated at Crook. His third son, John Lewis Count Eyre, who died Nov. 11th, 1880, was father of Mgr. Vincent Eyre, priest at Chelsea ; of Rev. John Lewis Eyre, who was educated at Ushaw, ordained priest July 25th, 1840, and died at Newcastle-on-Tyne, October 15th, 1842, at the early age of twenty-seven ; of his Grace, Most Rev. Charles Eyre, Archbishop of Glasgow ; and of Rev. Father William Eyre, S.J., late Rector of Stonyhurst College. In regard to the last named I erred in stating (p. 71) that he received the early portion of his education at Ushaw. He was educated in his early years at Prior Park ; went to Ushaw for a few months only ; thence to Oscott, attracted thither by the fame of the then President, Dr. Wiseman. He ultimately proceeded to Rome, where, after six years' course of study, and at the age of thirty, he was ordained priest in the Basilica of Saint John Lateran. He afterwards entered the noviciate of the Society of Jesus, at Hodder Place. In May, 1879, Father Eyre was appointed Rector of Stonyhurst College, from the duties of which office he retired in September, 1885. In connection with Mgr. Vincent Eyre, of Chelsea, I omitted to state that at the time Dr. Baggs was Rector, Mgr. Eyre, from 1841-3, was Vice-Rector of the English College, at Rome. Others of the Eyres, to the number of eight, cousins to the four brothers above named, were educated at Ushaw : among these was Vincent, priest, who died at Bradford, September 28th, 1850. He had previously served the missions of Granby Row, and Mulberry Street, Manchester ; and was also at Stella ; whence he went to Bradford, Yorkshire, in 1845. To his brother, Lewis Eyre, 78, Redcliffe Gardens, London, I beg to express my acknowledgments, having by his aid been enabled to trace, as above, the genealogy of the worthy family of the Eyres.

The Most Rev. Charles Eyre, the Archbishop of Glasgow, was born at Askham Bryan Hall, York, November 7th, 1817. In Easter Week, 1826, not yet nine years old, he, with his brothers Vincent and John, was sent to St. Cuthbert's College, Ushaw, where he pursued his studies assiduously and diligently : he commenced his theology, and received Minor Orders in 1836. Having completed in 1839 his theological course at Ushaw, he went in December of that year to Rome, where he remained and studied three years and a half. On the 12th of March, 1842, he was ordained deacon, having previously, at Ushaw, May 25th, 1839, been made sub-deacon. On the 19th of March—the Feast of St. Joseph, 1842—he was ordained priest, and appointed by Pope Gregory XVI. one of his Chamberlains. After Easter, 1843, he returned to England, and till the completion of St. Mary's Church, Newcastle-on-Tyne, was placed at St. Andrew's, in that town. In the following year he was appointed to St. Mary's. The year 1847 was the terrible fever year. The subject of our memoir, the young and devoted priest of St. Mary's, caught the epidemic, and nearly fell a victim to it, his life for several days being despaired of. In order to recruit his health, he was placed from 1850 to 1856 in charge of a country mission, that of Haggerston, in Northumberland. In 1856 he returned with restored health and vigour to St. Mary's, Newcastle. In 1875 Mgr. Eyre visited Egypt and the Holy Land, during which visit he had the honour of being made a Knight of the Holy Sepulchre. In 1861 he was appointed one of the Canons of the Cathedral Chapter, and in 1866 Vicar-General of the diocese of Hexham and Newcastle. Early in December, 1868, Mgr. Eyre was appointed by Pope Pius IX. Delegate Apostolic for Scotland, with the dignity of Archbishop in *partibus infidelium*. Before the severance, on the 26th December, 1868, of the Archbishop's connection with Newcastle, his congregation presented him with an exceedingly handsome pectoral cross and chain, and crosier. On January 31st, 1869, he was consecrated Archbishop of Anazarba, in the church of St. Andrea-della-Valle, at Rome, the consecrating Prelate being Cardinal Reisach, assisted by Archbishop Manning, and Mgr. De Merode, Archbishop of Mitylene. By brief bearing date April 16th, 1869, Archbishop Eyre was appointed Administrator Apostolic of the Western District of Scotland. In order to attend the Vatican Council, convened by Pope Pius IX., he again, in 1870, proceeded to the Eternal City. In 1874 he founded at Glasgow a diocesan seminary for the education of students in philosophy and divinity. Early in the month of January (January 5th, 1878) the Archbishop was called to Rome by the Pope, in order to make the preliminary arrangements for the establishment of the hierarchy in Scotland. He was most cordially and affectionately received by the Holy Father, Pius the IX., but before the arrangements entered into, though completed, were signed by the Pope, Pius IX. died. On the succession of Leo XIII., February 20th, his Grace, on the following day, had a private audience of his Holiness. In the month following, by brief dated March 15th, he was translated to the Metropolitan See of Glasgow, founded as an Episcopal See by St. Kentigern about 543; and erected into an Archiepiscopal See, with four Suffragan Sees, in 1492. It was vacant 275 years, from 1603 to 1878. Archbishop Eyre received the pallium on the 31st of March; and on the 23rd of May, 1878, he consecrated in his Pro-Cathedral at Glasgow, the Bishops of Galloway, and of Argyll and the Isles. In July, 1879, a congratulatory address was presented to him by the Catholic laity, together with a handsome carriage, and a sum of £400. For this example of liberality and esteem the Catholics of Glasgow are in a high degree to be commended. The Archdiocese of Glasgow comprises a large and increasing Catholic population, and for its progress and prosperity owes much to the zeal, energy, and devotion of the worthy Archbishop. May he be spared many years to govern the Church of God in this important portion of North Britain, and may his labours continue to be crowned with success, and receive their reward in due season. To the pen of the learned Archbishop we are indebted for "The History of St. Cuthbert, &c.," which I have had previous occasion to notice, and which, says Montalembert in his "Monks of the West," "is written with great care and elegance." "Monsignor Eyre," as stated in a reviw of the book, "has achieved a task of no small difficulty, and labour of no small research; and that in the most complete and masterly manner. As an eloquent, painstaking biographer of one of the greatest of the Church's Saints; as an antiquarian; as a local historian —he stands in the first class—has perfected his task right well, and deserves the warmest commendation and approval: . . a charming right beautiful book in which treasures of holy comfort are garlanded together, and in profusion." Pity so interesting a work is no longer in print, and copies scarce.

On the 27th July, 1882, he laid the foundation stone of the new church at St. Cuthbert's, Ushaw, being a worthy Alumnus of that College. His unavoidable absence on occasion of its solemn opening, July 29th, 1885, was deeply regretted. In Easter week 1885 his Grace set out on another journey to Rome, whence he returned early in June. On the 28th October, being the Feast of SS. Simon and Jude, he consecrated, in St. Mary's Pro-Cathedral, Edinburgh, the Most Rev. William Smith, Archbishop of St. Andrew's and Edinburgh.

During the School year 1883-84, 27,062 children were presented for religious examination in the "centre of Catholicity in Scotland," giving an annual increase, during seven years, of 1261.

BISHOP BRIGGS.

This venerable and "most ancient" Bishop, "*vir pietate, ætate, et forma venerabilis*," as the inscription on his tomb describes him, was born at Pendleton, Salford, in the year 1789, and was educated at Crook Hall and Ushaw. It was in the autumn of 1804, October 13th, that John Briggs came to Crook. From Crook, when that establishment ceased to be occupied as a college, he went with the other Crook students to the new college at Ushaw, and completed there his course of studies for the priesthood. He was ordained priest July 9th, 1814, at Ushaw, by Bishop Gibson, where he also received the four minor orders, the subdiaconate, and diaconate from the same Prelate. In 1816 he left Ushaw for the mission. For many years he was priest at Chester, until the year 1833, when, on the feast of SS. Peter and Paul, June 29th, he was consecrated at Ushaw by Bishop Penswick, as his Coadjutor in the Northern District, and Bishop of Trachis. Bishops Baines and Walsh assisted. On the death of Bishop Penswick, January 28th, 1836, Bishop Briggs succeeded as Vicar-Apostolic of the Northern District; was appointed to the newly created Yorkshire District, in 1840; and in 1850, on the introduction of the Hierarchy, was translated from Trachis to Beverley. On the 7th of November, 1860, in consequence of failing health, Bishop Briggs resigned the see of Beverley, and on the 4th of January, in the year following, fortified with the sacraments of the Church, he departed this life at York, in the seventy-second year of his age. The deceased Prelate was buried in the chapel at Hazlewood, a solemn Requiem Mass having been sung in St. George's Pro-Cathedral, York, by his friend, Dr. Grant, Bishop of Southwark, at which the Bishops of Hexham and Newcastle, Birmingham, Salford, and Liverpool were present. God in His goodness receive his soul!

BISHOP BROWN.

George Hilary Brown was born at Clifton in the Fylde, 1786, and was educated at Crook Hall and Ushaw. He went to Crook Hall, as a student, September 25th, 1799, in the fourteenth year of his age. Dr. Brown was first cousin of Bishop Gradwell, and of the Very Rev. Henry Gradwell, priest at Claughton-on-Brock. He was ordained subdeacon at Crook in 1808; on December 4th of the same year, at the new college of Ushaw, deacon ; and on June 13th, 1810, he was raised to the priesthood by Bishop William Gibson. Remaining at the college after his ordination, he was successively Prefect of Studies, Vice-President, and Professor of Theology. He left Ushaw on the 8th of April, 1819, to take charge of the mission of Lancaster, as successor to Dr. Rigby, where he laboured about twenty years, with much zeal, for the salvation of souls. In 1840 he was appointed Bishop of Bugia, and Vicar-Apostolic of the newly-created District of Lancashire; was afterwards translated from Bugia to Tlos, *in partibus infid.*; and in 1850 was appointed first Bishop of Liverpool. Broken down with age and infirmity, Bishop Brown died at Liverpool, January 25th, 1856, aged seventy years, and was buried at St. Oswald's, the Old Swan. In his declining years and health, the venerable Bishop had reason to be consoled and comforted by the reflection that, during his episcopal rule in Lancashire, the faith had spread, religion had flourished, education been promoted, and its importance more universally recognised. It was in the early part of his episcopate that St. Edward's College, Everton, was established and opened for the education of ecclesiastical and other students, January 16th, 1843, under the presidency of the Very Rev. John Henry Fisher (Right Rev. Monsignor Fisher, D.D., V.G., Provost of the Cathedral Chapter of Liverpool), who, with four of his brothers, was educated at St. Cuthbert's College. With Dr. Fisher was associated as Vice-President of the college the Rev. Alexander Goss, subsequently Bishop of Liverpool. Mgr. Fisher, D.D., having, in 1884, retired from the presidency of this college, the Very Rev. James Canon Carr, V.G., succeeded him in that office. When Bishop Brown became Bishop, Liverpool contained six Catholic churches ; at his death there were sixteen.

BISHOP SHARPLES.

The Rev. James Sharples, in 1843, was appointed Coadjutor to Bishop Brown. A Lancashire man by birth, he received his education at Ushaw and Rome. He commenced his studies at Ushaw, at the end of January, 1809 ; thence he went, September 21st, 1818, to study at the English College, Rome, where, with the late Cardinal Wiseman, he arrived December 18th, 1818. At Rome he pursued his studies with great success and distinction, and obtained both in Philosophy and Theology several first class medals and prizes. Cardinal Wiseman once speaking of Bishop Sharples referred to him in the following terms :—" He was a faithful, loyal son of this house (Ushaw) ; he was my schoolfellow and fellow Bishop. I remember, upon one occasion, when engaged at the examination or concursus at the Roman College, and when he and myself had the good fortune, I will say, to obtain the prize, he remarked to me at the time—' we owe all this to having been under Dr. Newsham, as our master and our pedagogue. The rules which he gave us have guided us both, and secured to us the medals.' " Dr. Sharples was ordained priest November 30th, 1823, and on July 12th, in the following year, he left the English College to labour on the mission of his native county of Lancaster, succeeding at St. Alban's,

Blackburn, the Rev. Richard Albot. He remained at Blackburn till 1839, when he went to St. Marie's, Sheffield, and was there till 1843, when he was made Bishop of Samaria, and Coadjutor to Bishop Brown. In July, 1847, he was delegated by the English Bishops to proceed, with Bishop Wiseman, to Rome, to negociate the restoration of the Hierarchy. At Rome his health became impaired; and, after his return, he retired, probably about the beginning of 1850, to Singleton, a small old mission in the Fylde, long vacant. On the 11th of August, 1850, he departed this life at Great Eccleston, on his road home to Singleton, having devoutly received the sacraments of the Church. His remains lie buried in the grave yard, adjoining the Catholic church, at Great Eccleston. When Bishop Sharples was removed from Blackburn, a very handsome testimonial was presented to him in hard cash, which caused Dr. Briggs to assure him that two or three removes would be as good as a fortune. The Rev. Henry Sharples, educated at Ushaw, coming there as a patriarch about the year 1828, was brother of Bishop Sharples. He was a man of solid and mature judgment; of staid and grave character: quiet and retiring in his habits; and a most good and holy priest. He built the present church of St. Michael, Alston Lane. On February 17th, 1874, he peaceably rendered up his soul to God, and his remains were laid in repose in the cemetery attached to the church which he had erected. He came to Alston Lane in 1849.

BISHOP HOGARTH.

The Right Rev. William Hogarth was born at Dodding Green, near Kendal, on the feast of the Annunciation, March 25th, 1786, at the house adjoining the little chapel of St. Robert, then occupied as a farm dwelling by his family, his father being, as they are called in Westmorland, a "statesman" in that county. Dodding Green, and the beautiful sylvan valley in which it is situated, is a charming spot. The valley is watered by the river Mint, gliding and coursing with babbling glee along its stony channel, over red sandstone strata, and between banks shaded with trees and coppice wood, to mingle its waters with the Sprint and the Kent. Bishop Hogarth and his elder brother, Rev. Robert Hogarth, who died at Dodding Green, 1868, and was interred there, commenced their studies at Crook Hall, and completed them at Ushaw, William being ordained priest by Bishop Gibson, December 20th, 1809. When ordained, he was destined for the mission at Blackburn, but his services—so useful were they considered—were retained at Ushaw, where he was made one of the professors, and appointed General Prefect. In 1816, at the end of October, he left Ushaw to go on the mission at Cliffe, where he remained eight years. Thence he removed to Darlington in 1824, where he resided till his death, endeared to, and respected, on account of his saintly life and labours, by persons of every class and creed. On the feast of St. Bartholomew, August 24th, 1848, he was consecrated by Bishop Briggs, in the collegiate chapel of St. Cuthbert, Bishop of Samosata, and Vicar-Apostolic of the Northern District. In a memorial to Propaganda, 1848, he was described by Bishop Ullathorne "as a man of energetic character, who had evinced for long years a marked capacity for business, had been Vicar-General to Bishops Briggs, Mostyn, and Riddell, and was then Administrator of the District." Bishop Hogarth was translated to the see of Hexham September 29th, 1850, and was the first of the restored Hierarchy to sign a public document with his new title, " William, Bishop of Hexham." He was a most vigilant and faithful Bishop, led a saintly, blameless, temperate life ; was a wise and prudent prelate ; minded not high things, but condescended to the humble.

After saying the parochial mass on Sunday, January 28th, 1866, at St. Augustine's, Darlington, which church was built by him in 1826, and where he resided and performed parochial work, until the day of his death, he was seized early in the afternoon of that day with paralysis, and in the afternoon of next day, he calmly rendered up his soul into the hands of his Creator, having lived to the age of eighty years. Darlington and the whole diocese mourned, with deep sorrow, his departure, but nowhere more than at St. Cuthbert's, Ushaw, was his death lamented, for to that college he had ever been a stedfast friend, a faithful patron, and trusty counsellor. It was in the cloisters of the cemetery of Ushaw that his remains found sepulture, among the other Bishops who lie buried there. On the brass tablet affixed against the wall near his tomb is inscribed—" *Ejus memoriam Alma Mater grato animo veneratur. Pater venerande vivas cum Jesu.*" An elegant obelisk of polished granite, 30 feet high, was erected at Darlington by his flock and fellow townsmen, as a monument to the deceased Bishop's memory. The monument bears this inscription :—" To the Right Rev. William Hogarth, D.D., first Bishop of Hexham and Newcastle, the Father of his clergy and the poor, who by a saintly life, great labours and charity unbounded, won love and veneration from all, this monument was erected by his flock and fellow townsmen of every creed and party. Born at Dodding Green, Westmorland ; died at Darlington 29th of January, 1866 ; buried at St. Cuthbert's College, Ushaw, aged 80 years. R. I. P. .

BISHOP GRANT.

Quo nemo vir melior natus est, nemo pietate præstantior. —Cic.

Thomas Grant was born November 25th, 1816, and came to Ushaw from Chester, where, under the care of Dr. Briggs, with whom he spent upwards of three years, he received his early education and training. He was a pious, docile, diligent student, and was generally at the head of his class. In his second year of philosophy, he was sent by his superiors to Rome, and was there ordained priest, November 28th, 1841. Immediately after his ordination, he was created Doctor of Divinity, and became secretary to Cardinal Acton, which office he filled for rather more than three years, when, in 1844, he was appointed to succeed Dr. Baggs, as Rector of the English College. He was the first Bishop of Southwark, being consecrated to that See, July 6th, 1851, in the church of the English College, Rome, by Cardinal Fransoni, at that time Prefect of the Propaganda. The

"Papal Aggression" frenzy was at its height when he took possession of the See of Southwark. Bishop Grant was a man of extraordinary piety, great learning, wonderful and saint-like humility; had a ready, well stored, retentive memory, and a remarkable facility for writing Latin. His sufferings for several years from a painful malady were often most excruciating, so that, worn out with labour and sickness, this saintly Bishop, who went to Rome to attend the Vatican Council, there, in the fifty-fourth year of his age, expired, June 1st, 1870, being the first day of the month of the Sacred Heart, towards which he ever cherished a loving and tender devotion. "What a consolation at death," says B. Margaret, "to have ever cherished devotion to the Sacred Heart of Him who is to be our Judge." On hearing of his death, the Holy Father, Pius IX., exclaimed with emotion—"*Un altro Santo in paradiso.*" His body having been brought to England, was buried in the cemetery of the Orphanage, at Norwood, in which Institution, during life, he had taken the deepest interest, so that he might justly be called the Father of the Orphans.

"*In memoria æterna erit justus*": with Bishop Grant's memory, and the regard I entertain for him, are associated many bright and sunny remembrances, "*Virtutem illius viri amavi, quæ extincta non est;*" no, the example of his many virtues will long survive; his humility, cheerfulnesss, patience, purity, love of prayer, devotion to Jesus in the Adorable Sacrament, to His Immaculate Mother, and to the holy souls in Purgatory, will continue to diffuse an aroma more fragrant than nard or cassia, for

"Only the actions of the just,
Smell sweet and blossom from the dust."

By such virtues "that soul devoted to God was green as the spring, becomingly and abundantly."

One of his favourite and oft repeated ejaculations was *Credo, Amo, Spero*, brief, but most suggestive. "A great example and a great light have gone from us when we most needed them," wrote the Bishop of Birmingham, on the occasion of Bishop Grant's death.

The schoolroom at Ushaw now occupied by the "Grammarians" was, in days of yore, assigned to the class of "Low Figures." It was called the "black school"—having a great propensity for smoking—(it has been cured of this defect, cleaned and renovated), and was the scene of many a chivalrous exploit, and deed of adventurous daring. Through respect to the memory and virtues of that good and sainted Bishop, Dr. Grant, the writer never fails, when he goes to Ushaw, to make a visit to this school. It was in this school he taught Thomas Grant his rudiments of Latin, &c., being appointed his pedagogue, when he first came a boy to college. He came on New Year's Day, 1829:—it was a severe and very hard winter, and the little fellow's hands used to be blue with cold. He was of a quiet, meek, and gentle disposition, and his application to study and love for learning were soon manifested. Although he left Ushaw to continue and complete his studies at Rome, he always preserved a sincere attachment to Ushaw—his *Alma Mater;* and for nearly 20 years before his death, he never let a New Year's Day pass without writing to remind me of the anniversary of his going to college, and to thank me for what he was pleased to term my patience and painstaking with him. The last letter I had the honour of receiving from him was dated from the English College, Rome, New Year's Day, 1870—the year of his decease. If "sanctity is greatness," then Bishop Grant was truly great.

BISHOP TURNER

was born at Whittingham, near Preston, September 25th, 1799; educated at Ushaw and Rome from 1813 to 1825; ordained priest in St. John Lateran's, December 17th, 1825; served one or two missions in Yorkshire temporarily, on arriving from Rome. He was appointed by the Right Rev. Dr. Penswick, V.A. of the Northern District, to Rochdale and Bury, 1827; to St. Augustine's, Granby Row, Manchester, 1832, and volunteered to Leeds during the cholera for a period of three months. He next was placed at old St. Chad's, Rook St., Manchester, in 1835; was appointed by the Right Rev. Bishop Brown, V.A. of Lancashire, senior priest of St. Augustine's, Granby Row, Manchester, in 1841; Vicar-General of the Hundreds of Salford and Blackburn, the same year. He was consecrated first Bishop of Salford, in St. John's Cathedral, by Cardinal Wiseman, July 25th, 1851; created Assistant at the Pontifical Throne, June 8th, 1862; and attended the Vatican Council from December 8th, 1869, to May 28th, 1870. The venerated Bishop calmly expired, after two hours illness, at Salford, July 13th, 1872; was buried at the Salford cemetery, July 17th, 1872; and translated to the new Catholic cemetery, Moston, near Manchester, with five priests, two or three years afterwards. Dr. Turner built the church of St. John, Rochdale, under great difficulties. He had to pawn his watch one Saturday night to pay wages. He used to walk from Rochdale to Manchester to go to confession, a distance of 12 miles. When he first appeared in the pulpit at St. Augustine's, he was so delicate that people gave him no more than a few months to live, but by regularity and care he lived and worked hard to the age of nearly 73 years. The Archbishop of Westminster (Cardinal Manning), in his sermon at the Bishop's funeral, spoke regarding him as follows :—" Such was the life of your Pastor—a life of beautiful, exquisite, tender charity, and of a piety which sprang from the Holy Ghost. He had a conscience void of offence towards God, and he lived a life without censure before his fellow men. His life was a luminous example of a true christian and fervent priest, of a faithful and loving Bishop. Blamelessness of life, inoffensiveness of spirit and heart, great spiritual industry, great respect for his clergy, and a tender love of souls were the special characteristics of your late Bishop. Without pain, and as if gently touched by the hand of a spirit saying—'Come up hither,' he became unconscious, and a little after noon, entered into rest." Bishop Turner was priest at St. Augustine's, Granby Row, when he was consecrated Bishop, and remained there for about a year afterwards. The great end and aim of his life was—" *Servire Deo et prodesse populo.*" Hence he was most devoted to the spiritual interests of his flock, and in the service of God most fervent and constant. In patience he possessed his soul—a soul peaceful and serene, broken in its perpetual calm by no cloud, agitated by no storms, disturbed by no emotions; ever mindful to preserve an equality of mind both in prosperity and adversity.

BISHOP ROSKELL.

Richard Roskell, who was of the respectable family of the Roskells, was born at Gateacre, near Liverpool, August 15th, 1817. When scarcely nine years of age he was placed, July 20th, 1825, at St. Cuthbert's College, Ushaw. In 1832, on leaving Ushaw, he repaired to Rome, to continue his studies for the Church, and was ordained priest in June, 1840. From Rome he came on the English mission; was placed at Manchester; and subsequently was given charge of St. Patrick's, in that city. When elected Bishop of Nottingham, he was Provost of the Cathedral Chapter of Salford, and Vicar-General to Bishop Turner. He was consecrated by Cardinal Wiseman, at Nottingham, September 21st, 1853. Bishop Roskell, on account of failing health, resigned the see of Nottingham, in 1874, retiring to the quiet and secluded retreat of Whitewell, in Bolland, where, the world forgetting, and almost by the world forgot, he continued to reside, until he was removed from this vale of tears, dying in peace, January 27th, 1883, in his sixty-sixth year. His remains rest in the cemetery at the little church of St. Hubert, in the same romantic valley, where, in the decline of health and life, he had fixed his abode.

Pie Jesu Domine, dona ei requiem.

Bishop Roskell was endowed with a well-stored and well-cultured mind; was learned and eloquent; respected and beloved by his flock; and esteemed by a numerous circle of friends.

BISHOP GOSS.

He was a great priest and prelate—*Sacerdos et pontifex, pastor bonus in populo;* renowned and much revered in his day and generation; as right worshipful a Bishop as ever wore mitre or wielded crosier; and to the bishopric and church of Liverpool an ornament and honour:—

"*Ovilis ille pastor, et rector gregis,*
Vitæ recludit pascua, et fontes sacros,
Ovesque servat creditas, arcet lupos."

On the 25th of September, 1853, he was consecrated Bishop of Gerra, and Coadjutor to Dr. Brown, Bishop of Liverpool, by Cardinal Wiseman. The ceremony took place in the Pro-Cathedral Church of St. Nicholas, Copperas Hill, Liverpool, at which many bishops assisted, and a numerous and respectable congregation attended. Dr. Goss was born at Ormskirk, in Lancashire, July 5th, 1814. To his virtuous mother (his father having died when he was young) he owed his early religious education and training. She moulded with assiduous care his mind and manners to virtue, and fixed in the breast of her young boy generous purposes, and high-minded aspirations. How many great and holy men have owed their eminence to the fostering care of a pious mother. There is no power or influence so great as that possessed by a mother over the infant years of her son. "A mighty influence for good or for evil." Edmund, Archbishop of Canterbury, was a great saint. Mabel, his mother, was herself a saint, and worthy to be the mother of a saint. Hence she trained up her child in the way he should go;

devoted him early to God's service; inured him betimes to abstinence and penance, and gave him and his brother, on their going to Paris, each a sackcloth shirt, enjoining them to wear it next their skin twice or thrice a week. At the age of twelve years the boy, Alexander Goss, was sent by his venerable uncle, the Rev. Henry Rutter,* to St. Cuthbert's College, Ushaw, which he entered at the end of June, 1827. Here he greatly distinguished himself in his studies, to which he applied with persevering diligence, giving unmistakeable evidence of considerable talents, and good promise of a successful career. At the end of his course of humanities and philosophy, he was appointed to teach the class of Syntax; and by his scholars, among whom he infused great zeal for study and love of learning, he was regarded with much esteem and affection. Having in the month of September, 1838, left Ushaw, in the following year he proceeded to Rome to study theology. He was received into the English College October 30th, 1839; and July 4th, 1841, he was ordained priest by Cardinal Fransoni. On the 3rd of March, 1842, he took his departure from the Eternal City, and in October of that year, he was selected by the Bishop as one of the Superiors of St. Edward's College, being appointed Vice-President. Bishop Brown having passed to his reward, " Alexander, by the grace of God, and favour of the Apostolic See," succeeded him as Bishop of Liverpool. During the term of his Episcopate, religion in the diocese of Liverpool, like a tree planted by running waters, put forth deep roots, and wide-spreading branches; burgeoned, bloomed, and fructified. New missions were founded, new churches erected, new schools established, education promoted, and Catholic claims urged and advocated. Bishop Goss was truly " a man of lofty counsel, strict in rule, learned and eloquent; of dignified stature; of known and approved reputation; and worthily endowed with the knowledge of literature." He was fond of diving into old records, ancient chronicles, mildewed and worm-eaten manuscripts; of ransacking dusty folios, and the solemn volumes of the fathers and schoolmen. "*Legit libros, non libellos;*" hence he never thought of running away from a folio, however ponderous the volume might be. It is inconceivable how great an amount of historical, ecclesiastical, and antiquarian lore Bishop Goss had amassed. He took special interest in the study of natural history, and its cognate subjects; and was well read in hagiology and biography. I remember the delight he experienced in listening to the reading in the refectory at Ushaw, of Knolles's History of the Turks, wherein are recited the achievements and valorous deeds of Scanderbeg; Foissart's Chronicles, and Irving's Conquest of Granada, &c. Dr. Goss was strictly conservative; disliked novelties and innovations; and was wholly in accord with Pope Zachary II., who said—" *Nihil innovetur nisi quod traditum est.*" He was the type of a thorough Lancashire man, and felt proud of his native county and its catholicity. He used to say that, after crossing Ribble bridge, and experiencing the genial warmth of faith and

---

*One of the old race of Douai priests. He was author, among other writings, of "Help to Parents in the religious instruction of their children;" of the "Life of Christ," &c. The last years of his missionary life were passed at Dodding Green, at which place he died a holy death, September 17th, 1838, at the good old age of 85.

devotion which pervaded Preston, and was diffused over all the Fylde and neighbourhood, he invariably, having passed through Lancaster, buttoned his coat, because he found, as he pursued his journey northward, faith grow cold, and piety wax lukewarm. Like Robert Grosseteste, Bishop of Lincoln, Bishop Goss was a most uncompromising opponent of every abuse wheresoever it existed, and in what he considered duty enjoined, and conscience dictated, firm and unbending. Error and heresy, under whatever phase they appeared, he most strenuously opposed ; and with St. Jerome he might say—"*Fateor me nunquam hæreticis pepercisse, et omni egisse modo ut hostes ecclesiæ mei quoque hostes fierent.*"—His Lordship had moreover an awful sense of the responsibility of the episcopal office. In the visitation of his diocese the Bishop was most regular, exact, and observant. Whatever he saw out of place in a church, were it even a cobweb, he would point attention to it. By his decease the church lost a most distinguished prelate, and Lancashire a learned and notable celebrity, whose mind was by no means narrowed, but comprehensive and penetrating. His loss was greatly deplored, and he was mourned alike by friends and opponents. For some time before his death his health had been failing ; but he laboured to the last. On the 29th of September, 1872, he opened the new church of Coniston, the last of his episcopal functions, and on the evening of October 3rd, while at dinner with Dr. Fisher, at St. Edward's College, he was seized with sudden illness, became unconscious, and passed to a better life, there to rest from, and reap the reward of his labours. He was buried with much honour and solemnity : Archbishop Manning preached ; Archbishop Errington and six other Bishops were present ; a crowded congregation thronged the pro-Cathedral. His remains were laid in the cemetery of St. Sepulchre, at Ford, where a simple inscription over the tomb marks their place of sepulture. *Da ei Domine requiem æternam, et locum indulgentiæ.*

BISHOP CORNTHWAITE.

This estimable Prelate succeeded Bishop Briggs as Bishop of Beverley, and was born at Preston, May 9th, 1818. Thus two Lancashiremen, under the restored hierarchy (Bishop Briggs, be it remembered, having been born in Lancashire), were successively appointed to govern the Church in Yorkshire. They went there as "ambassadors from heaven's court sent," not with the sword of strife and warfare, but bearing the olive branch of peace, commissioned to establish an eternal league of friendship—the truce of God, between the two whilom rival factions of York and Lancaster, and on one stem—the stem of holy Church, to engraft the red and white roses. O happy union ! O sacred bond of amity and peace ! To Preston, as stated, belongs the honour of being the birthplace of Bishop Cornthwaite. Before the suppression of the old religion,

"Ere Gospel light first shone through Boleyn's eyes,"

Preston, or "Priests' Town" would, without doubt, from time to time, give Bishops to the Church of God ;

―― " *Sed omnes illacrymabiles
Urgentur, ignotique longa
Nocte, carent quia vate sacro.*"

Since that direful and disastrous event, I can only find two natives of Preston, who have been raised to the dignity of Bishops, *viz.*, the subject of this memoir, and Gregory William Sharrock, O.S.B., Vicar-Apostolic of the Western District. He was born in 1742 ; deceased 1809 ; to whose soul may God grant mercy.

Robert Cornthwaite, at the age of twelve, commenced his studies in 1830, at St. Cuthbert's College, Ushaw. From Ushaw, in 1842, he went to Rome, and was ordained priest there, November 9th. 1845. He returned to England in 1846, and was sent on the mission to Carlisle. In 1851 he succeeded Dr. Grant, Bishop of Southwark, as Rector of the English College, which office he resigned in September, 1857, and left Rome for England, where he was appointed to the mission of Darlington, and Secretary to Bishop Hogarth. In 1858 he was made Canon Theologian of the Chapter of Hexham and Newcastle, and on the 10th of November, 1861, he was consecrated by Cardinal Wiseman to the See of Beverley. The diocese of Beverley, in 1878, was divided into the dioceses of Leeds and Middlesbrough, Leeds being assigned to Bishop Cornthwaite, Middlesbrough to Bishop Lacy. Of Bishop Cornthwaite it may be with truth asserted that he is a man of irreproachable life and reputation ; and to be mentioned with the highest honour. Religion flourishes in his diocese ; his priests are devoted to their duties ; and he possesses, for the education of his young ecclesiastics, St. Joseph's Seminary, founded by him. *Ad multos annos vivas, eximie Præsul.*

BISHOP CHADWICK.

He was a High Priest : a good and virtuous man, modest in his looks, gentle in his manners, graceful in his speech, exercised in virtues from a child : who, holding up his hands, prayed much for his people, and the city of God.—2 MACH., xv., 14.

And in his faith and his meekness was sanctified.—ECCLUS. xlv., 4.

The aged, energetic, and vigilant Prelate—William, Bishop of Hexham and Newcastle, was succeeded by the meek, mild, and kind-hearted Bishop Chadwick, second Bishop of the above named See—a man of becoming life and learning, of saintly and venerable deportment, of dignified and commanding presence, and most humble withal. " He looks every inch a Bishop" was the exclamation of all who saw him for the first time. At the Vatican Council, where Bishops from every quarter of Christendom were assembled, the Bishop of Hexham and Newcastle was conspicuous amongst them all for the dignity of his appearance. For the various outlines of his life, and traits of his character, I have not to look far, a sketch being given of him in the *Northern Catholic Calendar* of 1883, so exhaustively and ably drawn, that I have much pleasure in reproducing it in its entirety, or nearly so.

"The Right Rev. James Chadwick was descended from an honourable Lancashire family, the Chadwicks of Burgh Hall, in the township of Duxbury, parish of Standish, and Hundred of Leyland, about two miles from Chorley. The family was noted for its fidelity to the ancient faith in ages of persecution and of penal laws, and for its loyalty to the Stuart throne. Some of its members rose to high ecclesiastical rank. The great-uncle of the Bishop, the Rev. John Chadwick, son of the purchaser of Burgh Hall, held for many years the office of Vicar-General, in the Northern Apostolic Vicariate, and was also one of those proposed to the Holy See as successor to Bishop Walton. He resided with his brother at Burgh Hall, where a chapel attached to the mansion afforded the opportunities and the consolations of religion to the Catholic yeomanry and people of the neighbourhood. To the fostering care of the family of the Chadwicks, and to the untiring zeal of the Rev. John Chadwick, it is due, under God, that a large remnant of old English Catholicity survived the crushing effects of the unhappy '45 in that part of the county. When the late Cardinal Weld presented the Church with the property now known as Weld Bank, for the purpose of establishing a more permanent mission, the Rev. John Chadwick removed from Burgh Hall to Weld Bank, which is at a little distance from it, and there opened the first chapel, and founded that mission. About the beginning of the present century, John Chadwick, the father of the Bishop, emigrated to Ireland and settled at Drogheda, where he married a Miss Frances Dromgoole, of the County Louth. Hence his son James, the future Bishop, was born in that town on the 24th of April, 1813. As his great-uncle had been an alumnus of Douai College, in the diary of which we find him mentioned as taking the college oath on June 3rd, 1748, in the presence of Dr. Walton, at that time one of the professors, so young James became an alumnus of St. Cuthbert's College, Ushaw, the successor and inheritor of Douai, in all that remained to it after the French Revolution. James Chadwick was educated from a boy at this college, which he entered on the 26th of May, 1825. After passing through the various lower classes of the college, he finally chose the ecclesiastical state, and received the tonsure and four Minor Orders, from the hands of the venerable Bishop Briggs, on the 18th of December, 1835. On the day following he was promoted to the sub-diaconate, and on the 28th of May, 1836, he was ordained deacon ; and priest on the 17th of the following December. The President of the college, the Very Rev. Dr. Youens, appointed him General Prefect, and during the years he filled that important office he endeared himself to the students, while he maintained the discipline of the house. He was afterwards professor of humanities, mental philosophy, and pastoral theology, and continued to reside at Ushaw till 1850. He then joined a community of diocesan missionaries established at Wooler, and for near seven years gave missions in most of the larger towns of the North of England, till the community was broken up by the fire which destroyed their house and chapel, with all their books and effects. This took place while Dr. Chadwick was giving a mission at St. Augustine's, in Preston, and the news was brought to him as he was about to preach the opening sermon of the mission. The next three years of his life, from 1856 to 1859, he spent at Ushaw as professor, and then, for four years, he was chaplain to the late Lord Stourton. In the year 1863, the president of Ushaw, the Right Rev. Dr. Tate, invited Dr. Chadwick to the chair of pastoral theology; however, for one year he filled for the second time the chair of mental philosophy, and then in the following year began his course of pastoral theology. As a professor, the Bishop had always been beloved by the students, for his kindness and amiability, and there is not a part of the world where Ushaw men are to be met with, where his name and memory are not held in respect and veneration. His knowledge, too, of ascetic theology, brought him into constant communication with the religious communities, and there is hardly a convent in England wherein he has not given retreats. The death of Bishop Hogarth caused a vacancy in the episcopacy, at the beginning of the year 1866. The canons of Hexham met for the first time to exercise their right of nomination, and one of the names sent up to Rome was that of the Very Rev. James Chadwick, Canon of Beverley, and professor at Ushaw. He was elected Bishop on the 12th August, and was consecrated as Bishop of Hexham and Newcastle, at Ushaw, on the 28th of October, 1866, by Archbishop Manning, assisted by the Bishops of Salford, Beverley, Southwark, Shrewsbury, and Northampton. The consecration sermon was preached by the Right Rev. Dr. Amherst, Bishop of Northampton. Upon this occasion a pectoral cross was presented to him by the professors of Ushaw. The episcopal ring, which was designed by Geo. Goldie, Esq., was given to the Bishop by his brother, Jno. Chadwick, Esq, and the students of St. Cuthbert's afterwards presented his Lordship with a new crosier. On the 8th of the following month, Dr. Chadwick was solemnly enthroned in his cathedral church, Newcastle-on-Tyne, the sermon being preached by Canon Consitt. We can hardly pass over a remarkable fact in his episcopacy—his return to Ushaw as president, at the same time retaining his administration of his diocese. This arrangement, though, perhaps, not very grateful to his clergy, as it removed their Bishop from more immediate contact with them, was hailed with delight by professors and students, who were always so deeply attached to him. During the year of his presidency, he evinced the great interest he took in the students by the many arrangements he made for their comfort and convenience. During the sixteen years of his episcopate, the churches and schools in the diocese multiplied, and the number of priests increased to a remarkable extent."

As leaves have their time to fall, and flowers to fade and decay, so it is appointed for all men once to die,—kings and potentates, bishops and priests, the loved and the loving ones, the friends of our youth and our manhood—"*Nos nostraque morti debemur.*" At length, therefore, the silver cord was broken, the golden fillet shrunk back, and the spirit of the venerable and beloved Bishop of Hexham and Newcastle, Dr. Chadwick, returned to God who gave it. He expired after a short illness at his residence in Newcastle, on the morning of Sunday, May 14th, 1882, in the 70th year of his age, having piously received the Sacraments of holy Church. Prior to the interment of his remains at St. Cuthbert's College, Ushaw, a solemn requiem mass was celebrated in St. Mary's Cathedral, Newcastle. The celebrant was Dr. Cornthwaite, the Bishop of Leeds. There were present at the solemn service the Archbishop of Glasgow and four other Bishops. The chief mourners were his brothers, Mr. John and Mr. Frank Chadwick, both in their youth educated at Ushaw. The clergy of the diocese, to the number of 150, occupied the front seats of the church. The sermon was preached by the Right Rev. Mgr. Provost Consitt, an attached friend of the deceased Prelate's. For the text of his sermon he selected the words—" *Memento, Domine, David, et omnis mansuetudinis ejus.*"—Ps. 131. A numerous and imposing funeral *cortége* left the cathedral, and proceeded *en route* to Ushaw. Every where on the way crowds of spectators assembled ; every where there was a manifestation of sorrow and respect for the dear, departed Bishop. "At Ushaw the students were assembled in the College cemetery, and while the solemn chant and funeral rites proceeded, the representative of each school advanced, and placed on the coffin a wreath of flowers, as the last mark of their affection for him who had been to every Ushaw boy, not merely a Bishop, but a father."

"He rests in the home of his youth, where he had made his first communion, where he was ordained priest and consecrated Bishop. He rests in the spot he had chosen in life, beneath the shadow of the cross, and near to those who had been his guides in youth, his dear friends throughout life."

Deus Christus Omnipotens refrigeret spiritum tuum.

His place of sepulture is at the west end of the secluded college cemetery, close to the cross erected over the grave of the Rev. Thomas Crowe, an alumnus of Ushaw, and a benefactor of the college. The deceased Bishop had selected the spot himself, three months previous to his death, as his last resting place. "There," he said— in much the same words as were uttered by St. Waltheof, Abbot of Melrose, pointing to the spot where he wished to be buried—" is the place of my rest ; here will be the habitation among my children, as long as the Lord wills. Under the shadow of the cross I will repose—the cross my only hope in life, and my consolation, I trust, in death. There let my remains lie, that flowers may grow around my grave ; that the rain and dew may fall upon it, and the winds sweeping from the hills and woods around may chant my requiem." So died and was buried this good and virtuous Prelate—a Prelate meek and humble of heart ; in disposition mild as a gentle spring day ; in temper playful as a sunbeam on pellucid stream or fountain. On the raised tombstone covering his remains—fashioned after the one placed over Godfrey de Bouillon—is inscribed :—

J. C.

Illms. et Rvms. Jacobus Chadwick,

Epus. Hagulstad. et Novicastrensis,

Obiit die 14 Maii, A.D. 1882, æt. 70.

Pater eximiæ mansuetudinis vivas cum Xto.

For one so beloved and kind-hearted many a prayer has, doubtless, been offered ; many a suffrage made by friends who have stood or knelt by that tomb whence, could his tongue find utterance, you might readily imagine him addressing you in these words, or words of similar import : "*Je meurs, mais ma tendresse pour vous ne meurt pas ; je vous aimerai dans le ciel, comme je vous ai aimé sur la terre.*"

Some two years after the Bishop's death, when on a visit to Ushaw, I repaired to the cemetery, and standing close to the spot where he reposes in the sleep of death, it was most gratifying to behold the numerous floral wreaths which pious hands continued to place on his grave, as "love's last gift" to the saintly dead.

"Peace to him be, for I loved him, and love him for ever."

BISHOP O'REILLY.

Bishop Goss of happy memory having been gathered to his rest, the Cathedral Chapter of Liverpool elected the Vicar-General, Very Rev. John Henry Canon Fisher, D.D., President of St. Edward's College, to be Vicar-Capitular and administrator of the diocese, while the see remained vacant. In the month of February, 1873, Bernard O'Reilly, the zealous, self-sacrificing, and esteemed priest, superior of the Mission of St. Vincent's, Liverpool, and Canon of the Cathedral Chapter, to which dignity he received the appointment, December 24th, 1860, was instituted, in succession to Dr. Goss, Bishop of the important, populous, and extensive diocese of Liverpool. The extreme length of the diocese, from the head of lake Windermere, three-fourths of whose coast line is in Lancashire, to the river Mersey, is 76 miles. At its greatest width it measures 28 miles. The inhabitants at the last census in 1881 were 1,490,853; of the Isle of Man attached to the diocese of Liverpool, 53,492; total, 1,544,345. In 1885 the Catholic population in Lancashire whithin the Hundreds of West Derby, Leyland, Amounderness, and Lonsdale, was 350,100; of the Isle of Man, 1,530; total, 351,630. Number of churches in the diocese, 145; of priests, 322—on the Mission, 192; in Colleges, 15; Society of Foreign Missions, 1; invalided, retired, &c., 12. Catholic population of Lonsdale Hundred, 10,736; of Amounderness, 41,583, or 25.6 of the population. This Hundred contains the Union of Garstang, with a Catholic population of 1,828, or 14.7 of the population; and the Fylde Union, in which the Catholics number 6,199, being 15.1 of the population. It comprises also the town of Preston, with its 7 churches, and a Catholic population of 31,644; or 32.7 of the population. Catholic population of Amounderness, 41,583, or 28.6 of the population. Leyland Hundred has a Catholic population of 14,650; 16.8 of the population. The Hundred of West Derby may be termed the heart of the diocese of Liverpool. Although barely one-third of the diocese in extent, it contains 1,123,729 inhabitants, or three-fourths of the population of the diocese, and 284,131 Catholics, or four-fifths of the Catholics. The number of Catholic Missions in the episcopal city of Liverpool is 23, of people 169,187, or 30.6 of the population. In this Hundred there are 87 Missions :—West Derby Hundred with its multitudinous Catholic population is quite enough of itself to tax the energies, engross the time, and exercise all the vigilance of the most devoted and laborious bishop. Its clergy, people, churches, and missions would well suffice to constitute a separate and independent diocese. In the same Hundred are the heights or eminences of Billinge and Ashurst, each of which is crowned with a beacon, visible from a great distance, and commanding a most extensive and picturesque prospect. These beacons were constructed at a time when the scare of a French invasion of England by Bonaparte had seized the minds of Englishmen, at the beginning of the present century. Below Ashurst beacon stands the Diocesan College of St. Joseph, occupying one of the finest sites in the Hundred of West Derby. Of this new college more anon. Although, prior to the overthrow of the ancient hierarchy, there were but few religious houses in Lancashire, there has always been, notwithstanding, a numerous Catholic population in this county. There was truth therefore as well as wit in the answer of Bishop Milner to the question why so many Catholics remained in Lancashire, "because there was nothing to tempt the thieves"; or, as Cobbett remarked, "where there are no carcases to prey upon, no vultures are to be found flying about." Such, as regards population, is the important diocese of Liverpool, the government of which rests on the shoulders of the honoured and esteemed Bishop, the Right Rev. Bernard O'Reilly, to whom his servant, the writer of this memoir, sendeth greeting and obedience.

In days of old, the country lying between the Ribble and the Mersey was called "Christ's Croft." But between these rivers there is in our days a tract of land, in a state, alas! of spiritual desolation and darkness; a vineyard bleak, barren, and neglected; where there are no labourers even at a penny a day; where not a scintillation of the true faith glimmers through the darkness; where the tenets and maxims of the ancient religion are effaced and forgotten; where error, heresy, and dissent prevail and dominate; and where innumerable tares and superabundance of cockle have sprung up and choked the growth of nearly every blade of good corn. Hence few Catholics are found to inhabit this land of desolation, of solitariness, and separation from orthodoxy and truth. True it is railway enterprise has penetrated it; it is to be hoped that ere long religious zeal and enterprise will penetrate it also; and that its products will consist not of fruit, vegetables, and cereals alone, which in its soil grow so profitably and abundantly, but that there will be the ingathering of a spiritual harvest of souls, fed on the Word of God, nourished with the living bread that came down from Heaven, and feasted on the corn and wine of the elect. The land, that with the spiritual desolation above described lieth desolate, is that extent of territory, reaching from the vicinity of Southport to the neighbourhood of Preston, a district traversed by the West Lancashire Railway, and skirted on its east side by the Lancashire and Yorkshire Railway. The district comprises North Meols, Crossens, Hesketh Bank, Martin Mere, Holmes Wood, Tarleton, Sollom, Much Hoole, Longton, Hutton, Howick, and part of Penwortham,. It may be objected that in this benighted district Catholics are *rari nantes*. True, but like a skilful husbandman, who causes two blades of grass to grow where one only grew before, let an effort be made to create and establish a Catholic population, and a centre of Catholic worship. Thither, if unable to supply parochial instruction and ministration, send forth, as suggested by Cardinal Wiseman, for the work of the ministry, "men of mystified looks and placid demeanour, girt with the cord of a St. Francis, or bearing on their breasts the seal of Christ's Passion, as on their countenances the marks of its mortification; and with bare heads and feet, holding the emblem of redemption, let them preach judgment and death, and future punishment, and penance, and justice, and charity."

To resume our memoir of Bernard, third Bishop of Liverpool :— Bernard O'Reilly was born at Ballybeg, Co. Meath, January 10th, 1824. His father was Patrick O'Reilly, of Ballybeg, and his mother was Mary, daughter of John Blundell, merchant, of Lord St., Preston, and grand-daughter of Richard Blundell, of Carrside, near Ince, a lineal descendant of the Blundells, of Ince Blundell. Mary Blundell was born at her father's residence, in Lord St. ; her father, John Blundell, subsequently removed to and settled in Ireland. It is worthy of remark that the several families into which the Blundells intermarried, notably those of Chadwick, Gradwell, Worthy, O'Reilly, &c., have, all of them, furnished several priests to the English Mission for at least 150 years. By birth and parentage, therefore, Bishop O'Reilly may be said to be half Celt and half Saxon ; and a scion of an ancient, respectable, and patriotic stock, the family of O'Reilly—*clarum et venerabile nomen*. "There are some," it is stated in the Book of *Ecclesiasticus*, "of whom there is no memorial." Of the O'Reillys this cannot be predicated ; and it may truly be said regarding them—"*Quæ regio in terris nostri non plena laboris ?*"

In the first Crusade preached by Peter the Hermit, and originated by Pope Urban II. at the Council of Clermont in 1095, there figures a young Irish knight, Philip of Brefney by name, "light of heel and quick of hand," armed with hauberk and battle axe, and much lauded Irish arrows, with points as sharp as bodkins. This brave Irish knight had assumed the cross, and marched under the standard of that leader of leaders, Godfrey of Bouillon, together with old Guy of Mascon, the Burgundian, Hugh of York, the illustrious Tancred, Bohemond, Prince of Tarentum, Hugh the Great, Robert, Duke of Normandy, Robert, Duke of Flanders, and the valiant Baldwin, Duke of Boulogne, and Raymond, Count of Toulouse. There was also among these Aldemar, Bishop of Puy, representing his Holiness in the army of the Crusaders, courageous as the bravest of warriors, and who, before setting out on the expedition to Jerusalem, composed for himself, his followers, and fellow Crusaders, the glorious hymn, "*Salve Regina.*"

"There was for centuries," as stated in *Florine*, a tale of the first Crusaders, "after the conquests won by the Crusaders in the Holy Land, a branch of the ancient gallant and princely sept of the O'Reillys, in the Irish Kingdom of Meath, long remarkable for their dark skin, brilliant black eyes, and bluish raven hair, and the tradition was that they were descendants of a noble Brefney knight, who had won fame, wealth, and a foreign bride, at the time Antioch was captured by Bohemond of Tarentum, unto which, the rumour ran, that the Irish knight or his bride, or some one of the bride's family, had mainly contributed."

Though we have no historical evidence or proof, we are justified from a careful consideration of the facts and circumstances in stating that the present Bishop of Liverpool is a descendant of the above Brefney O'Reilly. There was also the illustrious Archbishop of Armagh, Hugh O'Reilly, schoolfellow of Father Luke Wadding, the Fransciscan annalist, who lived in the seventeenth century. Hugh O'Reilly was a lineal descendant of the ancient princely house of Brefney O'Reilly; and was a man of wonderful proficiency in classical knowledge and philosophy. After a course of theology in his native land, he was ordained priest in 1618. In 1625, in consequence of his great talents and high character, he was consecrated Bishop of Kilmore, by Fleming, Archbishop of Dublin. In 1630 he received the pallium as Archbishop of Armagh and Primate of all Ireland. The Archbishop, in the midst even of penury and persecution, attempted, though unsuccessfully, to have the Gregorian Calendar adopted throughout Ireland, being the first Irish Bishop who endeavoured to supplant the Julian Computation. Archbishop O'Reilly took an active part in the Kilkenny Confederacy (1642), together with Fleming, Archbishop of Dublin, Patrick Comerford, Bishop of Waterford, and Luke Wadding, but the Confederacy proved a failure, and poor Ireland was destined still to suffer oppression and persecution. The good old Primate, in the year 1652, calmly and quietly resigned his soul into the hands of his Creator, at the venerable age of seventy-seven years.

In his early years Bernard O'Reilly was placed in the well known seminary of Navan, in which so many priests have been educated, and where he received his elementary education. Though the county Meath abounds in rich and verdant pastures, "Navan is a straggling provincial town, flanked by damaged houses or mud cabins, such as one could hardly expect to meet with in a smiling country. At one end of the town may be seen the seminary. This institution, opened in 1802, seems to have already grown old in the service of literature, but like the ivy on the very ruin, the wrinkles on its brow give it a venerable appearance. But the beauty of this ancient seat of learning is 'within in golden borders.' If not the very first, it was one of the first seminaries built in Ireland after the repeal of the penal laws, and since then it has been the cradle of a succession of learned and holy priests, who have given Meath a foremost place in the Irish Church." From this seminary no small number of ecclesiastical students have been drafted into St. Cuthbert's, Ushaw; have become pious and useful priests, working with much zeal and self-abnegation on the mission in England. The first President of Navan Seminary was Father Eugene O'Reilly, from 1802 to 1827; then he became parish priest of Navan, and died in 1852, at the age of eighty-four years.

From the seminary of Navan Bernard O'Reilly was sent to Ushaw, being received there as a student, June 10th, 1836. During his college course he pursued his studies with steady attention and diligence; and was regular and exemplary in the performance of all his duties. In 1845, February 15th, he received the tonsure and four Minor Orders from Bishop William Riddell. By the same Bishop he was ordained at Ushaw sub.deacon, September 20th, 1845, and deacon, September 19th, 1846. In the following year, May 9th, 1847, he was raised to the priesthood; and on the 17th of the same month of the same year he took his departure from his *Alma Mater*, St. Cuthbert's, and next day, May 18th, commenced missionary work at St. Patrick's, Liverpool. It was the fatal fever year, following close on the Irish famine. The malignant malady prevailed in Liverpool with terrific virulence, its ravages being most destructive and appalling. The aged and the young; the strong man and the weak; parents and children,—fathers and mothers of families, became its victims, and succumbed to its attacks. Death scattered its arrows on every side—thick as snow flakes on a wintry day. In the populous district of St. Patrick's the malady raged with intense violence. In this district— among its fever dens—Father O'Reilly, like a strong man armed, and exulting like a giant to run his course—"*Da mihi, Domine,*" was his prayer, "*virtutem tuam, ut mecum sit, et mecum laboret, et mecum usque ad finem perseveret*"—sought out the suffering, the plague-stricken, and the dying, to afford them spiritual aid and consolation; nor relaxed he day or night in his work of mercy and apostolic zeal, until, the good shepherd himself was not long before he was prostrated by the fever. Three of his fellow priests, Parker, Grayston, and Hagger, all like himself educated at Ushaw, fell victims to it. Out of the number of 24 priests at that time stationed in Liverpool, 12 of them at the call of duty laid down their lives on behalf of their flocks. The other 12 would, had God so willed, sacrificed their lives in a similar manner. Fr. O'Reilly recovered, and was spared to perform further work in the vineyard, and to become an ornament and dignitary of holy church. Having regained his health, he continued his labours for a few years at St. Patrick's: then after much toil and anxiety, trials and difficulties, he founded the mission and built the church of St. Vincent of Paul, in a thickly inhabited part of the parish, and at considerable distance from the church of St. Patrick. The church, dedicated to St. Vincent of Paul, and built mainly by the pence of the poor, and the self-denial and exertions of their pastor, Fr. Bernard O'Reilly, was solemnly opened on the 20th to August, 1857, at which opening the writer of this notice was present. It was a glad and auspicious occasion for the good priest, and it gladdened also the hearts of his flock. In connection with St. Vincent's he built excellent schools, and introduced as teachers the Christian Brothers, and Sisters of Mercy. Father O'Reilly presided over St. Vincent's till he was elevated to the episcopate, and was consecrated Bishop of Liverpool by Archbishop Manning March 19th, 1873, in the church which he had raised. At this period the number of secular priests in the diocese of Liverpool numbered 133; in 1885 their number had increased to about 220. Nor does the old faith, the faith in which Lancashire Catholics gloried, the faith once delivered to the Saints, remain infructuous. Bishop O'Reilly, his zealous clergy, and faithful people keep it alive and burning. Numerous churches have been built, the number of clergy much increased, schools erected, education extended. The Bishop, since the commencement of his Episcopate, has held, at stated intervals, his Diocesan Synods, made his episcopal visitations, issued his pastoral instructions, and governs his diocese with vigour and godly prudence. He has opened from October 17th, 1875, to July 27th, 1884, 20 new churches; from March 30th, 1873, to December 14th, 1884, 18 schools and temporary chapels; and from 1875 to 1884, 5 churches after enlargement. His Lordship, since 1873, has ordained the following number of priests:—

1873—4 Secular Priests and 3 Redemptorists.
1874—3   ,,   ,,
1875—4   ,,   ,,   3   ,,
1876—3   ,,   ,,
1877—4   ,,   ,,   10 Jesuits, 4 Passionists.
1878—5   ,,   ,,   13   ,,
1879—1   ,,   ,,   12   ,,
1880—3   ,,   ,,   11   ,,
1881—6   ,,   ,,   16   ,,
1882—1   ,,   ,,   3   ,,
1883—14   ,,   ,,   13   ,,
1884— 6   ,,   ,,   5   ,,
1885—13   ,,   ,,   5   ,,

As, from the year 1874 to 1882, the returns each year of the numbers confirmed in the diocese are incomplete, an uncertainty existing in regard to some missions, as to whether confirmation was held at them, and at others as to the number confirmed, I date the confirmations as under:—from January 8th to April 20th, 1882, number confirmed, 1151. In the spring of that year the Bishop was attacked by a serious illness, which obliged him to interrupt his pastoral labours, and to absent himself from his diocese. In June, 1883, he returned home, and from August 8th to December 19th, he administered confirmation at several missions, principally in Liverpool, Preston, and Lancaster, where 6363 persons were confirmed. From January 3rd to December 31st, 1884, total number confirmed, 9828; from January 11th to November 19th, 1885, total confirmed, 4093. Many converts were included among those confirmed in the lists, both of males and females.

The great and crowning glory of Bishop O'Reilly's episcopate is unquestionably the foundation and erection of St. Joseph's Diocesan College, Walthew Park. The erection of this college will hand his name down to posterity, and be regarded as a monument of his zeal for the propagation of the faith, and the salvation of souls; as well as of the munificence and charity of the Catholics of Lancashire:—"*Illum aget penna metuente solvi fama superstes.*" In a letter addressed to the clergy dated 27th March, 1877, his Lordship writing respecting his projected new seminary, said—"In cheering words they (the clergy) have told me to begin, and in munificent contributions they have promised me help": the amount promised being £5615, afterwards raised to £6725. "With such promises, and from men who are prepared to make the sacrifices that the fulfilment of these promises must entail, why should we longer hesitate? In the name of God, and trusting to the prayers of our Mother, Mary, and our Protector, St. Joseph, we will begin." The Bishop next appealed to the laity for aid in his undertaking, placing before them the example of the clergy, and his appeal was most heartily and liberally responded to. Towards the end of the year 1878, a statement was published showing that the large sum of £38,826 8s. 9d. had been promised, and of this amount £17,982 had been paid.

Some delay necessarily occured in selecting a suitable locality for the new college. At length a farm, Walthew Park, measuring 153 statute acres, being offered for sale, was purchased for £8,000. On the

estate was a good freehold quarry, from which the college was built ; and the situation left nothing to be desired. The college is situated 4 or 5 miles to the N.W. of Wigan, and 1 mile N. of the ancient village of Upholland. The old church in the village, dedicated to St. Thomas of Canterbury, is a stone building of the 14th century. It was showing great signs of decay, but it has recently been renovated and repaired, both externally and internally. In the reign of Edward 2nd Sir Richard Holland founded here a college or chantry consisting of a dean and 12 secular priests ; but it was shortly afterwards changed into a priory of 12 Benedictine Monks. At the time of sequestration by Henry VIII., it contained 5 ecclesiastics and 26 servants. The registers date from 1600. The priory was sold in 1546 to John Holcroft ; and of the ancient structure little now remains except the church.
"I do love these ancient ruins ;
We never tread upon them, but we set
Our feet upon some revered history."
The present so-called *Priory*, adjoining the church, is a dwelling-house of more modern construction.

On the top of the hill rising above the college to the west is Ashurst beacon, and to the south about four miles distant is Billinge beacon. Between Ashurst hill and Harrock hill, which is about 6 miles distant to the N., is the valley of the Douglas ; in this valley there are the Liverpool and Leeds canal, and the Wigan and Southport railway.

One of the objects which Bishop O'Reilly had in building St. Joseph's College was to create a great future for Catholic Lancashire ; so that from this seminary "as from a great reservoir would be poured out streams of missionaries among the people." A most laudable object, which it is devoutly and sincerely to be hoped may be fully realised. A more eligible, healthy, and secluded site could not have been selected. "Schools, colleges, and convents," as we have read, and as must be apparent to all who have 'right notions' on these matters, "should be placed in beautiful and healthy situations, in order that the purity of air, and loveliness of scenery around may conduce to the mental and bodily refreshment of the students."

On the 18th April, 1880, the foundations were blessed by the Bishop, on the feast of the Patronage of St. Joseph, when an eloquent address on the progress and prospects of Catholicity in England was delivered by Very Rev. William Canon Walker, missionary rector of Lancaster. There was a large attendance of clergy and laity. Soon after the foundations were laid a considerable legacy was left by Mr. Gilbert Heyes, of Liverpool, to the Bishop, out of which legacy the north wing of the college, with its spacious ambulacrum, was built. The wing is known by his name, and there is a tablet placed in it recording his charitable bequest.

Fervet opus—the work proceeds with uninterrupted progress. The Bishop took the most lively interest in the work of erection : he frequently visited the place ; and scarcely a course of masonry was laid without its being inspected and examined by him, as long as his health allowed him to continue his visits. The college, on the 22nd of September, 1883, being ready for opening, thirty-one students were received, sixteen in philosophy, and fifteen in divinity. The Very Rev. Canon Teebay had been appointed Rector, and the Rev. John Bilsborrow, Vice-

Rector. The Bishop was present on occasion of the opening, and the college was solemnly blessed by him, in every apartment through which he passed in procession.

The cost of erecting St. Joseph's College has been considerable, but it was a great undertaking, and required a large outlay :—

	£	s.	d.
Cost of Land	8,000	0	0
College Buildings, about	40,000	0	0
Waterworks, Lodge, Cottages, Roads, Plantations (about 7 or 8 acres of new plantations), Walls, Grounds, Gates, Gas, Heating, Furniture, Architect's Commission, and sundries	10,000	0	0
	£58,000	0	0

Included in the expenditure is the cost of two large covered reservoirs and a filter bed, formed to contain half a million of gallons of storage ; besides there is a constant spring below the level of the reservoirs. The sum of £3,871 7s. 8d. was absorbed by this work. But an abundance of good water has been secured, and is supplied at a pressure of 100 ft. above the college, in case of fire, in 4 inch iron pipes. The plans for the new buildings were prepared by Mr. James O'Byrne, architect, Liverpool, and the work is most creditable to his talent and experience, and cannot fail to add to his reputation. To the Very Rev. Canon Worthy, of Euxton, a most worthy, practical, and experienced man, the meed of no small praise must be awarded. He planned, he planted, he watered, he designed, he superintended, and directed. In the year 1885, at Pentecost, eight of St. Joseph's *Alumni* were raised to the priesthood : in the August following another student was ordained priest. A report and balance sheet, with a new and complete list of subscriptions, was issued on the 31st July, 1885, from which it appears that there was still a debt of £2472 4s. 3d. on the college, with unfilled promises of subscriptions to the amount of £5021 16s. 6d. May debt and all encumbrance in speedy course of time be removed from this noble establishment, and may it flourish under the hills where it has been placed, and become a beacon of religion and learning, far more conspicuous and glorious than those that crown the eminences of Ashurst and Billinge. May each successive year a band of young, learned, and pious priests issue forth from it, to be the joy and the crown of Bishop O'Reilly, whom may God long preserve in health and safety for his church, and the benefit of the faithful people committed to his pastoral care ; and may his throne continue to be established in justice, and his seat in equity.

The Rev. Gerald O'Reilly, of St. Oswald's, Ashton-in-Makerfield, a most kind-hearted and respected priest, who attends with unwearied zeal to the spiritual welfare of his flock, is brother of the Right Rev. Bishop O'Reilly. He was educated at Ushaw, and entertains an unabated and ardent attachment to his *Alma Mater*. Fr. O'Reilly went as a student to St. Cuthbert's College, in 1838 ; and having completed his course of studies, and taught several years as a minor professor, he was ordained priest in the year 1856. His first mission was

St. Vincent's Liverpool. He was next appointed to St. Mary's, Wigan, where re remained 14 years ; thence he was transferred to Ashton, where loved and esteemed by his people and neighbours, he has been upwards of other 14 years. In proof of the respect and confidence in which he is held at Ushaw, it may be stated that he is one of the Trustees of St. Cuthbert's Society, is among its Vice-Presidents, and ranks as a member of the Society's Council. In the Society's welfare and progress he takes especial interest, has been a member since its institution, and seldom, if ever, absents himself from its meetings.

In regard to Bishop O'Reilly, I was nearly omitting to make mention of a most commendable and notable trait in his character. Not only has he attended with unwearied and watchful solicitude to the concerns and interests of his diocese, edifying by his zeal and piety both priests and people, rebuking, when occasion arose, the wayward and the backslider, enforcing discipline, inculcating submission to authority, and reminding the faithful, especially the well-to-do and the opulent, of their duty to contribute to the support of schools and missions, to the erection of churches, to the establishment of benevolent and religious institutions, but his solicitude extended to each individual priest of his diocese, and when any one among them fell sick, and became invalided, the Bishop, with a heart full of kindness and compassion, would hasten, how great soever the distance, and however inclement the season, to visit and console him—" I was sick and you visited me ;" and should he happen to die, he rarely failed to attend his obsequies.

BISHOP ANGUS MACDONALD.

Though the youngest of the Bishops whose lives I am writing, Bishop Angus Macdonald ranks next in precedence of consecration. For the nonce, therefore, my readers will be pleased to accompany me to Scotland, the land of the Gael, the land of Wallace, Bruce, and Douglas ; to the

" Land of the mountain and the flood,
Land of brown heath and shaggy wood."

I find there a learned and honoured *Alumnus* of Ushaw, the Right Rev. Angus Macdonald, enthroned as Lord Bishop of Argyll and the Isles, to which See he was appointed when the Hierarchy of Scotland was restored, March 4th, 1878, by Letters Apostolic of Leo XIII.

Bishop Angus Macdonald was born at Borrodale, Inverness-shire, the 18th September, 1844. He went to Ushaw in 1857, for the commencement of the Academic year ; and so his first Grand-week was that of the College Jubilee in 1858. He began his studies in First Class Underlow, under James (now Very Rev. Canon) Taylor. He was in Rhetoric when the venerated Dr. Newsham, the President, died, and was one of the " Forlorn Hope" sent up immediately after that event for matriculation, under the system then started, and since continued, of affiliation to the London University. After graduating in 1865 (either Oct. or Nov.) he continued that year at Ushaw, reading Moral Philosophy, which had been interrupted by the B.A. studies, and at the long vacation in 1866 he left, and was three years at home, after which he decided to continue his studies for the Church. Angus returned to Ushaw for theology in autumn, 1869, and was ordained priest by Dr. Chadwick on the 7th July (Feast of the Precious Blood), 1872. In course of a few months he was stationed (Oct. 1872) at St. Patrick's, Glasgow, where he remained till the spring of 1876, when he was sent to Arisaig, his native place, to assist the Rev. Wm. Mc.Intosh. He reached Arisaig on Holy Saturday of that year ; and on Whit-Sunday, Father Mc.Intosh having resigned through old age, Father Macdonald entered into full charge, and remained there till his nomination to the restored Diocese of Argyll and the Isles by Brief of 22nd March, 1878. On the 23rd May following he was consecrated (with the Bishop of Galloway) at St. Andrew's Pro-Cathedral, Glasgow, by Archbishop Eyre, the assisting Bishops being Dr. Chadwick and the Bishop of Aberdeen (John Macdonald, no relation). Bishop Angus Macdonald then took up his residence in Oban.

His Lordship's family are a younger branch of the Macdonalds of Clanranald. His brother, Hugh Macdonald, the Redemptorist, and Provincial of the Order, entered Ushaw three years before Angus, viz., in 1854, and completed his whole course there, being ordained priest in 1867, on the 21st September. After spending two years at Glenfinnan in delicate health, he was appointed to St. Mary's, Greenock, as curate, and joined the Redemptorists, which he had for years contemplated, and only deferred in compliance with wishes which he felt it right to defer to for a time,—in the year 1870.

The Diocese of Argyll and the Isles, including Argyllshire, South-half Inverness-shire, and all the *Western* Isles of Scotland, is territorially very extensive, the islands being scattered over a wide extent of sea. In length it is over 200 miles, and in breadth nearly 150. The Catholic population which consists mainly of the inhabitants of districts and islands which never lost their faith, numbers only about 12,000 at the outside. In Argyllshire there is (at Glencoe) a small body of native Catholics ; but the other missions in this county are town ones, and the Catholics are not natives, but persons attracted thither by better facilities for employment. The same holds of Rothsay mission in the Island of Bute. The See of Argyll was founded about 1200, and was vacant 299 years, from 1579 to 1878. The See of the Isles is said to have been founded about 447, by St. Patrick ; and was vacant 325 years, from 1553 to 1878. Within this diocese is "Old Iona's holy fane," an island (one of the "storm-vexed" Hebrides) which St. Columba, the apostle of Caledonia, has made immortal, and which took from him the name of I-Colm-kill (the island of Columb-kill), but is better known under that of Iona. It was here St. Columba, a voluntary exile from Ireland, established his monastery. "It was from this point," to quote from Montalambert's 'Monks of the West,' "that he was to assail the Land of the Woods, that unconquerable Caledonia, where the Romans had been obliged to relinquish the idea of establishing themselves, where Christianity hitherto had appeared only to vanish, and which for long seemed to Europe almost outside the boundaries of the world." On Columba was to devolve the honour of introducing the blessings of religion, civilization and learning into stony, sterile, and bleak Scotland. St. Columba lived during thirty years in his adopted island (Iona). From Iona he ventured to carry the light of Christianity among heathen people, and he planted the standard of the cross in the Orkney Isles, in the Hebrides, among the Northern Picts, and beyond the mountains, over the Lowlands, and into Northumberland. He is said to have built 300 abbeys, and to have written as many manuscript books. The famous cemetery of Iona was for many centuries the last asylum of kings and princes, nobles and prelates, and of the chiefs of the clans and communities of all the neighbouring districts; and, as a report made in 1594 says, "of the best people of all the isles, and consequently the holiest and most honourable place in Scotland." Within sight of Iona is the neighbouring isle of Staffa, which contains the famous grotto of Fingal.

Ages have come and gone; St. Columba and his monks have disappeared from the scene centuries ago; their monastery and church have been reduced to ruins by the effacing fingers of time, and the ruthless hand of the spoiler. The ruins, sombre, sad, and desolate, of this "Glory of the West," remain, it is true; but how melancholy are such memorials. *"Perierunt etiam ruinæ;"* and the very grave stones in the cemetery, defaced and broken, have in most instances forgot the names of those who are buried underneath them.

Under the pontifical rule of Angus, Lord Bishop of the Isles, to whom God grant a prolonged, prosperous, and happy life for the exercise of his episcopal office, may religion revive and again flourish among the Isles, so that they may become isles of the blessed, the centre once more, as in the days of Saints Columba, Aidan, and others, whence apostolic missionaries went forth to evangelize barbarous tribes of people.

The Bishop towards the close of the year 1885 journeyed to Rome, to visit the threshold of the Apostles, and to pay homage to the successor St. Peter, Pope Leo XIII. Bishop Macdonald, writing to me shortly before his departure *ad limina Apostolorum* says:—" I was greatly disappointed that I could not get up to the opening of the new Church at Ushaw. But I hope that the expansion of St. Cuthbert's College chapel may be only a foreshadowing of the increased greatness, splendour, and usefulness of *Alma Mater."—Hæc tua vota Deus secundet.*

To meet the pressing needs of the widespread and poverty-stricken diocese of Argyll and the Isles, a Committee has, at the request of the Bishop, taken in hand the work of forming a diocesan fund, the main objects of which will be to provide some certain maintenance for the clergy of the existing missions, to render possible the opening of new missions where they are urgently needed, and to provide a cathedral with accommodation for the requisite staff of clergy, at Oban. In the course of a statement the Committee observe that it is not easy to convey, in a few words, any adequate idea of the laborious nature of the ministry in the diocese of Argyll and the Isles, or of the privations which the clergy have to undergo in the discharge of their duties. The bulk of the Catholic population inhabit the islands and remote parts of the mainland; and it is no unfrequent occurence, during winter time, that sick calls are made by crossing a raging sea at the imminent peril of all engaged in the enterprise, including of course the priest himself, who may be storm-stayed for days together before he can return home, all the while subsisting on the scantiest food which the poor people can often supply only with considerable difficulty. Many of the missions extend over wide areas of mountain and moor, without roads, and passable only on foot during the winter, in consequence of the storm and flood. Such is the poverty of their missions that, with few exceptions, even in the comparatively speaking more favoured cases, the life of the priests is a struggle for existence. Many of the clergy are largely, and some almost wholly dependent for a meagre support on external aid. Their duties entail great bodily fatigue, and constant exposure to cold, wet, and storm, in their long journeys on foot or in open boats across boisterous seas, and to these unavoidable hardships are added a constant preying anxiety as to how they are to provide, not merely for the maintenance of their churches, or the adornment of the altar, but for the barest necessaries of life.

BISHOP LACY.

The diocese of Middlesbrough, formed December 20th, 1878, by the division of the diocese of Beverley into the two dioceses of Leeds and Middlesbrough, comprises the North and East Ridings of Yorkshire, and that portion of the city of York, with the Ainsty, North of the Ouse. Middlesbrough, the centre of the north of England iron manufacture, is situated in the North Riding of Yorkshire, at the mouth of the river Tees. The town is of recent growth; at the census of 1831 it was an obscure hamlet, with 383 inhabitants. Since then the population has increased prodigiously, being 50,000 or upwards, the Catholics numbering more than 13,000. The Catholic population of the diocese is computed at about 40,000. The subject of this biographical sketch, the Right Rev. Richard Lacy, is a native of the Emerald Isle, having been born at Navan, Co. Meath, January 16th, 1841. In the year 1855 he left home and country to study for the priesthood at St. Cuthbert's College, Ushaw. He was a pious, painstaking, and promising student; obedient to rule, submissive to superiors; loving God with his whole heart, and cherishing an ardent devotion to Mary, "Mother of our Gracious Lord." In course of the year 1864 he went from Ushaw to pursue and complete his studies at Rome, where he was ordained priest December 21st, 1867, in the Basilica of St. John Lateran, by H. E. Cardinal Patrizzi, then Cardinal Vicar of his Holiness Pius IX. On his return to England from Rome in May, 1868, he was placed at St. Patrick's, Bradford, as assistant priest to Canon Scruton, where he remained until August, 1872, when he was sent to Middlesbrough to take temporary charge of the mission. The scholastic excitement consequent on the Education Act of 1870 was then at its height. It was found necessary to provide school accommodation for some 2000 children without delay. Two large schools were accordingly built, and so generously did the flock correspond with the efforts being made, that in a short time £4000 had been raised for the purpose. The next work was to enlarge the presbytery for the accommodation of four priests or more; but in 1876 the most important work of all was begun, when the foundation stone of the present

Cathedral was laid by His Lordship the Bishop of Beverley. In 1878 it was solemnly opened by H. E. Cardinal Manning, who came again in the following year, Dec. 18th, 1879, and consecrated Dr. Lacy as first Bishop of Middlesbrough.

May he who so lovingly called himself the "Good Shepherd ;" who said, "I know mine and mine know me," guide, guard and direct the honoured, watchful "overseer of God's house," and the flock of which he has charge ; and conduct them to more refreshing and abounding waters than those of Tees, or Ouse, or Ure, or Swale,—to no other than the crystal waters of the river of life, " *Cujus impetus lætificat civitatem Dei.*" May she, who is "our life, our sweetness, and our hope ;" to whom, under the title of " Our Lady of Perpetual Succour," Bishop Lacy has dedicated his cathedral and confided the spiritual and temporal concerns of his diocese, shield and throw around him her benign and loving protection. His Lordship says :—" A special blessing seems to have descended on Middlesbrough since the church was dedicated to her, and more particularly since her picture was exposed in the Lady Chapel. Some of the most abandoned and inveterate sinners have had the grace of conversion, and some have been changed into saints. The tone of Catholicity is much improved in the town ; the faith of the people has completely revived. Our good priests labour very zealously among the people, but the success belongs to our Lady. If you ask me for miracles, I can give you only one, *viz.*, the wonderful progress religion is making in spite of very great difficulties." Dr. Lacy when in Rome in 1884 was vouchsafed through our Lady of Perpetual Succour a miraculous cure of an internal ailment, which for nine years had caused him much trouble and suffering, and been a sad drawback to him in his work. The cure was instantaneous and complete.

With his flock I unite in praying that his Lordship, in health and sickness, in life and death, may continue to be favoured with our Lady's perpetual succour ; and through her hands receive abundance of good things—even the good things of Israel :—*Cujus sint omnia bona Israel.*

BISHOP RIDDELL.

The Right Rev. Arthur Riddell is a scion of the ancient family of Riddell, of Felton Park, Northumberland. The Right Rev. William Riddell, Bishop of Longo, and Vicar-Apostolic of the Northern District, created in 1840, and comprising the counties of Northumberland, Cumberland, Westmorland, and Durham, was his uncle. This apostolic and zealous prelate died at Newcastle-on-Tyne Nov. 2nd, 1847, after a very short episcopate, from fever caught in visiting the sick. Arthur Riddell, his nephew, third son of Edward Widdrington Riddell, Esq., son of Ralph Riddell, Esq., of Felton Park and Swinburne Castle, both in Northumberland, was born in Paris, September 15th, 1836. His mother was the Honble. Catharine Stapleton, sister of Miles Thomas Stapleton, the eighth Lord Beaumont, and aunt to the present peer. The saintly Curé of Ars predicted to her that one of her sons would one day be a Bishop, and the truth of the prediction has been realised, her son Arthur becoming the third Bishop of Northampton. The Bishop's early education was received at Downside, whence, in 1851, he and his elder brother, the Very Rev. Edward Widdrington Riddell, Canon of the Cathedral Chapter of Middlesbrough, were removed from Downside to Ushaw. In 1859 Arthur was raised to the priesthood, and for thirteen years and a half he discharged at Hull, as assistant to the Very Rev. Dean Trappes, the duties of an exemplary priest. After Dean Trappes's death, June 7th, 1873, and on the death of the Very Rev. Canon Walker, of Scarborough, June 26th of the same year, he removed from Hull to take charge of the mission of St. Peter's, in that town. Whilst there he was appointed to fill the See of Northampton, in place of Bishop Amherst, resigned ; and was consecrated in the Cathedral of that town by Bishop Cornthwaite, June 9th, 1880. Bishop Riddell, on the death of Dean Trappes, was elected Secretary of St. Cuthbert's Society, which office he held till his elevation to the episcopate, having performed its duties most satisfactorily and advantageously. Under Bishop Riddell's episcopal rule may holy discipline, religion, and piety grow and flourish in the diocese of Northampton, and the upas tree of atheism and agnosticism be rooted up, so as no longer to encumber and poison the ground.

The Diocese of Northampton has an extensive area, but the number of its Catholic inhabitants are few and far between. The counties comprised in it are Northamptonshire, Bedfordshire, Buckinghamshire, Cambridgeshire, Huntingdonshire, Norfolk, and Suffolk. That learned and distinguished Prelate, Dr. Milner, in whose district (Midland) Northamptonshire was formerly situated, knowing the desolate condition as to spiritual concerns of that county, determined to establish a mission at Northampton, and the Rev. Wm. Foley, of Oscott, was appointed to the place. The number of Catholics in the town was 80. Mr. Foley at length succeeded in erecting a convenient chapel, and commodious house for the priest. The chapel was opened on the 25th of Oct., 1825. On the establishment of the hierarchy Northampton became an Episcopal See, its first Bishop being the Right Rev. William Wareing, who resigned in 1858, and died in 1865. Bishop Wareing considerably enlarged the chapel built by Mr. Foley, making it a part of a small but respectable Gothic building. The Right Rev. Francis Kerril Amherst succeeded Bishop Wareing, as second Bishop of Northampton, and built the present elegant and much larger structure, to which the portion, as left by Bishop Wareing, forms an appropriate entrance. This (the addition made by Bishop Amherst) was opened by Cardinal Wiseman of glorious memory, in the year 1863 or 1864. There are two convents in Northampton, viz., the convent of the Sisters of Notre Dame, and that of the Sisters of Nazareth, who have a house near, and on the same side of the road (Leicester Road) as the Cathedral. Bishop Amherst brought into the town the Sisters of Nazareth ; he also bought an old Catholic Hospital (Alms' House) with chapel adjoining. It has been fitted up as a Catholic chapel again, and Mass is said and Benediction given there. It was originally called St. John's Hospital. The Catholics of Northampton have increased in number to about 1600. Within the diocese there are many places of interest ; where numerous traces of the good old times remain ; where traditions of the ages of faith are still found ; and where, though obscured by the mists of heresy, the ancient religion, in spite of the persecution it has undergone, still lingers, and is not altogether obliterated, but like down-trodden grass, will spring up again with renewed freshness and verdure :—

"*Duris ut ilex tonsa bipennibus,*
Per damna, per cædes, ab ipso
Ducit opes animumque ferro."

Northampton is not only the episcopal seat of the Bishop of that See, but with Northampton are connected many religious and historical associations. It was here blessed Thomas à Becket stood out alone against the so called " Royal Customs," and would not crouch before Henry II. In opposing the pretensions of that King, he struggled for law, right, and justice, and finally afterwards witnessed for his faith in his blood. Listen to St. Thomas addressing the nobles in the great hall of Northampton Castle on the subject of the " Royal Customs :"

" I war not, Sirs, with ways traditionary ;
The Church of Christ herself is a tradition ;—
Aye, but 'tis God's tradition, not of men !
Sirs, these your customs are God's laws reversed,
Traditions making void the Word of God,
Old innovations from the first withstood,
The rights of Holy Church, the poor man's portion
Sold, and for nought, to aliens,—customs ! customs !
Sirs, I defy your Customs ; they are nought ;—
From them I turn to our old English laws,
The Confessor's, and theirs who went before him ;
The Charters old, and sacred oaths of Kings."

While the Parliament, with the King and the nobles, was sitting at Northampton, the Archbishop took up his abode at the convent of St. Giles, in that town. He was attended by his faithful friend and secretary, Warel, Sub-prior of the Abbey of St. Augustine, Canterbury. And Warel attended him in his flight from Northampton, where he had set at nought prince and prelate, accompanied him into France, returned with him to England, nor departed from his side even when undergoing death and martyrdom at the hands of the four wicked knights.

Again, there is Peterborough—Medehamstede—or " the Home of the Meadows," with its old abbatial church, that has been replaced by the present majestic cathedral, and which stands in the midst of gardens, lawns, and groves. The monastery was originally built in the seventh century by Mercian Kings, in honour of God and St. Peter. Its first Abbot was Sexwulf, much beloved by the Mercian Saxons. At its dedication were present Kings and Bishops, and all the Earls, Thanes, and landed proprietors of the Kingdom. St. Wilfrid, who might be considered one of its founders, also assisted at the solemnity, and afterwards obtained a charter from the Pope in favour of this great abbey. The monastery of Peterborough was one of the richest houses and most famous schools in England. St. Wulstan, Bishop of Worcester, the last of the Anglo-Saxon Bishops, was there educated.

There is also Ely, the monastic metropolis of East Anglia, with its beautiful Anglo-Norman Cathedral—Ely, where in 673 St. Etheldreda founded her monastery, and received the benediction as abbess of St. Wilfrid—a monastery which grew into speedy greatness, and where many Anglo-Saxon virgins joined her, among whom were a number of princesses of her family, having at their head her elder sister, Sexburga, the queen of Kent, who succeeded Etheldreda as abbess, and after her mother Sexburga, Ermenilda, queen of Mercia. The fourth abbess was Wereburga, only daughter of Ermenilda.

Within the jurisdiction of Bishop Riddell's diocese is ill-omened and tragical Fotheringay; the "fair town of Oundle," where once stood St. Wilfrid's monastery and the cell wherein he died; Cambridgeshire, where formerly existed 36 religious houses, and Cambridge with its ancient University, where, before the so-called new learning, literature, science and religion went hand in hand. Nor must Bury St. Edmund's (St. Edmundsbury) be passed over, which, prior to the suppression and dissolution of the monasteries could boast of its magnificent abbatial church, built by Abbot Baldwin, and dedicated "in honour of Christ, the Virgin Mother, and St. Edmund." This church is supposed to have been built of stone brought from Caen in Normandy. It contained altogether twelve chapels, the shrine of St. Edmund being preserved in a semi-circular chapel at the east end. To the abbey there appear to have been four grand gates of entrance; and its lofty embattled walls enclosed, besides the body of the monastery, &c., the splendid monasterial church, extensive cemetery, three smaller churches, and several chapels. Beyond the circuit of the walls were many hospitals, chapels, and other religious edifices, under the patronage of the monks, and depending on them for support. The monastery was a Benedictine establishment, and has generally been supposed to have exceeded all other ecclesiastical and monastic establishments in England, Glastonbury excepted. It remained 519 years in the possession of the Benedictine Monks, and during that time was governed by thirty-three abbots, among whom ranks the famous abbot Sampson, who in 1198 founded at St. Edmundsbury a school for 40 poor boys. He was a man of great force of character; "an eloquent man both in French and Latin; could read English manuscript very critically, and was wont to preach to the people in English, as well as in the dialect of Norfolk, where he was born and bred." The last abbot was John Reese, pious and learned, and a lover of his vow and his religion, who died of a broken heart, when he had seen the thirty-first year of the reign of Henry VIII., 1540. In the town there were fourteen guilds established in the several churches and chapels, and the alms houses for the poor were very numerous.

Norwich, with its beautiful Cathedral, its forty churches, its historical and religious associations; its boy martyr, St. William, seized and crucified by Jews in 1137, according to the Saxon chronicle; its sainted anchorite, Mother Juliana, who lived in the time of Edward III.; and coming down to present times, the magnificent church which is being erected in that city by the munificence and piety of the Catholic Duke of Norfolk for his co-religionists—the Catholics of Norwich, who number about 1400, claims a passing notice as being in the diocese of Northampton. The learned and venerable Alban Butler, author of "The Lives of the Saints," and a native of the county of Northampton, had, from the year 1754 to 1756, charge, as chaplain to Edward, Duke of Norfolk, of the congregation attached to the chapel in the Duke's palace. St. Felix in the seventh century having converted and baptized Sigebert, King of East Anglia, converted also nearly the whole of the East Angles—Norfolk, Suffolk, and Cambridgeshire. On being made Bishop, he fixed his See at Dunwich in Suffolk, then the capital of the kingdom. It was afterwards removed to Thetford about 1070; then Bishop Herbert of Losinga, who came from Normandy with William Rufus, removed the See to Norwich from Thetford, and laid the foundation of the Cathedral 1096. Before he died Bishop Herbert erected the presbytery or eastern arm of the church, apsidal chapels, choir, transept, and lower stage of the tower. Norwich Cathedral is celebrated as an interesting specimen of the Anglo-Norman style, and is one of the finest examples of the skill of the various periods, from the end of the 11th to the beginning of the 16th century, in which it was founded, enlarged, and repaired. The tower and spire are the most important features of the exterior of the Cathedral, the former being the loftiest and most elaborate of the Norman period remaining in England. It is square with turrets at the corners. The spire, with the single exception of that of Salisbury, is the highest in the kingdom. The cloisters form one of the largest and most beautiful quadrangles of the kind in England; they comprise a square of about 174 feet, and are 12 feet wide. They were commenced by Bishop Walpole about 1297, and although proceeded with by succeeding prelates, were not completed until 1430. The style of architecture is the decorated mixed with traces of the perpendicular. The under named Bishops of Norwich, who loved the beauty of God's house, and under whose hands the stones "assumed life and were spiritualised;" and became what Coleridge calls "the petrifactions of religion," and a French writer "*La pensée chrétienne batie*," were those mostly concerned and interested in the structure and architecture of Norwich Cathedral and cloister, on the various parts of which, interiorly and exteriorly, they have left the impress of their genius, conceptions, zeal, and devotedness :—Herbert, Eborard, Walter Suffield, Ralph Walpole, John Salmon, Thomas Percy, John Wakering, William Alnwick, Walter Lyhart, James Goldwell, Richard Nix.

Bishop Suffield died at Colchester, and his remains were brought in great state to Norwich, and laid before the high altar of his own Lady Chapel. Miracles are said to have been wrought at his tomb. He was consecrated in 1245; he died in 1257, *temp.* Henry III.

Thetford, in ancient times the seat of a Bishopric, until it was transferred to Norwich, and Ramsey in Huntingdonshire, where an abbey of considerable extent, and reputed to possess great wealth formerly existed, are within the limits of the diocese of Northampton. The town itself of Northampton is situated on the river Nen. Father Faber in the life of St. Wilfrid, which he wrote for the series of "Lives of English Saints," prior to his conversion to the Catholic faith, thus describes the pastoral beauty of the country through which the Nen flows:—"For quiet pastoral beauty the Nen is a sweet river, winding like a serpent, not in the romantic prison of a narrow, woody vale, but claiming as its own a region of blythe green meadows, multitudinous churches, and full often fringes of deepest summer foliage, varying its usual border of wide, sheep-spotted fields. The frowning front of Peterborough Minster looks up this smiling valley; and to one who wanders up the stream, turning his back on the abbey, the spires of Fletton and of Stanground, and the little tower of Woodstone, many a sweet sight presents itself. When the woods of Milton give way to the hedgeless fields, the "mother church" of Caistor, where St. Kyneburga dwelt, is seen, and the churches of Water Newton, Stibbington, and Wansford, come to the river's brink; then the low tower of Yarwell succeeds, and the beautiful spire of Nassington, hiding itself amid the poplars it so much resembles; while through the whole reach a beacon never missing, the tall and lordly tower of Elton on its hilltop shoots up out of the bosom of princely woods, looking down on the octagon of Fotheringay, where Queen Mary laid "her tired head upon the block;" there to the left the interesting church of Warmington stands a little retired from the stream, while Cotterstock and Tansor stand opposite each other on the shore: and as Peterborough Minster looks up this quiet valley, so down it visible for many a mile, the fretted spire of Oundle, shooting up into the blue sky, looks like a sentinel, from every point a beautiful, indeed an exquisite thing for the eye to rest upon. Over this region Wilfrid's spirit once rested, and hither did he come to die; the gates of his monastery of Oundle, or Avondale, closed upon the care-broken abbot; and they opened for his holy body to be borne in funeral pomp to Ripon."

Alas! that this beautiful country, and that portion of it known as the "Fens," now so fertile and cultivated, should be enmeshed in the toils of heresy, and estranged from the faith our fathers once held.— "*Exoriare aliquis nostris ex ossibus ultor;*"—and, not by breaking the bruised reed, and extinguishing the burning flax, but by "kindly words and virtuous life," let him strive to win back to the one fold this portion of English ground, and leave no means neglected to resuscitate the faith which, though apparently dead, only sleepeth; and to restore to the beauty and perfection of holiness a country that once was holy Church's inheritance. Then shall the face of the earth be renewed; then shall the meek inherit the land, and delight in the abundance of peace:— "*Tunc flumina plaudent manu, simul montes exultabunt a conspectu Domini.*"—Ps. 97. And may Bishop Riddell's Episcopate, here established, be as "a spring that bubbleth fast, and give out saving waters in abundance." May the people rejoice to receive from him the knowledge of salvation, and under his paternal guidance may their feet be directed into the ways of peace and santification.

> "*Auferte gentem perfidam,*
> *Credentium de finibus;*
> *Ut unus omnes unicum*
> *Ovile nos Pastor regat.*"

To the liberality and charity of Mrs. Lyne-Stephens, of Lynford, Norfolk, the diocese of Northampton is largely indebted—indebted for the splendid new Gothic church of our Lady at Cambridge ; for the churches at Wellingborough, Bedford, and Lynford ; for new schools at Thetford ; and for the Bishop's house, at Northampton, erected at the west side of the cathedral, at a cost of £10,000.

BISHOP BEWICK.

A worthy Northern, found most worthy to be advanced to the episcopal dignity, and to occupy the See which blessed Cuthbert sanctified ; which Paulinus, the Apostle of Northumbria, Aidan, the first Bishop of Lindisfarne, Acca, Eata, Alchmund, and Eadbert, Chad, John of Beverley, and though last not least the stout-hearted Wilfrid—all eminent for sanctity, magnified and adorned. "Gold," writes the Abbot Rupertus, "comes from the North"—"*ab aquilone aurum venit.*" It is not therefore unreasonable, by reason of the election of the present honoured Bishop of Hexham and Newcastle, John William Bewick, as successor to Bishop Chadwick, to foreshadow for the church of Northumbria a *golden* and prosperous career ; and to cherish the hope that, having been born in the North, religion, under his pastoral sway, like

"The oak, and the ash, and the bonny rowan tree,
That grow best at home in the North countrie,"

will become firmly rooted, and flourish ; faith be propagated, piety and devotion promoted, zeal for the house of God, and the extension of His worship increase ; and at length, a restoration of the Church's ancient ways, and a return to the unity of faith, take place throughout the extent of this grand old diocese. In a Pastoral Letter addressed to the clergy, and all the faithful of his diocese, Bishop Bewick, in taking a survey of the said diocese, of its extent, its population, and its resources, says—"The diocese of Hexham and Newcastle is wide, and far-stretching. The distance from Berwick-on-Tweed in the north, to Millom, our most remote mission in the south of Cumberland, entails a fair day's journey by railway. Again to travel from our residence at Tynemouth on the east coast, or from our cathedral to the Solway Firth or the Irish Sea in the west, we must pass through portions of the four counties which form the diocese, namely, Northumberland, Durham, Cumberland, and Westmorland. The total population of these four counties is computed at more than a million and a half. Of these we may fairly conclude that 180,000 are Catholics, that is, '*are of our fold and hear our voice,*' and own allegiance in things spiritual to us. To minister to this vast mass we have at this moment upon our clergy-list 156 priests. The diocese comprises an agricultural, a sea-faring, a manufacturing, a mining, an iron-working, a labouring population. The rich and opulent are few—the hewers of wood and drawers of water are many. If there are not in the diocese large cities, there are some of the busiest hives of industry in the world. Few rivers can vie in importance with the river Tyne. It and its estuary form the largest fishing ground in the world—on its waters float ships from every sea and port—

its banks and its quays supply the world with some of the staple commodities of trade and commerce. Then further inland there are the great coal fields and iron and lead producing localities. Amid all these resources of wealth, this stir and turmoil of business and manufacture, our labourers and artisans are exposed to manifold and serious dangers. Then, for the educating and training of our young clergy through twelve years of collegiate life, it is the glory of our diocese that it possesses one of the largest, grandest, and most efficient colleges in the land. Ushaw College holds highest rank for its success in competitive examinations, and contributes yearly an admirable contingent to the ranks of the clergy in the six Northern Dioceses of England. It is 'our joy and our crown.' Throughout the length and breadth of our Bishopric there are 90 schools, with 165 departments, for the primary or elementary education of our poor children, affording accommodation for 27,500 scholars. These (several of which are under the charge of members of Religious Communities) are able to hold their ground in competition with the schools of the land ; but every day reveals the necessity of enlargement or multiplication."

In extending this survey of the portion of the vineyard committed to the pastoral charge of Bishop Bewick, what notable places, what grand and glorious names crowd upon us ! Durham and Lindisfarne, Jarrow and Wearmouth, Tynemouth and Hexham, Finchale and Newminster, Chester-le-Street and Monkcastre (Newcastle) ; " merry Carlisle" also, where St. Cuthbert kept his Pentecost, recall a period when the Church flourished in light and peace, throughout Northern England, blossoming like a lily, and sanctified by a galaxy of Saints and servants of God, who, like northern lights streamed across the hemisphere of Northumbria. Besides the saintly Bishops, previously enumerated, who does not recall with love and veneration such men of holy lives and learning as Venerable Bede, Benedict Biscop, Ceolfrid, Edelwald, Colwulf, who exchanged his crown for a cowl in the abbey of Lindisfarne, Edwin, Oswald and Oswin, Godric of Finchale, and his friend Robert of Newminster ; Godwin the hermit ; and Herbert, priest and hermit of lake Derwentwater, friend of St. Cuthbert, both of whom, on the same day and hour, passed from earth to heaven. Nor must mention be omitted of the learned Ælred, abbot of Rievaux, nor of Waltheof, descended from the old kings and earls of Northumbria, friend of Ælred, and many years abbot of Melrose. That was a time when the north of England was the home of Saints, when "there was a light and a beauty upon its hills and its wolds, its valleys and its coasts ;" when kings were the nursing fathers of the Church, and queens and devout women retired to the seclusion of cloisters to pray for its prosperity, and " for the peace of Jerusalem." These were goodly days for the Saxon church of Northumbria (would that they might return— *talia currite secla)* ; when men had leisure for life and time to die ; when " we see kings counting thrones as nothing, and casting away their crowns to follow in simplicity the poverty of the Cross."

But to return to our immediate subject :—Bishop Bewick "one of the most widely esteemed members of the English Hierarchy," is a native of Northumberland, born at Minsteracres, on the 20th of April,

1824. On his father's side he is related to Thomas Bewick, the celebrated wood engraver, whose productions are held in such high estimation, and are so much sought after. A nobler art and calling than engraving on wood was destined for John William Bewick. His vocation was to engrave on the hearts and souls of men, the truths of religion, the love of God and a reverence for His holy law :—his to

" Bend the stubborn heart and will,
Melt the frozen, warm the chill ;
Guide the steps that go astray."

" *Tu regere imperio populos, Romane, memento ;
Hæ tibi erunt artes, pacisque imponere morem,
Parcere subjectis, et debellare superbos.*"

In the year 1837, in the month of September, he became a student at St. Cuthbert's College, Ushaw. In that great seminary of religion and learning he studied with earnest diligence, and in his studies made great proficiency, exhibiting talent of high order and excellence. At Whitsuntide, in the year 1850, he was advanced to the dignity of the priesthood, and appointed assistant priest at St. Mary's Cathedral, Newcastle. Shortly afterwards he was removed to North Shields, on which mission he laboured with much fruit, great zeal, and edification, for fifteen years. On account of his literary attainments, he had been named one of the classical examiners of St. Cuthbert's College. The venerable Bishop Hogarth, in 1865, appointed him Bishop's Treasurer ; in the same year he was made a Canon of the diocese ; and subsequently was chosen by Bishop Chadwick as his Vicar-General, between whom and the Bishop the most friendly relations existed for a long period of years. He then removed from North Shields, and took up his abode at Tynemouth, where, in 1871, he founded the present mission, and continues to reside there at the " Martyr's Peace :—"

"——For many an age,
The pilgrim from far countries came in faith,
To that still shrine—they called it ' Oswin's Peace,'—
Thither the outcast fled for sanctuary :
The sick man there found health. Thus Oswin lived,
Though dead, a benediction in the land."

Through a jealous animosity on the part of Oswy, king of Bernicia, against Oswin, the good King of Deira, the latter was cruelly assassinated by Oswy. The body of the royal martyr was deposited in a chapel dedicated to the blessed Virgin, and situated on a granite headland almost surrounded by the sea, at the mouth of the Tyne, a river which was then the boundary line between the two Northumbrian states of Deira and Bernicia. Eanfleda, cousin-german of the murdered king Oswin, and wife of king Oswy who killed him, obtained permission from her husband to build a monastery on the spot where the murder had been committed, that prayers might be offered there for ever for the souls of the victim and of the murderer. Through his wife's influence a happy change appears to have been wrought in the character of Oswy from the day on which she induced him to found this monastery. The monastery was placed under the invocation of the Blessed Virgin Mary, and St. Oswin, king and martyr.

In the eleventh century Tosti, Earl of Northumberland, with his pious lady, caused the re-erection of the abbey, and placed within its sacred walls the far-famed shrine of the royal saint and martyr. This magnificent monument to the departed saint was the favourite resort of the devout for many centuries. The most costly jewels of silver and gold, the offerings of kings and queens, and all ranks of the faithful, bedecked the shrine of the holy Oswin. In the twelfth century considerable further additions were made to the Norman church, and in the fourteenth century, a small beautiful chapel, which still exists, was added to the conventual part of the abbey. Tynemouth Priory was long the wonted haunt of the nobility of England as well as of royalty, especially when in adversity they sought the consolations of religion. From the time of its re-erection by the Earl of Northumberland, until its suppression, the Priory continued to receive the most extensive benefactions. The conventual chapel has, for some years back, been used as a store room for the garrison at Tynemouth; its beautiful windows have been filled with stone; and the whole of the walls and ceiling of the chapel have been covered with whitewash. The old doorway, beautifully recessed, to the east of the high altar, still remains, and is an object of deep interest to the antiquarian. It is generally supposed that beneath the old church are extensive crypts, where the sainted dead were interred for centuries. After the deed of surrender to the crown, in 1539, the ex-prior Blakney received a pension of £80 per annum, with leave to reside on the land, which formerly belonged to the abbey, at Benwell on the Tyne. The other monks who signed the deed were similarly pensioned by the crown. Bishop Bewick's residence at Tynemouth, and temporary chapel, are in the immediate neighbourhood of the Priory ruins. The actual ruins are not now occupied by the military, but the grounds are. New barracks have been erected within the last fifty years, and the ruins are within the batteries and fortifications, and can only be approached through the gateway of the Elizabethan Castle.

In 1875 the Holy See conferred upon Canon Bewick the degree of Doctor of Divinity, and on the death of Bishop Chadwick he was appointed Vicar-Capitular and Administrator of the affairs of the diocese. For the vacant See he was chosen by the Chapter as one of the *Terna*, and his name was recommended to His Holiness by the unanimous approval of the English Bishops. The clergy of the diocese likewise prayed that their Vicar-Capitular might become their Bishop, and in the month of August, 1882, Dr. Bewick, priest of Tynemouth, was appointed to fill the vacant See of Hexham and Newcastle. He was consecrated on the Feast of St. Luke, October 18th, 1882, in St. Mary's Cathedral, by His Eminence Cardinal Manning, assisted by the Archbishop of Glasgow, and the Bishop of Leeds. The Archbishop of St. Andrew's and Edinburgh; five other Bishops, and upwards of one hundred of the clergy were present at the consecration of his Lordship. The clergy, after the ceremony, presented him with an address of congratulation, assuring him of the love and esteem in which they held him. Numerous addresses were also presented to him from the laity in testimony of their reverence and affection. At the luncheon, which was given on the occasion, and at which Cardinal Manning presided, His Eminence, in course of his address said "I rejoice that there has been by the Vicar of Our Lord selected a pastor, whose heart is in St. Cuthbert's College, and one who for so many long years has been the centre of his brethren, to whom they have been united so intimately in the bonds of affection and of confidence."

The Diocese of Hexham and Newcastle had in 1884 an estimated Catholic population of 180,000. The See of Hexham, so named at the restoration of the Hierarchy, in 1850, was by Rescript of May 23rd, 1861, called Hexham and Newcastle. We read in Dolman's Magazine for May, 1849, that " Few towns can boast of more glorious records of 'the days of faith' than are yet traceable in Newcastle-upon-Tyne. Such was its renown in those days for religion, and for its religious houses and splendid temples, that pilgrims from all parts of Europe visited the good old town. Amongst other visitors it is quaintly recorded, in the eleventh century, that Aldwine, prior of Winchester, with two monks of Evesham, travelled on foot to the banks of the Tyne, leading a small ass, carrying some books and vestments, necessary for the celebration of mass. They were met at Tynebridge by some monks, and conveyed to the Pilgrim's Inn, in Pilgrim Street, where after visiting the principal confraternities in the town, they left to visit the monks at Girsoz (Jarrow)." In the year 1705, according to a return made to Parliament, the grand total of "Papists," in all the parishes of Newcastle, amounted to 49! A different state of statistics, as regards the number of Catholics in Newcastle, exists in the year 1886. Brighter days, and brighter prospects have dawned for the old faith that erstwhile flourished with such lustre in the city of the Tyne:—

" *Venit dies, venit tua,*
In qua reflorent omnia."

Who does not most earnestly pray that for Bishop Bewick many years of a vigorous and useful life may be in store—*multos annos felices lætitiæque dies ;* and that after his term of labour and conflict, he may enjoy, as his motto bids him hope, the "*quies in cælo,*" for which in "the pomp and rush of life" we all most ardently long. " Peace was not made for earth," nor is rest found here. We shall, having performed our task work in life, have all eternity wherein to rest :—

"Our folding of the hands is in the grave,
And fixed in Heaven the Sabbath of our rest."

BISHOP LARKIN.

The name of Bishop Larkin will not, I opine, be familiar to many of my readers. In the list of Bishops, who are recorded as having received their education at Ushaw, I have discovered no mention of the name of this Prelate. However, Bishop Larkin was one of the early Ushaw students. The names of Charles Larkin, and John Larkin, his brother, appear in the college diary, the former in 1810, in the second class of Rudiments, the latter in the same year in the third class of Rudiments. In the year 1812, August 3rd, Edward Larkin, a brother, it is to be presumed, of Charles and John, came as a student to St. Cuthbert's. By a numerous class of the inhabitants of "canny Newcastle," the name of Charles Larkin is well known and remembered. He was a prominent Tyneside Radical, and an eloquent speaker and writer. His name is inseparably connected with the great Parliamentary Reform movement of 1830, as well as with other social and political movements in the North of England. He died after a lingering illness at the age of seventy-nine, February 28th, 1879, at his residence in Newcastle. One of the other brothers Larkin (which of them I have not been able to ascertain) became a priest—a hard-working, virtuous priest, in North America ; but the only trace I have been able to meet with of him appeared in the " Weekly Register," December 22nd, 1849. It is as follows :—" The Bishop of Toronto, Upper Canada, on a mission from Canada to Rome, on important ecclesiastical matters connected with the Church in North America, paid a visit to his brother, Charles Larkin, Esq., of Newcastle, at the end of December, 1849. The arrival of his Lordship in his native town created a great sensation of interest, not only in Catholic but Protestant circles, his patriotic refusal to connect himself in any way with Mr. Poulet Thompson's Administration in Canada, his missionary labours in the prairies of his mission, his refusal, for some time, of episcopal dignity, and desire to end his days a 'poor priest,' preaching in the wilds of America, have rendered, especially in his native district, his Lordship an object of great veneration, as one worthy to be classed with that venerable order of which he is now so distinguished an ornament. Dr. Larkin preached on the Sunday morning, within the rails of St. Andrew's Church, in Newcastle, at which rails there are still members of the congregation who remember his appearance at catechetical instructions, when under Father Worswick. His Lordship proceeded to deliver a very eloquent address, amidst the most profound attention of a very numerous congregation. In the evening Bishop Larkin again preached to a still more crowded audience, from the words of the Royal Psalmist, 'O Lord, make me to know mine end,' and illustrated, in a strain of logic and impassioned eloquence, the vanity of all here on earth, as compared with that great fundamental requirement, for which alone this spacious world and man had been created, for which our Blessed Redeemer came from heaven, for which he suffered an ignominious death, all to induce man to consider his last end, and thus to become partaker of inexpressible glory in heaven, with God and the saints, for all eternity. The Right Rev. Dr. Larkin was educated at Ushaw (in the earlier part of his college career), and adds another name to that of the long list of distinguished personages who reflect honour on their far-famed *Alma Mater*." This distinguished Prelate preached on the following Sunday, in the same church, from the text "What went ye out to see ? A reed shaken with the wind," &c. The congregation was large, the building being crowded to overflowing. The sermon was delivered extemporaneously, and with great fluency, animation, and earnestness ; and was listened to with deep attention.

These details concerning the worthy Bishop of Toronto are few and scanty. I beg my readers to be satisfied with them, as they form the sole record I have of him at present, or can gain access to. With this brief sketch of his Lordship I bring to a conclusion the memoirs of the several episcopal celebrities, who adorn the pages of Ushaw's history, and add lustre to "our glorious college ;" and whose lives I have endeavoured, though imperfectly, but I hope truthfully, to portray.

My notice of the above named episcopal dignitaries, connected by education with Ushaw, has caused me to digress from my more immediate subject, to which, having halted long enough on the road, I now hasten to return. "*Dimittamus et exempla clarorum hominum, et illorum virtutis impressam historiis memoriam, quorum in vestigia pedem ponere oportet, qui laudabiliter vivere, quique honestis in actionibus exerceri volunt.*"

The Rev. Thomas Eyre, the first President of the new College at Ushaw, died, as I have previously stated, May 9th, 1810. At Douai he had taught Poetry and Rhetoric, and having left Douai October 11th, 1775, he was appointed to the mission of Stella Hall, near Newcastle-on-Tyne. From Stella, in the month of October, 1792, he went as temporary chaplain to Mrs. Silvertop, at Wooler, in Northumberland; thence to the mission at Pontop Hall, near Lanchester. Mr. Eyre was a liberal benefactor to Ushaw—"*benefactor munificus,*" and at his death left an income to the college of £305, to be apportioned for stipends to four Professors, for educational funds, and for the purchase of theological books. He left behind him a great number of MS. sermons for every Sunday; edited the spiritual works of Gother; and translated Gobinet's Instructions of Youth, 2 vols.

REV. JOHN GILLOW, D.D.,

succeeded the Rev. Thomas Eyre as President, being installed in that office June 11th, 1811. He was the son of Robert Gillow, of Westby, in the Fylde, and his wife, Agnes Fell, and was born March 25th, 1753. His father, Robert, was a younger son of Richard Gillow, of Singleton. The family originally sprang from Yorkshire; came to Lancashire; and settled at Bryning. Thence they removed to Singleton, where they increased and prospered, and were honourable in the land. They were moreover firm, practical adherents of the old faith— the faith which they had inherited from their forefathers, and gave to the Church a succession of virtuous and exemplary priests,—none more so than John Gillow, D.D., the second President of Ushaw, educated at the College of Douai, to which renowned seminary he went October 3rd, 1766, and when in Rhetoric, in the Presidency of H. Tichborne Blount, took the college oath, December 27th, 1772. When ordained priest, he remained at the College, and taught Philosophy and Divinity for eleven years. In the autumn of 1791 (Oct. 3rd), he left Douai, and we find him in 1792 in charge of the mission at York, where for nineteen years he laboured zealously and indefatigably, and built the chapel in Blake Street, in that city. It has been said that Dr. Gillow was desirous of having as his successor at York, or as Vice-President of Ushaw, the Rev. Thomas Penswick, but neither appointment had the approval of Bishop Gibson, and was consequently not made. In 1823 Dr. Penswick was chosen Coadjutor to Bishop Smith ; and consecrated at Ushaw as Bishop of Europum, on the Feast of SS. Peter and Paul, 1824. Bishop Smith died at Ushaw, July 30th, 1831, aged sixty-nine; Bishop Penswick succeeded him as Vicar-Apostolic of the Northern District, and died January 28th, 1836, at the age of sixty-four. His remains rest in the old Catholic cemetery of Windleshaw, where others of his ancestors are interred.

The College of Ushaw was planned to be a quadrangular structure, but up to the year 1812 three sides only of the quadrangle had been built and occupied. In that year Dr. Gillow caused the foundations of the west wing, or fourth side of the quadrangle to be laid, but the work, owing to the want of funds, was subsequently suspended. Within a short time from that period £65,965 18s. 5½d, it is stated, had been expended on lands and buildings connected with the erection of St. Cuthbert's, and that the good old President placed his private fortune, nearly £5000, at the disposal of Bishop Gibson. In 1819 the new wing of the College was partly completed, and by its construction, accommodation for 140 students was provided. In 1812 the number of students in the College was 125.

The duties of his office were discharged wisely and well by the venerable President, and his memory is perpetuated and cherished at St. Cuthbert's with affectionate veneration, for he was a "priest of much worth," deserving to be mentioned with the highest honour. Although, as not unfrequently happens, at the inception of important undertakings, that pecuniary difficulties and other obstacles arise, by these Dr. Gillow was in no wise daunted, but encountered them manfully and energetically. He not only completed the west wing, but for shelter and ornament to the College, he planted trees, formed plantations, caused the pond to be made in front of the house, and effected sundry improvements, always having particular regard and consideration for the comfort and happiness of the students. The College for some time continued as it were in *statu pupillari*, in an elementary or rudimental state, without much apparent development, but from this condition it gradually emerged, and went on from strength to strength—"*ibat de virtute ad virtutem*," until it acquired a name and a prestige as a nursery of learning and a school of letters, of no mean importance—

"Like tree that of the soil took healthy root,
It grew on every side, and shadowing wide,
It spread its ample boughs."

Youths from home and abroad resorted thither to be educated, or to make their studies for the Church. The names of many foreigners, who came when Dr. Gillow was President, are to be found in the College diary. In 1811, the year of his installation as President, 31 students were received ; in 1819, the year when the west wing of the quadrangle was completed, 25 were admitted.

The good old President was a man of sterling excellence, the veritable model of a priest of the old school. In person he was tall and stout, and very dignified in appearance; forehead largely developed; hair blanched by the snows of age, and rendered whiter still by the use of hair powder. His whole aspect was most benign and venerable, and his deportment truly kind and affable—"*vir pietate, benignitate, aspectu venerabilis.*" While he upheld and maintained discipline, and insisted on the observance of rule and order, his behaviour to the students—from the highest to the lowest—was most just, impartial, and paternal. He was accustomed to say that "one drop of honey was worth a spoonful of vinegar." In his whole life and actions he exhibited a conspicuous example of devotedness to duty, of ecclesiastical zeal and piety; nor was he one who conformed to the world, nor to the things of the world; who "flattered its rank breath, or bowed to its idolatries." Every morning he was to be seen offering up, with intense fervour and devotion, the holy sacrifice, at the right hand side altar in the old chapel; and on no account whatever, though he took snuff, would he take a pinch until after saying mass and commencing his thanksgiving. When in Holy Week, during the retreat he took his turn to preach, his sermons were full of unction and feeling; eloquent and impressive; and earnestly listened to. The original portrait of Dr. Gillow, painted by Ramsay, may be seen in the refectory at Ushaw; it is a faithful and unmistakeable likeness of him, so are the engravings, of which I am fortunate in possessing one, taken from it. I remember him on one occasion coming into the Underlows' School, and observing the words "*Quis habet signum?*" chalked on the wall, he looked at us more blandly than sternly, saying, as he struck the floor with his gold-headed cane, "*Quis habet virgam?*" It would be here irrelevant and insulting to Ushaw boys, of a past age at least, to explain the meaning and signification of the "*signum.*" Woe to the luckless wight who took the symbol with him to class Dr. Gillow was a great stickler for Douai rules and customs; believed in the old traditions; and was a veritable "*laudator temporis acti.*" It is recorded of him that, when the pond, in frost, would bear, and was safe to skate upon, he never refused a skating play day. Revered and beloved by all over whom he presided—by Professors, masters, and students, and even the smallest boys, his memory may well deserve to be honoured and cherished—"*erat enim in illo viro comitate condita gravitas.*"

In 1824, while he was President, the consecration took place on the Feast of SS. Peter and Paul, of the Right Rev. Thomas Penswick, Bishop of Europum, as Coadjutor to Bishop Smith, and at that period of Ushaw's history it was a memorable occasion. It may be noted also that at the latter end of the summer of 1812, namely, on the 21st of August, there was a meeting of Catholic Bishops, at Durham. Bishop Moylan, of Cork, was there, and Bishop Milner was there; so were Bishops Gibson, Poynter, and Smith. At this episcopal meeting, Dr. Gillow was present; and after the business for which they had met was terminated, they paid a visit to Ushaw. This event was signalised by a series of play-days granted by the President, in honour of his distinguished guests.

Periodical visits to his friends in Lancashire used to be paid by our old President. When he went thither he used to make his journeys on horseback—on old Ball, his favourite and well-remembered steed. He was uncle to Robert Gillow, Esq., of Leighton Hall ; great uncle to the Rev. Robert Gillow, who died at Copperas-hill, Liverpool, in the fatal fever year ; to the Rev. George Gillow, of Preston, the Right Rev. Mgr. Charles Gillow, of St. Cuthbert's, Ushaw ; and their elder brother, R. T. Gillow, Esq., of Leighton Hall. All these brothers received their education at Ushaw.

In the first month of the fourteenth year of Dr. Gillow's Presidency, I was placed as a student at St. Cuthbert's College. I was a very small boy, and not 12 years of age ; there was no railway at that time to Durham, nor for many years afterwards ; and the journey from Lancashire had in those days to be made by coach. A long, and tedious journey withal over Stainmore, through Brough, Bowes, Barnard Castle, and Bishop Auckland, by the Lord Exmouth coach, in which I started at 4 o'clock in the morning, from "time honoured Lancaster," arriving at Durham late on in the day. I was there met by appointment, and conducted on a balmy evening in July (July 11th, 1824,) to the College. The General Prefect, Rev. John Pratt, received me ; and having provided me in the refectory with "a portion" of bread and milk, he consigned me to the care of two "play-fellows," who for the next three days had to be my constant companions, go out walking with me, teach me the rules, and instruct me in the duties and details of College life. A delightful task to them, as during those three days they became entitled to divers privileges and indulgences—such as leave out, studies off, afternoon tea, and matutinal "aristotes." My play-fellows were two Fylde boys—John Latham from Kirkham, and John Lund from Bartle. Both became priests, and both died young ; the former at Manchester, the latter at Blackbrook, St. Helen's. Poor Lund ! not very long ago I was wandering and musing among the ruins and tombs of Windleshaw Abbey, when, not knowing at the time that he was interred there, I accidentally came upon his grave in an isolated corner of the burial ground. A plain, flat stone, inscribed with name, age, and date of his death (June 18th, 1838,) marked the place of his interment. The grave and gravestone were overgrown with grass and weeds, and nearly concealed from sight. From that day I have made a memento in my prayers of John Lund among departed friends.

The Rev. John Pratt, who was of tall, slender form, and light complexion, did not remain long at Ushaw as Prefect after my arrival. He went on the mission to Copperas-hill, Liverpool, and subsequently established the mission at Birkenhead, where he died, August 4, 1840. The other superiors and professors, when I went to Ushaw, were Dr. Gillow, President, Dr. Youens, Vice-President, Rev. John Kirk, Procurator, Rev. Joseph Brown, Prefect of Studies, Rev. Charles Newsham, Professor of Natural Philosophy, Rev. Thomas Billington, of Moral Philosophy, Rev. Robert Tate, of Rhetoric ; Prefect of Study place, Rev. Walter Maddocks, then in Deacon's Orders. Of the above named not one is left ; all have been removed by death from the toil and strife of life.

A few words respecting the Rev. Joseph Brown :—He was born at Greenside, near Stella, in the county of Durham, on the 10th September, 1794 ; commenced his studies at Crook Hall, whence he proceeded with the other students, when the college was ready for their reception, to Ushaw, where in the year 1809 we find him in the class of Grammar. On being raised to the priesthood he continued in residence as a professor at Ushaw, and subsequently was made Prefect of Studies. In the year 1825 he was appointed by Bishop Smith Rector of the English College, Valladolid, and remained there eleven years, when he came to England, merely as he considered to recruit his health, impaired by the climate and a late attack of fever. This was in 1836 (August). In February of the year 1838 he attempted to return to his college, but on account of the revolution in Spain, he found it was attended with such difficulty that he ultimately abandoned his design. In the ensuing year, on the 2nd of July, 1839, he was appointed by Bishop Briggs assistant chaplain at Carmel House, Darlington, to Rev. James Roby, who was in a very infirm state of health; and resigned his office of Rector of Valladolid College. On the 29th November, 1841, Father Roby died, having been chaplain to the community of Carmelite nuns 51 years, and Father Brown remained sole chaplain till his death, 15th February, 1877. The deceased was a Canon of the Diocese of Hexham and Newcastle. God rest his soul in peace.

I remember how, when Prefect of Studies, the Rev. Jos. Brown endeavoured to cure one of my schoolfellows, a Northumbrian, of the "burr," or the inability so peculiar to the natives of that county to pronounce the letter *r*. As a test whether the young boy, from north Tyneside, was mastering his impediment of speech, Mr. Brown used to say to him—" Now, so-and-so, pronounce 'Glororum,'" but 'Glororum' was a stumbling block, a regular poser to my Northumbrian school-fellow.

The long vacation had just commenced at Ushaw, on my arrival. Its duration then was only three weeks—till the first of August, when the schools re-opened. During those three weeks I had assigned to me an exceedingly kind and considerate pedagogue, Mr. Clement Fisher, so different to the one under whose charge I was afterwards placed. *He* believed in scolding and terrorising; Mr Fisher was the very opposite: he was gentle and patient, conciliatory and encouraging. Mr. Fisher left Ushaw to continue his studies at the English College, Rome, in the autumn of that year. On his return to England he was appointed to St. Anthony's, Liverpool, on the first great visitation of cholera, from an attack of which he never perfectly recovered. Early in the spring of 1835 he sailed for Australia with his uncle, Father Wilfrid Fisher, O.S.B., and Bishop Polding, and died at sea when the ship was passing near St. Helena, May 26th, 1835, aged twenty-six years. His heart was buried in Sydney Cathedral. Deceased was brother of the Rev. Thomas, and George Fisher; of the Right Rev. Mgr. John Henry Provost Fisher, D.D., and the Very Rev. James Canon Fisher, good men and true, true to holy Church, true to the rock on which it is built, true to all sacred traditions; men of edifying lives and manners, whom "*elegit Deus in hereditatem sibi*," and made "fishers of men." The elder brother, Rev. Thomas Fisher, was several years a professor at Ushaw, taught Rhetoric and Moral Philosophy; and was also Prefect of Studies. He went a student to Ushaw in November, 1817; was ordained priest in 1829; and on leaving the college in July, 1833, was appointed to the mission at Sheffield, where he died of fever, October 4th, 1835, at the age of thirty-one years. James Canon Fisher, the youngest of the five brothers, entered St. Cuthbert's in the month of January, 1828; received the priesthood on the 24th of June, 1838; and departed this life January 15, 1883, of his age sixty-eight years, whilst on a few days visit, at St. Edward's College. He was ordained priest when teaching Rhetoric at Ushaw; then for two years he filled the office of Procurator; left Ushaw in July, 1840, and was appointed chaplain to the Liverpool hospitals. Next the mission of Congleton was placed under his charge in November of that year. In 1850 he removed to Great Crosby; in January, 1871, to Burscough; in October, 1877, he retired from missionary work to Birkdale, to devote himself to the finance department alone of the diocese. In this work he had been associated with the Very Rev. Dr. Crook, in the year 1851. The other brothers, George and John Henry Fisher, went to Ushaw on June 7th, 1826, and entered High Figures in August of the same year; George was promoted to the priesthood the 19th of December, 1835. His first mission was Oldham, and he built the first church there, which was opened in March, 1839. From Oldham he removed to Dukinfield, in March, 1840, which he left in November, 1847. From this time to March, 1848, he supplied at intervals three missions, then vacant on account of the prevalence of fever, and the dearth of priests to fill the places of those who had fallen victims to it. He was next temporarily four months at Bootle; in July, 1848, he was appointed to Appleton, where he built two schools, half a mile apart from each other. On removing from Appleton he was inducted in July, 1875, on the death of the Rev. George Gibson, to Hornby, near Lancaster, in whose historical and classical retreat all his friends pray he may be blessed with health, and his life be prolonged to a patriarchal age. Numbering now between seventy and eighty years, he is tranquilly awaiting the end of this life, in expectation of the heavenly one. His brother, the Right Rev. Monsignor Fisher, D.D., a learned and discreet ecclesiastic, was raised to the priesthood at Whitsuntide, May 26th, 1836, and went, on June 19th, to be the private chaplain of the Hon. Charles Stourton, at Biddlestone, Northumberland, where he remained till the 15th of January, 1837. After leaving Biddlestone, he was placed at Macclesfield, and was there three years, doing duty at Bollington, and once a month at Knutsford. This necessitated a walk of four miles and back to Bollington, and twelve miles to Knutsford. In the year 1840, owing to the depressed state of trade in Macclesfield, the mission was unable to support a second priest, so Dr. Fisher was transferred to Dukinfield, and was there until October, 1842, when he was appointed by the Right Rev. Dr. Brown to be the first President of St. Edward's College. On 13th September, 1851, he was appointed Canon of the Liverpool Chapter by the Bishop of Liverpool. On the 28th of August, 1854, he was created by Pius IX. Doctor of Divinity; on October 20th, 1871, he was made Vicar-Capitular; in 1866 he was appointed Pro-Vicar, and in November, 1868, he was made Vicar-General: Provost Cookson dying in 1878, Monsignor Fisher succeeded him as Provost of the Cathedral Chapter of Liverpool. In July, 1884, Dr. Fisher resigned the Presidency of St, Edward's College, which office he had filled with much honour and distinction, retired to Southport, where as an old friend and schoolfellow, the writer may be allowed to wish him *multos felicissimos annos.*

On Easter Tuesday, April 7th, 1885, the Secular Clergy of the Liverpool Diocese, in order, on his retirement, to show the esteem and regard which they entertained for the Right Rev. Provost, presented him with an address most beautifully illuminated, and a golden testimonial of £100. To this mark of their respect they considered Dr. Fisher was eminently entitled, because as a priest he had borne for forty-eight years complete, "the burden of the day and the heats," and had been selected by three successive Bishops, and in one instance by Capitular election, to fill very high and arduous offices; and was numbered by the Holy Father among his domestic Prelates.

On May 26th, 1886, he celebrated the golden jubilee of his Priesthood, on which occasion he received numerous kind and cordial congratulations from friends and acquaintances.

At page 159, it is stated that Clement Fisher sailed with his uncle, Fr. Wilfrid Fisher, O.S.B., and Bishop Polding, to Australia. It was not so: he sailed with Dr. Polding and some priests who were going out with the Bishop to Sydney, but Fr. Fisher, O.S.B., was not of the number.

The two last named priests, Rev. George Fisher, and the Right Rev. Monsignor Fisher, and one layman, Henry Riddell, Esq., alone remain of a numerous class of schoolfellows. The last named is the only one left of those who commenced their studies with me, *tertia classe Rudimentorum.* Our master at the opening of the schools, in August, 1824, was Mr. Thomas Parker, who, when ordained priest, went on the mission to St. Chad's, Rook Street, Manchester; was also at Ellingham, Northumberland; and in August, 1845, was placed at Stella, where he died July 22nd, 1847, aged forty-two years, and was there interred. Among others of my schoolfellows at this date (August, 1824,) were Ralph Platt, Richard Gillow, John Fitzpatrick, and Joseph Dent, who all became priests, walking worthy of their vocation; and Edward Charlton, who attained to considerable eminence as a physician in Newcastle-on-Tyne. Alas! these are all departed, and have left this fleeting world of shadows.

> "I have had playmates, I have had companions,
> In my days of childhood, in my joyful school days,
> All, all are gone, the old familiar faces."

> "Thou unrelenting Past!
> Thou hast my better years,
> Thou hast my earlier friends—the good—the kind,
> Yielded to thee with tears——
> The venerable form, the exalted mind."

Such was my introduction to College life, with the actualities of which I was not long in becoming acquainted; and though my years are now few, and the infirmities of age warn me that my days are fast declining—

> "*Jam proprior leto, fessusque senilibus annis,*"—

I still cherish a grateful remembrance of the happy time I spent, and the pursuits and studies to which my boyhood and youth were devoted, in the academical shades of Ushaw. "*Quis est nostrum liberaliter educatus, cui non educatores, cui non magistri sui atque doctores, cui non locus ille mutus, ubi ipse altus est, cum grata recordatione in mente versetur.*"—CIC. *pro Planc.*

From my first tasks in the old Douai "Introduction to Latin Grammar," familiarly called the "Figures;" from lessons in "Selectæ e Profanis, &c. ;" Cæsar and Cicero ; Quintus Curtius, Livy and Tacitus ; to what we considered a great achievement, *viz.*, the reading of the whole of Virgil, Horace, Herodotus, and the Iliad of Homer, besides other classical and literary work, these studies have, through all tides of chance and change, been a source of delight and solace to me :—"*delectant domi, non impediunt foris, peregrinantur, rusticantur.*" Nor has my ardour for such studies, even in the winter of life and the occupation of business, in any wise abated. The friendly rivalry, emulation, and contention, which were called forth by them, at this distance of time even, cause many pleasant recollections to spring up,

"precious memories won
From the bright hours for ever gone ;"

remembering how each one, when he was praised for application and diligence, rejoiced, and how his emulation was enkindled when, in his regard, kind words of commendation were spoken : "*accendunt hæc omnia animos ; et alit æmulatio ingenia :—*"

"Ah ! happy days of old which now are gone !
A memory and a dream !"

I cannot here refrain from quoting from one of the lyrics of Scotia's rustic bard, the following beautiful lines—so apposite to this part of my subject :—

"Still o'er these scenes my memory wakes,
And fondly broods with miser care ;
Time but the impression deeper makes,
As streams their channels deeper wear."

I return now to our worthy old President. It was an unprecedented and novel event in those days, and most worthy to be recorded, when in the Ember Week, of September, 1826, Dr. Gillow presented for promotion to the priesthood eight divines—all Ushaw students, whose names I subjoin :—John Ball, William Carter, John Dixon, William Fletcher, Philip Orrell, Thomas Maddocks, Nicholas Rigby, John Walker. Such a number of Priests ordained at the same time, and all with the exception of two, Lancashire men, how much did it rejoice the venerable President's heart ! "*Tunc repletum est gaudio cor nostrum, et lingua nostra exultatione.*" He was so delighted that he considered, and expressed himself to that effect, that the Northern District would now, at least for many years, require no further supply of priests. Had he lived a few years longer to witness the progress and advancement of religion, the new missions that one after another were established, their requirements, and the demand for priests, he would have found his prescience sadly at fault, and would have entertained a very different opinion. Having asked the blessing of each of the newly ordained, he said "Receive in your turn the blessing of an old man;" and he blessed them all as they knelt down before him.

Dr. Gillow having at this time, *viz.*, in 1826, attained the age of more than three score years and ten, was fast hastening to the term of his pilgrimage. For a brief space his sojourning was prolonged, when full of years and merits, he peacefully closed his days on the 6th of February, 1828, in the seventy-sixth year of his age. His departure was greatly lamented; and on account of his saintly life, and the veneration in which he was held, many of the students treasured up any little memorial or relic which they were able to possess of him.

Of the eight priests presented for ordination, not one, in the year in which I write, survives. The last of them, the Rev. Nicholas Rigby, of Ugthorpe, died 7th September, 1886. He was the sole remaining and most ancient link, after the death of the Rev. Thomas Danson, connecting the present with the past generation of Ushaw's alumni. The death of Father Danson occurred on the night of Thursday, May 27th, 1886, at Birkenhead, whither he had retired from missionary labour some seven years ago—

"One night awaits us all, and all must tread
This road unknown, the pathway of the dead."

This venerable priest was in his 89th year, having been born in 1797. He was sent at an early age to Crook Hall, and was among the first students, who on the opening of St. Cuthbert's, Ushaw, entered that college, being at the time in the third class of Rudiments or Underlow. He had been upward of sixty years a priest, and among other missions on which he was placed, was Minsteracres, in Northumberland; his last was Howden, in the then diocese of Beverley. The Rev. Nicholas Rigby was born at Walton-le-Dale, near Preston, Lancashire, about the year 1798, and received his elementary education in a school at Preston. From his early youth Nicholas Rigby showed considerable aptitude for learning, and was much esteemed among his schoolfellows and companions. Being destined for the Priesthood, he was sent in December, in the depth of the severe winter of 1812, to St. Cuthbert's College, Ushaw. His elder brother, John Rigby, was his pedagogue; the late Richard Canon Hodgson was his fellow pupil. Both youths went to Ushaw in the same year, Richard Hodgson three months before Nicholas Rigby. There the latter pursued his ecclesiastical studies with praiseworthy diligence, and soon became distinguished among his fellow students. His ability as a reader and elocutionist, his constant attention to study, and his general good conduct, soon attracted the notice of the President, the Venerable and Rev. John Gillow, D.D., and the other superiors, who successively appointed him to fill several offices in the college, among others that of Professor of Elocution. In the year 1824 he made the acquaintance of the celebrated historian, Dr. Lingard, on the occasion of a visit of the latter to Ushaw. This acquaintance afterwards ripened into intimate friendship, which continued during the remainder of the great doctor's life. In the beginning of the year 1825, Nicholas Rigby received the Tonsure and Minor Orders, and towards the close of the same year was ordained Sub-deacon and Deacon. In the following year, September,

1826, he was ordained Priest by the saintly Bishop Smith, Vicar Apostolic of the Northern District, and appointed to the charge of St. Mary's, Wycliffe. Here the newly ordained Priest laboured assiduously for the space of six months, at the expiration of which time he was appointed to the more important charge of the united districts of Egton Bridge and Ugthorpe. Great was the regret of the congregation of St. Mary's on being informed of the intended removal of Father Rigby from their midst. They had learned to appreciate his many excellent and amiable qualities, his learning and his piety. But ever obedient to the voice of authority, he hastened on his way to the scene of the former labours of one of the last of the English martyrs, Father Postgate.* The inhabitants of Egton Bridge and Ugthorpe welcomed the young priest with every mark of favour and confidence. From his first coming amongst them, he manifested unwearied solicitude both for their spiritual and temporal welfare, and his labours were crowned with such success that in seven years it became necessary to divide his district into two. On the occasion of the division, Bishop Penswick paid a marked compliment to the ability, energy, and piety of Father Rigby, and appointed him to the charge of St. Ann's mission, Ugthorpe. Here there was ample room for all the exertion and zeal he could exercise. There was only a small congregation with a very poor chapel, and a presbytery scarcely deserving of the name. Nothing daunted, but putting his trust in God, and confiding in the prayers of his martyred predecessor, he commenced the erection of a church which in point of architectural beauty, completeness of its fittings, its stained glass windows and handsome decorations, yields to none in the north of England. The church was opened on Thursday, October 25th, 1855, by the Right Rev. Dr. Briggs, Bishop of the Diocese. In the year 1856, the Rev. N. Rigby turned his attention to the erection at Ugthorpe of a middle-class school. The want of such an institution had long been felt throughout the northern dioceses of England. The natural beauty of the place, its seclusion, and the bracing air of Ugthorpe, rendered the situation admirably adapted for the purpose. Encouraged by his Bishop and several of the clergy, Father Rigby issued an appeal for the necessary funds, and was fortunate in meeting with a generous response. Accordingly the noble pile of buildings which to day stands in the midst of the Yorkshire moors—like an oasis in the desert—was commenced, and in the space of three years completed. The opening ceremony was an interesting one, being graced with the presence of Cardinal Wiseman, Archbishop of Westminster, the Bishop of Beverley, and a large attendance of the clergy, all of whom were unanimous in testifying to the good priest's pastoral activity in the cause of souls, and to the energy displayed by him in erecting those large halls, spacious dormitories, beautiful rooms, and extensive corridors—affording accommodation for about eighty students. Since that day hundreds of students have received within those halls a sound

---

*Father Nicholas Postgate was educated at the English College, Douai. He laboured fifty years as a priest in his native county of York. His residence, a dismal hermitage, was on a bleak moor, about five miles from Whitby, and two miles from Mulgrave Castle. He suffered martyrdom at York, on the 7th of August, 1679, aged eighty-two years, having been a priest fifty-one years.

religious and secular education ; and having gone forth into the world, have in their various spheres of life eminently prospered. In 1867, Ugthorpe received a visit from Cardinal Manning, who greatly admired and was much pleased with Father Rigby's undertakings and labours in the cause of religion, learning, and civilisation. As a writer on religious and especially controversial subjects, and as a preacher, Father Rigby in his younger days attained considerable eminence. A list of his publications is here given, which will, no doubt, be found interesting to many.

1.—The Real Doctrine of the Catholic Church on the Scripture.

2.—A Sermon on the Birth of Christ.

3.—A Sermon on Purgatory, with a Preface and Appendix.

4.—The Principles of the Catholic Religion.

5.—Two Addresses to the Gentlemen of Whitby, and the Protestant Clergy, on the Papal Aggression.

6.—Four Controversial Sermons addressed to Protestants and Dissenters.

7.—Reflections on the Great Truths.

8.—A little book on the Fall of Man, the Redemption, and the Mass.

In the year 1876, the Rev. N. Rigby celebrated the golden jubilee of his Priesthood. To him it was a memorable and interesting event. From far and near came ecclesiastical dignitaries, fellow labourers in the vineyard, and a multitude of sincere and admiring friends, who were all anxious to offer him their hearty congratulations on that auspicious occasion. The Holy Sacrifice of the Mass was offered up in thanksgiving to Almighty God for all the graces and blessings which He had so liberally bestowed upon His servant during his long and eventful life. Before taking their departure the numerous company united in an earnest prayer that God would spare Father Rigby to live yet many happy years. But "the plough came at last to his furrow." He had enjoyed vigorous health, and was in full possession of all his faculties, nearly to the time of his death, which occurred in the 88th year of his age. Two years from this date he retired from the active work of the mission of Ugthorpe, to which the Rev. Edmund J. Hickey, who for five years previous had been Father Rigby's curate, was appointed, and who in his last illness ministered to, and attended him with assiduous and affectionate devotedness. He expired at the presbytery, Ugthorpe ; and right peaceful and tranquil was the aged pastor's end, dropping into the grave like a withered leaf that falls noiselessly on a calm autumnal evening, beneath the shade of its parent tree, or like ripe fruit that has been ungathered in the orchard and left to drop on the ground. The deceased was of a lively, genial, and kindly disposition ; humourous, jocose, and facetious ; admitting with Horace, that " *Dulce est desipere in loco.*"

The seven other priests ordained with Rev. N. Rigby, whose names are previously recorded, having fulfilled their earthly duties, have all passed away—gone to render an account of their stewardship and to receive their reward. "Their years are at an end, and are folded up as a shepherd's tent," or as an Arab's in the wilderness. " As a thread by a weaver their life has been cut off," and like a mist in the morning they have disappeared from the earth. For them the winter is past—life's winter with its trials and its toils—and the rain is over and gone. The troubles and temptations, which, with the violence of wintry storms, assailed them, are at an end, and have ceased to disturb their tranquillity and peace. "*Jam hiems transiit, imber abiit, et recessit ;*" and serenity and sunshine have succeeded.

REV. THOMAS YOUENS, D.D.

The Very Rev. Dr. Youens was elected to fill the vacancy in the office of President, created by the death of Dr. Gillow. The new President was born 1790, at Windilaw, near Ellingham, Northumberland. At the age of thirteen he began his studies at Crook Hall, April 27th, 1803, and on the 19th of July, 1808, proceeded with the other Crook students to the new *Alma Mater* at Ushaw, where he was ordained Sub-deacon and Deacon in 1814. The year 1816, (March 30th,) saw him raised to the Priesthood, and appointed Professor of Moral Philosophy. I find among his schoolfellows in Rhetoric, in the year 1809, the names of Thomas Hodgson, Henry Gradwell, George Corless, John Ashhurst, and John Anderton. On the retirement of the Rev. George Brown from the office of Vice-President, to take charge of the mission at Lancaster, Dr. Youens was appointed Vice-President, and Professor of Dogmatic Theology. Dr. Gillow dying in 1828, Dr. Youens succeeded him as third President of St. Cuthbert's, governing with wisdom, gentleness, and prudence, and unostentatiously and noiselessly fulfilling the duties of his office. "Shallow rivers," it is said, "glide away with noise ; the deep are silent." To fervent and solid piety Dr. Youens united a large store of varied information, a love for scientific pursuits, an extensive knowledge of history, sacred and profane; and was profoundly versed in patristic, dogmatic, and moral theology. Notwithstanding his great literary and scholastic attainments and other endowments, his humility and diffidence were especially notable. He was of a singularly absent turn of mind, occasioned, doubtless, by deep and studious thought. It is recorded of him, that, on several occasions, on being awakened in the morning, a folio volume of St. Thomas has been found lying open on his bed, and the candle on a table by his bed side, burnt down to the socket.

Dr. Youens having presided over the college five years, vacated the office of President on the 27th March, 1833, in favour of the Rev. John Briggs, of Chester, who was appointed co-adjutor to Bishop Penswick, and whose consecration as Bishop of Trachis took place on the 29th of June following. The stone parapet surmounting the front of the college, and the lodge erected at the entrance gates, were the work of Dr. Briggs. No large scheme of improvement was formulated, no great undertaking was projected by him. From Ushaw Dr. Youens went on the mission to Liverpool, and was placed in charge of the church of St. Nicholas, Copperas-hill. Here he won golden opinions and favour from both priests and people. Bishop Briggs, after the death of Bishop Penswick, retired from the presidency, and in August, 1836, fixed his residence at York. Dr. Youens was recalled from Liverpool to resume the office of President; but "a change had come o'er the spirit of his dream." He preferred labouring for the salvation of souls in the busy world of Liverpool to literary ease, seclusion, and retirement within the peaceful walls of Ushaw. In six months therefore we find him again labouring among the masses in Liverpool, with much sacerdotal zeal and activity.

"A very little while," says the author of the 'Following of Christ,' "and all will be over with thee here. Man is to-day, and to-morrow he is seen no more." Within a dozen years from his return to Liverpool, Dr. Youens departed to his rest, May 31st, 1848. *"Thou shalt rest and stand in thy lot to the end of the days."*—Dan. xii., 13. His death resulted from typhus fever, of a most malignant character, occasioned by a severe cold, which was brought on during a short excursion into Wales, where he got over heated by walking, and had the misfortune of being exposed to a heavy downpouring of rain. He died at the convent in Mount Vernon Street, attended in his sickness by the Sisters of Mercy, whom he had established in Liverpool, and whose convent he had built. His funeral took place at St. Nicholas's, Copperas-hill, on the 2nd of June. The Right Rev. Dr. Brown, the Bishop of the District, between whom and the deceased, who was his Vicar and chief adviser, an attachment of forty years had subsisted, sang the Requiem Mass. Dr. Errington was the assistant Priest, the Rev. George Gillow, Deacon, and the Rev. John Walmsley, Sub-deacon. Between forty and fifty priests in surplices, were present at the obsequies, and the church was densely filled with a sorrowing congregation. When the coffin was slowly borne to its last resting place in the vault, there arose from the vast multitude a wail of grief and lamentation, and tears flowed from every eye. His friends, and they were numerous, were mindful of him, and offered prayer to God for him with pious earnestness and supplication.

RIGHT REV. MONSIGNOR NEWSHAM, D.D.

"*Vir potens in opere et sermone coram Deo, et omni populo, cujus memoria in benedictione est.*"

I now approach an important and eventful epoch in the annals of Ushaw.

"The old order changeth, yielding place to new,"

and my "Records and Recollections" of *Alma Mater* bring me in contact with a great mind, a great and notable name, a name not to be mentioned without grateful remembrance, profound respect and veneration, in consideration of the conspicuous improvements and changes which he introduced, and the numerous useful works and undertakings which he commenced and carried to a successful issue, more fully thereby developing the status, and increasing the efficiency of St. Cuthbert's College, as a great centre of classical and ecclesiastical learning. It is to one who may rightly be called the second founder of Ushaw that my narrative refers—to The Right Rev. Monsignor Charles Newsham, D.D., whom by consent all called " *The Doctor ;*"

" Aye, *The old Doctor* was their name of love."

Nor was he undeservedly thus named, for he was truly a Doctor in Israel, a Doctor of the Church, who so many had led on wisdom's path ; "so many had sustained up virtue's steep ;" so many in fact had "allured to brighter worlds and led the way." The good old Doctor was a man of learning, well skilled in things both human and divine ; well read in Sacred Scripture, and who learnedly and lucidly expounded it. By those theological students, who attended his Scripture lectures, his exposition and annotations were esteemed extremely valuable, and were carefully transcribed by them for subsequent reference. He was no less profoundly versed in ascetic and mystic theology, and in whatever related to the science of the interior and spiritual life. Hence his counsel and guidance were much sought ; and as an enlightened director—skilled in the "*ars artium regimen animarum*"—he was held in goodly estimation. "All that pertained to life eternal he exemplified in deed as he preached in word," as related of St. Willibald, the kinsman of St. Boniface, and missionary to the Germans under St. Boniface.

Dr. Newsham was pre-eminently a man of prayer and meditation, who did all things with a view to God, and in order to please Him ;

"And as the needle to the starry pole
Turned constantly, so he is heart to God,"

knowing well that nothing was more calculated to spiritualize the soul than prayer, and that

———"More things are wrought by prayer
Than this world dreams of . . . .
For so the whole round earth is every way
Bound by gold chains about the feet of God."

Those under his charge, profiting by his example, became imbued with a spirit of piety and recollection, were trained in the practice of holy obedience, and submission to rule and superiors. Actuated by this religious spirit, discipline was maintained, and authority reverenced among the students. Rarely was insubordination or opposition to authority heard of at Ushaw. Pliny describing his own unhappy age asks who now is ready to yield to authority? And how few young men in this our age are so disposed.—"*Statim sapiunt, statim sciunt omnia : neminem verentur, imitantur neminem, atque ipsi sibi exempla sunt.*"

Dr. Newsham compiled and edited for the use of the students, unto which was prefixed a singularly beautiful preface in Latin, addressed "*Ad alumnos Collegii Sti. Cuthberti,*" by Cardinal Wiseman, a treatise on the spiritual life—"*Manuale Vitæ Spiritualis,*" containing select portions of the spiritual works of Blosius. It was published in 1859. No wonder that under so spiritual a guide and master, piety grew, blossomed, and bore fruit ; and that an ecclesiastical gravity, enhanced by the sublime ceremonies, devotional exercises, and solemn offices of the Church, pervaded the entire body of students, and diffused its aroma throughout the whole college. Oh, how sweet is the holiness of youth ! how beautiful is the chaste generation with glory !

Turning at this point of my narrative from the building up of the spiritual to the extension and enlargement of the material edifice of the college over which, on the final departure as President of Dr. Youens, Dr. Newsham was appointed to preside, it is meet that I should advert to, and humbly attempt to describe the almost magical transformation and marvellous works which Dr. Newsham accomplished, not for self-glorification, but for the sole purpose of developing the educational resources, and raising the character and prestige of *Alma Mater*.

In a sermon preached by Dr. Manning, at the opening of the Church of St. Godric, in Durham, November 15th, 1864, occurs the following well-timed and beautiful allusion to Ushaw: " Fifty years ago, a Bishop of the Church, in the time of its bondage and poverty, laid, with the power of a primitive faith, upon a bare hill, overlooking the splendours of Durham, the first stone of a Catholic College. It was a great venture—almost a rashness—in such days of weakness and oppression. Nevertheless, it was done, and the work prospered. A college rose in fair proportions ; but its founder, with all the confidence of his faith, little thought what should be the expansion of the work which he then began in poverty and straitness. At this day, this slender beginning has ascended and unfolded itself into a vastness and a splendour of which no one ever dreamed. The single college of fifty years ago has multiplied itself into a cluster of halls and chapels, of cloisters and quadrangles, for stateliness and beauty surpassing almost any modern work in England. There it stands with its three hundred students, the spiritual mother of a multitude of priests. It renews before us the creations of the Church in other days, when it reigned over the English people in wealth and majesty, possessed of lands and baronies, of political power and ancient privileges, in Courts and Parliaments." The remarks quoted below are equally apposite to the associations and memories which cluster round Ushaw. " Ushaw is the representative of Douai and Rheims, the great seminary, which Cardinal Allen founded in Elizabeth's reign, to provide priests for the English mission. If coal pits and blast furnaces have begrimed the once fair face of the neighbourhood, they cannot destroy the sacred memories which are all around it, of St. Cuthbert, of Durham, of St. Godric, or the interesting historical memories of the home of the Nevilles at Brancepeth, of Chester-le-Street, or of Lumley Castle. The buildings, though irregular, because of various dates—library, church, museum, exhibition hall, refectory, are all worthy of an Oxford or Cambridge college."

It is said that the Emperor Augustus found Rome a city of brick, and left it of marble. But though Dr. Newsham did not embellish or re-build Ushaw with marble, and material hewed from costly quarries, his projects and schemes of improvement, works of beauty and gracefulness, and the numerous trophies of his zeal for St. Cuthbert's, surround his name with a halo of enduring renown.

It is with much distrust, diffidence, and apprehension lest I fail in the attempt, that I proceed to enumerate and describe the divers improvements which Dr. Newsham planned and accomplished, the undertakings which he set on foot, the additions which he made, the designs which he formed and compassed, in order to place Ushaw in the first rank of the collegiate institutions of the country. This was the Doctor's great aim and purpose—a noble purpose, the outcome of a progressive and expansive mind, full of energy and lofty conceptions; of a mind averse to useless pursuits; on no account allowed to stagnate,—

"*Nam capiunt vitium, ni moveantur aquæ;*"

always employed on what he considered of beneficial and useful tendency. Like St. Stephen, Abbot of Citeaux, "contemplative and spiritual as he was, he was still a man of action; he had the head to plan, and the calm unbending energy to execute a great work." As change has her periods, and earth changes momently, he discarded all such resolve as "emanates from an unwillingness to adopt any manner of change, but to rest in a dead immutable routine— cultivating the mind of the past, in whatever form, whether of literature, of art, or of institutions, without any regard to the present or the future."

St. Cuthbert's College, as originally constructed, formed a large quadrangular building, solid and substantial in its masonry, but plain and no wise attractive in appearance; with little pretensions to architectural grace and beauty, being built more for convenience and utility than for show and ornament. Its measurement from east to west was 180 feet; from north to south 230 feet; and it enclosed an extensive court, round which are spacious ambulacra or corridors. The additions of other buildings have considerably increased the length from east to west of the south front, which is now fully 470 feet. Dr. Newsham with much decision of purpose and energy of character resolved to inaugurate a new era, introduce a new order of things, and create of Ushaw a college worthy of the name, a centre of light and learning, in regard to which those who were there educated might feel proud, and honoured in being Alumni of an institution, commending itself by the efficiency of its education, rules, and discipline, and by its exquisite adaptibility for all the purposes, arrangements, and conveniences of a superior first-class college. Hence he completely transformed, amplified, extended, renovated, and adorned the original college, its surroundings and its precincts, its external and internal belongings. The front or south wing of the college is the most imposing portion of the original structure. It is three storeys high, and its elevation is bold and lofty. In the centre of the structure, in the uppermost storey, is the clock, that was made and placed there in the year 1812—"*Joannes Bolton fecit, 1812,*" so that it has told the time and struck the hours for a period of nearly fourscore years. It is on the same elevation, but considerably above the front entrance doors into the college. This entrance was narrow and confined; it has been opened out and extended: the stairs have been widened, rendered more easy of ascent, and more ornamental. The bell that was placed under the stairs, and used to ring for prayers, study, meals, but especially sonorously for play days, has been removed, and fixed elsewhere in a suitable bell turret. Ranged along the south side of the corridor or ambulacrum, forming the lower basement of this part of the college, *viz.* the south wing, were formerly the study place, the Professors' parlour, and the Divines' school (now the reading room); and at the east end were doors opening into the bounds or play ground. This ambulacrum was not at one time even flagged, but was laid with common bricks or tiles. The second storey contained the President, Vice-President, and the Bishop's rooms, Professors' and other rooms. In the same storey used to be situated the Divines' library. The topmost storey (top gallery) had at the east end the Prefect's room, its windows looking southward and eastward respectively. The other rooms in this storey were chiefly occupied by Professors and Divines. The room adjoining the Prefect's was used for the purpose of a museum. All these rooms were airy, lofty, and spacious, and from those on the south side was obtained the prospect of a wide and diversified range of country. At the east end of the north wing was the old chapel, in all its primitive simplicity—plain and unadorned, having its high, and its two side altars, severally unenclosed. In the same were the old kitchens, and the refectory. In the west wing were to be found the old writing and ciphering school, the lavatory, and several class-rooms. In the east wing was the principal entrance to the bounds or play ground; this wing also contained the Philosophers, Poets, and Rhetoricians' schools, and other schools or class rooms. From this part of the college there was access to the large dormitory.

I must now pass from the old order of things to the reforms and improvements introduced by Dr. Newsham in regard to St. Cuthbert's. To carry these into effect there was one requirement, *viz.*, money—"*quærenda primum pecunia est,*" and on this quest towards the close of the year 1837, the Revs. Thomas Cookson, the Vice-President, and Thomas Witham, were deputed to solicit contributions in the Northern Vicariate.

The Rev. Charles Newsham was appointed President of Ushaw, May 24th, 1837. On being installed in the office he considered it to be an especial part of his duty to provide the college with all requirements befitting and needful for a large institution "There were," says the Rev. Henry Gillow, in his Historical Introduction to the Chapels at Ushaw, "no kitchens and offices, properly so called, no room of large dimensions, where all the students could assemble for public speaking or examinations. The dormitories were in the attics, the lavatory too primitive for description, the playground was a confined space, badly provided with ball places and racket courts. There was no reliable supply of water, no bath rooms, and the refectory arrangements were shabby and insufficient. The only large rooms were the chapel and refectory, and both were low roofed, the latter having a dormitory above it." To remedy these inconveniences, and provide more ample and better accommodation necessarily required a great outlay of money ; but Dr. Newsham proved himself equal to the task he had undertaken, and to any emergency that might arise during the progress of the work which he had in hand. Both clergy, laity, and friends most generously came forward with pecuniary aid, but however liberal their contributions, they were not sufficiently ample to cover all the expenses incurred. The President, whilst engaged in carrying out the various works commenced by him, in order to advance the interests and influence of Ushaw, and raise it in the "scale of perfection," was fully alive to the imporance of improving and adapting the course of studies to the requirements of the age, as well as to the necessity of providing such facilities and means for imparting a superior and first-class education, that so Ushaw, in the march of intellect and educational progress, might maintain an honourable and prominent position. Hence in 1840 the College was affiliated to the London University; and each year examiners are sent to preside over the Matriculation and B.A. examinations. At the first examination for the degree of Bachelor of Arts, after the career of University honours was laid open to our Catholic colleges, among the successful candidates were Messrs. Frank Wilkinson and Richd. Wilson, who were deservedly complimented by the examiners, though they had but a few weeks' time to prepare for their examination. Their course of studies had been directed and superintended by the then Prefect of Studies, the Rev. Ralph Platt. This office of Prefect of Studies Mr. Platt filled for six years at Ushaw, with signal credit and ability. The teaching staff of the college was considerably increased; and in place of an annual outing, a pic-nic and feast, as in past times, in other words "a good lad's Cornsay day," books and medals were substituted and awarded at the annual examinations to those who had obtained the requisite marks of excellence. It is, if I rightly remember, Demosthenes who states that if you award prizes to the few and the deserving, and give them under certain regulations, you will have many competitors striving to merit and obtain them. In our college days neither medals, honours, prizes, nor fellowships were obtainable. But we had a higher and more enobling motive to cheer us on in our studies, than a "Cornsay day"—a motive prefixed to our themes—"*Ad majorem Dei gloriam.*"

In the new order of things, and as knowledge advanced and education made progress, improved and annotated editions—with English notes and vocabulary—of the classics got introduced. These were great aids to learning. There were no such aids and auxiliaries in my time: we had to work out the problem as best we could, by brain power, dictionaries, and lexicons, aided by scholia and notes in Latin, not unfrequently more difficult than the original text. For us there was no royal road, no *faciliores aditus* to learning. We had to work our way through involved passages, like woodmen penetrating through the tangled undergrowth of a crowded forest. Translations were sealed books, interdicted. But "*labor omnia vincit improbus;*" and I respectfully submit that the race of yore—the old Ushaw students, were not much inferior to those, who in later times, have had presented to them so many advantages and facilities for acquiring knowledge.

Having previously alluded to the discipline which, firmly but kindly enforced, prevailed under Dr. Newsham's regime, and to the obedient spirit, docility, and piety of the students, to whom the words of the Psalmist might aptly be applied—"*hæc est generatio quærentium Dominum,*" I may state *en passant* that Dr. Newsham introduced among them a love for music—particularly sacred music, and composed several Masses, Litanies, and Benediction pieces, which by eminent judges and directors of choirs were received with much favour and commendation.

To return to the consideration of the material work undertaken by Dr. Newsham for the development and expansion of St. Cuthbert's. The old play grounds being found too small for the recreation and exercise of the students, he extended their area to six or seven acres each, erected new ball places and racket courts, and introduced cricket, which was little known at Ushaw before his time. The popular game is now played there with much spirit and animation. Within the few last years a splendid cricket ground—one hundred yards square, has been formed in the centre of an eighteen acre field—the field known as "the Football Field." The buildings grouped round the old quadrangular edifice were so numerous and striking, that, as we learn from Mr. Gillow's "Introduction to the Chapels at Ushaw," Pope Pius IX. on seeing the bird's-eye view of Ushaw said with astonishment that it looked more like a town than a college :—and he showed his appreciation of Dr. Newsham by making him one of his Domestic Prelates. "The lighting of the house with gas," continues Mr. Gillow, to whom I beg to express my indebtedness for the following particulars, "was one of the President's first objects, and for this purpose he erected Gas Works in 1839. In that and the following year he improved the dormitories, opened a Library and Museum for the use of the boys, and, instead of the narrow passage at the front-door, formed the present entrance hall and added a handsome staircase. In 1844 the Chapel was commenced, to replace the old one in the north wing, now transformed into an Exhibition Room. The Refectory was gothicised and adorned by A. W. Pugin in 1846. It was afterwards enlarged, and, on occasion of Dr. Tate's Jubilee in 1873, the present beautiful west window was put in. In 1849, a series of important works were taken in hand—the Exhibition Room with its magnificent roof by Joseph Hansom, and other buildings down to 1854, by Messrs Joseph and Charles Hansom combined. The Great Library and Study Hall were begun in 1849 ; the Playground, Ball-places and Racket-courts in 1850, the Farm in 1851, the Terrace and Cemetery in 1852, and the Lavatories in 1854. The elder Pugin gave the design for St. Joseph's Chapel in 1852, but left it for his son, E. W. Pugin, to finish. The latter continued to do all the architectural work of the College until his death. During the ensuing four years still greater advance was made. A Laundry was begun in 1854, and a Chemical Laboratory in the same year, Professors' Parlour in 1855, Infirmary and Museum in 1856, new College for Junior Students and St. Charles's Chapel in 1857, St. Michael's Chapel, the Kitchens and Offices in 1858."

I may be permitted here to reproduce from the *Tablet* the following account relating to Ushaw ; the "*mutatas formas,*" the extension and improvement that there took place while Dr. Newsham was President. It was written by me at the time of and in reference to the celebration of the College Jubilee, July, 1858, the twenty-second year of the old Doctor's presidency, and was as follows :—Any person visiting Ushaw after an absence of several years would scarcely be able to recognise the college, so changed, improved, and extended has it become. He would find the old chapel, where he had so often knelt, metamorphosed into a splendid public hall, and a new church erected of most elegant design, and enriched with every ornament. He would see a magnificent library stored with about 20,000 volumes, a large and commodious study place, a fine and noble refectory, dormitories, spacious and well ventilated, libraries and reading-rooms for each class, and new and conveniently planned lavatories, the walls of the ambulacra covered with maps and pictures, the playground enlarged and fitted up with new ball places and racket courts, the old farmhouse and buildings fronting the college removed, and another farmstead, with all convenient and suitable appurtenances, erected. Then he would have pointed out to him the splendid new range of buildings on the west side of the college. These consist of museum, 180 feet long, entered by an archway, where the stairs leading to the west gallery once were; a noble infirmary, with every convenience; another college on a magnificent scale with its chapel, schoolrooms, refectory, study, dormitories, lavatory, ambulacra, kitchens, &c. This portion has been designed with great skill, and exhibits an exquisite fine specimen of the decorated period. Having gazed with amaze and wonder at all these additions and transformations, as if some enchanter's wand had waved and a new Ushaw had been called forth; having wandered from structure to structure, from corridor to corridor, he next quietly strolls into the bounds or round the ambulacra, or paces up stairs through the galleries, and wherever he goes he cannot help being struck with the order and decorum, the dutiful and submissive demeanour, the pious and excellent spirit, the mutual regard and good understanding observable among the students. So far Ushaw has fulfilled its destiny nobly. It has grown with a steady growth, and by the care and exertions of others, trained in the school, and cheered by the example of its earliest guardians, it has attained noble and imposing dimensions. Two years only previous to the jubilee have elapsed since this pile of buildings was commenced, the architect who had the honour of designing them being Ed. Welby Pugin, Esq., Knight of St. Sylvester. The infirmary and the museum, above which is placed a suite of rooms for the divines, are completed; the others are rapidly advancing towards the same end. At the extremity of the museum, and placed in the centre, between the old college and the new schools, is the Procurator's room, accessible also to the infirmary by means of a covered cloister. The infirmary, museum, and new schools are situated on the west side of the College, wash-houses, and laboratory on the east, and kitchens on the north. The most complete, if not the most beautiful, of the entire range, is the infirmary, placed on the highest land, and looking southwards into a magnificent court, 200 feet square. This building contains separate suites of apartments for every class of students either in the college or seminary, and is connected with each by means of separate cloisters. The principal room of each suite measures 25 feet long, 17 feet broad, and 15 high. These open into a general ambulacrum, running the entire length of the building. On the first floor the chapel forms an appropriate and beautiful centre to the whole, and contains windows opening into the chief bedrooms. At the lower part of the chapel is a small sacristy, which is intended to be fitted up with every convenience. Attached to the infirmary is a kitchen for immediate requirements, but in case it should be necessary a covered communication is secured with the principal kitchen of the college. The building also contains distinct apartments for the chaplain, so that during any infectious illness a priest would devote his entire time to the students, and have no connection with the students in the college.

The museum next claims our attention. It is a magnificent room, 180 feet long, 20 feet wide, and 18 feet high. It is divided into fourteen compartments by means of framed and wrought principals. These compartments are again subdivided by wrought and moulded ribs, at the intersection of which small centres are placed. Every other compartment is occupied with a three light window, below which the cases containing antiquities will eventually be arranged. This building is extremely simple both in the exterior and interior, and derives its effect from the grandeur of its size and justness of its proportions.

The building terminating the museum is somewhat different in character, and is much more elaborate than the rest of the structure. It contains a bay window, plinth, buttresses, elaborate mouldings, chaste and symmetrical tracery; in short on this work the architect, Mr. Pugin, appears to have made his greatest effort, and we cannot but admit that he has achieved a great success.

From this point a connecting cloister runs westward to the schools, and enters the eastern end of the main cloister, 200 feet long. This is the main artery of the new schools. On the first turn to the right, entirely separated from the rest of the building, are situated the chapels, and chambers for quiet study; on the left, the refectory, parlour for the professors, kitchens, and other offices. Returning to the main cloister, and proceeding westward, we enter the writing and other schools. Our next turn to the right brings us to the entrance hall, where reception rooms are provided for the friends of the students. Again, proceeding westward, we turn down to the right, passing the several class rooms, until we reach the study place capable of containing 100 students, for which number the seminary is erected.

Returning again to the cloister we find on the left the lavatories; these are in immediate connection with the dormitories by means of the principal staircase, which leads directly to the dormitory, where there is sleeping accommodation for the whole of the students. It measures 200 feet long by 38 feet wide, and 17 feet high. The west wing is devoted to the professors' rooms, all of which are large and commodious. Besides the principal staircase there are two spiral ones, one in each wing. The exterior of the main Chapel, that of St. Aloysius, evinces considerable purity of style in its conception; the internal portion is as yet incomplete.

The new kitchens in connection with the college have only lately been commenced, but from what we have seen of the plans we venture to state that, although extremely simple in design, they will be a masterpiece of convenience, and will contain every modern improvement, which may tend to diminish manual labour.

The new wash-houses and laundries well repaid inspection, and are entirely worked by steam power, thereby reducing the persons employed to almost half the number formerly engaged in this department.

The laboratory is situated at the extreme north-east corner, has an open wooden roof, lower in the centre, and every necessary arrangement.

The whole of the buildings are of stone from the quarry on the college estate, and constructed in courses, tuck-pointed. The natural beauty of the material, combined with the skill of the architect, has tended to give the buildings a solid as well as beautiful appearance.

Some portions of these buildings, and of the private chapels or oratories in connection with St. Cuthbert's Collegiate Chapel, at the date of this record—the year of the Jubilee, were not completed. But no long time elapsed before they stood forth in all their completeness, symmetry, and beauty—like the king's daughter, "*in fimbriis aureis, circumamicta varietatibus.*" The chapel of St. Michael built by Michael Gibson, Esq., of Leamington, to receive the body of his son, the Very Rev. Dr. Gibson, Vice-President of St. Cuthbert's, who died on returning from Rome, in the year 1856, promised to be one of the most chaste pieces of groining yet produced. The columns supporting the same were intended to be of marble and porphyry. In short nothing, it appears, had to be spared in order to make a monument worthy of the virtues and memory of the deceased. To the life and death of this learned and estimable priest I shall have occasion to recur in a subsequent portion of my narrative.

The old college chapel, where so many of the past generation of Ushaw's worthies had knelt and prayed before its humble altar and unenclosed sanctuary, where most of the good old priests with whom we were acquainted said or sung their first mass—*primitias Deo offerentes*,—where the late venerable Bishops of the North, Drs. Penswick, Briggs, Mostyn, Riddell, and Hogarth were consecrated, was disused as a chapel in 1848. The foundation stone of the new College Chapel of St. Cuthbert was laid on the 23rd of April, A.D. 1844, by the Right Rev. Wm. Riddell, coadjutor Bishop of the Northern District. The chapel was entered by the community on Christmas Day, of the year of our Lord, 1847. It was consecrated in honour of St. Cuthbert by the Right Rev. Wm. Hogarth, Bishop of the Northern District, on the 27th of September, A.D. 1848, and on the 11th October, A.D. 1848, was solemnly opened. The Right Rev. Wm. Hogarth celebrated Pontifical High Mass on the occasion, and the Right Rev. Nicholas Wiseman (afterwards Cardinal Archbishop of Westminster), then coadjutor Bishop of the London District, preached the opening sermon. The plan of the building was arranged after the models of some of the collegiate chapels at Oxford. The old chapel was transformed into the Exhibition Hall, which presents a large and highly decorated interior. The roof is of open frame work of the most superb character; the pillars, beams, and pendants being beautifully carved, and the principals terminated by grotesque heads. A spacious gallery for spectators rises by progressive steps from the floor, affording an uninterrupted view of the proceedings at general meetings, the distribution of prizes, and other important public occasions. Several large valuable paintings adorn its walls. The south front of the college is flanked on the west by St. Cuthbert's beautiful chapel; and the library, built in or about the year 1851, by the Messrs. Hansom, forms at the extreme east end a wing corresponding with the church. It is approached from the south-east angle of the front ambulachrum by a noble staircase, and is a capacious and lofty room, elegant in its architectural details, and well lighted from the south, whilst on the east and west are stately windows ornamented with stained glass. The coved ceiling is appropriately painted and decorated. Underneath the Library is the Study Place, or Hall, as it is termed in modern parlance, 70 ft. long by 30 ft. wide. The Library measures internally 120 ft. long by 30 ft. wide, and contains nearly 50,000 volumes, with many valuable manuscripts, some of them beautifully illuminated. It is also rich in choice editions of standard theological, patristic, historical, and other works. What stores of literature, what treasures of wisdom are here encased in cedar wood! A large proportion of the books were presented by the Rev. Thomas Wilkinson, and are the fruit of many years' patient collecting. Towards the erection of the new Library, and other objects connected with St. Cuthbert's, he contributed most generously of his substance. Father Wilkinson was priest at Kendal from 1793 to 1853: he died at Ushaw, where he spent his last years, on the 30th December, 1857, at the patriarchal age of ninety-three years: a place of sepulture was assigned to him in the cemetery cloister. Before his death he was the last living priest ordained within the walls of venerable old Douai, which he had left previous to the outburst of the French revolution. It is supposed he was born in the neighbourhood of Hornby.

Of the works undertaken for the extension of the college, the Very Rev. John Gillow had in conjunction with the architect the immediate direction. He also undertook the whole of the engineering department with the most encouraging success. Dr. Gillow possessed a wonderful mechanical genius, much scientific knowledge, and great aptitude for scientific pursuits. By him an almost unfailing supply of water for the college and the farm was provided from large reservoirs, which he caused to be made for the purpose. He devoted much attention also to the irrigation and the utilisation of sewage; and under his supervision the garden comprising about five acres was surrounded with a wall, against the whole extent of which he caused fruit trees to be planted.

Such is Ushaw, started by Bishop William Gibson with the slender resource of only £5, and which, in fifty years, under its fifth President, the Right Rev. Monsignor Newsham, became a great, a flourishing, and prosperous establishment. He has left his footprints upon it and upon all its surroundings. Nor will his memory there perish, but for years yet to come it will be revered and cherished, since, as was said of Abbot Sampson, "these and all other things worthy to be kept in remembrance and recorded for ever, did Dr. Newsham."

MONSIGNOR NEWSHAM'S JUBILEE.

Years roll on in their course—*more labentium aquarum*—
"The lapse of time and rivers is the same,"
and the fiftieth year, the jubilee year of Monsignor Newsham's college life, at length arrived. He commenced his studies at Crook Hall early in the present century, and in 1808 was transferred with the other Crook students to the new college of Ushaw. On Wednesday, June 22nd, 1853, his jubilee was celebrated at Ushaw with much festivity and joy, for it was a joyful occasion, and was honoured by the presence of His Eminence Cardinal Wiseman, Archbishop of Westminster, Dr. Hogarth, Bishop of Hexham, Dr. Briggs, Bishop of Beverley, Dr. Gillis, V. A. of the Eastern District of Scotland, Dr. Turner, Bishop of Salford, Dr. Errington, Bishop of Plymouth, and a numerous assemblage of clergy and gentlemen, friends and visitors. At half-past seven High Mass commenced, being celebrated by the Right Rev. Dr. Hogarth, Bishop of Hexham. After the gospel, His Eminence, from the altar steps, delivered a beautiful and eloquent discourse. He selected his text from Psalm xliv., 5.—"*Specie tua, et pulchritudine tua, intende, prospere procede et regna.*" "*With thy comeliness and thy beauty, set out, proceed prosperously and reign.*" Although this may seem, he said, to be an occasion of a personal commemoration, and we have assembled to do honour to one whom all that know him must esteem and reverence, still does the motive carry us back to a distant period with which this day is necessarily connected. It bears us back, some of us perhaps in memory, but all in thought, to that period when what we now see so increased, both in extent and in magnificence, was but a small and poor commencement. It takes us back to the day when not one stone was laid here upon another, when even the site on which this noble college should stand had been scarcely decided on. And we, therefore, either from the tradition of but a few months, or from the recollection of our own thoughts, can all carry ourselves back to that moment when a beginning was about to be given to this great institution. And we may imagine to ourselves one whom God had gifted with the sight and knowledge of the future, looking on, humble indeed at the meanness of what he was then commencing compared with what we possessed in past times, but still foreseeing what it would be after he had been gathered to his fathers, and what he himself might live to see,—we may imagine him casting his glance at the foundation stone as it rolled into the trench prepared for it, and saying, "In thy comeliness and thy beauty set out, proceed prosperously in thy grand career." But where was the beauty then? Where was the comeliness? Where was the grace? A few weeks ago you saw one of those plants which now is covered with beauty, which now sparkles in the sun; and what did you see then?—That the beauty which is now so luxurious, so gratifying to the eye, was yet enfolded and shrouded in the plant itself, so that the eye of man could not see it. But it was no less certainly therein contained; and when the hour should come for it to break forth as it has done, sure to blossom, as if we had been enabled to count its petals, and see the hidden tints which now suffuse them; and so small and plain, simple and insignificant as might be the beginning of this

great work, God's eye was on it, and saw enfolded and enwrapped in it all those treasures of art, all those beauties of design, all that grandeur of conception, and all those holy thoughts which, from that small beginning, were one day, under the influence of better times, and still more, under the blessing of Divine Providence, to come forth and array themselves in that dignity and splendour in which they now appear. We who have seen its infancy, we who know its small beginnings, and have watched the growth, the gradual increase of this structure, have, indeed, heartily said from time to time, " Go on and prosper, go on and increase ; increase not only in greatness, increase not only in that amplitude which is necessary to render thee useful, but increase in beauty, increase in comeliness, and instead of this increase being a token that thou shalt perish, it is, on the contrary, a sign that thou shalt endure !" We who from early youth have been acquainted with its course,—we who with jealous eye have watched every change,—we who therefore can bear witness that although some of those rudenesses which were necessarily connected with an infant and a struggling establishment may have been removed, yet not a particle of all this beauty, or grandeur, or luxury that has been displayed, has been applied to the personal advantage or the personal comfort of the superiors of the establishment,—we who know that there still prevails the same simple mode of life, the same generous and disinterested devotion to their duties in them, and the same strictness of discipline, the same assiduity in study in the scholar, cannot but feel assured that every development of beauty has been only an addition of enduring vigour, and an omen of perpetuity. For we who there see that what is done for the great and high purposes of education, feel that every addition of beauty, every step in even outward improvement, is a step also in the elevating and ennobling of that most important pursuit. You see the Library, not only vast in its dimensions, but beautiful likewise in its architecture, and rich in its ornamentation. And what shall we hope from this, but that it will remind the student as he enters in—that wisdom is the gift of God, to be preferred to kingdoms and to thrones —that learning is a treasure, accumulating through ages, far more valuable and far more imperishable than the gold of this earth,—that it deserves to be prized, and to be well preserved in a treasure-house which testifies our estimation of it? It will make him feel that genius, ability, skill, whatever else man may possess from God, is a holy gift, a *talent* which must be accounted for. It impresses him, also, with the awe of sacred learning and solemn knowledge, and makes him feel the immense difference between that wisdom which makes a man wise before God, and that which the puny stream of daily and hourly literature dribbles into the ears of men. And so it is with the noble Academic Hall. Its roof is splendid and rich. The youthful student as he casts upwards his eye while engaged in the occupations of this place, sees looking down upon him the effigies of those saints who, in addition to the crown of sanctity, have borne up to heaven the badge of a science, worthy to be held in their hands with the palm branch or the lily before the throne of God. And he comes to know that even the pursuits of his academical course are under the patronage of heavenly saints, and that his very thoughts are gazed down upon by them, and that, above all, Heaven is his guide, his light, his perfection, and his only reward. In fine, he learns, what the inspired word has taught us, that—" In the hands of God are both we and our word, and wisdom, and knowledge, and skill in works."—*Wisd. vii.* And the Chapel. Can too much be done to separate it from that which is homely, daily, and profane—to make it in every respect distinct from the house of man ; so that whoever shall traverse the whole of this magnificent pile of buildings, coming at last to what may be considered the residence of the Most High, shall see that He truly is reputed as first and greatest of this house—that He has a tabernacle here as disproportioned in beauty to man's abodes as was the Tabernacle amid the dark tents of the Arabian Desert, or the Temple amid the meaner buildings of Jerusalem? And is it not important, too, that we should have so much compassion on poor human frailty and weakness, as that they who come in to adore their God, or to pray to Him, should have but small difficulty in realising to themselves that they are no longer in the midst of the ordinary places of study or recreation, no longer in the midst of the dwellings of men, but in the house of God, where all that they see around them speaks to them of God, and where, if distraction should disturb them, it may lead the eye to dwell on some religious representation which may re-kindle their devotion, and renew their fervour? It is right and salutary that all this should be: and whatever thus tends to raise and sanctify the character of ecclesiastical education, whatever most particularly is directed to increase that most essential part of education—sincere devotion, gives security, stability, and permanence to whatever is done. And therefore, I say, " Go on, never consider your work accomplished ; proceed prosperously ; for to you is given by God, not merely this first assurance of success—but go on and reign." Then, indeed, shall this day be one of happy festivity for us all. And then let us remember that we are the children of the saints, "*filii sanctorum sumus ;*" and on this day of England's Protomartyr, St. Alban, we may renew within ourselves the spirit of that long line of glorious martyrs, from whom this college sprang, earnestly praying that having preserved or regained that beauty of holiness with which God here once filled our souls, and prospered us in our career, we may go on to reign with Him and His martyrs and saints in heaven. I ask you not, in these sacred walls, to disturb your thoughts with the enumeration of what has been done by that Superior whose jubilee calls you here together; I ask you not to distract your minds by recounting the many personal acts of kindness which I am sure he has exhibited to so many of you ; I do not ask you even to take into consideration what has been done for religion by his zeal and wisdom, but I ask you to pray,—this day, that God may long preserve him among you in health, in strength, and in that energy of mind by which he has already done so much—that this day may be to him a day of consolation and of joy not merely through his own feelings and the consciousness which he must possess of what he has done, but by feeling that through your prayers he will be more strengthened to exert himself even more and more to prosper in his holy undertaking. Yes, in the spirit of humility and of devotion, may he continue to prosper and go on in those works of beauty and of gracefulness with which his hands have always been filled—go on and prosper here, until one day his reward shall come, and he shall reign with God and His saints for ever.

Immediately after Mass, breakfast was served in the Refectory; after which the students and visitors repaired to the splendid Lecture Hall. At eleven o'clock His Eminence, accompanied by the President and the Bishops present, entered the Hall, when he was hailed with the most enthusiastic cheers and applause. The proceedings were opened with music. After the music, the Bishop of Hexham rose and said—My Lord Cardinal, Right Rev. and Rev. Brethren, and Gentlemen, we have met this day, as you are aware, to celebrate an extraordinary event. It is the completion of fifty years of the college life of our venerable friend, the President of this college Well do I remember his entering the college; and I have seen him, I may say, go through boyhood, youth, mature age,; and now you see him yourselves, perfect, I may say, as a President of this grand establishment. Gifted by Providence with more than ordinary talent, he is also possessed of something which is ever requisite to make a very great man—he was always industrious, he was always energetic; but above all, he had indomitable perseverance. This has produced the wonderful effects in the great changes and improvements which have been effected in this magnificent college There never was anything which he did not succeed in accomplishing while a boy by that same indomitable perseverance. Indeed, I cannot recollect anything in which he ever failed. And now, you who are here present, you have seen his progress in all the difficulties with which has had to contend; and you have seen all, one after one, fall before his great perseverance. His energy is something extraordinary, something which seems to have been particularly committed to him by Providence, from the very first of his entering here, for effecting all those great and wonderful improvements of this college, and which I hope will be continued by him until he has accomplished all the grand views which I know he entertains towards this establishment. We trust that Providence will guide and protect him, will give him health and strength, and continue that blessing that seems to attend his labours and his endeavours, and that he will yet live many and many more days.

A number of students next sang Collin's "Ode to the Passions :" then followed

THE JUBILEE ODE,

SPOKEN BY MR. E. MANSFIELD.

Fifty long years have passed since in the prime
Of boyhood's spring his college course began.
Fain would I trace along the vale of time
  The stream through which his life's calm current ran;
As yet, where Ushaw stands the eye could scan
  Nought save a barren waste; for many a day
Yon Hall at Crook within its narrow span
  Held Douai's glorious sons, who wou their way
From foreign chains, through blood and battle's stern array.

But, where the need his early course to trace?—
  The hundred trophies which his zeal can claim,
In characters that time will ne'er efface,
  Have stamped a prouder record to his fame
Than e'er adorned the laurelled victor's name.

Fame did I say? He asks not human praise;
  Zeal for God's glory was the beacon flame
  That kindled each resolve, and shed its rays
On his triumphant path—the star that fixed his gaze.

Who can recount these trophies of his zeal?
  You who 'neath Ushaw's shade dwelt years ago
  And view her now, to you do I appeal.
  Yon glorious church and library which throw
  Such stateliness around her—the rich glow
  Of yon refectory, and this gorgeous hall—
  Whose works are these? Oh! much indeed we owe
  To friends whose names our loving hearts recall,
But HIS the mind that planned, HE was the soul of all.

But these are deeds which speak to every eye,
  His hidden worth his sons alone can tell—
  The loving zeal, the unwearied energy
  Which labour daunts not, nor can sickness quell,
  Those burning words which make the bosom swell
  And urge us on the path to virtue, where
  His bright example ever points as well;
  All this endears him to the hearts that share
His ever watchful love for those beneath his care.

The snows of age are falling on his brow;
  Still the fond hope and prayer our hearts must own
  That many a year as yet may come and go
  To swell the ripening harvest he has sown;
  For though his summer days of youth are gone,
  Yet not youth's vigour, or the unshaken will,
  Or kindling eye, for age that striketh down
  The shrub that blossoms by the winding rill,
Gives to the mountain oak a healthier vigour still.

Then let us not regret the snows of age,
  Since wisdom crowns the brow on which they fall,
  And since this day will ever gild a page,
  The brightest Ushaw's annals can recall.
  And oft, when gathered in this lofty hall,
  Her sons in ages yet to come shall tell
  In glowing strains of this great festival,
  And speak of Him whose name remembered well,
Shall with her Founder's name in deathless honour dwell.

A congratulatory address was then read from the students to their "most respected and beloved President," availing themselves of the opportunity to express some portion of that respect and admiration which was felt by every member of St. Cuthbert's College towards its venerated President.

The Right Rev. Bishop Gillis on behalf of the visitors and himself begged Dr. Newsham to receive their most heartfelt and warmest congratulations on that joyous occasion. There were many present, who, although not educated at Ushaw, were not the less alive to the glories of that magnificent establishment, and to those feelings which must animate every heart on an occasion like the present.

His Eminence the Cardinal Archbishop addressing Dr. Newsham said—My most revered and dear Dr. Newsham, I have been chosen to address you to-day on behalf of a numerous body of your friends, who, consulting rather the interest of ages to come than your own modest wishes, have desired to add one more precious recollection of you to the numerous ones which already surround us. You have built churches, and libraries, and other beautiful edifices, which both add to the integrity and the honour of this establishment. You have built them according as our fathers raised them of old. You have not built for jubilees, you have built for centuries ; and we can easily imagine that after one century has passed over, and your name remains essentially and necessarily connected with the whole of this splendid structure, there will arise in the minds of those who either visit and admire them, or who still more derive from them and in them the benefit of a good ecclesiastical education—there will arise naturally in the minds of men that desire which will thus express itself : " I should have liked to have seen that good and glorious President ; I should have been glad to have lived in his time ; I should have rejoiced to look upon the countenance which was the expression of so much kindness, of so much energy, of so much virtue, as is described in those traditional records which die not in any Catholic house." And we have wished to procure for those that shall come after us, some small recollection at least of that which we have the pleasure of enjoying in its fulness, in the sight and knowledge of your features, some idea of what you were when you lived amongst us. Your portrait, therefore, has been secured : secured in a way which will bear the resemblance and the memory of you to posterity, in as exact a form as the skill of the artist can transmit the likeness of one that is well loved. And it will be a pleasure, I am sure, to all those who have joined in procuring for those that shall follow us, the gratification we enjoy to see and know that the work is not unworthy of him whom it represents. I therefore speak in the name of those who present the portrait to you, knowing well that it is to remain as one of the most cherished monuments of St. Cuthbert's College, one upon which the students will love to gaze, one which posterity will not fail to revere and to love. In this room I see persons connected with you by the most various ties. There are those who have known Dr. Newsham when himself a youth. Then comes another generation, to which I belong ; and I feel a pride in saying that in it I am connected with him in a more special manner. I belong to that generation, now verging into old age, which had the happiness of seeing and knowing him as a superior, though not as yet the head of the college. I say, I have to claim a peculiar rank and place in that class, because not only had I the advantage of possessing him as a Professor for several years, and those the most important of my course, but because I had that more peculiar and close connection with him, so well known to you here—that of pupil and pedagogue. Day after day have I sat at his fireside while he was engaged in graver pursuits, and while I was conning my lessons for the next day, and applying to him for assistance in the little difficulties which stopped my way. Day after day have I gone to him, at the old familiar quarter, to obtain such help as you know a good natured pedagogue is ever ready to give to an idle pupil. I thus can say that I had opportunities which few have had of studying and appreciating the character of your most amiable President ; and I say it with pleasure, because from the day that that more intimate connection ceased, and that, choosing my portion in a distant land, I left the college to complete my studies at Rome : from that day to this, there has been established a firm bond still, I trust, of uninterrupted friendship. It seems as if in a moment the tie between us was changed into one more valuable. The dependence which I had for so many years upon him, and marked as it had been with mutual confidence, in one moment seemed to place us in a state of equality. We corresponded together : we have treated one another as friends ; and there are few friendships I can say that I value more highly than his. And if, indeed, it has pleased Almighty God that this separation should have led us into divergent courses : that he should remain here on the spot where I left him, still attached to the old walls, but soon after called to develop an energy and greatness of ideas which few thought were lurking in him,—if he remained so as to complete his jubilee, as the President of this college, and as he may well be called its second Founder,—if he has well used those gifts which God gave him to make great, bright, and beautiful one spot : if, on the other hand, it has pleased Him that, after passing many years of my life far away from the scenes of my youth, I should have returned to bear my share in that pastoral solicitude which as it was unsought, so has it been well tried, it is now a true consolation to me, to return back to the scenes of earlier life, and to renew again the impressions of more tender affection ; and if I return, confused not a little at seeing the pupil placed where his instructor and guide perhaps ought to have been —if I see myself invested with a mark of honour and ecclesiastical distinction which would have much better suited him, I say, it is one of the mitigations of that confusion which I feel, if that dignity to which it has pleased the Head of the Church to raise me, however unworthy, reflects any honour upon the jubilee of my estimable and most beloved friend, I am glad that such an opportunity of thus employing it should have been afforded me. I will take the liberty of concluding this offering to our worthy President—the portrait which you have joined in presenting him with, by embodying in a few lines the thoughts which strike me in witnessing what, in past years, has been done by him. They are in the form of a sonnet ; and it is the only way I have of placing in his hands what I have endeavoured to express :—

TO THE VERY REV. MGR. NEWSHAM,

On his College Jubilee, June 22nd, 1853.

How few upon one spot the time have spent,
　Which gives to noblest plants maturity :
　From the lithe sapling building up the tree.
But here thy mind received its early bent
Full fifty years ago. Thoughts inly pent
　At first, have since grown quietly with thee,
　Till they expanded into what we see,
Of great and fair, for highest purpose blent.

For chapels, cloisters, libraries, and halls,
　Alive with youthful intellect and grace,
Glowing with art, awake to music's tones
To-day, by festive echoes from their walls,
　Proclaim that in thy mind their form had place,
Ere art impressed it on enduring stones.

The portrait, by J. R. Herbert, R.A., is an excellent likeness, and exceedingly well executed.

The President having in the kindest and most affectionate terms thanked the students, who he knew would be glad to be called his children, for their address, and expressed a hope that if their prayers for the lengthening of his days be heard, and their kind wishes for his future health and strength be fulfilled, it would be only to enable him to spend them on their welfare, or at least to witness the happiness of their own future career, and the accumulation of the many blessings which God would not fail to award to virtuous youth. He next thanked his numerous friends assembled there to give him proof of their friendship and kindness. Among these were two of his first masters (Rev. Mr. Bradley and Rev. Mr. Cock), and his pedagogue (Very Rev. Robert Hogarth). There was his old schoolfellow also, the venerable Bishop of Beverley, Dr. Briggs. How could he sufficiently thank them? Of the others some were acquaintances or friends from early youth, who had shared with him the fostering care of their common mother; some had been labourers in the same field, and had contributed much to her prosperity. To all he tendered sincerest thanks, and fervently wished to all the blessings of health and happiness. To the subscribers to his portrait he would beg to say, he felt they had a double right to his gratitude. For, first, they had shown him by their gift a kindness which he must ever highly appreciate. To know that even death will not separate him from the walls—sacred to him—within which he had passed so many years of happiness, and devoted his life to its appointed duties; to anticipate that they who now are young will, perhaps, when grown old, and returning here, have recalled to their mind the lineaments of one who wished to be their early friend; to be sure, at least, that the sight of this likeness would secure for him a place in the short prayer for the departed, which closes every meal enjoyed beneath it -these are considerations which might justly overcome the natural repugnance one must experience to a mark of honour that is generally reserved for much higher dignity or far greater merits. But, further, he felt that this repugnance was still more overcome—and he owed the subscribers on this sacred ground still further thanks for it—by the selection made of England's most distinguished artist; for thus he had felt that, in bestowing this portrait on the college, he was enriching it with a splendid work of art. He begged now to conclude with one general expression of gratitude to all present: to all the members of the house, superiors, professors, and students,—to all who had honoured him by joining them in this commemoration of his jubilee, and especially to His Eminence the Cardinal Archbishop,—and to all the illustrious prelates who had condescended to shed a splendour, and to call down a blessing on that day's proceedings, and thus, while they honoured him by their friendship, gave to the college the countenance and encouragement which it will be proud to deserve.

After this, the students, to the number of 70, sang the Jubilee Song, which was given with great taste, and highly applauded. The song composed for the occasion was set to music by John Richardson, who presided at the piano. The whole was conducted by the Rev. Roger Taylor.

These interesting proceedings having been concluded, the whole of those present sat down to a sumptuous dinner in the refectory. Upwards of 300 sat down, His Eminence taking the chair; supported on his right by the Bishops of Hexham and Plymouth; and on his left by the President, the Bishops of Beverley, Salford, and Edinburgh. The refectory was tastefully decorated with banners and evergreens.

The cloth having been removed,

His Eminence the Cardinal proposed "The health of our Holy Father, Pope Pius IX.," who had been pleased to number their revered and beloved President among his domestic prelates, a mark of favour unexampled in England, as no other superior of a college ever received it before him.

Bishop Hogarth gave "The health of His Eminence Cardinal Wiseman," who had done great things for Ushaw, and to whom they were indebted for much of the hilarity of that meeting, and for the splendour of the ecclesiastical ceremony which they had witnessed.

His Eminence having returned thanks for the honour they had done him in drinking his health, and for the kind welcome they had given him, observed that it was to him a source of pride and satisfaction to be singled out to propose the health of one to whom he felt such great and continued obligations, and whom he had always, throughout his life, considered it an honour to himself to be able to call his master and his pedagogue. When separated from him in early life, and while pursuing the course of his studies at Rome, the words he had spoken to him, the principles he had instilled, the counsels he had given, the directions of study he had received, again and again recurred to his mind, and he found them always sure guides to follow. He begged them to drink the President's health with all their hearts and souls.

The Vice-President, Dr. Gibson, replied on behalf of the President.

The Very Rev. Dr. Tate proposed "the health, with all the honours, of the Bishops, and long life to them."

The Right Rev. Bishop Briggs rose to reply, and alluding to his schoolfellow, their revered President, and his much esteemed friend, Dr. Newsham, said he (Dr. Newsham) was pleased to mention him as his schoolfellow; and it was true that they were fellow scholars until the close of their theological studies; and if there be any one who may be supposed to have had a most intimate acquaintance with their worthy President, it should be himself. They travelled their course together, and he was delighted to have that opportunity of bearing his humble testimony to his merits and his worth. When it pleased the Almighty to raise him to the Episcopacy, and he returned to the college, and presided over it three years after his predecessor died, he resigned the charge, and proposed Dr. Newsham as his successor; and he craved some degree of credit to himself for having made such an election.

Bishop Gillis returned thanks for having been elected an honorary alumnus of Ushaw, and stated there was no college in this country with which he would feel more proud to be linked than with that of Ushaw.

Rev. J. Walker replied to the toast of "The Clergy," a body of men than whom, whether for merits, whether for distinction of any kind, whether for devotion to that establishment or devotion to their own duties, he knew no other body to surpass them. They felt they were met, not to celebrate the jubilee of a retiring prelate, not to bid farewell to a man who had given them fifty years of service and from whom they would receive no more, but they were expressing their gratitude and veneration for one whom he thought qualified to give them another jubilee of services or more, and he begged to join in fellowship with the noblest and sincerest enthusiasm they could express that that establishment might long continue under Dr. Newsham's sway, a sway which had been truly admirable, admirable from the familiarity of the President with conventual life, admirable from his (Dr. Newsham's) own intrinsic wisdom combined with the gifts of gentleness and energy, and from the blessing of God which had been manifestly given.

Sir W. Lawson on behalf of the laity responded to the toast of "The Visitors"—observing that the occasion would be one of the most happiest days of his recollection in future times, and he had felt immense gratification at having been present.

The Right Rev. Dr. Errington, Bishop of Plymouth, gave "The Superiors and Students." He did not wish to flatter them, and yet he had to be complimentary; bnt he would not attribute the wonderful changes and improvements they had seen either to the general or to the army. They came mainly, he believed, from the glorious constitution of Ushaw; it was because Ushaw stood so firm to those regulations made in ancient times that Ushaw had risen to greatness. The constitution of Ushaw makes it impossible to have those sudden, unconsulted changes which are so dangerous; but at the same time, it allows full scope for the matured consideration which will keep it always up to the level of the time. But it would be impossible for either the constitution to keep up and work well, or for the rules to be observed, if there were not good officers to see after them, and if there were not willing subjects to obey. The labours of the Superior were self-sacrificing, energetic and persevering; but unless the boys corresponded heart and soul with the professors, their labours would be in vain.

A display of fireworks took place in the evening.

ST. CUTHBERT'S SOCIETY.

I must not pass unnoticed this Society, which was founded July 19th, A.D. 1854, the year after the celebration of Mgr. Newsham's jubilee, the forty-sixth anniversary of the opening of the college, primarily with the view of forming a bond and centre of union for the alumni and friends of St. Cuthbert's College, Ushaw, in whatever part of the world they reside, and thus perpetuating that spirit of brotherhood which has ever existed among them; and secondly for the promotion of religion and learning among the students of the college, by the foundation of scholarships and by grants for prizes and for the expenses of Matriculation, and other University Examinations. It awards prizes in Theology for Latin Essay—Jubilee Fund Prize, £20; English

Essay—first prize, £10, second prize, £7, third prize, £5; Dogmatic and Moral Theology—first prize, £10, second prize, £6, third prize, £4; Sermon Writing—first prize, £7, second prize, £5, third prize, £3. In Moral Philosophy—English Essay—first prize, £7, second prize, £4; in Natural Philosophy—English Essay—first prize, £7, second prize, £4; Matriculation—highest in Honours—prize £10. The Society is placed under the special protection of our Blessed Lady—*Sedes Sapientiæ*—and of St. Cuthbert, the patron of the college, and is entitled "St. Cuthbert's Society." It has its Patrons, its President (the President of St. Cuthbert's College), its Vice-Presidents, and its Officers. The Patrons of the Society are such Archbishops, Bishops, and other distinguished members of the Society as have consented to accept the honour. The Officers of the Society are its Council of twenty members, its five Trustees, a Chaplain, an Honorary Secretary, and an Honorary Treasurer. The duty of the Chaplain is to say Mass once in each month for the members living and dead, and for the welfare of the Society. He has also to say Mass for the same intentions on the day of the General Meeting, and one Mass for the soul of each member deceased as soon as possible after the death has been notified to him by the Secretary. The Society both in funds and numbers flourishes and prospers, and has large invested capital. Each year it adds to its ordinary and extraordinary members: amongst its members it has had His Eminence Cardinal Antonelli, the Right Rev. Mgr. Nardi, Right Rev. Mgr. Talbot, Mr. Justice Shee, &c. His Grace the Duke of Norfolk, E.M., and Lord Mowbray and Stourton, were also members. To the Very Rev. Dean Hogarth, who died at Dodding Green early in the year 1868, St. Cuthbert's Society was under great obligation. He was one of five persons who were most active in forming the Society, and he it was who interested himself in a particular manner in founding the Scholarship Prize. His brother, the Right Rev. Bishop Hogarth, was the first to join the Society, and to become a life member. The Right Rev. Prelate was never absent from its meetings, and took the most lively interest in its prosperity. On the 1st of May, 1867, His Holiness Pope Pius IX., in answer to the humble petition of the President and Secretary of the Society, was pleased to grant to all the members of the Society, who had duly paid their subscription, a Plenary Indulgence, to be gained once a month by complying with the usual conditions of Confession, Communion, and Prayers for the Church, and saying five Our Fathers and five Hail Marys for the intention of the Sovereign Pontiff.

In 1879 the Silver Jubilee of the Society was celebrated by a more than ordinary meeting of its members, and by an event that will prove a lasting memorial. In commemoration of the occasion, a statue of Our Blessed Lady, as the *Sedes Sapientiæ*, of alabaster, was fixed in a niche of the same material facing the entrance into the college, and on the 30th of July of the above year, was solemnly unveiled in the presence of the Bishop of Hexham and Newcastle, the Professors, and Students, and more than eighty members of the Society. This memorial was erected at a cost of nearly £400. Hence on entering the college the image of Mary "solace of sinners, loadstar ever nigh" is before us—

"But in a higher niche, alone, but crowned,
The Virgin Mother of the God-born child,
With her Son in her blest arms looked round,
Making the earth below seem holy ground."

"*O mater nivei flos intemerata pudoris, utinam mea mens spiret odore tuo.*" To mark still further the year of the Society's first Jubilee, one pound to each of the various prizes in Divinity and in Moral and Natural Philosophy was added, and grants were made of five pounds for a prize in Sacred Scripture, and of five pounds for a prize in Canon Law. The Council also inaugurated a yearly prize of £10 to be awarded to such student who obtained among competitors from St. Cuthbert's College, the highest place in Matriculation Honours at the London University.

In connection with the Society especial interest attaches to the Very Rev. Michael Trappes, Rural Dean and Rector of St. Charles's, Hull, who, from its foundation in 1854, to his death in 1873, was its worthy and respected secretary. To the great interest which he took in the Society, and to his unremitting exertions on its behalf, its health, vigour, and flourishing condition are in a great measure attributable. I know few who deserved better of Ushaw than the Very Rev. Michael Trappes; his heart and soul were centred in St. Cuthbert's Society, and in the welfare and good estate of his *Alma Mater*, to whose interests through a long course of life he was most devoted, and seemed almost part and parcel of the establishment. Hence, on this and other accounts does the good old priest and venerable secretary deserve to receive in these pages grateful and honourable mention, and it is particularly gratifying to me to render this tribute of respect to his memory.

Michael Trappes was of goodly and gentle birth, the historic family of Trappes being able to trace its lineage as far back as the Plantagenets; and when to be a Catholic was a crime and a dishonour, they—the Trappes—clung unflinchingly to the faith of their fathers, in spite of centuries of persecution, sequestration of lands and property, and deprivation of honours and emoluments. He was the seventh son of Francis Michael Trappes, Esq., of Nidd Hall, in the West Riding of Yorkshire, and Elizabeth (*née* Lomax) his wife. He was born at St. Trinian's, Richmond (Yorks.), on the feast of St. George, April 23, 1797, and was baptized the same day by the Rev. Thomas Lawson. Nidd Hall is situated on the river of that name, near to where St. Bertwald, Archbishop of Canterbury, about the year 705 called a council, "and Wilfrid was there, and Bosa, and John of Beverley, and Eadbert of Lindisfarne," respecting rendering obedience to Rome, and to this principle that day by the dark silent waters of the Nidd men bowed in fear and reverence, a principle for which the indomitable Wilfrid had so long and strenuously battled. And on the occasion, Mass was sung on the side of the Nidd, Holy Communion was received, and the kiss of peace given by the adverse bishops, and perfect concord and reconciliation effected between them. Though only eight years of age, little Michael Trappes, young and tender sapling as he then was, was, in 1805, transplanted from the home of his ancestors on the banks of the Nidd, and placed at Crook Hall, there to commence his college life, and to pursue his studies. On the opening of the college of

Ushaw, the boy Michael was among the band of students who, in 1808, migrated from Crook and established their abode beneath the old Ushaw yew tree. In the year 1809-10 his name is to be found in the list of those who had reached the first class of Rudiments (High Figures). As a student he is represented as being always exact and industrious, kind and obliging to others, and joining in the college games with great spirit and energy. In the twenty-fifth year of his age, on the 21st of December, 1821, he was ordained priest, and began his missionary life at Monkwearmouth, Sunderland, where he remained six months. Thence he went to St. Mary's, Mulberry Street, Manchester, which mission he served four years; Bury and Rochdale two years; Broughton Hall, as chaplain to Sir Charles Tempest, eleven years; Huddersfield, another eleven years. Lastly, on May 20th, 1848, Father Trappes was placed in charge of the flock of St. Charles's Church, Hull, and here in the midst of his flock this venerable, grey-haired priest, and faithful pastor, on the 7th day of June, 1873, having attained the good old age of 76 years, entered into his rest, and, as we trustfully hope, into the joy of his Lord. Two years before his death he celebrated the golden jubilee of his priesthood, when the congregation presented him with a congratulatory address, together with a purse of £175. He had also in 1861 received from the Catholics of Hull an address of thanks and congratulation for his unwearying exertions to provide for the religious and educational wants of his flock, and a purse containing £100. It is testified of him that after the practices of religion, the cause of education occupied the next and dearest place in his heart. To increase the means of imparting knowledge to the children was one of the grand aims of his life. To effect this he laboured late and early, and he was spared to see the fulfilment of his aspirations, and ample means for education placed within the reach of every Catholic child in Hull. In the same year Father Trappes was promoted to a deanery, on Dean Hogarth leaving Marton for Dodding Green, near Kendal. The death of Dean Trappes was deeply and universally lamented, and his praise and good name were upon every one's lips. By all who knew him he was regarded as a perfect gentleman and a most excellent priest—"*dilectus Deo et hominibus, cujus memoria in benedictione est.*" His charity, generosity, and benefactions were unbounded, and his heart and his ear were ever open to the cry of distress. "*Manum suam aperuit inopi, et palmas suas extendit ad pauperem.*" "*Dispersit dedit pauperibus,*" therefore "*cornu ejus exaltabitur in gloria.*" In an account of his death, the *Hull Evening News* thus alluded to the worthy Dean's affection for and connection with Ushaw.—"In one other little spot—amid the hills of Durham—will a sadness and gloom be 'spread. Year after year Father Trappes was accustomed to spend his holidays in the cherished home of his youth and early manhood. To Ushaw College he would retire for a time from the fatigues of missionary life, and there would he grow young with the brightness of early days. To sleep again within the precincts of *Alma Mater* was a most genuine pleasure to the worthy old gentleman. It was happiness for him to see "his boys" at their games, and if he could secure the house a holiday he was more delighted than they. Every one knew and loved the old familiar face, for every one, from the 'Philosopher' to the least boy in the lowest 'form,' he had kind words and a courtly greeting. In all things relating to Ushaw he took the liveliest interest. He loved Ushaw, nay, the very air of Ushaw, beyond aught else. There it was his wish to be buried, and in the picturesque little cemetery of Ushaw College, in the shadow almost of its many spires, and in the perpetual remembrance of her alumni, all that remains of Michael Trappes find an appropriate abiding place. A long life of singular tranquillity and peace has placidly ended, and in bidding farewell the Catholic body can say with truth that there has gone from them a thorough gentleman and a perfect priest." On the Tuesday morning following his death a solemn Requiem Mass was celebrated in the church of St. Charles, in the presence of the Bishop of Beverley, Right Rev. Dr. Cornthwaite. His remains were then conveyed by express train to Durham ; thence in a hearse to St. Cuthbert's College. Next morning the Requiem Mass was celebrated by the Lord Bishop of Hexham and Newcastle, Right Rev. Dr. Chadwick. The funeral discourse was preached by the Very Rev. Canon Consitt, his text being taken from the inscription on the coffin—" *Dilectus Deo et hominibus.*" After Mass the body was borne to the college cemetery, and there interred besides the guides of his youth, and the friends of his old age— in the spot which, on all the earth, he loved most dearly, and which he had chosen. He had died peacefully and tranquilly, as his fathers had died—

"It is enough, O Lord ! now let me die,
Even as my fathers did."

The Rev. Arthur Riddell, afterwards appointed Bishop of Northampton, who had been his assistant priest at St. Charles's, Hull, succeeded Dean Trappes in the office of Secretary of St. Cuthbert's Society.

Dr. Newsham's jubilee had passed, St. Cuthbert's Society was founded, and through the aid and exertions of Father Trappes, the indefatigable Secretary, had taken root and was extending its ramifications among an honourable people, when, in a very few years the joy that prevailed at Ushaw, became mingled with sorrow. True it is,

"*Surgit amari aliquid medio de fonte leporum* ;"

and no less true that oftentimes our sincerest laughter and rejoicing " with some pain are fraught," and that not unfrequently a gloom comes over us like an occasional cloud that ever and anon is seen floating across a serene summer sky. In the third year following the President's jubilee, the Very Rev. Michael Gibson, D.D., the Vice-President, a most saintly, amiable, and learned priest, the esteemed friend, the *fidus Achates* of Monsgr. Newsham, departed this life—

"Removed from earth's rude strife and weary ways,
To live in memory here, in heaven by love and praise."

Michael Gibson was born at Salford, Manchester, 25th August, 1816. His father, Michael Gibson, came from York to Manchester, about the beginning of the century, and was engaged in the cotton trade. His mother, Elizabeth Reeve, was a member of the old Catholic family of that name, which furnished many priests to the

Church in the last century. Her uncle, Rev. Joseph Reeve, S.J., was the author of the "Bible History" and the "History of the Church." Michael, their son, went to Mr. Dobson's school at Broadwood House Academy, Maghull, at the age of 7½ years, on the 26th of March, 1824, his father having removed his residence to the neighbourhood of Liverpool in the year 1822. He made his first Communion at Netherton Chapel, on the 26th of March, 1826. In March, 1828, he left Broadwood House, and in the following month, April, he was sent to Ushaw College to study for the Church. He was in the same school as the late Bishop of Liverpool, Dr. Goss, and the present Archbishop of Glasgow, Most Rev. Chas. Eyre, and the late Dr. John Gillow, V.P. He distinguished himself in his studies, and always held the first or second place in his class. He received Minor Orders, 17th December, 1836, at the hands of Bishop Briggs, the same day that the late Bishop Chadwick was ordained priest. He was ordained Sub-deacon, 23rd December, 1837. In March, 1839, from Ushaw he went to the English College, Rome, to finish his theological studies. He was there ordained Deacon, 17th December, 1839, and on the 9th June, 1840, he was raised to the Priesthood, by the late Cardinal (then Dr.) Wiseman, who had been the day before consecrated Coadjutor Bishop for the Midland District. He returned to England along with Dr. Wiseman, Dr. Roskell, late Bishop of Nottingham, and Monsignor Thompson. In December, 1840, he was appointed Professor of Poetry at Ushaw, and in September, 1844, commenced teaching Moral Theology. In January, 1850, he became Vice-President, Dr. Newsham being President of the college. On the establishment of the Hierarchy he was made Canon Theologian of Hexham, and Doctor of Divinity, October, 1850. In May, 1856, Dr. Gibson went to Rome on business connected with the college and the Diocese of Hexham. In the month of August, he was attacked by fever which caused him to hurry home. He reached his father's house at Leamington, 14th August, in a very prostrate state; and said Mass for the last time on the Feast of the Assumption. The Roman fever was too much for his exhausted frame to contend with, and in spite of every care on the part of his devoted parents, he sank under the attack, and died 27th August, 1856. His body was conveyed to St. Cuthbert's College, and is interred in the Mortuary Chapel, built by his father as a tribute to his memory, and where a few years later, the Right Reverend President of the college, Dr. Newsham, was also buried.

I have great pleasure, in loving remembrance of my friend, the Very Rev. Provost Platt, in here inserting a portion of the discourse delivered by him, then Canon Platt, V.G., at Dr. Gibson's funeral, 2nd September, 1856. It was as follows :—

"*I grieve for thee, my brother Jonathan, exceeding beautiful, and amiable to me above the love of woman. As the mother loveth her only son, so did I love thee.*"—II. Kings, i., 26.

MY LORDS AND REV. BRETHREN,

I do feel it a painful task to break in upon your grief on this distressing occasion. But if at the request of your Reverend President I am compelled to utter a few, a very few words, I know not what language to make use of but that of holy David when he had sustained a similar loss—" I grieve for thee," &c. A dear bosom friend, who had long lived under the same roof, and partaken of all his joys and sorrows, was prematurely stricken down in the battle field. All the endearing qualities of his beloved companion flashed at once upon his mind, and thinking of his sudden bereavement, he could only repeat in broken accents "how beautiful, how exceeding beautiful, and amiable" was the dear friend he mourned, whom he prized above every other earthly attachment. He can call him by no other name than that of "brother." "I grieve for thee, my brother Jonathan." Nay further he adds, "As the mother loveth her only son, so did I love thee." My dear Rev. Brethren, you will, I feel assured, bear with me, when I say that I and many of you bore the same sincere affection to our dear departed friend. And was he not "exceeding beautiful and amiable?" Was there ever any one in whom was more strikingly displayed that amiability of disposition which wins hearts and unites them in bonds indissoluble. Nor was it any earthly attachment. It was something purer, holier, stronger far, which the grave will not bury, nor time efface. In truth he never seemed really to belong to this world. In the words spoken of the first martyr, we may say of him, "We beheld his face as that of an angel." As an angel we always looked upon him, both in the days of his boyhood, when he was our schoolfellow and playmate, and in the vigour of his age when ministering at the altar; or when revisiting the college, we saw him with such heavenly grace and dignified humility discharging the duties of that exalted station to which he was so deservedly raised. There are two distinguishing characteristics of the ecclesiastical vocation, which, if possible, should be still more pre-eminent in the Superior and Professor of an Ecclesiastical Seminary. With both of these, namely virtue and learning he was most abundantly endowed. Trained to piety from his earliest infancy by parents well deserving of such a son, I well remember how from the day he first entered within these walls, we always looked up to him as a bright example to us all. Though brought up in all the comforts of opulence, not a murmur of complaint ever escaped his lips, when placed under strict discipline, and experiencing many privations, which of necessity must have been trying to his delicate frame. No, always cheerful, quiet, meek, and amiable, and above all, most sensitively conscientious, shrinking from the least appearance of evil, he was a model of piety, docility, and obedience. The extent of his learning could be known only by those to whom in a manner he was compelled to disclose it. Suffice it to say that in cases which could be solved only by the greatest depth of learned research, combined with the most solid judgment, no one, either in the college, or out of the college, ever had recourse to him in vain. He was for several years Professor and Doctor of Theology; too short a time he was our Canon Theologian, and it is the highest commendation to say, that for both offices he was well qualified. In training the minds of the young ecclesiastics committed to his care, his bright example and sweet words of counsel were most successful, and it was delightful to hear them, when they came amongst us, dilating on the merits of their good Vice-President, and rehearsing the maxims of wisdom which they had treasured up from his lips to direct their future conduct. Alas, my dear Brethren, in the very flower of his age, when most efficient, and apparently most wanted, God, who orders all things for the best, has been pleased to take him from us. But if his death was premature for us, it was not so for himself. "Being made perfect in a short space, he fulfilled a long time. For his soul pleased God"- therefore, as St. Chrysostom remarks, the very reverse has happened to what we should naturally expect. "His soul pleased God," therefore we might suppose he would be allowed to remain amongst us for our example and encouragement—no, because his soul pleased God, therefore did God hasten to bring him out of the midst of iniquities, and transfer his pure soul to a more congenial sphere. To fit him for his departure hence, he was privileged to revisit before his death those holy sanctuaries and tombs of the Apostles, where, as a student at the English College in Rome, he loved so much to go and pray. With the benediction of the Holy Father on his head, and animated with the spirit of the illustrious Saints and Martyrs, whose shrines he had just venerated, he returned to his native land. We welcomed him back with joy as a burning and shining light for us all, to he raised, at some future day, we expected, some distant day we hoped, to a still higher station in this house, perhaps eventually to the highest dignity in the diocese. So men thought, and spoke, but God had otherwise ordained, and destined him for a station still more exalted. The pious parents rejoiced to see once more the glory of their house, and an honour to God's Church, returning to his paternal roof. He had been their consolation during life, he was come now to edify them by his holy death. And if ever the consolations of religion were ministered in abundance to a departing soul, he was certainly pre-eminently favoured. Those good parents who had so cheerfully given him to the service of the church, prayed incessantly for him till they resigned him into the hands of God; his dear sister by blood, and dearer still by religion, like a consoling angel ministered to him to the last. A bosom friend, a beloved brother Professor, was also privileged to attend upon him, to be edified by his holy death, and to impart to him the last blessing of the Church. After having calmly arranged his temporal affairs, he received in the most devout dispositions the Holy Sacraments and last Rites of the Church. He knew well what was about to happen, and expressed himself perfectly content. "Never," said he several times, "never did I know what it was to be happy, before this hour." He felt the agonies of death, yet in the midst of them he turned his eyes towards his dear sister, and said with a sweet smile, "I have had too easy times during life; it is well that I should suffer something before I die." "Jesus, Mary, Joseph," were constantly on his lips and in his heart till he expired. My dear Brethren, do we wish to die such a death? Let us then endeavour to copy to the best of our weak ability his holy life. My young friends, the happy inmates of this noble college, you prayed fervently that your good Vice-President might be spared. It was well to do so, and all of us most heartily joined in your prayers. Life was asked for him, and life was given him, for not as the world gives, does God give. "Vitam petiit a te, et tribuisti ei in longitudinem dierum." You asked for him a few more years of this miserable life, and God gave him life eternal. But though removed from us, his memory will long be held in benediction. His bright example will still animate our faint-heartedness, and long live in the memories of those who have had the happiness of being educated by him within these walls, where, as his good father truly said, his heart and soul always were; and whither now, as a precious treasure his mortal remains have been brought to repose. Let us conclude this solemn service by repeating again those words of Holy Church, uttered in the Masses we have said for him this morning. "May the blessed Saint Michael, the standard bearer of Heaven, and his dear Patron, conduct him into the holy light of God's presence."

To his parents and friends, to his fellow priests, to his *Alma Mater*, and to all the students, Dr. Gibson's death was a source of heartfelt sorrow and affliction—"*multis ille bonis flebilis occidit*"—but by Dr. Newsham his loss was deeply felt, and most sincerely lamented.

"What saint was there ever in the world," asks the author of the *Following of Christ*, "without his cross and affliction?" Great saints have great trials: like them Dr. Newsham had his troubles, vexations, and crosses, but he shrank not from them; he took up his cross and carried it manfully, going on his way rejoicing; amplifying and enlarging the accommodation of the college, beautifying its buildings, improving its status, adding even to its territorial possessions. Biggin, 176 acres, lying among the green pastures, meadows, and cornfields of Lanchester valley through which the Browney stream meanders; and Bromholme, 197 acres—these estates became the property of Ushaw, being purchased during the time of Dr. Newsham's presidency. Bromholme (Broomehall) has a history; Biggin has none. On certain recreation and feast days the junior boys used of late years to go to Biggin instead of to Cornsay, the former not being so far distant as Cornsay House from the college. We learn from Hutchinson's *History of Durham* that Broome, or Bromeholme, as mentioned in ancient records, is situated near Aldan-Grange (Aldyngrenge). By an inquisition taken in the third year of Bury, Bishop of Durham, it appears lands in Broome were in possession of Constantia del Brome. Thomas del Brome was her son and heir. In the 31st year of Bishop Hatfield, by an inquisition taken on the death of Thomas de Hexham, whose heirs are named in the survey before noted, we find he died seized of the Manor of Broome, held of the prior of Finchale by fealty and four shillings rent— "Heredes Thomæ de Hexham tenent ii acr. juxta Bromeholme." In the beginning of the fifteenth century, the 27th year of Bishop Langley, it became part of the great possessions of the Fossour family, of Kelloe and Harberhouse, near Finchale, who afterwards wrote their name Forcer. Surtees in his *History of Durham*, says "I have little doubt that this name (Broomehall) is derived from the native broom which overspreads the western uplands." The mansion house and tenements are mentioned by Camden. They are situated about three miles west of Durham. In the eighteenth century from the Fossours the property passed into the hands of the Tempest family. It was afterwards sold to Mr. Frank Taylor, of Aldin Grange, at whose decease it was incorporated by purchase into the Ushaw domains. The house (Broomehall) has the appearance of a respectable farm house, but scarcely so good as you would designate as the abode of a gentleman farmer; one of the old small property holders might have occupied it.

There hangs in the college refectory at Ushaw a portrait— the portrait (an oil painting) of Thomas Carr, *alias* Myles Pinkney, who was born at Broomehall at the close of the sixteenth century, in the year 1599. The inscription underneath the portrait reads thus "*Revdus. Myles Pinkney ('Thomas Carre') primus Monialium Canonissarum Anglarum, Parisiis, Confessarius et hujus Seminarii studiosissimus, natus 1599, obiit 1674.*" The seminary mentioned was the English College of Douai, from which no doubt the portrait passed into England. The mention of the name of Myles Pinkney carries us back to a remote period of history— to the rueful times of persecution, when, on account of their religion the blood of Catholics was poured out like water, when Catholic priests were hunted like wild beasts, racked, tortured, doomed to death, and executed with cruel butchery. His name moreover transports us to the early days of Douai College, and its records, "Mylo Carrus" being therein entered anno 1625. From the time of his birth 1599, to his death in 1674, the undernamed were the Presidents of this renowned and time honoured institution:—Dr. Thomas Worthington 1599, Dr. Matthew Kellison 1613, Rev. Geo. Musket 1641, Dr. Wm. Hyde 1646, Dr. Geo. Leyburn 1652, Rev. John Leyburn 1670. Next Presidents in succession were Dr. Francis Gage 1676, Dr. James Smith 1682, Dr. Edward Paston 1688, Dr. Robert Witham 1714, Dr. William Thornburgh 1738, Dr. William Green 1750, Rev. Henry Tichbourne Blount 1770, Rev. William Gibson 1781, Rev. Edward Kitchen 1790, Rev. John Daniel 1792. Previous to the first mentioned (in this list) Dr. Worthington, Douai had for its first President and founder, Dr. William Allen 1568, who was succeeded by Dr. Richard Barrett 1588.

The statement below is to some extent at variance with that of Bishop Challoner, in a previous part of our "Records and Recollections." Douai College produced one Cardinal, two Archbishops, thirty-one Bishops, and Bishops elect, three Archpriests, about one hundred Doctors of Divinity, one hundred and sixty-nine writers, many eminent men of religious orders, and one hundred and sixty glorious martyrs, besides innumerable others, who either died in prison, or suffered confinement or banism for their faith. Many also of our Catholic nobility and gentry received their education at Douai College. After Douai had sent fifty-two priests to labour on the English mission the college was compelled to remove to Rheims; but in 1593 it returned to Douai and continued for two centuries from that date to supply priests to the English mission. The New Testament, translated by Dr. Gregory Martin, was published at Rheims in the year 1580; the Old Testament in 1609, after the return of the college to Douai.

At an early age Myles Pinkney became a student at Douai College, that venerable parent of confessors and martyrs. Having completed his studies, and on being raised to the priesthood, he remained several years as Procurator at Douai. He then went to Paris, where he founded the convent of Augustinian nuns, along with Lady Tredway, and the College of St. Gregory. From this convent, through Cardinal Wiseman's mediation, came the episcopal ring of St. Cuthbert, now in sacred keeping at Ushaw. Fr. Pinkney was the active business agent for the English Bishops and Catholics, crossing the channel 58 or 60 times, as Dodd states, on matters of ecclesiastical importance. He enjoyed the confidence of the Bishop of Chalcedon (Dr. Smith), who for the last 15 years of his life resided as his guest at the Augustinian Convent. St Vincent of Paul was often seen walking with Mr. Carr *alias* Pinkney in the convent garden. He was likewise an intimate friend of Cardinal Richelieu, and the author of many works of piety. Dodd in his *Church History of England* relates that "Thomas Carr *alias* Myles Pinkney, (the latter being his true name,) was of an ancient family at Broomhall, in the Bishoprick of Durham, and was sent very young to the English College at Doway, and was admitted among the clergy *per tonsuram*, June 13th, 1620. He proceeded in his studies with good success and was no less remarkable for his religious behaviour. When he had completed his philosophical lessons, some domestic affairs required his presence in England, but before he undertook the journey, it was judged proper to promote him to holy orders, which was done by a particular dispensation, being first instructed in the ceremonies of the sacred functions; so that June 11, 1625, he was made Sub-deacon; on the 14th he was made Deacon; and the next day ordained Priest. The 9th of July, the said year, he set out for England, and having completed his affairs returned back to Doway, September the 8th. He afterwards finished his Theological studies, and being excellently qualified for economy, was made Procurator of the college. He behaved himself in this office to the general satisfaction of his brethren, and remained in it till 1634, when he undertook the project of founding a monastery of nuns, at Paris, of St. Augustine's order, where he resided as their confessor, till he died. The foundation of this monastery proved a work of incredible labour and charge to Mr. Carr. It is recorded that he crossed the seas sixty times, between England and France, to bring it to perfection, and bestowed all his time, money, interest, learning and piety, for forty years together for the same purpose. At last being seized with a palsy, he became almost unserviceable for nearly twelve years before he died, during which time Mr. Edward Lutton, formerly also Procurator of Doway College was appointed his coadjutor, and succeeded him upon his death, which happened October 31st, 1674, when he was seventy-five years of age. Mr. Carr appears to have had all those qualifications required in his station of life; a public spirit, moderation in domestic controversies, indefatigable patience in taking pains, and firmness in all oppositions, which are always customary where the honour of God and the good of religion are concerned. The clergy never failed to consult him in all matters of consequence. He laid down the first sum of money towards purchasing a residence for such of his brethren as were designed to take degrees in the University of Paris, an undertaking afterwards completed by Dr. John Betham. He was much respected by the Court of France, especially by Cardinal Richlieu, who was a singular benefactor to the English abroad, through his mediation; and though his life was much spent in action, yet he found time to publish the following works :—

1.—Pietas Parisiensis; or a Description of the Hospitals, &c., in Paris, 8vo., 1666.

2.—Sweet Thoughts of Jesus and Mary; or Meditations for all the Sundays and Feasts of Our Blessed Saviour and Blessed Virgin Mary; for the use of the daughters of Sion; 2 parts, 8vo., 1665.

3.—The Draught of Eternity; a translation from the French of Bishop Camus, 8vo., 1632.

4.—Soliloquies of Thomas of Kempis; a translation dedicated to Lady Tredway, 12mo., Paris, 1653.

5.—Occasional Discourses; 1st, of Worship and Prayers to Angels and Saints; 2nd, of Purgatory; 3rd, of the Pope's Supremacy; 4th, of the Succession of the Church; chiefly—with Dr. Cosens, 8vo., Paris, 1646.

6.—A Treatise of the Love of God; a translation from the French of St. Francis of Sales, in 2 vols., 8vo., Paris, 1630.

7.—The Spiritual Conflict; a translation from the French of Bishop Camus, 1632.

8.—A Christian Institution; or Cardinal Richlieu's Catechism; a translation from the thirtieth edition, 8vo., Paris, 1662.

9.—Cardinal Richlieu's Controversies; a translation, 1662."

A tradition exists that the Pinkneys had fallen from the faith, and that Myles Pinkey was a brand snatched from the burning, being converted by seeing a man exorcised by a Catholic priest; and that afterwards he went to Douai. Whether the tradition is authentic or legendary, I know not; I had the statement from an authority which I respect and will not impugn. Some years ago an old man named Pinkney lived at or near Hill Top, in the neighbourhood of Ushaw, who was supposed to be a relation of Fr. Pinkney. Among the number of " Romanists and other Sectarians" proceeded against in the court of Dennis Granville, Dean and Archdeacon of Durham, from 1673 to 1677, in the parish of Eshe, occurs the name of Thomas Pinkney, sen., *Papist*.

THE COLLEGE JUBILEE.

We have now reached the stadium of fifty years, "*currit enim volubilis ætas*"—since S. Cuthbert's College was founded, since the exodus from Crook Hall and the wild and desolate country round about, took place, and the little colony of students entered the walls and corridors of Ushaw. It was on the 19th of July in the year 1858 that the Jubilee or fiftieth year of this auspicious event was commemorated, and this Jubilee was the culminating point of Mgr. Newsham's life. I had the honour of being present as one of the visitors and guests; hence—"I have some rights of memory in this kingdom;" and I flatter myself —*ævi non inscius veteris*" that the account which I then wrote of this festival, will not, after the lapse even of thirty years, have altogether lost its interest :—

> "*Quo semel est imbuta recens servabit odorem*
> *Testa diu.*"

There was high pageant in dear old Ushaw on the occasion of its Jubilee, and its joyful celebration will long be remembered. The feast of St. Vincent of Paul, on Monday, July 19th, A.D. 1858, was a bright sunny morning, and Ushaw rang with the notes and noise of preparation for the approaching solemnity. There was the tread of busy feet, the sounds of merry voices, and every heart beat high and rejoiced exceedingly. A mighty flag was planted in the centre of the playground, and floated triumphantly in the air. Another flag waved on the top of the south wing of the college, and others of smaller pretensions might be seen streaming here and there from different points of view. From the "green gates" or porter's lodge to the front door, a series of triumphal arches, formed of branches of trees and evergreens, and flowers, had been erected. They were surmounted with small flags, and the word "Welcome" traced in large letters, was conspicuous among their leafy garniture. The front door and steps were completely embowered in foliage and flowers, and immediately over the door was placed, tastefully bordered with flowers, and surmounted with the armorial bearings of the college, a tablet on which was inscribed "*Salvete hospites diem auspicatissimum celebraturi. Esto procul a limine quidquid nocet vel angit: quin vobis advenientibus occurrant pax et gaudium Dimidiatum sæculum quæ signat lux det felicem annis anteactis exitum, lætum venturis omen. Quare et vos domum intrantes omnia fausta adprecamini, et una mente atque voce conclamate—Havete vos.*" His Eminence Cardinal Wiseman, who took the liveliest interest in the festivities, was among the earliest arrivals, and was welcomed with music and cheers. His arrival was quickly followed by that of others, young and old mingling like the tribes of Israel in one great crowd, and in a full chorus of jubilee. Never were seen so many visitors, strangers, and alumni of *Alma Mater* in Ushaw's walls before. It was most cheering and delightful to witness the welcome accorded to old friends and acquaintances ; to note the mutual congratulations and hearty greetings that passed between them, and the old time memories, traditions, and associations, that their meeting of one another after years of absence awakened, and which like ghosts of the past crowded around them. Upwards of 200 additional beds had been provided, and the new Infirmary for the nonce had been converted into a dormitory. The house, as His Eminence the Cardinal observed, resembled more the commissariat of a regiment than a college, yet good order and arrangement prevailed in every place and department. Bishops, Provosts, heads of colleges, nobility, gentry, &c., were there; and together with His Eminence Cardinal Wiseman, were Dr. Briggs, Bishop of Beverley, Dr. Hogarth, Bishop of Hexham, Dr. Gillis, Vicar Apostolic of the eastern district of Scotland, Dr. Roskell, Bishop of Nottingham, Honble. Dr. Clifford, Bishop of Clifton, Dr. Amherst, Bishop of Northampton, Honble. and Right Rev. Monsgr. Talbot, Dr. Weedall, President of Oscott, Dr. Russell, President of Maynooth, Rev. H. Vaughan, Vice-President of St. Edmund's, &c., &c.

The festivities may be said to have commenced on the Monday evening, a concert being given in the Hall by the choir, the brass and string band of the college, consisting of 50 or more performers. Next day at 11 o'clock all met in the Hall to hear an address to his fellow students by one of their number, after which followed the reading up, and a musical performance "Les deux Aveugles." Then the meeting of the committee of the Jubilee Fund, by which a Theological Scholarship of £25 per annum was established. At 8 p.m. in the Hall were performed "Taming a Tiger," "The Chorus of Mr. Tomkin's Whitewashers," all more or less musical. Various scenes from "William Tell" were also performed with *éclat*. But the great day of the Jubilee Festival was Wednesday, July 21st. Immediately after breakfast the solemnisation of the Feast commenced with High Mass, celebrated by the Lord Bishop of Hexham, in presence of the Cardinal Archbishop and of the other assembled Bishops. What a magnificent procession of mitred Bishops, surpliced priests, and other ecclesiastics, issues from the sacristy, and, wending its way through the cloister, enters the choir of the Collegiate Chapel of St. Cuthbert! The Cardinal follows last with his full state of attendants, dispensing his blessing as he passes along: and, as if the age of chivalry were revived, Ed. Waterton, Esq., girded with his sword as a Knight of Malta, and in the military costume of that order, brings up the rear of the stately procession. Solemn Mass was then sung with thrilling music and glorious ceremonial. After the gospel His Eminence the Cardinal, taking his text from Leviticus, xxv., 10, delivered an eloquent discourse on the Jubilee which they had met to commemorate, and on the espousals about to take place between the college and its patron St. Cuthbert, by the solemn recognition, authentication, and veneration of St. Cuthbert's ring. The ring of gold enclosed a sapphire stone of great beauty; from the saint's shrine it passed at the Reformation to the last Catholic Dean of Durham; from him to Lord Viscount Montague, to Dr. Smith, Bishop of Chalcedon, to the English Canonesses at Paris, from them to Cardinal Wiseman, and from him to the college (Ushaw). After Mass, a meeting commemorative of the Jubilee, was held in the Public Hall, at which His Eminence presided. An introductory address written it is said by Cardinal Wiseman, and remarkably beautiful in its composition, was delivered by Mr. Arthur Wilberforce. The Right Rev. Dr. Gillis then came forward, and spoke of Ushaw and the Jubilee in a strain of great eloquence, and amidst enthusiastic cheers. Most vociferous however did those cheers become when, at the conclusion of the address, he claimed and obtained, it being the year of Jubilee, a prolongation of the annual vacation. The Very Rev. Canon Oakeley followed, and spoke on the subject of collegiate education; the Honble. Charles Langdale on the political history of Catholics during the last half century; the Very Rev. Dr. Russell on Dr. Lingard, the great literary glory of Ushaw, the historian, the scholar, and the priest, introducing also the subject of historical studies; Sir W. Lawson on Douai College and the foundation of St. Cuthbert's; the Very Rev. Dr. Manning on the future prospects of Ushaw during the next 50 years, and the influence it was probable this college would exert on the Catholic Church in England. The Cardinal wound up the several topics, and added a few of his own experiences and recollections of college life at Ushaw. He passed a warm eulogium on Dr. Lingard, and recorded several instances of Dr. Lingard's friendship and kindness towards him.

At the conclusion of his address the College Ode, by the Cardinal, was sung with orchestral music.

THE ODE.

No breezes play, no sunbeams smile
Throughout the length of Britain's isle,
Upon a more loved, honoured pile,
    Than this our college home ;
Heir of the rays, which no more shine
In Finchale's vale, on banks of Tyne,
Round holy Cuthbert's rifled shrine,
    On Bede's yet hallowed tomb.

CHORUS.—Then join in chorus, man and boy,
    Long reign in this our noble college,
    Celestial truth and earthly knowledge,
Study's toil, and virtue's joy.

We love our church, its image, stalls,
Our graceful chapels, noble halls,
Our ambulacra's pictured walls,
    Our library's rich lore ;
We love our ball-place, lake, and bounds,
Our merry games' perennial rounds,
The hubbub of their joyful sounds,
    Shouts, cheers, and laughter's roar.

CHORUS.

But hush ! good spirits fill the air :
They come our joy and love to share,
Great Lingard, Gibson, Gillow, Eyre,
    Who sleep beneath our sod,

And many a one, whose youthful head
Soon drooped above the tainted bed,
Then sank among the martyred dead :
    The path here taught who trod.

CHORUS.

Then up, up cheerily, dash we on !
Not words, but deeds, mark Ushaw's son ;
The world's wide battle field upon,
    With evil deadly strife !
In faith uncompromising zeal,
Devotion to our country's weal,
Charity, honour, virtue—seal,
    Brothers ! our coming life.

CHORUS.

The Jubilee Banquet next followed, when 600 sat down to dinner ; toasts were proposed in honour of Pius IX., and the venerable President, Mgr. Newsham. Evening came, and at 8 o'clock the Hall was filled with a dense assembly, anxious to witness the performance of "The Hidden Gem," a drama in two acts, written for the celebration of the Jubilee by an "an old collegian," (His Eminence Cardinal Wiseman). This drama, which is certainly a *gem*, and worthy in every respect of its illustrious author, was listened to with most intense interest. The several characters were excellently sustained, and frequent applause testified the approbation and delight of the audience. In one of the scenes occurs an exquisitely touching allusion to Ushaw, and the worthy President of the College, Dr. Newsham, and it was here the company rose *en masse* to cheer and applaud. At the end of the performance nine cheers were called for and given to the "old collegian." The festivities of the day were wound up by a magnificent display of fireworks in the front of the college. A perfect illumination was caused by them, the display terminating in a brilliant device, representing St. Cuthbert's cross, with the words "God bless St. Cuthbert's" emblazoned above it. Thursday was the College Festival. The company again met in the Hall when a concert took place, and scenes from "The Heir at Law" were enacted with much spirit and humour. The Annual Meeting of St. Cuthbert's Society was then held in the Reading Room, the Cardinal Archbishop presiding. Among its early patrons was the Cardinal, who in a letter to Dr. Newsham, says he thinks it a high honour to be counted among its patrons, and adds, " I cannot therefore consider the acceptance of the proposed office in any other light than of a duty of grateful affection, in return for the many advantages and blessings which I owe to St. Cuthbert's. I believe and hope that every one educated there will feel the same, and become members of a Society which will not only keep up through life the kindly feelings that should unite the sons of the same *Alma Mater*, but will enable them to secure and increase her well earned prosperity." The Cardinal Archbishop, and the President, having received the thanks of the meeting, the proceedings terminated. The Cardinal then distributed the prizes for classics, &c., remarking that the books received by them (the students) as prizes ought to be treasured up by them in their libraries as memorials of the Jubilee, as it was no small distinction to receive them in the year of that festival. A beautiful new medal had also been struck, commemorative of the Jubilee, which each successful student would receive. The medals, some silver, others bronze gilt, are very large and beautiful ones. On the obverse, is a bust of Cardinal Allen, the words " *Gulielmus Cardinalis Allanus*" being inscribed in the inner circle ; and in the outer circle " *In memoriam tanti viri Collegium apud Ushaw hoc præmium meriti excudi fecit, mdccclviii.*"—C. F. Voit, Rome.—On the reverse is represented the Blessed Virgin, with the infant Jesus, St. Cuthbert on her right hand, and St. Joseph on her left, the former presenting an ecclesiastical, the latter a lay student. At the top of the medal is the inscription "*Hic est filius meus dilectus, ipsum audite ;*" below, "*Da mihi sedium tuarum adsistricem sapientiam.*"

When the Cardinal had finished distributing the prizes he declared the Jubilee at an end, feeling sure that all had been delighted. The present was the root of a great future, and augured well for the prosperity and renown of St. Cuthbert's. The Lord Bishop of Hexham, amid loud cheering, thanked the company for their attendance on that joyful occasion. The Lord Bishop of Clifton returned thanks on behalf of the visitors, for the honour and the hospitality which they had received. This was the first occasion he had visited Ushaw, but it was a memorable occasion of which he should long cherish the remembrance.

At the meeting in the College Hall, to commemorate the Jubilee, on the Wednesday of the Great Week, His Eminence the Cardinal announced to E. W. Pugin, Esq., architect, who was present, that on the previous day, a Brief Apostolic, sent by Cardinal Antonelli to Mgr. Talbot, had arrived from His Holiness the Pope, addressed to Mr. Pugin, making him on account of his distinguished talents and services to religion, a Knight of the Order of St. Silvester. The announcement was received with cheers and congratulations.

Subjoined is a copy of the Programme issued on occasion of the Jubilee Festival:—A. M. D. G.—Programme of the Annual Festival and celebration of the Jubilee of St. Cuthbert's College, Ushaw, July 20th, 21st, and 22nd, 1858, the fiftieth year since the opening of the college.—Tuesday, July 20th.—Eve of the Jubilee.— Eleven a. m. —Public Meeting in the Hall, *Cohortatio ad condiscipulos; Solemnis locorum assignatio post confectum studiorum curriculum.*— Music, and a French piece (morceau comico-musical,) entitled "Les deux Aveugles."—Half-past One (after luncheon) :—Meeting of the committee for the Jubilee Fund in the Reading Room.—Five.— Dinner.—Eight.—Meeting in the Hall, concert, scenes from "William Tell."—Half-past Nine (after tea) night prayers.—Wednesday, 21st.— The Jubilee Festival.—Nine (after breakfast) Solemn High Mass, *(coram Episcopo,)* and in the presence of His Eminence the Cardinal Archbishop of Westminster, who will preach, and of the other assembled Bishops. After Mass will take place the solemn recognition, authentication, and veneration of St. Cuthbert's ring.—Eleven.—Commemorative meeting in the Hall, introductory address by a student, addresses by friends of the college, clergy, and laymen, "The College Ode," the words composed by His Eminence Cardinal Wiseman, the music, with full orchestral accompaniment, by Mr. John Richardson.—Three.—Dinner in the New Museum.—Eight.—Meeting in the Hall, performance of "The Hidden Gem," a drama in two acts, written for the occasion, by an old collegian. At night prayers, the *Te Deum*.—Thursday, 22nd.—The College Festival, exhibition, and distribution of prizes.—Ten.—Meeting in the Hall, concert, and scenes from "The Heir at Law."—Twelve.—Annual Meeting of St. Cuthbert's Society, in the Reading Room.—Half-past One.—Meeting in the Hall, distribution of medals and prizes, by His Eminence Cardinal Wiseman; and proclamation of the candidates for classical and mathematical honours.—Three.—Dinner in the college Refectory.—L. D. S. This Programme is intended to convey to the receiver of it a special invitation to attend the week of the Jubilee, with a most earnest request of a reply, whether he can give the honour of his attendance or not.—Charles Newsham, D.D., President.—St. Cuthbert's College, June 21st, 1858.

Feasts and festivals like all temporal and sublunary things come at length to an end—"*nihil est annis velocius,*"— and Ushaw's grand Jubilee passed away and became an epoch in history. In zeal for the glory and exaltation of Ushaw, in solicitude for the welfare of the students, and in order to keep alive that spirit of piety, docility, and obedience, which existed among them, and which it had always been the end and aim of his life to foster, Dr. Newsham persevered with unabated and patient energy to the end. The last noticeable incident in his eventful life was to secure for the college, through the recommendation and agency of Mgr. Talbot, a magnificent collection of Sacred Relics, which were in possession of a private individual at Naples. "The Roman Basilicas," said Mgr. Talbot, writing to Dr. Newsham, "have not a finer, nay, not so fine a collection." After some preliminary arrangement, the Relics became the property of St. Cuthbert's, and arrived at the college on May 21st, 1860, being met at the lodge by a solemn procession of the students, singing the Litany of the Saints. Mgr. Talbot further remarks, "I cannot help thinking that the Saints, whose Relics you will possess, will redouble their prayers for the conversion of England." The Chapel of the Holy Family was prepared for their reception, and on the Feast of St. Boniface, June 5th, 1861, was celebrated their translation to their new resting place. Pontifical High Mass was sung by the Bishop of the diocese, the Right Rev. Dr. Hogarth, and a sermon on devotion to the Saints was preached by the Rev. Ed. Consitt. After a procession round the ambulacra, in which the principal Relics were carried by the Bishop and clergy, they were enshrined in the Chapel of the Holy Family, where they still remain, with the exception of a few which have been transferred to the Chapel of St. Aloysius. A descriptive and very useful catalogue of the Relics has been compiled and published by the Rev. Robert Laing, one of the Professors at the college. Excluding the names of our Lord and the Blessed Virgin, the list contains the names of 480 Saints. There are 20 Relics of our Lord, 3 of our Blessed Lady, and of the Saints, 860; so that the total number of separate Relics is 883. "*Dominus custodit omnia ossa sanctorum.*" Two generous benefactors, the Misses Orrell, of Blackbrook, piously came forward and aided Mgr. Newsham to acquire these precious treasures.

The venerable President, as was said of blessed Stephen, Abbot of Citeaux, "had stoutly administered the office committed to him, and having passed the great trials of life, he now lived in comparative peace, quietly watching the growth of the mighty tree into which the grain of mustard seed had grown." But the allotted term of his life was hastening to its close. The day was far spent, the evening was come, his dissolution was at hand. Having therefore reached the last line in the last chapter of Dr. Newsham's memorable life—"*mors est ultima linea rerum,*"—little now remains to add, except to record the death of the worthy and illustrious old Doctor. It is right he should sleep in peace and take his rest, for he has fought a good fight, and supported the tribulations of life with fortitude and patience ; he has finished his course and accomplished the work he was set to do ; he has kept the faith, and has trained up a chosen generation, a kingly priesthood, to transmit and teach it to others ; hence for him we trust "is laid up a crown of justice."

"Man's portion is to die and rise again—"

depart therefore and sleep in peace. In a meditation on death attributed to Dr. Newsham, and entitled "Peace to men of good will, and their death made sweet," occur such words of holy import as "Sweet Mother Mary ! I have long since put my death under thy special patronage. Death is the only friend that will bring me to the God of my heart ! and shall I not desire to die ?" "To die is nothing else than to live ; to die is my gain—the gain of my God and my all—the morning star of my happy eternity." Sweetly and peaceably, on Sunday night, the 1st of February, 1863, at the age of seventy-one years, Dr. Newsham breathed his last—"*placida tum morte quievit ;*"

"So gently gliding round the curvature
Of life from youth to age,"

he passed from this land of exile to his true country, to his Father's house, in which there are many mansions. Enfeebled by long infirmity, his death was neither sudden nor unexpected, and as a shock of corn in the golden harvest time, he was gathered to his fathers, ripe in years and virtue.

The Right Rev. President was a native of Lancashire, having been born at Westby, in the Fylde— a country where the old heroic race of men, heroes of priestly fortitude, were nurtured, and, who leaving the homes of their ancestors, departed to mature their vocation, and to be trained for the ecclesiastical state. The first years of Mgr. Newsham's ecclesiastical education were passed at Crook Hall, and after the foundation in 1808 of the new college, at Ushaw, he removed with the professors and the rest of the students from Crook to St. Cuthbert's. The late venerable Bishop of Beverley, the Right Rev. Dr. Briggs was one of his schoolfellows. He had three brothers who were priests— Revs. Matthew, Joseph, and Robert Newsham. Matthew Newsham died at Houghton Hall, Yorks., May 20, 1848, Joseph Newsham, S.J., at Stonyhurst, February 8, 1849, in his 68th year, and Robert Newsham, at Dorchester, about the year 1859 or 1860. Having completed his course of Philosophy and Theology, Dr. Newsham, after being ordained priest, remained at the college, holding successively various professorships, then the office of Vice-President, and in the year 1837, on Dr. Youens's resignation, he was appointed President. All who are acquainted with Ushaw know with what wonderful efficiency and zeal, with what superior talent and discretion he administered that important office; all know the affection and reverence in which he was held, not only by those under his immediate charge, but by all others who approached him, or had the happiness of his acquaintance.* To great and fervent piety the Doctor united a deep store of wisdom, and possessed a remarkably well informed and highly cultivated mind. The interests of Ushaw, the prosperity of Ushaw, were paramount with him, and he might have said, in the words of Cicero in Lælio—"*mihi autem non minori curæ est qualis respublica post meam mortem futura sit, quam qualis hodie sit.*" I well remember the joy, and gratitude, and affectionate greeting with which, both on the occasion of his own and of the College Jubilee, he welcomed to *Alma Mater* so many of her sons, and so many distinguished guests. He considered, and insisted that it was the duty of the college and all who held office in it to be hospitable, kind, and considerate towards all friends and visitors. This duty the late kind and respected Procurator, Rev. Thomas Croskell, failed not to perform, conformably with Dr. Newsham's enlightened teaching. Writing to me in 1855, the Doctor says—"It was a very great pleasure to me, and to us all, to see you at Ushaw: I am sure we were all quite as much pleased with you, as you were with us. We shall at all times be delighted to see you."

Having finished his pilgrimage, and passed from the domain of time into that of eternity—"man shall go into the house of his eternity," his funeral obsequies were performed with becoming honour, and with solemn and sacred rites his remains were committed to the grave. A resting place was prepared to receive them in the Mortuary Chapel, dedicated to St. Michael, access to which is through an arched doorway, and down a short flight of steps on the north side of the cloister, near the Ante-Chapel door. Two marble slabs, inscribed with brass lettering M. ✠ G. 1856, and C. ✠ N. 1863, mark the vaults under the floor of this chapel, in which the Very Rev. Michael Gibson, D.D., and the Right Rev. Mgr. Newsham, D.D., are interred. Mural tablets on each side of the door, inlaid with crosses of brass, are inscribed as follows:—

---

*The late Sergeant Murphy who was in part educated at Ushaw, and went the Northen Circuit, when at Durham used always to visit his old friend Dr. Newsham. On one occasion, when a Sunday occurred during the Assizes, one of the Barristers asked Murphy what he was going to do with himself that day. The Sergeant said he was going to visit his old friend Dr. Newsham, at Ushaw. "What can there be in common between you and that old priest at Ushaw?" exclaimed his legal friend. "My dear fellow," replied Murphy, "You don't know that every saint has his pet sinner." For this anecdote I am indebted to the "Oscotian." I remember Frank Murphy, at Ushaw; I was in the class of Underlow; he was in Philosophy. Frank had the reputation of being a great wag. He was a clever Greek scholar, and agile and dexterous at most of the games.

"Signifer S. Michael representet eum in lucem sanctam. Revdus. admodum Dominus Michael Gibson, D.D., Canonicus Diœceseos Hagulstadensis, Vice-Præses Collegii Sti. Cuthberti, obiit Die XXVII. Augusti, A.D. MDCCCLVI. Ætatis suæ XL."

A kneeling figure of Dr. Newsham has a label on which is inscribed—

"Sancte Cuthberte, Protector noster Respice Gregem tuum. Revmus. Dnus. Carolus Newsham, S.T.D., Sanctitatis suæ Pii IX., S.P. Prælatus Domesticus, Collegii hujus Sancti Cuthberti annos fere XXVII. Præses, ejusdem Fundator alter merito dicendus, pie obiit in Vigilia Purificationis B. M. V., Anno Dni. MDCCCLXIII. Ætat. LXXII. Cujus Animæ propitietur Deus."

Precious was the death of these two holy priests. They loved each other mutually in life, and in death they were not divided. There was a very large attendance of alumni and friends of the college at Dr. Newsham's funeral—specially large considering the time and season of the year, when the weather is cold, and the days are short. The venerable Bishop Hogarth and other Bishops were there; Provost Cookson also, who came from Lancashire to testify his respect to the memory of his deceased friend.

I conclude this notice of Mgr. Newsham with the following extract from the preliminary account of the College Jubilee, prefixed to "The Hidden Gem," composed for that occasion by His Eminence Cardinal Wiseman :—"Of all the marvels which that half century had wrought, none, perhaps, was greater than the marvel of St. Cuthbert's itself. A college, no unworthy compeer of the noblest of our mediæval institutions, had spread its goodly amplitude. A magnificent chapel, with its cluster of tributary oratories, a noble library, a museum of vast length, a refectory of stately proportions, a spacious theatre of literary exhibition, ample rooms, lines of dormitories, and almost a mileage of cloister, had sprung up as if by miracle." Yes, all had sprung up, and Dr. Newsham was the magician's wand which called them into existence.

RIGHT REV. MGR. TATE, D.D.

"A man of worthy life, excellently well learned, pleasant in talk, gentle in manners"—

"*Doctor pius et insignis.*"

I know not how I can in more appropriate terms characterise the Right Rev. Mgr. Tate, D.D., the next President of Ushaw, than in the words which I have prefixed to this memoir of him. Robert Tate was born on St. Andrew's day, November 30th, A.D. 1800, hence he used to say his age kept pace with the age of the century. He was a native of York—no mean city, the most ancient of British cities, the Eboracum of the Romans, and the principal seat of their dominion in Britain. Here Hadrian lived, and Severus died; here too died Constantine Chlorus the father of Constantine the Great, the first Christian emperor, supposed to have been born here. At York resided St. Helen, the empress; and the most distinguished scholar of the 8th century, Alcuin, the friend of Charlemagne, was born here, about the year 735. " In my youth," said Alcuin, " I sowed the seeds of learning in the prosperous seminaries of Britain; and now in my old age I am doing so in France, without ceasing, praying that the grace of God may bless them in both countries." For its Bishops York had St. Chad, St. John of Beverley, St. Paulinus; the heroic and magnanimous Saxon, St. Wilfrid, the venerable Thurstan, who founded the Abbey of Fountains, and St. William of sacred memory. Blessed Cardinal John Fisher was a native of Yorkshire, born at Beverley. The first metropolitan church in England, which finally developed and grew in beauty, till it became an august and noble temple—the present York Minster, was built here: it was commenced by Edwin, king of Northumbria, and finished by St. Oswald. The first English Parliament was held at York in 1160 by Henry II. The British Association for the Advancement of Science was organized at York in 1831. In the list of martyrs who suffered death on account of their religion, York furnished a noble army, not only of holy priests, but of men and women—saints of God, who went forth "with dyed garments from Bosra," crowned with the glory of martyrdom. Of York's renowned city and its antiquities; of Yorkshire's pastoral hills, old woods, and verdant dales; its rivers, its valleys, its ancient castles, and ruined abbeys, Dr. Tate used to speak with manifest delight and attachment—

"Nescio qua natale solum dulcedine cunctos
Ducit, et immemores non sinit esse sui."

Robert Tate, in the twelfth year of his age, quitted his native home in York's ancient city to commence his studies for the priesthood at St. Cuthbert's College. His talents were of a very high order; his application to study, his diligence, love of learning, and eagerness to acquire knowledge could not be exceeded. According to the Ushaw diary he was in 1818 in Natural Philosophy, and in the same college year 1818-19, he became, on the 11th of April, Professor of Grammar. In 1820, at the age of twenty he is teaching Rhetoric, and received the tonsure On the 21st September, 1823, he was raised to the Priesthood; was made Prefect of Studies in 1825; in 1826 taught Moral Philosophy; and was Vice-President from 1828 to 1830. In the latter year, August 9th, he went on the mission to Whitby; thence in 1831 to Sheffield; from Sheffield in 1833 to Hazlewood. In the month of September, 1839, he returned to Ushaw and again became Vice-President, which office he held till 1849, and conjointly with it, from the departure of the Rev. R. Platt to Rev. F. Wilkinson's appointment, he discharged the duties of Prefect of Studies. In 1849 he again left the college to resume the duties of missionary life at Hedon and again at Hazlewood. Shortly after the death of Mgr. Newsham, Dr. Tate was appointed to succeed him. Writing to me from Hazlewood, February 28th, 1863, he says, " I hope to be at Ushaw on Tuesday next, March 2nd, where in memory of days long gone by, it will always be a pleasure to see you." Affairs at Ushaw, under Dr. Tate's rule, proceeded smoothly and auspiciously. The college continued to prosper, and the number of students to increase. The President was much loved and esteemed, for he was kind, considerate, and indulgent. In the fourth year of his Presidency an event occurred that will long be remembered and recorded in the annals of Ushaw. It was in the year 1866, and the first day of August in that year was rendered memorable on account of the visit paid to the college by His Eminence Charles Augustus von Reisach, Cardinal Priest of the Holy Roman Church of St. Cecilia, Prefect of the Congregation of Studies, &c. ; and His Grace the Most Rev. Henry Edward Manning, Archbishop of Westminster—a most happy inauguration of Dr. Tate's Presidency. Leaving Stonyhurst College on Wednesday morning, where they had been on a visit, attending the day previous the celebration of the Feast of St. Ignatius, they travelled by Normanton, York, and Darlington, and between four and five o'clock reached Durham, the city of St. Cuthbert,

" Where his cathedral, huge and vast,
Looks down upon the Wear."

They were met at Durham station by the Very Rev. Dr. Tate, and the Very Rev. Professor Canon Consitt, and thence in a carriage drawn by four greys, were conveyed to St. Cuthbert's College. They arrived at the college at a quarter past five. The bells rang ; professors, students, and visitors, hastened to pay their respects to the distinguished guests, and to receive on bended knees their blessing. They had come "to crown Ushaw's Academic Year," and they received an Ushaw welcome. Immediately on their arrival a procession was formed to the church, and the Cardinal and the Archbishop were met at the doors by cross bearer and acolytes, and presented with holy water. The solemn strains of the organ burst forth, and the two dignitaries, attended by Dr. Tate in a rich cope, having entered the sanctuary and adored the Blessed Sacrament, the *Te Deum* was sung by the united voices of the choir and the students. With this truly ecclesiastical reception Cardinal Reisach and Archbishop Manning expressed themselves highly gratified. Shortly afterwards dinner was liberally and sumptuously served in the college refectory, grace being said by His Eminence the Cardinal. The evening's entertainment, at which the two distinguished prelates were present, and who, on entering the Exhibition Hall, were loudly cheered, was the "Merchant of Venice." The entertainment was eminently successful, Shakespere having evidently been well read and studied by the actors. In fact we heard one of the Ushaw *corps dramatique* afterwards declare that he considered no education perfect without a knowledge of Shakespere, and no household complete without a copy of his works. Thursday was the crowning day of all, when the distribution of honours, medals, and prizes, and the meeting and dinner of St. Cuthbert's Society took place. At half-past seven o'clock, High Mass was celebrated by the Archbishop, and a High Mass at Ushaw on such occasions is accompanied with imposing ceremonial and solemnity. After Mass the *Te Deum* was chanted. Previous to the guests sitting down to breakfast, an exceedingly rich and elegant chasuble, presented to the college by the Rev. Michael Trappes, of Hull, was exhibited. It belonged to Cuthbert Tunstal, the last Catholic Bishop of Durham—1530—1559—and the thirty-sixth in succession from Aldhune—995. From the family of the Tunstals it had passed into that of the Trappes. The vestment was regarded with much curiosity, and was much admired. Soon after ten o'clock, the Exhibition Hall was filled with the visitors, professors, and students, for the purpose of witnessing the distribution of honours, medals, and prizes. The Cardinal and the Archbishop were present, being greeted on their entrance with enthusiastic cheers. Mr. Charles Croskell, in an exhortation to his schoolfellows—"*Cohortatio ad Condiscipulos*"—begged to be allowed, in his own name and in the name of all the students, to thank in the first place the most eminent and illustrious Cardinal, for gracing by his presence their festivities, and doing such honour to Ushaw by his visit, beseeching His Eminence to convey to the feet of His Holiness the Pope the earnest expression of their love and duty, and their heartfelt devotion and fidelity to the Holy See; praying also that he would obtain for the college the Holy Father's blessing. The speaker then turned to His Grace the Archbishop, and thanked him also for his kind condescension in coming amongst them, and for the honour which he had done them by his distinguished visit. The occasion of the visit of two such illustrious personages will be long remembered at *Alma Mater*.

The reading up of places obtained by each student in the several classes next took place, and the medals and prizes were subsequently distributed to the successful competitors by His Eminence the Cardinal. The prizes having been awarded, the Archbishop addressed the assembled students—both successful and unsuccessful competitors, inculcating the importance of study and application, and furnishing them with some excellent instructions on the method of study. Attention, intention, and intensity, were three words, three points of meditation, which he wished to impress upon their consideration, and which he hoped they would dwell upon not only during the vacation, but ever afterwards. On these several points the Archbishop eloquently enlarged, and he was listened to with most earnest attention. The Cardinal also addressed the students in Latin on the importance of uniting piety with learning. He stated that he had experienced the greatest pleasure in coming amongst them, and had been inexpressibly delighted with all that he had seen and heard in his visit to Ushaw. He assured them that he would take the earliest opportunity on his return to Rome to make the Holy Father acquainted with their devotion and fidelity, and to lay before him their wishes and their prayers.

The annual meeting of St. Cuthbert's Society was then held in the public reading room. The Very Rev. Dr. Tate presided, and the meeting was attended by the Cardinal and the Archbishop, who both kindly consented to become patrons of the Society. Dr. Tate expressed the great pleasure he felt in opening the twelfth annual meeting of the Society in presence of the eminent and illustrious Cardinal, and of His Grace the Archbishop of Westminster. It was an honour to the Society to have present amongst them two such illustrious visitors, and he considered it an augury and an earnest of the Society's success. The Very Rev. Provost Platt, in the name of St. Cuthbert's Society, thanked the Cardinal and the Archbishop for honouring their meeting by their presence, and expressed a hope that, as it was now a long time since a foreign Cardinal had paid a visit to the shrine of St. Cuthbert, in Durham Cathedral, His Eminence would take that opportunity, in company with the Archbishop, of visiting the shrine of that great Saint. The Cardinal briefly expressed his acknowledgments, and the Archbishop, in returning thanks, spoke in very high terms of St. Cuthbert's as an educational and ecclesiastical establishment, stating that since his first visit—twelve years ago—his heart had been with Ushaw in all sincerity and sympathy. The dinner of St. Cuthbert's Society afterwards took place in the college refectory, where nearly 100 guests were entertained. The Very Rev. the President took the chair, having the Cardinal on his right, and on his left the Archbishop. The Most Rev. Dr. Manning having proposed the health of His Holiness the Pope, which was most enthusiastically received, begged to give the health of the Very Rev. Dr. Tate, the President of Ushaw, and the worthy successor of him whose portrait they saw before them, the Right Rev. Monsignor Newsham, D.D. They had all had unmistakeable proofs of his courtesy and kindness, and had all experienced his generous hospitality. He deserved to receive *laude plena et sonora* their grateful thanks, and most justly might it be said of him what Horace said of Proculeius, the Roman knight—

" *Vivet extento Proculeius ævo,
Notus in fratres animi paterni.*"

Dr. Tate's health was drunk with rapturous applause, and he thanked the Archbishop and the company in feeling and eloquent words. The college bell at eight o'clock summoned the students to the Hall. It was an unexpected summons, but the secret soon oozed out. The Archbishop appeared amongst them, and amid uproarious cheers announced that at the request of the Cardinal, the President had been pleased to grant them an additional week of vacation, extending it to Michalmas term, the 29th of September. " *Viva il Cardinale*" re-echoed on all sides. After this joyful surprise, nothing but light-heartedness and congratulations prevailed, until it was time to repair to the church, when Solemn Benediction was given by His Eminence, at which the Archbishop assisted. Next morning early, Ushaw's ingenuous youths bade farewell for awhile to the yew tree's shade, to their games, to their books, and to their class rooms, to enjoy the society of their parents and friends, and the recreation of prolonged holidays:

" *Ite domum pastæ, nunc ite capellæ.*"

Having " browsed on the thyme and the cytisus of the Durham hills," now that summer had come with fervent heat, and flowers, and fruitfulness, these happy youths—the flock of Ushaw's fold—had departed, and gone to seek another range of pasture and other herbage; had repaired to the shade of the arbutus, to the mossy fountains, and to grass more soft than sleep—

" *Muscosi fontes, et somno mollior herba,
Et qua vos rara viridis tegit arbutus umbra.*"

On the same day Cardinal Reisach and Archbishop Manning, accompanied by Dr. Tate, proceeded to Durham to visit the Cathedral, the Castle, &c. They also paid their respects to the Dean, and to the Very Rev. Provost Platt, the Vicar Capitular of the Diocese of Hexham and Newcastle. On their return to Ushaw the Cardinal planted a yew tree in front of the college as a memorial of his visit—

Be it thy care, soft spirit of the gale !
To fan its leaves in summer's noontide hour ;
Be it thy care that wintry tempests fail
To rend its honours from the sylvan bower.
Then shall it spread, and rear th' aspiring form,
Pride of the wood, secure from every storm,
And grow, as years roll on, a consecrated tree.

His Eminence Cardinal Charles Augustus von Reisach was born on the 6th of July, 1800, at Roth, near Eichstadt, in Bavaria, and was created Cardinal in 1855. He subsequently became Cardinal Bishop of Sabina, and was Prefect of the Sacred Congregation of Studies, at Rome. His secretary, Monsignor Luigi Matera, honorary Private Chaplain to His Holiness, and assistant in the secretary's office of ecclesiastical affairs, accompanied him. His *cameriere* was also in attendance upon him. The Cardinal by his affability and kindness won the hearts of all who were brought in contact with, or introduced to him ; and his impressions and hopes of England were most favourable. He died about the year 1870.

Pass a few years, and the Golden Jubilee of the venerable and respected President's elevation to the Priesthood arrived. Fifty years since his ordination in 1823 had elapsed, and occasion was taken to celebrate the event with thanksgiving, festivity, and rejoicing. The alumni of St. Cuthbert's, the friends of Dr. Tate flocked from the remotest parts, anxious to join in the celebration—

"*Sit hæc dies festa nobis,*
Sæculorum sæculis ;
Sit sacrata, digna laude,
Nec senescat tempore."

Venerable dignitaries of the church, archbishops and bishops, priests grown grey with age and missionary labour, priests in the vigour and prime of manhood, and others—younger toilers in the vineyard— these, with a large number of Catholic gentlemen, assembled at *Alma Mater* to commemorate the jubilee, or fiftieth anniversary which the Right Rev. Mgr. Tate, D.D., the President of the college, had completed of his priesthood. They came to testify to that worthy and distinguished prelate their respect and devotion, to tender him their warmest congratulations, to wish him with full sincerity of heart, health and length of days ; and by their presence withal to manifest their fidelity and attachment to St. Cuthbert's, where most part of them had been educated in all goodly learning. Hence this gathering of friends, this congregation of people who surrounded Ushaw's venerable president—a people faithful and true to the traditions which they had there learnt—*viz.*, of honour and respect for superiors, of love for holy Church, and of submission to the authority of Rome and its teaching. All these—old students and schoolfellows, classed together from Under-, low to Philosophy —some of them even companions and associates to the end of their ecclesiastical course, gladly availed themselves of this occasion to repair to *Alma Mater*, tending thitherward as to the home of their youth like divisional streams which, having gushed from the mountain side, murmur and meander through glen and glade, fret and foam over rock and precipice, and onward roll with expansive current through plain and valley until they find repose in the ocean which receives them.

> "*L'onda dal mar divisa*
> *Bagna la valle e'l monte;*
> *Va passiagiera*
> *In fiume,*
> *Va prigionera*
> *In fonte;*
> *Mormora sempre e geme*
> *Fin che non torna al mar;*
> *Al mar dov'ella nacque,*
> *Dove acquisto gli umori,*
> *Dove da lunghi errori*
> *Spera di riposar.*"

The rejoicings in honour of Dr. Tate's jubilee commenced on the 14th day of October, 1873, and during two days' celebration there were present no fewer than 200 persons. Lancashire was most respectably represented by its two bishops—the Right Rev. Dr. Vaughan, Bishop of Salford, and the Right Rev. Dr. O'Reilly, Bishop of Liverpool—numbers of its clergy, and many lay gentlemen. Among the priests was the Very Rev. Dr. Hall, of Macclesfield. He commenced his studies at Tudhoe, continued them at Crook Hall, and completed them at Ushaw. There were also present the Most Rev. Archbishops Errington and Eyre; the Right Rev. Dr. Chadwick, Bishop of Hexham and Newcastle; the Right Rev. Dr. Brown, Bishop of Newport and Menevia; and the Right Rev. Dr. Cornthwaite, Bishop of Beverley. The two archbishops and three of the bishops received their education at St. Cuthbert's.

The Right Rev. President, Dr. Tate, round whom friends in such numbers assembled to offer him their affectionate congratulations, and their tribute of grateful respect, came a boy to Ushaw, on the 16th of July, 1812. From the period of his entering college as a boy to the date of his installation as President, what a series and succession of changes had he not lived to witness!

"*Omnia, proh! quantum longis mutantur in annis.*"

To the college he had seen added a magnificent church, chapels, altars, and oratories; a splendid library, museum, and academic hall; he had seen the new seminary arise, a new infirmary built, the long vistas of cloisters extended and decked with works of art, the refectory enlarged and beautified, spacious farm and other buildings erected, plantations around and coeval with the college grown up into sheltering woods, the number of students increased threefold, and the staff of professors in proportion, while learning and piety, advancing hand in hand, had flourished with most satisfactory and gladdening results. Then, in his peaceful seclusion at college and while on the mission, he had beheld his fellow Catholics restored to freedom, and their captivity turned "like a torrent in the south;" and after a long and dreary winter it had rejoiced his heart to behold the church rehabilitated and arrayed in springtide freshness and verdure, lengthening its cords, extending its stakes, and like the "lopped tree," budding anew, and spreading its branches far and wide—

"The Spring rose on the garden fair,
Like the spirit of love felt everywhere,
And each flower and herb, on earth's dark breast,
Awoke from the dreams of its winter's rest."

He had seen the glory of the hierarchy restored, converts added to the fold, the number of the faithful multiplied, churches and chapels, schools, convents, and other institutions spread over the length and breadth of the land, and places "that have been waste from of old," restored and raised up from their ruins. It is true old friends had departed, and passed away "like shadows o'er the hearth ;—"

"They are gone, they are fled, they are parted all."

To his surviving friends it was most gratifying to notice how hale, fresh, and vigorous Dr. Tate in his seventy-fourth year appeared. Most true it is

"*Ampliat ætatis spatium vir bonus ;—*"

and as a belated flower, says an old writer, blooming during the fall of the leaf rejoices the gardener's heart, so shines a wise old age in the wilderness of life. From early youth Mgr. Tate, knowing well that wisdom is far above rubies, had been constantly applying his mind to acquire it. With Baptist, the Mantuan, it was permitted him to say,

"*Plurima perlegi, didici, docuique, nec ullum,
Dum licuit, studii tempus inane fuit.*"

It is related of Suger, Abbot of St. Denis, that his eloquence and learning were so great, that not only could he quote the Fathers, but even could repeat two or three hundred lines together of Horace by heart. With the Fathers and the old classic authors Dr. Tate had held continual converse; their study had been to him a source of recreation and delight, and their writings as famlliar to him as household words.

To proceed with my narrative of the jubilee. Two days were devoted to its celebration, and on each day the weather was all that could be wished for. Autumn had decked the woods and thickets in gold and russet vesture, and hill and valley, rustic lane, hedgerow, and orchard, were robed in rich and varied embroidery. On every side the landscape exhibited features of beauty—the bright but mournful beauty of October. On the second day, the feast of St. Teresa, October 15th, the students, guests, and visitors assembled early in the church, and Pontifical High Mass was celebrated by the Bishop of Hexham and Newcastle, at which the two Archbishops, and the rest of the Bishops assisted, each attended by a chaplain. Mass over, a solemn *Te Deum* was sung by the choir. The company afterwards proceeded to the refectory for breakfast. At mid-day, the presentation of the jubilee memorial window to the President took place in the same refectory, at which all the visitors, Archbishops, Bishops, &c., and the whole of the students were present. This window adorns the west end of the refectory. It is a splendid window, filled with stained glass, and consists of six main lights divided by a transom, with tracery above, and is of the late fourteenth century period of architecture, the glass having been designed and executed in strict accordance with it by Messrs. J. Hardman and Co., Birmingham. The treatment that has been adopted for the window is a single figure one. The six upper lights are filled with the patron saints of the six presidents of the college, together with the names and dates of their appointment and termination of office. Reading from the right they are as follow :—1. St. John the Baptist, in memory of Rev. John Daniel, who was the connecting link between Douai College and Ushaw. 2. St. Thomas the Apostle, patron saint of the Rev. Thomas Eyre, the first president of Ushaw (1808), and successor at Crook Hall of the Rev. John Daniel, the last president of Douai. 3. St. John the Evangelist, patron saint of the Rev. John Gillow, D.D., the second president—from 1811 to 1828. 4. St. Thomas of Canterbury, the patron saint of the Rev. Thomas Youens, D.D., president from 1828 to 1833, and again from 1836 to 1837. 5. St. John of Beverley, patron saint of the Right Rev. Dr. Briggs, president from 1833 to 1836. 6. St. Charles Borromeo, patron saint of the Right Rev. Mgr. Charles Newsham, D.D., president from 1837 to 1863. Of the lower tier only the second and fifth lights are at present filled with figures, the second with St. Andrew the Apostle, the patron saint of the Right Rev. Mgr. Tate, D.D., the scroll underneath being inscribed with the words "*Nunc feliciter regnans*—made President in 1863—*orate pro felici statu Roberti Tate.*" The fifth light has the figure of St. Cuthbert, the patron saint of the college. It is intended to fill the four remaining lights at some future time with the patron saints of the succeeding presidents, but they are at present treated with quarries richly powdered, alternately with St. Cuthbert's cross and *fleur de lis*, the heads of the lights terminating in handsome foliage on colour, through which runs an inscription. The centre of these four lights also contains a medallion having a large St. Cuthbert's cross on colour. The four principal openings of the tracery contain the arms of Cardinal Allen, Douai College, Ushaw College, and of the diocese of Hexham and Newcastle. The whole of the lights are bordered with the coneys taken from the arms of the college. Besides this memorial window, the presentation included six splendid gaseliers by Messrs. Hardman, and are fine specimens of ecclesiastical art. They were designed for the college refectory and represent a St. Cuthbert's cross, the arms of the cross being each inscribed with the motto "*Christi Crux est mea Lux*," and from each end of the arms springing a rich cluster of lights. Under the stained glass window, in order to complete the memorial, is placed a brass plate, with appropriate inscription, that the fact of its having been presented to the President may be commemorated and made known to posterity. The refectory of which the ceiling had recently been richly decorated with the coats of arms of the bishops and others connected with the college, is a magnificent room, 100 feet long, 38 feet wide, and 25 feet high. The floor is laid with white Sicilian and black Galway marble. There are seven two-light windows, and two with three lights. The President's window at the west end I have already described. The shields of various benefactors are emblazoned on the several windows, and the walls are adorned with portraits—most of them life-size. Among the portraits is a splendid full length figure of his Holiness Pope Pius IX. It was painted by Durani, and represents his Holiness walking on Monte Mario, holding up his hand as in the act of blessing the people. He is attired in scarlet cloak, hat, and shoes, with white soutane, and pectoral cross. There is a majesty in his step, a sweetness and affability in his countenance, and the whole contour of the figure, the drapery—its colour and arrangement—are exquisite. The portrait was purchased by Bishop Chadwick for the college during his sojourn at Rome, attending the Vatican Council. His Holiness through Dr. Chadwick sent to St. Cuthbert's his own copy of the Raccolta of indulgenced prayers. It is richly bound in red morocco, with the Papal arms upon it. Instead of simply inscribing his name in the book, as he was asked to do, he wrote these words,— "*Indulgeat Deus debita vestra, et liberet vos a malo.*" Being staunch "Infallibilists" at Ushaw, they sent an address through their Bishop, praying that the doctrine might be forthwith defined in its full integrity. The Pope was much consoled by the warm-hearted expressions of their faithfulness, remarking that Ushaw had always been most devoted to the Holy See, and he desired the Bishop (Dr. Chadwick) to convey to the President, Professors, and Students, his Apostolic Benediction. When the Dogma of Infallibility was defined, they intoned the *Te Deum* in thanksgiving. His Holiness, also in compliance with the petition which they had sent to him, asking for a play day, had, with his own hand, written on their address that he granted three instead of one. The Holy Father granted the favour in the following words:— "*Benedicat vos Deus, et gratiam petitam non tantum pro uno die, sed etiam pro tribus diebus benigne concedimus.—Pius P.P. IX.*" Among other portraits with which the refectory walls are adorned are those of Bishop Gibson, founder of the college, Cardinals Allen and Wiseman, Dr. Lingard (the portrait by Lonsdale), the Rev. Thomas Eyre, the first President, Dr. Gillow, Dr. Youens, Dr. Briggs, Dr. Newsham, Dr. Tate, Presidents of the college in succession; also of Bishops Smith, Riddell, Hogarth, and Chadwick. The portrait of the last named Bishop was given by his Lordship, as the inscription underneath the frame states, to his *Alma Mater*, "*Memor multorum beneficiorum.*" There is also the portrait of Dr. Gillow, Vice-President, and of the Very Rev. Dean Trappes, through whose exertions the enlargement and decoration of the refectory took place. I have given above the measurements of this magnificent room. But neither in length, breadth, or height can it compare with the refectory in the Abbey of St. Germain, which was 115 feet long, 32 feet wide, and 47 feet high, and on eight immense windows were emblazoned the arms of Castille.

Occupying the principal seats at the ceremony of presentation were Archbishop Eyre, Archbishop Errington, the Bishops of Hexham and Newcastle, Beverley, Salford, and Liverpool, Monsignore Searle, Monsignore Thompson, Monsignore Croskell, &c. The proceedings commenced with the choir and orchestra performing "The Heavens are telling," from the "Creation."

The Very Rev. Canon Consitt, after referring to the origin of the memorial, and to the various presents of venison, game, fruit, wine, and spirits, which had been sent to Dr. Tate, proceeded to state that it was necessary to tell them what had been done in the matter of this jubilee. In the first place, the window having been put forward as the prominent memorial, was provided for it. It was ordered at the request of the President and superiors of the college from Mr. Hardman, of Birmingham. With regard to the subject of the window, the idea was to put up memorials to all the Presidents of Ushaw, and as there had been six Presidents, they filled the six main lights of the window. But it was thought that it would not do on this occasion to pass over that which connected them by so close a link to the great mother of Ushaw—the mother of them all, he might say—Douai College. The Rev. John Daniel was the last President of Douai and first President of Crook, and he was therefore inserted in the first space, which now contained the figure of St. John the Baptist, the patron saint of the Rev. John Daniel. The Rev. Canon then briefly touched upon the disruption of Douai College, and traced the history of the foundation of Ushaw. After explaining the details of the window, he apologised for any neglect he might have been guilty of in the course of the arrangements, stating that everything he had done had been for the good of old *Alma Mater*, and for its venerable and Right Rev. President.

The Right Rev. Dr. Chadwick esteemed it both an honour and a privilege to be called upon to ask the Right Rev. President to receive these tributes of their sincere regard and affection on this the day of his jubilee of 50 years in the priesthood. Referring to early associations, he said that if the venerable and Right Rev. President remembered him as a little boy, he (the speaker) could certainly remember Dr. Tate as a very young man—and he was assured that the estimate he then formed of his qualities had not proved to be a false one. It was now receiving additional proof as evidenced by the presence of this numerous assembly, whose appearance there was a justification of the existence of these qualities. It must indeed be exceedingly satisfactory to the worthy recipient of the memorial to see so many friends—both clerical and lay—around him, and when they reflected that now he had completed 50 years in the holy priesthood—and that during that period of time he had ever been an honour to it—the venerable and Right Rev. President would be assured of this—that the esteem and affection for him was in no way diminished. They sincerely congratulated him upon having seen that day, and he hardly need say how earnestly they all wished he might have happy years to come. He could not express the delight he, together with the rest of that company, felt in asking him to accept these tributes of their esteem and regard which, but for his love and generosity to *Alma Mater*, would have taken the form of a testimonial to himself personally. He begged him now, therefore, to accept these as tributes of their admiration, hoping that for years to come he might preside over the college as he had done in the past, and was yet doing in the present.

The Rev. Charles Gordon, on behalf of the students and friends of the college, read the following beautifully illuminated and framed address to Dr. Tate :—

To the Right Rev. Mgr. Tate, D.D.—Dear Dr. Tate,—When the friends and alumni of St. Cuthbert's are assembled to congratulate you on this memorable day, we who have the happiness to live under your rule cannot content ourselves with merely joining in the universal congratulations. There are doubtless many around us who cherish your memory as affectionately as we, but the ties that bind us to you are unlike all other ties, and the feelings they excite can find no adequate expression even in the warmest congratulations of surrounding friends. We know indeed that you would much prefer the silence of our respectful obedience to any formal address, still we trust that it will give you pleasure to hear from our lips how deeply sensible we are of the debt we owe you, above all for that affectionate solicitude which ever makes our interest and our happiness your own, and seems to change the rule of authority into the guidance of a father and a friend. As a memorial therefore, and a token of our gratitude, affection and esteem, we beg your acceptance of a silver remonstrance, designed and made in commemoration of your Jubilee. We feel assured that you would prefer such an offering to a more personal gift. And when we adore our Hidden God, enthroned within it for the love of us, each one amongst us will breathe a heartfelt prayer that he will be pleased to preserve you in health and strength for many a year to come, to encourage and to guide us still in the paths of virtue and of learning.

The remonstrance bears on its foot the following inscription :—

Reverendissimo Dno. Dno. Tate,
Decimum Sacerdotii sui lustrum complenti,
Alumni Collegii S. Cuthberti,
1873.

The Right Rev. Dr. Tate in reply said he felt himself in an exceedingly trying position. He knew of no circumstances more trying than those in which one had to return thanks and acknowledge gratitude for any favour. It was perfectly true, as had been expressed, that he would much rather give to *Alma Mater* than receive anything for himself. He was seventy-four years of age, and had been thirty-eight years at the college—the better half of his lifetime. *Alma Mater*, he assured them, presented a very different appearance then as contrasted with the present state of things. He lived in days very different to those of the students of the present day. There were then no grand chandeliers, but what they had they thought very good, namely, two pieces of wood made of good deal, and costing a great deal less than these would cost. In his day they might be said to have fed upon such works as those of Demosthenes, Cicero, Plato, and others. Their minds were occupied in thinking of these, and thus they paid less attention to the inconveniences they had to put up with. He concluded by again and again expressing the gratitude he felt for the great honour which they had all been pleased to confer upon him by the commemoration of his jubilee as a priest of the church.

The company, comprising bishops, clergy, and the rest of the guests, together with the professors and students of the college, were entertained to a sumptuous dinner. The large refectory was filled in every part, nearly 500 persons being seated at the tables. The chair was occupied by the Right Rev. President, Dr. Tate, having on his right Archbishop Errington, Bishop Chadwick, and Bishop O'Reilly, and on his left Bishop Brown, Bishop Cornthwaite, and Bishop Vaughan. The first toast—" The health of His Holiness Pope Pius the Ninth"—proposed by Bishop Chadwick, was most enthusiastically received, and drunk with bursts of applause. " Long live the Pope" was sung by the choir. Archbishop Errington, in a most gracious and emphatic manner, proposed " The health of the President," which was honoured with rounds of cheers. Dr. Tate returned thanks, and gave "The health of the Bishops." Dr. Brown, Bishop of Newport and Menevia, responded. The Vice-President, the Very Rev. Dr. Gillow, next proposed "The Visitors," to which Dr. Charlton replied. "The Professors" was given by Bishop O'Reilly, on behalf of whom the Rev. Wm. Wrennall returned thanks. "God save the Queen" was then sung, the company all standing. In the evening the comedy of "The Rivals" was performed in the Hall. The last scene of all in the festive drama was a display of fireworks in front of the college. This pyrotechnic demonstration afforded considerable amusement, and concluded what we heard it so called in Durham, the "great to do," at Ushaw. Next day most of the visitors separated, and the college subsided into its usual quiet state. They departed in various directions, scattered over the highways of the world, like leaves among the woodlands in the autumnal season. They departed, but all carried to their homes some "relics of joy," some pleasant memories and grateful recollections of their visit to Ushaw; and all wished success to *Alma Mater*, and long life to the venerable President, the acceptable year of whose Jubilee was so auspiciously brought to a close.

During the time Dr. Tate was President until within a few months before his death, I had the honour of receiving frequent letters from him. The number treasured up by me cannot be far short of a hundred. The familiar and friendly sentiments, the kind heartedness, candour and courtesy which these letters manifest in my regard, cause me with good reason to regard them as the legacies of a friend whom but to know was to love. In this dry, unanointed age it is most refreshing to re-open and re-peruse their contents;—they embrace such a variety of topics, treat on such diverse and interesting subjects, abound in such classical and literary allusions, apt and elegant quotations, remarks on passing events, notices of books, and of the authors who wrote them. They also evince a great love and admiration of the beauties of nature, which "never did betray the heart that loved her," an unmistakeable appreciation of the pleasures of rural life and rural scenery, of the delight which green fields, purling streams, embowering woods, sheltering plantations, fruit and flower gardens afforded him. It might truly be said of him that he "found tongues in trees, books in the running brooks, sermons in stones, and good in everything."

———"Every tree
And bush, and fragrant flower, and hilly path,
And thymy mound, that flings unto the winds
Its morning incense, is my friend."

The willows on the river's edge had a melody for him, and he enjoyed the hospitable shade of the pine and the poplar—

" *Quo pinus ingens albaque populus*
Umbram hospitalem consociare amant
Ramis, et obliquo laborat
Lympha fugax trepidare rivo."

He loved to meditate and wander among the beeches and broad oaks, "in forest wyld to space :"

"His walk the woods, his sport some foreign book ;
His resting place the bank that curbs the brook."

"In happy leisure," to quote from Digby's *Compitum*, "he enjoyed the sweet odours exhaled from the yew, and the foliage of the white poplar in the beautiful days of spring, when the plane and the young elm blend their murmuring sound."

"*Non omnes arbusta juvant, humilesque myricæ ;*"

but Dr. Tate admired and was interested in all trees and shrubs—the lofty and the low—from the cedar of the hills to the hyssop on the wall. It was his delight to speak and write about the different kinds of trees which he took a pleasure in planting in and around the Ushaw boundaries—from "the pine tree which the rain had nourished, to the hawthorns that cannot be allured by April warmth to blossom sooner than the time appointed for the swallow to arrive, when their sweet perfumes will be safe from storms." On one occasion he thus wrote: "There is a review at Durham on Whit Monday. Instead of going to hear the roar of cannons and of rifles, to have one's ears dinned and eyes bewildered by the *strepitum et strata urbis viarum*, I will have a ramble with my book and stroll to the neighbourhood of Hag Wood :—

"*Maluit umbrosam sylvam, musasque canoras.*"

As St. Jerome used to say, "to him a town was a prison, and solitude a paradise." "In what manner am I to suppose you employ your leisure?" says Horace to Tibullus—

"*An tacitum sylvas inter reptare salubres,
Curantem quicquid dignum sapiente bonoque est ?*"

EXTRACTS FROM LETTERS.

ORTHODOX CHRISTMAS CARDS.—I forgot to ask you the other day whether you will have any of the orthodox Christmas cards. Those eternal robins, although one has a traditional regard for the bird itself, seem to be the only idea Protestants have for wishing a happy Christmas and new year. If you get any of the orthodox kind, let me have a few for the benefit of my friends. Mind I don't reject robins as such. I go along with you in the deepest veneration for it, when it is treated in an orthodox way ; but hitherto one has not seen a Christmas card in this country without the robin simply perched on a gate or a bush, and happy Christmas supposed to be uttered by the bird. Surely there is a Catholic mode of handling the winsome little creature. The Germans surpass the French by many degrees in such matters. Their Christmas books are beautiful, and so Catholic. I have an A, B, C book in German. The design for each letter of the alphabet is charming. The Einsiedeln kalendar is very cheap, and the illustrations in it are most interesting and well done.

POPE SIXTUS V.—I must have Hubner's Life of Sixtus V., a great favourite of mine, and one who would have led Cavour a dance, and tired him down.

TRASIMENE OAK.—I am glad that you have a memorial of old Hannibal, the son of Hamilcar—*filius lactatoris*, as the boy translated the papa's name. We planted our memorial tree with due ceremony, on Tuesday last, Feb. 18, 1872.* How comes it that the Greeks shorten the *e*, and the Latins lengthen it? *Trasumēnaque littora testes*, Ovid says. What a sad piece of generalship it was on the part of the Romans! How delightfully old Livy's narrative contrasts the haste of Flaminius with the "cunctation" of Fabius. One can almost fancy old Ennius's lines to be poetical—

" *Unus homo nobis cunctando restituit rem,*
Non ponebat enim rumores ante salutem."

Some one says that the English poetry of the 17th century was prose, and the prose of the 18th century poetry. Ennius's verses are good sound prose, and hence sometimes very like Pope's verses. Since the young oak came I have looked at old Livy. What a beautiful lively style he writes. Is he not more of a poet than old Maro?

THE SEVEN PENITENTIAL PSALMS.—I will pardon your oversight on condition that when you next say the Seven Penitential Psalms you put in an Ave at the end of the last for my intention. What most serviceable substitutes they are for non-fasters.

PRAYER BOOKS.—If any of us miss our way to heaven, it will not be for want of Prayer books.

CANON WALKER.—Writing on June 26th, 1873, he says: at this moment the requiem mass will be going on at St. Peter's, Scarborough, for the late pastor, Canon Walker. How suddenly he has gone! I always gave him many years to come, he looked so healthy, and in appearance at least changed so little under the weight of years. God rest his soul. He took a position which will not be easily supplied by one *par* to Canon Walker. His death much widens the gap, made by the death of my still older friend of Hull. Mr. Trappes and I have been closely allied friends since 1813, when he returned to Ushaw after an absence of a year. Mr. Walker and I had only a few months between us, and such facts tell in very plain language what we ought to think of:— " *Valde cito erit tecum hoc factum.*" The good Bishop of Salford lately dead was ten months my junior—*Memento mori, &c.* Sixty years this day, July 16th, since I entered these walls !

REV. JOSEPH WRENNALL.—You will be sorry to hear of the death of the Rev. Joseph Wrennall. He seems in his spirit of zeal to have overworked his strength. God rest his soul. *Bene meritus est de Alma Matre.*

VITA VITÆ NOSTRÆ.—I am so much attached to the "*Vita Vitæ Nostræ*" as a fountain head of subjects for meditation that I seldom use any other. Beuvelet is very good, *mais &c.*

---

* Young trees from acorns of an oak growing at Hornby. This tree—SYLVÆ FILIA NOBILIS—was raised by Dr. Lingard, the eminent historian, from an acorn brought by him in 1820 from the scene of Hannibal's third victory, and which now SUOS TENDIT RAMOS in the garden at Hornby.

LANCASHIRE WEATHER.—Your muggy, misty, mizzly, murky Lancashire weather very much damped my desire to visit you in Fishergate during my visit to Claughton—Fishergate which a Preston youth had once the audacity to compare with the immortal Corso at Rome. In later years he entertained a different opinion, and *longe alio animo fuit.* I hoped to call in some morning upon you from Lancaster, but then we had a programme for each day which did not include the metropolis of the Fylde, and so I came home in *hunc portum tranquillitatis re infecta quantum res spectat civitatem illam satis claram, cujus nomen Latine redditum nondum est."*

GRANGE-OVER-SANDS.—What a beautiful place Grange is over the bay of Morecambe. Did you ever visit the island there? Some of the pines and grasses there are very fine.

PROLIFIC POTATOE.—At Hornby, Mr. Gibson showed us the produce of a single potatoe—somewhat of a revolutionary tendency—called the Bolivian red. The thirteen sets from one potatoe had produced $10\frac{1}{2}$ lbs. weight, all sound and firm.

DR. TATE'S JUBILEE.—Is it not just one year this very day (Oct. 14th, 1874), since our "merry meeting" for my Jubilee, of which I always think with the highest pleasure? *Horæ quidem cedunt et dies et menses et anni.*

BISHOP OF LIVERPOOL.—The Bishop of Liverpool (Dr. O'Reilly) left us this morning, *via* Tebay for Lancaster. What a very amiable kind manner he has. *Honores non mutant mores,* in his regard.

NEWMAN'S LOSS AND GAIN.—I am reading "Loss and Gain" for the twentieth time, and every time it interests me more than before. Is there a novel equal to it, whether on historical, social, or religious matters? I must have a copy of the new edition, the 6th, to see what the author has to say in the new advertisement.

L'ESPRIT LITTERAIRE.—Can you get for me a copy of Rollin's *"Traité des Etudes?"* You will have read it I dare say, and you will not thus be surprised that a writer such as Rollin of that old school be sought for. I do feel that that fine *esprit littéraire* which we in our early days relished so much, and to which our teachers were careful to draw our attention, is suffering from what is so mischievously as well as so inappropriately, if exclusive, denominated science. This is the *scientia quæ inflat* which St. Paul denounces, and the age is fast coming to it, there is reason to fear.

SKATING.—Our students have had good skating on the pond for a week, and it is a subject of earnest prayer with me that it may go on through the vacation (Christmas, 1874). Skating keeps them in good humour and in good health, two most weighty points *quoad adolescentes cum juniores tum seniores.*

A CORNSAY DAY.—I am just off to Cornsay for the day, an enjoyment in the routine of college life as grateful as it was 50 years ago. I feel just now that I should like to have you there and give you a dressing at long whist.

THE WEATHER.—The weather at this date, January 8th, 1875, is much milder, but we have dense fogs. Are they what Maro calls *densissimus imber*? The President's Feast on Wednesday, January 13th. If you can come, you know you will be most welcome.

LETTUCE.—Many thanks for the lettuce seed. Old Celsus, I see, attributes soporiferous properties to it. "*Lactuca, maximeque æstiva, cujus cauliculus jam lacte repletus est, somno apta est.*" How well and smoothly runs Martial's distich—

"*Claudere quæ cænas lactuca solebat avorum,
Dic mihi cur nostras inchoat illa dapes?*"

Does not the question which Martial asks touching *lactucæ* show that the old Romans like their *posteri* ate vegetables without an accompaniment? Some of the Valerian family were cognominated *Lactucini a studio colendæ lactucæ, juxta Plinium*.

LONG AND SHORT DAYS.—How little we should relish as we ought the long days, if we had no short ones. Take a morning walk in a wood when the sere and yellow leaf mingles so harmoniously with the red and dark green, forming a shade much better than the "*pinus ingens albaque populus,*" and you will love Autumn with its shortening days. The classics give no idea of the Autumn. They deal only in sunshine or in storm.

EDUCATION OF THE YOUNG.—With all the noise and bother there is about the education of the young, where but in the Holy Apostolic Church can be found such a galaxy of devout men who devoted their lives to the care and education of the young—SS. Camillus, Vincent of Paul, Jerome Æmillan? What heroes and what martyrs in the cause! The Forsters and the Gladstones—*taceant sileantque—labia comprimant scholarum tabulæ, et confundantur in æternum.*

CHRISTMAS NIGHT.—How is it Christmas night in my quiet chapel of Hazlewood—built 1286—always gave me a most solemn impression. All so quiet, no voice but my own heard on that night, very different from a large choir of young voices singing "*Collaudantes.*" So your duet with Provost Platt will be a sort of medium between the two—Ushaw and Hazlewood. Well, in that deep still valley (Dodding Green) the "*Collaudantes*" inspires very poetical and welcome feelings. A wind such as we had last night will give it something of the sublime. It is still blowing "great guns."

HEAVY RAINS AND FLOODS.—I hope you and others of my friends in Lancashire were not washed away by the floods of rain which fell on Saturday night and yesterday (November 14th, 1875). Here 1½ inch of rain fell on Saturday night, and went on in torrents till 1 p.m. yesterday. The Browney broke all bounds, and made a lake of Bear Park, and the Derness floated away the two bridges at Broadgate and Flass, modern structures to be sure, but which had stood the *extravagans* stream for many years :—

"*Expatiata ruunt per apertos flumina campos.*"—Ovid, Met. 1.

No doubt the Murgate *alias* Priestbeck which passes Newhouse, and the site of the old chapel, where lived Rev. Ferdinand Ashmall, and died æt. 104, and where good Father Boost, martyred at Durham, was saying Mass attended by a party of nobility from Brancepeth Castle, when he was seized by the sacrilegious villain who had confessed to him and communicated the same morning for the purpose of supplying himself with proofs of the good Father being a Priest—(you will have lost the thread of the sentence, so you must return *unde digressus es*)— the Murgate, no doubt, played its part in the flood where it joins the Derness near Flass, having left the classic shades of Cornsay.

FR. COLERIDGE'S LIFE OF OUR LORD.—I like the 1st volume of Fr. Coleridge on the Life of Our Blessed Lord better than the 2nd on the Beatitudes. He gives, it seems to me, too many interpretations from the earlier commentators, and thus overdoes his work.

THE POET WORDSWORTH ON THE B. VIRGIN.—In my copy of "Selections from Wordsworth" occurs the following passage from one of the sonnets:—

"Mother! whose Virgin bosom was uncrost
With the least shade of thought to sin allied;
Woman! above all women glorified,
Our tainted nature's solitary boast—"

words which will well bear the interpretation of the Poet's belief in the Immaculate Conception of the Blessed Virgin Mary. The reverent, loving words, in which the simple, truly poetical soul of Wordsworth speaks of our B. Lady, are very telling.

OLD ASSOCIATIONS.—A walk yesterday in the Esh country brought into fine view the vale of the Derness, and then that of the Browney, and gave me a most delightful fillip, which these material-minded dictionaries define to be a jerk of the forefinger and thumb, and then all the old associations crowd in, and at my time of life, one half lives upon such mental food.

POETRY OF THE PSALMS.—We are reading the Psalms in school just now, and one wonders how people can admire any other poetry, except as *longo proximus intervallo.*

GUESSES AT TRUTH.—The "Guesses at Truth" is a work which I used to read ever and anon some thirty-five years ago with the greatest relish, and the book you so kindly offer me is all the more valuable as it brings to my mind my late most valued friend, Dr. Youens, who used to dip into it with me. Your kind present has come safe and sound. Already I have brushed up my memory in several passages which one can read with such zest; and when I again say that you have indeed made me a most valuable and most welcome present, really no "Guess at Truth" can be more sure or more appropriate. When you again give me the pleasure of a call at my "lodgings" here, you will find the "Guesses" in possession of a permanent place on my table. Let me also beg you will accept my best thanks for the *Chronicle.* You always treat this theme ("The Grand Week") with so much *con amore,* that it is a great pleasure to travel with you in the route you describe, whether near or afar off, here or elsewhere.

COLD AND "RAINLESS" WEATHER.—The weather here is cold and "rainless"—a new word which however must have been in use in the good old Saxon English, before our vernacular began to grant liberty of citizenship to every Greek and Latin and French word that asked for the honour.

POPE GREGORY VII.—I have just finished Voight's Life of St. Gregory VII. With all the occasional misunderstandings of certain points of that Pontifical hero's character which you must expect from a Protestant biographer, what a magnificent character St. Gregory is in the pages of Voight. The noble sainted Pontiff's last quiet retreat at Salerno, and his last words "*Dilexi justitiam, et odivi iniquitatem, ideo morior in exilio,*" how true and how great they are in the mouth of S. Gregory. A Catholic would have given more room to such a Pontiff in his last days, but this you cannot expect from a Protestant, *quia non datur ei ut de tali re loquatur. Qui potest capere capiat*, but a Protestant *non potest capere quid tale.*

NEW MONSTRANCE.—The new monstrance was used at Benediction yesterday—the Feast of All Saints, and very handsome it looked. It is a most opportune and considerate offering on the part of my young friends, in commemoration of my jubilee, and gives me great gratification.

LOVE OF BOOKS.—I keep getting books as if I were only fifty instead of being on the sunny side of seventy. After all, what a pity it is that a few good books do not content us; but one must hunt out details in every catalogue that comes to hand. We ought to read less and ruminate more.

HARVEST SEASON.—We are in *mediis rebus quod spectat ad messes;* the wheat magnificent—"*Illius immensæ superant horrea messes.*" Did not the ancients make their corn stacks *sub dio*? Oh, what a fine sight a large field of ripe wheat is, waving in the breeze on a hill side!

CATHOLIC LEGENDS AND TALES.—I do relish good Catholic legends and tales, so will you get me the Household Stories from the land of Hofer, which the *Tablet* has in its notices of new books. It will have some nice bits for the Christmas vacation.

THE LATE EARL OF DERBY.—Poor Lord Derby! The death of such a man brings many thoughts to mind—much to please, much to speak of "*vanitas vanitatum.*" He was the orator of his day. His language was elegant, earnest, Saxon, and quite free from any thing like stiffness or study. This he owed to his taste for classical literature.

FURNESS ABBEY.—I spent a very agreeable week at Lancaster, and went to Furness Abbey. What a most splendid ruin, and how full of interest in its history and position. Visited Hornby also, a classic spot now by the memory of the good Doctor (Lingard.)

ST. CUTHBERT'S DAY.—This is St. Cuthbert's day (March 20), and most glorious High Mass we have had this morning. The choir was in high spirits, and their voices sounded as if they were looking for a play day to-morrow. Now St. Cuthbert does not order a play day except when his feast falls on a school day, but this day is so fine that I fully expect my stony heart will turn soft in the morning:—

"*Gutta cavat lapidem, non vi, sed sæpe cadendo.*"

ST. CÆCILIA.—St. Cæcilia's day! What a beautiful office the Breviary has for this day! Is not old Aristotle quite right when he tells us that poetry is more philosophical and attractive than history? So it is. The good cautious scholar Alban Butler wont admit the acts of St. Cæcilia; but what a picture they are of the spirit of those days, and of the privileges from heaven which in such times of peril and persecution the Church militant must have been blessed with.

PALEY'S HOMER.—Have you seen Paley's new edition of Homer? He has now a new maggot about the old poet who, as Paddy said of the Irish round towers, "puzzles posterity," and wrote for that purpose.

MODERN CIVILIZATION.—This modern civilization unsettles the mind sadly, and is always creating an appetite for more creature comforts.

BISHOP CHADWICK AND HIS PHOTOGRAPH.—When Dr. Chadwick was lately at Roulers, in Belgium, at the college there, he presented to the students what they had earnestly requested, his photograph. At dinner he found lying on his plate, when grace had been said, these lines—

"*Depictam solis radiis summa arte tabellam*
Præsulis eximii quæ vultum reddit amatum,
Pignus amicitiæ, læti salvere jubemus,
Ast alia auxilio solis nullius inusta,
Nobis corde manet, semperque manebit imago."

GREEK NEW TESTAMENTS.—When you pay us another visit you must see my collection of Greek New Testaments. With all their *lectiones variæ* what a striking proof their very "numerosity" affords of the care which *le bon Dieu* has taken of the Holy Scriptures, for they vary in nothing of consequence, or that affects the sense at all. What a fuss the *docti indoctique* have made about these various readings, and none save and except the famous I. Joan., v., 7, makes any matter at all. But there is a pleasure in seeing these small and unimportant, though numerous varieties, as an argument *de Providentia divina quoad SS*. I have two or three of Tischendorf's editions of the New Testament, but he is a sad anti-trinitarian; he places a full stop after *Sarka* in Rom. ix., 5, and omits Joa. v., 4, and viii., 1-11, in the Greek editions, though he does print it in other type in his Greek and Vulgate and German Polyglott edition. In I. Joa., v., 7, he leaves out v. 7 in all the three.

MARCUS TULLIUS CICERO.—Old Tully said of his vacation—"*In hisce litteris sine ulla interpellatione versor;*" and so I could say, if my letters did not come so thickly; so with a somewhat different translation of the word "*litteris,*" I may say the same thing.

EVENINGS OF ARCADIA.—I have read some of the "Evenings of Arcadia" with much pleasure. He makes out his assertion, I think, that Milton sings of pastoral subjects *not* from observation. Shakespeare could not have said

"How sweet the moonlight sleeps upon this bank,"

without having *seen* it.

LONGFELLOW'S DANTE.—Many passages in Longfellow's Dante show the advantages of literal translation, and the force of our Saxon tongue stripped of its adventitious German and Latin words. An article in the *Dublin Review* holds out Dante as a deep mystical Divine, and yet he was often in hot water, and did not speak always with due reverence of the Popes.

AUTUMN.—We have most lovely weather, quite a Michaelmas summer. Autumn has no attractive features in the Roman poets. *Lætifer Autumnus* it is in Juvenal; and old Horace is quite in the blues about it—"*per autumnos nocentem corporibus metuemus austrum.*" How delightful Autumn is in a fine season on the moors, with the heather in bloom, so rich in colour and so warm, more especially in the evenings when—"*summa procul villarum culmina fumant.*" Was it not a peat fire—*that* in one of the most lovely and graphic lines in the Odyssey?

DID HOMER COMPOSE THE ODYSSEY?—Hayman, in the preface to the 2nd vol. of the Odyssey, disposes of Paley's notion, which has haunted German critics for some time, that old Homer did not compose both Iliad and Odyssey, and very glad one is to see our old respectable ideas set fairly on their feet again. *Tempus plantandi, et tempus evellendi quod plantatum est*, and the latter is the pet aim of the critical world in this our day.

THE PRESIDENT'S FEAST.—On Wednesday, January 11th, is the President's Feast, and if you would come, the day before of course, very happy shall I be to see you, but suit your own will and convenience, and no apology is needed if you have no *promotio physica* in this direction at this season of the year. We are both of respectable ages, and to such all consideration is due. We have had, I may inform you, thirteen days of good skating, with a certain amount of sweeping and pushing to clear the snow sometimes. It began with the Christmas vacation and has ended with it, so the frost has shown a due regard for study.

CŒLUM CHRISTIANUM.—The Bishop, Dr. Chadwick, has presented me with a copy of the *Cœlum Christianum* which you will have seen advertised to be reprinted. I like it much—the meditations are short, much to the point, and suggestive of good practical resolutions. It contains a hundred meditations—none more than a page in length.

ST. IGNATIUS, MARTYR.—I like much to read some writing of a holy Father on or about the time of his feast. St. Ignatius, Martyr, has had my spare time this week (Feb. 4, 1874). What a fervent, noble strain the dear good old Saint, whose death disgraces the name of Trajan, much as that of Mary, Queen of Scots, disgraces that of Queen Bess, does pour out of his loving, reverent heart! And how striking that, whereas in all the other six epistles he insists so much, in a short style, but most emphatic, on dogma and obedience to Bishops, not a word of either in his epistle to the Romans, because at Rome the church is safeguarded, and has always been preserved from all foreign taint and error.

SHORT MASSES.—A great desideratum, at present. These long Masses that make the solemn liturgy a musical entertainment, and throw the holy sacrifice into the shade, are not to be borne any longer, and there is, I believe, reason to hope that the decrees of the last synod will speak out on the evil.

DISSERTATION ON WRITING INK.—I congratulate you on the darker hue of your ink. Old Pliny tells us that in his day there were three sorts of *melan graphicum, viz.*, the graphicum, the sutorium, the pictorium :—the first for writers, the second for tanning purposes, the third for painters, and according to the same authority, Apelles, the artist, used a sort of varnish for his *opera absoluta, ut idipsa repercussa claritatis colorem excitaret, custodiretque a pulvere et sordibus.* Your new fountain is of darker hue, I am happy to say, and so is not that *atramentum temperatum* of which Tully speaks in one of his letters. *Hactenus de atramento.* What a most delightful letter writer old Tully is! Quintilian says of him—"*Ille se profecisse sciat cui Cicero valde placebit.*"

HYMN FOR THE FEAST OF SS. PETER & PAUL.—The Hymn for SS. Peter and Paul is a most magnificent piece of poetry; the metre most noble. Have you seen what at Rome they call the *luce a'oro,* the *lux aurea* which spreads over the Campagna in an evening? How telling and beautiful the "crown" of the two Princes as the golden day of eternity sheds its light over them ; and then the fine line—the *libera via* opened to the penitent sinner by the keys which Peter bore. The *vitæ senatum laureati possident*—What a most happy classical allusion—what so seldom a religious sentiment will be in keeping with! The Roman warrior coming into the senate with his crown of laurel, emblem of his victories. You can imagine you can see the two glorious Apostles and Nero seated in the *senatus*—the curia of Heaven ;—but "*possident*"—what a *verbum vigilans*, as St. Augustine terms such words! *Possessio est non tantum corporis, sed juris est.* Livy says "*quod bello captum possidet,*" and this is the dictum of Roman law "*Tenes quod alieni juris est, possides quod jure habes, non clam, non precario.*" Then how grandly Rome, consecrated by the glorious blood of these apostolic Princes, is apostrophised, and proclaimed most happy in being thus empurpled, and thereby rendered more resplendent in beauty than all other earthly beauties. "*O Roma felix,*" &c.

THE FRANCO-PRUSSIAN WAR.—What a blessing it would be if the Prussians and French would find their way out of their sad dreadful war before Christmas comes. *Prope est jam Dominus*, the Church sings, and may our Lord's coming bring *in terra pax hominibus bonæ voluntatis.* But that *bona voluntas* is sadly wanting in such creatures as Gambetta, who keeps his place on the strength of war and carnage, and in the mean time many brave and devout Catholics are throwing away their lives in a struggle which all their bravery and heroism appear unable to assist in the cause of *la belle France.*

THE ABOMINATION OF DESOLATION.—After returning from Rome in 1867, Dr. Tate thus speaks of the "abomination of desolation" which he beheld in the holy places in Italy. "To see Monte Cassino deserted, the frescoes of Assisi left to chance, and noble monasteries with their beautiful cloisters abandoned, or only one or two old monks left there to eke out their subsistence as they can—reminding you of the 'widowed solitary thing' in Goldsmith's 'Deserted Village,' is sad indeed. Italy looks as if the age of barbarism were returning. Rome seems to be the only sanctuary remaining of the *Kalon kagathon.*"

THE PLEASURE OF A GARDEN.—I can well enter into the delight you must have in a garden, more especially in the early part of spring. What enjoyment you must have when leaving the *fumum strepitumque* of Preston—the only features it has in common with old Rome—you find yourself in the quiet of country life :—

"*O rus quando ego te aspiciam ? quandoque licebit,
Nunc veterum libris, nunc somno et inertibus horis,
Ducere solicitæ jucunda oblivia vitæ ?*"

However your enjoyment, according to the lot of all human enjoyments, would be much lessened if you had not the advantage of the daily contrast between town and country, for man made the one, and God the other. Ever since I lived in Sheffield it has been an article of faith with me that to relish the country fully, and drink in its "balmy breathing" air, you must have lived in a town. . . . . *Diffugere nives,* as you say, but you did not dare to finish the verse. For the "*redeunt jam gramina campis,*" we must wait awhile. As for the "*arboribusque comæ*" is there a more beautiful foliage than that of the larch ? The delicate green of the larch ushers in the *arbores,* as the snowdrop does the *flores,* but it requires some genial days. The snowdrop goes before and gives notice that it is time for spring to come.

PASCHALIA GAUDIA.—A very happy Easter to you and yours, and all Paschal joys and blessings, such as are symbolized by the beautiful flowers which enliven this season of the year, and as many more Easters such as you can wish and as many as will suit you. . . . . On May 22, he writes as follows :—"*Desinit tempus Paschale,*" the Ordo tells us. So let me wish you all happiness at the beginning of this prosaic season.

SPRING.—Poets have written very beautifully of the spring, but is there any passage more picturesque than that in the *Canticum Cantic.* which Catholic spiritual writers have so aptly and so feelingly applied to their own high purpose ? *Hiems transiit, imber abiit et recessit ; flores apparuerunt in terra nostra, tempus putationis advenit, vox turturis audita est in terra nostra ; ficus protulit grossos suos, vineæ florentes dederunt odorem suum.* How inviting ! Hence *surge amica mea, et veni.* Compare this with Virgil's 1st Eclogue—

"*Fortunate senex, hic inter flumina nota.—*"

Is not the Canticle much fresher in its description than the Roman poet is ? Virgil is quite intent on lulling one to sleep. The sacred poet is all wide awake to the scene before him both as to hearing and seeing. *Flores apparuerunt in terra vestra ;* no doubt snowdrops, perhaps the crocus. The only one I can find here at Ushaw (Feb. 6th, 1871), is the Christmas rose—the black hellebore, with its flower so little in unison with its name ; and during the frost and snow how beautifully it pops out its white rose, and invites you to take it to warmer air, where it will spread out its blossom in full glory. Do you think that any description of spring in the Latin poets takes so tight a hold of the *vis imaginationis* as that of old Maro, 2 Georgic—

"*Non alios prima crescentis origine mundi
Illuxisse dies, aliumve habuisse tenorem
Crediderim ; ver illud erat, ver magnus agebat
Orbis, et hybernis parcebant flatibus Euri.*"

There is no painting here, but the evidence of a mind imbued with a love of his theme. Again, what a beautiful description of spring does he give in two words—*nunc frondent sylvæ ;*—this speaks volumes, so he has a right to close the verse with an assertion rather than a picture. *Nunc formosissimus annus.* Look at any spring landscape, and the *frondent sylvæ* is the leading, the absorbing picture.

WOODS AND FORESTS.—To-morrow (Nov. 3rd), we must start with the filling up of young trees in the plantations, where failures have occurred. My walks at this season don't extend farther than our own ground, as the plantations always supply work for the pruning knife and saw. In sending me the book about forest trees, most truly have you hit upon my "weakness," for the very sight of a fine spreading tree is most elevating to the mind ;—what is it when one may roam through a forest of old oaks and hawthorns? Nothing after all more striking than a good gnarled hawthorn tree, one of the prominent features of the real old English forests. We have here an enjoyment of which the classic writers can give us no strain worthy of the theme. In Virgil it is little else but single trees and underwood—"*sub tegmine fagi*"—

"*Dumosa pendere procul de rupe videbo.*"—Virg. Ecl. 1.

Don't you think that one of the great charms in Tacitus's account of the Roman campaign against Arminius is that the German leader fought in his forests? How telling is that passage—"*Arminius colligi suos jussit, et propinquare sylvis monitos vertit repente: mox signum prorumpendi dedit iis, quos per saltus occultaverat.*" Then further on what a concise but speaking picture of a wood, where wood ought to be "*circum sylvæ paulatim acclives.*" Yes, the woods of England, and Germany, in the middle ages, how full of poetry and romance, and are to this day in books at least.* By the way in the Æneid, Bk. VI., Æneas does see a large forest, but he does not seem to care a jot about it :—

"*Aspectans sylvam immensam, et sic ore precatur ;*"

and then the more—he says his prayers instead of choosing some *sylvan vista* for a contemplative walk ! By the way old Lambert of Aschaffenberg has a most picturesque passage in his history of Henry IV.— "*Castellum in altissimo colle situm erat, et uno tantum itinere, ipsoque difficillimo adiri poterat. Cætera montis latera vastissima sylva inumbrabat, quæ exinde per multa millia passuum continua vastitate in latum extenditur usque ad confinium Thuringiæ.*" Old Lambert relished a good

---

*Cæsar also speaks of the barbarians taking refuge in the forests of Gaul and Germany—"SESE IN SOLITUDINEM AC SYLVAS ABDIDERANT ;" and in the middle ages, it was wise and learned men that flocked in exceeding great numbers to the forests, as yielding an asylum from the violence of the few under the standard of the Prince of the world.

forest, it is clear, for he speaks of the Harz forest with much zest. Yet, after all, Virgil does betray some taste for a walk through a wood—

"*Quale per incertam lunam, sub luce maligna,
Est iter in sylvis;*"

but he is off again in a second, though he might have taken us into the recesses of the wood.

Did you ever observe that of brooks, which run through or near a wood, each, when it "*laborat trepidare rivo,*" has its own special note? I fancy that if four brooks could be heard at once, you would have a murmur—a babble in complete harmony of four parts.

"*Claudite jam rivos.*" These extracts which I here bring to a close, to all who love Ushaw, to all who esteem Dr. Tate, venerate his memory, and admire his intellectual acquirements, cannot fail to prove most interesting reminiscences of him. Nor do they betray on my part, as evident from the selections I have made, any breach or betrayal of confidence in regard to the correspondence which took place between us. The subjects he discusses and treats of in his letters are numerous and interestingly diversified, affording evidence of his great power and faculty of observation, and of his extensive and varied range of reading. "He was a scholar, and a ripe and good one; exceeding wise, fair spoken, and persuading. A man of gentlemanliness, dignity of character, and high principle; of much courtesy and amiability;" endowed with great knowledge and erudition, and who had, in copious draughts,

——"Quaff'd knowledge from the founts of mind."

Mgr. Tate moreover was a thorough churchman, firmly and devotedly attached to the chair of Peter—to the central influence of truth and unity. Error and heresy under their multiform phases and disguises he hated with a holy hatred. For shams and charlatans he had a consummate contempt; neither had he much sympathy with total abstinence, which he considered a species of manichæism.*

The term of Mgr. Tate's life on earth was now nearing a close. In the spring and summer of 1876, it was apparent to those among whom he lived that the health of this estimable and learned priest, this worthy President of Ushaw, was impaired and failing, and that it was only a question of a brief space of time before the *immutatio venerit*— "*Expecto donec immutatio veniat.*" He himself appeared to be cognizant of his approaching dissolution. He who had purchased, had read, had pondered over so many books, who on one occasion, in one of his letters, said—"*Requiem quæsivi et non inveni nisi in angello cum*

---

*The law of the Carthaginians, which interdicted wine to all who bore arms, and obliged them to drink only water during the war, enjoining the same abstinence on magistrates, pilots, judges, and on all who assisted at a deliberative assembly, only draws from Plato the remark savouring of irony, that with such customs, a state however great, needs but few vineyards." As rhythmically expressed by the angelic doctor in his SUMMA—

"*Sobrietas circa potum,
Bona virtus, quæ non totum
Nobis vinum subtrahit.*"

libello," now informed me that his reading was exclusively confined to the New Testament and the Following of Christ. Scarcely had summer gone, succeeded by early autumn; before the leaves had begun to fall, and the harvest had been reaped, when, on the Feast of St. Louis, August 25th, 1876, in the seventy-sixth year of his age, death closed his eyes to this world—its vanities, illusions, and worthlessness— "'Tis but a worthless world to win or lose," said Lord Byron. But nothing in life became Dr. Tate like the leaving of it. It is true he did not like St. Louis and other holy men expire on a bed of ashes; but his death was no less precious and edifying. Finding that his departure was near at hand, by his special request, he was conducted into the church, and in presence of professors and students, and before God's altar, he was "iled, anoynt, and ihoulsed" by his friend Provost Consitt, by whom he was throughout his sickness most tenderly and affectionately attended. By the Provost also was preached a most eloquent and impressive sermon, on occasion of Dr. Tate's interment. The little and the great, emperors and kings, the literate and illiterate, all perforce must yield to death. *Dic mihi, ubi sunt modo omnes illi Domini et magistri, quos bene novisti dum adhuc viverent et studiis florerent?"* asks the author of the "Imitation of Christ." They have passed through the valley of the shadow of death, and their place on earth is known no more. Truly, "blessed is that servant who, when the Lord shall come, shall be found watching;" and God grant, that like to him, Mgr. Tate, Ushaw's sixth President, has been set over all his master's possessions. The remains of the venerable deceased were assigned a resting place in the cloister of the college's secluded cemetery, among the other Presidents interred there. The inscription, on the the mural tablet which marks his place of sepulture, reads as follows:—

R. D. ROBERTUS TATE, S.T.D.,
Præl. Dom. SS. D. Pii PP. IX.
Præses Sextus 1863-1876,
Vir ingenio doctrina urbanitate insignis,
Illustris vita, vitæ exitu illustrior:
Viatico et S. Unctione ante altare susceptis,
Patientia sua ac pietate,
Quo modo advenienti sponso obviam irent,
Egregium suis tradidit exemplum,
Ob. Aug. 25, 1876,
Ætat 76.
Pater carissime vivas cum Jesu.

The inscription that follows was composed at the instance and by request of Bishop Chadwick (of blessed memory), but being found too long for the purpose for which it was intended, it was superseded by the foregoing shorter one:—

PACI ET ÆTERNÆ QUIETI
RVDMI. DNI. ROBERTI TATE, S.T.D.,
Prael. Dom. SS. Pii IX. PP., et Sexti Hujus Collegii Præsidis.

Vixit annos LXXVI. Obiit diem supremum, cum pace Christi, die XXV. Augusti, anno ab Incar. MDCCCLXXVI., in festo Sti. Ludovici regis, cujus meritis et precibus adjuvantibus, Pie Jesu Domine, miserere animæ ejus, et perduc eum ad æterna gaudia vitæ.
Sacerdos scilicet magnus, qui in diebus suis placuit Deo :—dilectus hominibus, carus amicis, benignus in familiares, virtute et doctrina perillustris. Ecclesiæ, quam amore ardentissimo amavit, decus insigne et tutamen extitit. Sedi veritatis - Petri sanctæ sedi, firmiter ac fideliter adhesit, cunctas ita hæreses perosus, ut hostes Ecclesiæ ejus hostes fierent. Decorem domus Dei eximie dilexit; nec minore dilectione cantus Ecclesiæ, ritus, et cerimonias sacras. Assiduus in Dei legis meditatione fuit ; et quæ pie egregieque dicta in sacris Scripturis, sanctorumque Patrum scriptis commendata invenit, sedula lectione sua fecit. Tanto ardore hisce aliisque studiis operam navavit, ut in illis persequendis—plurima perlegendo, discendo, et docendo- "SPIRITU SAPIENTIÆ ET INTELLECTUS IMPLETUS"—consenesceret. Vitæ dimidium et amplius in hoc Collegio degit varia munera obeundo, doctrina sua et ingenio alleo se commendando at gratiam omnium et favorem merito adipisceretur. Tandem in vineam abiit, ubi multos annuos pietate et zelo animarum laboravit. Electus hujus Collegii Præses, hoc gravi et magno officio, per tredecim annos et circiter sex menses, honore et dignitate perfunctus est. Quod si in vita clarus et nobilis, in morte fuit nobilissimus ; quippe qui, ingravescente morbo et periculo mortis imminente, publice in Ecclesia coram professoribus et auditoribus Collegii, sacram ante Altare sedens unctionem recepit. Pie et placide postea obdormivit in Domino.
Vale, Sacerdos veneraude ; vale vir admodum colende ; vale desideratissime amice! Hodie sit locus tuus in Paradiso.

A characteristic trait in Dr. Tate was attachment to old friends. This attachment was most sincere, firm, and constant. Early in the year 1874 "I have lost," he says, "within the last nine months, four of my oldest friends." These were the Very Rev. Michael Trappes, Canon Walker, Rev. Andrew Macartney, and Provost Platt. So it is; we find those who set forward with us lovingly and cheerily on our pilgrimage, have one by one dropped from our side.—

" When true hearts are wither'd,
  And fond ones are flown,
  Oh! who would inhabit
  This bleak world alone?"

REV. ANDREW MACARTNEY.—To Dean Trappes reference has been already made, and a memoir given of him. Of Andrew Macartney, "we know little more" as the venerable Bishop Challoner in his meditation on St. George observes, "than that he was a Christian soldier." Mr. Macartney also was a soldier, having entered the army in early life, and held, during the Peninsular war, office and rank in the commissariat department of the service. But in 1819, abandoning the profession of arms " *militiam sæcularem in militiam spiritualis exercitus commutans*"—and laying aside cares and carnal obstacles, he commenced studying for the priesthood at Ushaw, and in 1824 he was raised to the sacerdotal dignity. After serving various missions in the North, in Lancashire, and in Yorkshire, he retired to Ushaw, there to end his days in peace. The end came at last ; "*finis mors est, et vita hominum tanquam umbra subito pertransit.*" He departed to his rest, January 27th, 1874, at the ripe of old age of 84 years, and his remains were interred in the cloister of the College cemetery. Father Macartney was one of that respectable class of students known at

Ushaw as "patriarchs," being persons who enter on their studies for the church late in life. The race at present is well nigh extinct— "blotted from the things that be." In my college days several held patriarchal rank at St. Cuthbert's, and became worthy, respected, useful priests and labourers in the vineyard.

JOHN CANON WALKER, SENR.—John Walker was the son of William Walker and his wife Helen Park, born in 1800, at Thistleton, in the Fylde. He came of a family that had kept their faith and their lands during a long period of years. He received the early part of his education under the care of Mr. Banks, then incumbent of Singleton, who kept a school in the parsonage house. He was the only Catholic boy there, and this fact alone was amply sufficient to attract the attention of the other scholars. But he possessed many other attractions which endeared him to his master and schoolfellows. His brilliant abilities were equalled only by the sprightliness of his manners and the kindliness of his disposition. George Long, born in the same year, afterwards the learned classical scholar and historian, was one of his schoolfellows; but after they left, their paths were divided, and they never met again. This was not the case with all. Mr. Segar, afterwards County Court Judge, kept up their intimacy through life. The difference between a Catholic boy from the other scholars had struck the mind of young Segar then, and facilitated or suggested his future conversion. The subject of this notice had at stated times to leave the school before the usual hour. This naturally excited the attention of his schoolfellows. Their curiosity was quite satisfied when they ascertained the fact that he had to go to confession at regular intervals. His kind and gentle master had to ask him occasionally whether he was not due, so much was it taken as a matter of course. In May, 1814, he was sent to Ushaw, and after a brilliant course was ordained priest. He was then placed at St. Patrick's, Liverpool, recently erected, and served some time under Father Murphy, who became subsequently Bishop of Adelaide. Being recalled from the mission, he was appointed Professor at Ushaw of Rhetoric, and afterwards of Logic and Metaphysics. In the summer of 1835 he was ordered to take charge of the mission at Scarborough, and built the church there which is an ornament to the town. He was wholly careless about his own comfort; he had great compassion on the poor and those in distress, and was most profuse in his charities. He would go from morning to night on botanical excursions without tasting food, and on being told by his housekeeper that there was no dinner for him but a red herring, his answer was that he never yet had a dinner that was not too good for him. He was an accomplished scholar, and an intimate friend, &c., of Lingard, with whom he exchanged letters twice a week. He was present when the historian of England breathed his last July 17th, 1851. He did not write much. He preached one of the opening sermons at St. Anne's, Leeds, on the 31st Oct., 1838. This was in the early days of the Tractarian movement. The subject of the sermon was the Apostolic Succession with reference to Dr. Hook, and Anglican claims. It excited a sensation at the time, and for beauty of style and force of logic could not well be surpassed. The sermon is printed in the Feb. No. of the *Catholic Magazine*, 1839. He wrote also a paper on Bede in the *Dublin Review*, and many letters in the Magazines on the questions of the day. He died suddenly at Great Eccleston, on the Feast of the Sacred Heart, June 22nd, 1873, being at the time of his death on a visit to his friends. His remains were removed for interment to Scarborough, where he had long resided and zealously laboured. An intimate friend of the Canon's has been kind enough to furnish me with a few reminiscences of him ;—they are as follow :—" I should say that one of his very special traits was a singular unselfishness and absence of anything resembling meanness. He was a man of great simplicity of habits, and of very unusual indifference as to food, living very sparingly, often almost forgetting his meals, and satisfied with anything when he returned home some hours after the dinner hour. Yet if friends were with him, he was most particular to entertain them well. For the greater part of the time he was in Scarborough his means were very straitened ; but he never appealed to his people for himself, though he always eloquently pleaded for the usual Diocesan and other collections. One who made his acquaintance not long before his death, was so struck by his singularly unworldly spirit and indifference to money, that he gave him at once a large sum to reduce the debt of the church, and afterwards not only made up what was required after the bazaar to clear it entirely, but in memory of him (for he had alas ! died meanwhile) decorated the church and supplied it with a fine organ. Another trait known only to those who, like myself, had the privilege of knowing him intimately, was a singular tenderness of soul. Any affecting incident touched him strongly. He was fond of reading Shakespeare and other favourite authors aloud to his friends ; often I have seen him struggle to restrain his emotion caused by a pathetic passage, and finally throw down the book, unable to proceed with choking voice and eyes filled with tears. His tenderness to the sick was well known, and he sympathised deeply with the troubles of his flock, and I have seen him quite dejected when misfortune of any kind overtook them. At the same time, like Venerable Bede, whom I often thought he much resembled, he was really terrible to the criminal and the hardened violators of God's law ; and no one that I ever knew could speak with such awful impressiveness as he could."

Canon Walker's nephew, the Very Rev. William Canon Walker, Rural Dean, is Rector of St. Peter's Church, Lancaster ; his nephew the Very Rev. John Canon Walker died *flore ætatis*, September 28th, 1873, in the 52nd year of his age, at Peel, near Lytham. He was buried at St. Ann's, Westby, near Kirkham. Both brothers were earnest and devoted priests, learned, loved, and much esteemed. Both had successively charge of the mission of St. Augustine's, Preston, and they live in the grateful remembrance of the congregation. They performed their studies at Ushaw, and went through their course with honourable distinction. William, the elder brother was a Professor there for several years, before coming on the mission to Preston. Contemporary with Canon Walker, of Scarborough, at college, and on the mission, were the Very Rev. Richard Gillow, and the Right Rev. Provost Cookson. The former was one of the Canon's oldest and most attached friends.

PROVOST PLATT.—The Very Rev. Ralph Platt was born of respectable parents at Warrington, on the 21st of March, 1812. The maiden name of his mother was Rigby; she belonged to an old Catholic family resident at Little Plumpton, in the Fylde. On his father's side (his father died while he was yet a child) he had two uncles, Revs. James and Ralph Platt, both priests, educated at Crook Hall and Ushaw. That venerable priest, an alumnus of the college of Douai, the Rev. Ralph Platt, of Puddington, near Chester, at whose school no small number of youths were trained up in virtue and learning, and received ecclesiastical vocations, was his great uncle. After the death of his father the young boy, Ralph, was consigned by his widowed mother to the care of her parents and relations at Plumpton; thence in his thirteenth year he was sent to St. Cuthbert's College, which he entered at the end of the summer vacation, 1824. He and I were related, and commenced our studies together; sat next to each other in study place, and had contiguous "pigeon holes;" were fellow pupils and school fellows until the end of High Figures, when on account of his ability for learning, and progress in his studies, he was transferred to the class of Syntax, at the head of which he was soon placed. Canon Bewick, V.G., in the sermon preached by him at Dr. Platt's funeral, on Feb. 10th, 1874, thus speaks of him :—" Having entered college, and having once placed his hand to the plough, he never looked back, but steadily and faithfully pursued his course, and after passing through the curriculum of twelve years' study and preparation, he was raised to the priesthood, and from a pupil he became a professor, from a student prefect of studies, in which honourable position he remained about six years, and then entered upon his career of a missionary priest, being appointed by Bishop Mostyn as assistant to the Venerable Father Wilkinson, of Kendal. Here his labours and his virtues are still held in remembrance and his name in benediction. Thence he removed to Stella, from Stella he was promoted to Durham, and finally, in 1868, he quitted Durham, and returned to Westmorland, to take charge of the little flock attending the chapel at Dodding Green, near Kendal. In these several places he has left marks and monuments of his fervent zeal—zeal for the beauty of God's house—zeal for the education of poor children—zeal for the memory of the dead, and for the relief of the suffering souls in Purgatory. He has erected baptismal fonts; he has enlarged, beautified, and built churches; he has founded new missions; he has opened two burial grounds, one at Stella and one at Durham, in the latter of which it was one time his pious wish to be buried, which nothing but the long distance could have gainsaid or frustrated. In the midst of his numerous missionary labours he attained to all the various honours, dignities, offices, trusts, and titles which his fellow clergy or his Bishop could confer upon him. He was successively Secretary and Treasurer and first Superior of the Clergy Fund, Missionary Rector, Dean, Vicar-General, Provost of the Cathedral Chapter, and Doctor of Divinity. He was also for many years a member of the old English Chapter."

Death, says St. Chrysostom, is a translation into life; and in the Imitation of Christ it is said :—" thou shalt labour now a little and thou shalt find great rest : yea, everlasting joy." The Very Rev.

Ralph Platt, D.D., Provost of the Diocese of Hexham and Newcastle, was, after a brief illness, overtaken by death, on the 4th of February, 1874, and translated, we hope, to a better life, "yea, to everlasting joy." His death was comparatively sudden, and unexpected; hence when apprised of it, his friends were much surprised, and greatly lamented his departure. I had spent, as was my wont, the previous Christmas with him, little deeming that it was the last occasion that I should be permitted to enjoy his company and hospitality. It had been our custom, for several years past, to recite together, in memory of the good days of old at Ushaw, the office of Matins and Lauds for the morrow's feast, Christmas Day, and when we were so engaged on the Christmas Eve before his death, and were repeating with fervour, and meditating for a brief interval on the words "*Natum vidimus, et choros Angelorum collaudantes Dominum,*" uttered by the shepherds, on their being asked "*Quem vidistis pastores,* &c.," suddenly a band of waits and minstrels made the valley resound with the strains of the "Adeste Fideles." Oh! how our hearts bounded with joy and exultation on the occurrence of this happy coincidence. The funeral of Dr. Platt took place on the Tuesday (Feb. 10) after his death, the spot chosen for his grave being on a grassy slope, under the sable canopy of yews and cypresses, in the grounds at Dodding Green, and adjoining the grave of his predecessor the Very Rev. Robert Hogarth. Mass was celebrated by his cousin, the Rev. W. Rigby; the funeral sermon was preached by the Very Rev. Canon Bewick, V.G. There was a numerous attendance, considering the season of the year, of the clergy of the diocese of Hexham and Newcastle, and other parts. St. Cuthbert's, Ushaw, his *Alma Mater,* also sent her representatives. It was a cold, bleak, gusty day, early in February, when this grave, learned, and goodly priest was laid to rest with a solemn *Miserere* and *De Profundis,* and a silent *Requiescat.* Old winter still muffled up his cloak; hurtling showers of hail and sleet rattled through the leafless woods; the ground was hard and frost-bound; no re-awakening of spring; no flower—not even the snowdrop, in bloom; not a bird twittering, or warbling its wood notes wild.

Dr. Platt, we are reminded by Canon Bewick in his funeral discourse, succeeded to the living of Dodding Green on the death of the Very Rev. Robert Hogarth, in 1868, so that he held the appointment six years. The Very Rev. Robert Hogarth died on the 7th of February, 1868, and Provost Platt preached the sermon at his funeral. "Possessed," observed Canon Bewick, "of a bearing at once gentlemanly and genial, the faithful index of his large heartedness, the Provost had the aptitude to win friendship from gentle and simple alike. His interest in whatever tended to the welfare of the humblest cottager in his neighbourhood, irrespective of creed, was easily excited, and his charity was as ready as his counsel. His ripe and varied attainments, and his wide field of reading made him a delightful companion to all who had the pleasure of his acquaintance. The grounds around the house and chapel of Dodding Green give proof of his taste in horticulture, and much of his leisure time was given to carefully training and tending his leafy favourites, growing around the beautifully secluded retreat, where the sunset of his life was spent." Than Provost Platt few had a more exquisite appreciation of the beauties of nature, and of nature's gracious harmonies. He loved the fields, the woods, the streams, the meadows, the lakes, and the mountains; the "*gelidi fontes*" and the "*mollia prata*." Knowing withal, as St. Augustine declares, that God is the beauty of all that is beautiful—"*Dominus pulchritudo pulchrorum omnium*," how truly might he say with the Prophet, "*Delectasti me, Domine, in factura tua, et in operibus manuum tuarum exultabo*." At college Dr. Platt was a laborious and painstaking student, and as a priest grave, wise, and holy. As a scholar he was profoundly versed in Greek and Latin; had made no small proficiency in Hebrew; and had a good knowledge of the French and Italian languages.

"He knew the Hebrew, Greek, and Latin tongue,
   And conn'd the Sacred Books assiduously."

He was well skilled in historical and antiquarian lore, in ecclesiology, geology, vegetable physiology, and botany. He was moreover a sound and clever theologian; well read in Scripture and the writings of the Fathers; was an able controversialist, a staunch upholder of orthodoxy, and most zealous in maintaining the old venerated Catholic traditions :—"*State super vias vestras, et interrogate de semitis antiquis.*" "The knowledge of a wise man," according to Ecclesiastes, "shall abound like a flood." Besides his abundance of knowledge, our friend possessed considerable large heartedness—"*dedit ei Deus*," as we read of Solomon, "*latitudinem cordis.*"

I well remember when travelling with him in Belgium, with what a glow of delight and interest we visited and admired the beautiful churches of that Catholic land; with what reverence we entered them, with what devotion we heard mass in Antwerp Cathedral, and assisted at Benediction of the Blessed Sacrament in the church of St. Gudule, at Brussels. Nor do I forget the joy we experienced in visiting the venerable ruins of Finchale and Tynemouth Priory; and at other times in wandering through the solemn aisles, the chapels, and monuments of Durham's glorious cathedral. Then, in our walks and rambles to gather wild flowers in field, on roadside, and the banks of the Mint, to examine their botanical structure, and familiarise ourselves with their names; and what pleasure he took in tracing and pointing out to me the stratum of old red sand stone in the bed of the river Mint, cropping up very noticeably at and near Laverock bridge. The Very Rev. Provost built the church of St. Godric in Durham, the little mortuary chapel in St. Bede's cemetery, in the outskirts of that city, and enlarged the accommodation of St. Cuthbert's church, at Durham, and of that at Stella, while he was resident priest at those places. He composed and published a number of hymns entitled "St. Godric's Hymn Book," and for the Northern Catholic Calendar of 1872, 1873, and 1874, he wrote "Introduction to some Memoirs of the Northern Vicars Apostolic," "Cardinal Allen and Douay College," "Memoirs of Tudhoe School and Crook Hall College," &c. Had he lived, papers written by him on cognate and other subjects would, no doubt, have graced in consecutive years the pages of that little useful and interesting publication.

While Dr. Platt filled the office of Prefect of Studies at Ushaw, and had the direction of them, he introduced a new departure, and considerably improved, re-modelled, and extended the course. It was at this period, in the year 1840, while the curriculum of studies was directed by him, that the senate of the University of London issued a decree admitting students from the Catholic colleges as candidates for Degrees in Arts, &c., and Ushaw was the first of these colleges to take advantage of the privilege. Dr. Platt, with his characteristic energy and devotion to the cause of education, at once gave his adhesion to the new movement, and selected for the London University Examination two students, Francis Wilkinson and Richard Wilson, whom he prepared for it with unremitting care and diligence. Although the time for their preparation was very limited, it was most gratifying to him and to *Alma Mater* that the two candidates passed a most successful examination and obtained a First Class Degree. Under Dr. Platt a great ardour in the pursuit of learning, and zeal for study arose in the college. He fostered, encouraged, and aided it, for he knew well — none better — the importance of intellectual culture :—

"*Doctrina sed vim promovet insitam,
Rectique cultus pectora roborant.*"

Through him, with the sanction and approval of Dr. Newsham, was established that useful institution the public Reading Room (occupied formerly as the Divines' School) which is so amply stored with books in every department of literature, and which by the higher students is resorted to with much frequency.

Dr. Platt was a clever Greek scholar ; Greek derivatives, particles, and roots he had at his finger ends. A story is told of him that on one occasion he was showing a former Ushaw student round his garden, and describing to him the various shrubs, plants, flowers, and roots, when the young man, who was somewhat of a waggish turn, inquired of the Doctor whereabouts in his garden he had planted the "Greek roots." "Well, Dr. Platt, and where are the *Greek roots?* They used to be great favourites of yours, and entered largely into your system of anthology."

Many were the happy days, alas ! now past and gone, I spent with my friend at the several missions where he was placed—Stella, Durham, and Dodding Green. In our visits to remarkable places, and places of interest in the respective neighbourhoods of the above localities, there was not a stream, a tarn, a crag, an ancient hall, secluded hamlet or village, old country church, cosy grange and farmstead, rustic cottage and garden, that we passed unnoticed. We went together to Kendal, thence pased Sizergh Hall, and journeyed onward to Levens Hall, where we were permitted to view, and wander through the quaint trim gardens of that mansion. At a short distance from the manse and chapel of Dodding Green is Skelsmergh Hall, an ancient seat of the Leyburns. James Leyburn, who was Lord of the Manor of Skelsmergh, died a martyr for his faith, being drawn, hanged, and quartered at Lancaster, March 22nd, 1583. John Leyburn consecrated Bishop of Adrumetum, and Vicar-Apostolic of England, September 9th, 1685, was of the same family. "The old Catholic family of *Leybourn*, or Leyburn is," Dr. Platt states in his Introductory Memoirs of

Northern Vicars Apostolic, "now, I think, extinct. Their estates in Westmorland were confiscated in the last century, for their faithful adherence to the Catholic cause. A portion of them fell into the hands of Lord Derby. At Witherslack,* Skelsmergh Hall, and Cunswick, may still be seen the old Catholic chapels, belonging to the Leybourns, now desecrated." In the same township of Skelsmergh is Giltfortrigs (Gilthwaiterigg) : here we visited the house where James Duckett, the martyr, who suffered at Tyburn, April 19th, 1601, was born. He was a younger son of Mr. Duckett, of Giltfortrigs, and was named in his baptism James, after his godfather, the above mentioned James Leybourn, martyr. He (James Duckett) was a bookseller in London, and was executed for publishing Catholic books. The same James Duckett, martyr, had a son, Father Duckett, Prior of the English Carthusians. "Of the Ducketts of Skelsmergh," writes Provost Platt, in the *Northern Catholic Calendar* for 1872, "one branch of the family still keeps the Faith though no longer resident in Westmorland. It is remarkable that one of this family is married to an eminent Catholic bookseller of our time, who, there is no doubt, if called upon, would be found no less deserving than his illustrious relative of the martyrs' crown." The house at Gilfortrigs where Mr. Duckett lived in early youth, and whence he went to be apprenticed in London, is a respectable looking farm house. As a memorial of the birth place of the martyr I carried away with me a root of the *vinca minor* (lesser periwinkle) and planted it on a border in my garden. Another martyr from the same township of Skelsmergh was Thomas Sprott, who was ordained priest in 1596, and was sent from the English college, at Douai, the same year, upon the English mission. He suffered death at Lincoln, July 1600, with a constancy worthy of a martyr. In heretical Protestant Westmorland, where Catholics are so few, and scarcely have a local habitation and a name ; a country where the old religion had been almost stamped out and obliterated, and until lately was an "*opprobrium abundantibus, et despectio superbis ;*" a land dark and covered with the mist of error, God grant that the blood of our English martyrs may become the seed of the church, that through their sufferings, merits, and prayers, the one true faith may revive and be rekindled, and Catholic truth and unity be resuscitated and restored ; then shall "the mountains skip like rams, and the hills like the lambs of the flock ;" then shall its fells, and tarns, and waterfalls, and all the trees of its woods exult with joy :—"*tunc gaudebunt campi et colles, et omnia ligna sylvarum exultabunt.*"

"*Quæ vox, quæ poterit lingua retexere,*
Quæ tu Martyribus munera præparas ?
Rubri nam fluido sanguine fulgidis
Cingunt tempora laureis."

The hymn, "*In Natali Plurium Martyrum,*" supplies the words above quoted. Happy and glorious the Church which has so many saints and martyrs in heaven to intercede for it :—"*O felix Ecclesia, quæ tot habet in cœlo sanctos intercessores et martyres.*"

---
* Lord Stanley of Preston resides at Witherslack.

Having paid this passing tribute of affection and gratitude to the memory of my esteemed and venerated friend, the venerable Provost of the Diocesan Chapter of Hexham and Newcastle, I here bring my memoir of him to a conclusion. His death, so unexpected, was sincerely lamented by his friends, and his loss much deplored by his fellow clergy, for no one stood in the midst of them greater than the Very Rev. Provost Platt, D.D. "*Quapropter nitar, faciam, experiar, denique animum relinquam quam illum deseram.*"—Terence, Adelph., iii., 4.

> "Green be the grass above thee,
> Friend of my early days,
> None knew thee but to love thee,
> None named thee but to praise."

In pace in idipsum dormias et requiescas.

Writing to me shortly after Dr. Platt's death, Dr. Tate thus speaks of him :—"The late good Provost had a *clarum et venerabile nomen*, and was so hearty and honourable in all he did and said. God rest the soul of our good friend." In loving memory of him and of the Right Rev. Mgr. Tate, D.D., I composed, not long after their death, the following verses :—

IN MEMORIAM.

Through Ushaw's academic bowers and classic halls I tread,
I seek for friends who once were there,—those friends alas! are dead;
Some in their distant graves repose, and some in peace are laid,
And take their rest in holy ground 'neath Ushaw's yew tree's shade.

Replete with years and honours, there has late one passed away,
Who ruled at ALMA MATER with paternal, gentle sway;
Among the sainted dead of old, beloved, lamented, mourned,
Within the solemn cloister's bounds his ashes are inurned.

Garner'd in heaven his virtues are, ripe as a sheaf of corn,
That homeward by the reaper in the harvest time is borne;
And all his gifts of mind and heart, a rich and copious store,
Shall now to full accretion be developed more and more.

Not like to talents buried, or neglected summer flowers,
That bloom unseen and fade away among deserted bowers,
None of these gifts were wasted, since their object and their end
Was to promote the cause of God, and holy Church befriend.

And long as ALMA MATER, of Northern land the pride,
The studious youths who gather there shall train, instruct, and guide;
So long his venerated name shall ever cherished be,
And treasured as a household word within their memory.

And he, friend of my early youth, and of my riper years,—
He too has gone, and left me in this lonely vale of tears;
But still his spirit lingers round about me night and day,
And I for his eternal rest and peace ne'er cease to pray.

I loved him as a brother, I revered him as a priest,—
Nor have my love and rev'rence e'en in death the least decreased;
And though our lines and lives were cast in widely different sphere,
Cognate pursuits and tastes made both unto each other dear.

He died upon a winter's day ; the snow lay on the hill,
And over fell, and moor, and tarn, the wind blew bleak and chill ;
The snowdrop, though just peeping, with much coyness glinted forth,
In face of hurtling sleet and shower, and storm cloud in the north.

'Neath shade of yew and cypress they laid him in the grave,
In Dodding's hallowed grounds that Mint's swift-rushing waters lave ;
There rests my friend ; and on the turf that hides his narrow cell,
A shrub grows here, a flower blows there,--flowers, shrubs, he loved so well.

Fair trees your branches spread apace around his silent tomb,
And you, fresh, fragrant flowers, there in sweet profusion bloom ;
And thou, dear, lovely Dodding, this I make my special prayer,
That thou wilt guard my friend's remains with sacred, watchful care.

When spring arrays the verdant vale, and sunshine gilds thy hills,
And each blithe bird that haunts thy groves its wood notes sweetly trills ;
In palmer's guise unto thy shrine a pilgrimage I'll make,
And offer there my vows and prayers,—all for his soul's dear sake.

RECOVERY OF DOUAI PLATE.

In the early part of Dr. Tate's Presidency an event occurred, whose importance deserves to be here recorded, since every thing connected with the old English College, at Douai, and its former occupants, is of especial interest to all alumni and well wishers of Ushaw, who are the representatives and perpetuators of the Douai traditions. The event I refer to was the recovery of the buried treasures which, before the college broke up, and the students were dispersed, were concealed there in 1793. In the *Tablet*, of June 6th, 1863, will be found the following particulars of the recovery :—"When the time for departure came in 1793, two trenches were dug hastily by night, and in them were deposited two chests, one containing church plate and vessels for the service of the altar, the other containing holy relics, and among them the hair shirt of St. Thomas à Becket, and the beretta of St. Charles Borromeo. The late Rev. Richard Thompson, V.G., of Weld Bank, bore the principal part in the achievement, and one of the eye witnesses was the Rev. John Penswick. About twenty-two years ago, Father Burchall, Father Swale, and the Rev. R. Thompson visited the college (which, in 1834, had been purchased by the French Government and converted into barracks for the artillery), and satisfied themselves that the deposits had not been disturbed during all the vicissitudes through which the college had passed. At last, however, it was determined to apply to the Emperor Napoleon III. for permission to search for and remove these treasures. The Right Rev. Mgr. Searle obtained an audience, and made his request which was willingly granted, and on the 18th of May all proper authorisations having been obtained, and in the presence of a French Commission and of Mgr. Searle, the Very Rev. Dr. Burchall, O.S.B., the Very Rev. M. A. Hankinson, O.S.B., Prior of the Benedictine College, Douai, and the Rev. T. M. Margison, O.S.B., the search began. At first it was unsuccessful, but a reference to Mr. Penswick fixed the site as being that of the old 'Low Figures' class room ; and at some depth were discovered the decayed remnants of the chest and the plate."

The extract below, from a letter of the Rev. Bede Rigby, O.S.B., Procurator of the English Benedictine College, Douai, addressed to the President, or to one of the Superiors of Oscott College, states :—" In September, in the year 1841, the Rev. R. Thompson, V.G., of Weld Bank, Chorley, one of the priests who had fled from Douai, in 1793, when the Revolutionary frenzy was at its height, and who had witnessed the burying of the 'Treasure,' came to St. Edmund's College, Douai, and confided to Father Burchall, who was then the Prior, and to the Procurator, Rev. Sir John Swale, Bart., the secret of the hidden 'Treasure.' He also took them to the old College, which is now a barracks, under pretence of a visit, and stood over the spot where the 'Treasure' was supposed to be hidden. The secret was faithfully kept, and the agent of the English Bishops, Monsignor Searle, in 1863, applied to the Emperor Napoleon III. in person, to authorise him to dig up the 'Treasure.' The necessary permission was given, and Monsignor Searle and the Very Rev. Father Burchall went to Douai, in May, 1863. The Rev. Father Swale sent a letter describing the place pointed out to him by Father Thompson. On May 18th they began to dig in a room on the right of the quadrangle ; but after digging for a whole day nothing was found. The next day, May 19th, the spot indicated by Father Swale was chosen. It was in the room adjoining the Officers' Mess Room. They dug about eight feet deep under the hearth, and then came across the remains of an oak chest all mouldered away. Beneath was the 'Treasure,' consisting of numerous table services, about a dozen drinking goblets, mostly inscribed with the names of English nobility and gentry. After certain formalities had been gone through, the 'Treasure' was handed over to Monsignor Searle in the month of August. The day after their first success they determined to dig for some relics which were supposed to be also hidden there. They had a plan of the ground. The place marked was then used as a dungeon or lock-up. The search was fruitless. The relics in question were the hair shirt of St. Thomas of Canterbury, and the hat (beretta) of St. Charles Borromeo. There was also a tradition, that there was the body of a martyr buried with these relics. Monsignor Searle brought the 'Treasure' to England. The silver goblets were distributed among the Colleges."

"The plate recovered," writes the Right Rev. Mgr. Canon Searle, "was the Refectory plate which was buried in the 'Low Figures' class room. The church plate was buried in the grounds, in a plot (farm yard) which was sold for the site of a beet root sugar manufactory, and perhaps some of the men employed in digging for the foundation, could tell something about it. The great Sanctuary lamp was buried at Esquerchin, the country house, about three miles distant from Douai, and the farmer, it was asserted, had discovered and taken possession of it. Some relics, and the body of Father Southworth[*] were buried in

---

[*] John Southworth, priest, was born in Lancashire, in the year 1592, being a younger son of the ancient family of Southworths, of Samlesbury. He was sent for his education to the English College, of Douai, from whence he went on the English mission, the 13th of October, 1619. After some years employed in his functions, he was apprehended, and condemned, in 1627, to death for being a priest. However he did not suffer at this time, but was reprieved, and kept a close prisoner in Lancaster Castle, where, in the following year, as Father Arrowsmith was going to martyrdom,

the kiln. Researches were difficult from the change of the internal structure, and the heaps of debris on which the present floor is laid. We excavated through all this, but from the nature of the soil beneath, every thing we came upon was decomposed, and I decided to go no further in the excavations. The tradition among the people is that there is a body in the building."

From the summary here subjoined, for which I am indebted to an esteemed friend and Professor at Ushaw, the Rev. Henry Gillow, it appears that a visit was paid to Douai, in September, 1841, by the Very Rev. Richard Thompson, V.G., of Lancashire and Cheshire, who had been present as a boy when the treasure was buried by some of the Douai students before leaving the college in 1793. There was no other witness of the act then living, except the Rev. John Penswick, and he was too old to attempt so long a journey. The Very Rev. R. Thompson was accompanied to the English College, Douai, then used as a barracks for artillery, by the Very Rev. Provost Crook, and Fathers Burchall and Swale from the Benedictine College in the town, where the Vicar had been staying. The object of the visit was to make Provost Crook and the others aware of the exact spots where the treasure was buried. In case officers or soldiers should be present, and to prevent their learning where the objects were buried, it was pre-arranged that the Vicar should indicate the localities by putting himself in a certain posture when standing upon them. In this manner the position of the silver for domestic uses was discovered under the hearth stone in the "Low Figures" class room. It was stated in the *Tablet* of June 6th, 1863, that the Rev. John Penswick was the one who gave the information as to the precise spot where the treasure lay, but the Rev. Sir John Swale declared in a letter to the *Tablet*, June 13th 1863, that the information came from himself. His claim to the honour of having provided the sole clue to the discovery was not contradicted, and he must therefore be credited with having faithfully preserved the secret confided to him by Vicar Thompson, and with putting it at the disposal of Canon Searle and the rest who finally unearthed the treasure, in May, 1863. Vicar Thompson appears to have been at fault when he attempted to indicate the spot where the other treasure lay. Owing to the building of a new wall he could not recognise the surroundings, so as to be in any way clear where the box was buried. The Rev. Sir John Swale is the only person (but he is now dead) who might be able to point out the locality where Vicar Thompson was at fault. If the whole floor in the neighbourhood of his attempt were laid open, the relics and sacred vessels might possibly be recovered. The valuables discovered undoubtedly belonged to the two colleges, Ushaw and Old Hall, which alone inherited the funds and other property of Douai College. In the division of them, however, made by Cardinal Wiseman and Canon Searle,

---

Father Southworth gave him the last absolution. From Lancaster Castle he was removed to London, and committed to the Clink, but being afterwards released, he returned to his Master's work. In 1654 he was finally apprehended, and suffered death at Tyburn, on the eve of SS. Peter and Paul of that year, being the first of the usurpation of Cromwell. The aged martyr's body was sent over to the College at Douai, by one of the illustrious family of the Howards of Norfolk, and deposited in the church near St. Augustine's altar.

whilst a larger share of the objects went to Ushaw and Old Hall, a third portion was sent to Oscott, a college which had never been in any way connected with Douai.

LIST OF DOUAI SILVER AT USHAW COLLEGE.

Five silver handled knives, five table forks, fourteen table spoons, one large gravy spoon, nine goblets, two salt-cellars, one sugar duster, one coffee-pot, one tea-pot, one cruet-stand, one lamp-stand. Of these solid silver objects, the most noteworthy are the large and handsome coffee-pot and tea-pot. The sugar duster which stands nine inches high is well designed and engraved with the words "Given by the Honourable Henry Howard of Norfolk." All the cups, which are tulip shaped, are more or less engraved, six large ones with the names of the donors, and three small ones with the initials of the college, C.A., above a shield bearing St. George's Cross. No. 1. President's cup, engraved with shield bearing St. George's Cross and inscription "Ad usum Præsidis." No. 2, Engraved shield of donor, with inscription "Teney Le Vray, ex Dono N. D. Caroli Towneley, 1753." No. 3 bears shield of donor, with inscription "Ex Dono Nob. D. G. Heneage, Phiam Defendentis sub R. D. Ioan. Lodge, 1749." No. 4. Shield with St. George's Cross; initials C.A. above it; inscription "Ex Dono D. Antonii Canezas." No. 5. Shield as above; inscription "Ex Dono R. D. Thomæ Daniel, Alumni et Sacerdotis hujus Collegii, 1747. No. 6. Shield as above; inscription "Ex dono D. Hen. Wilkens, 1751." Nos. 7, 8, and 9, small cups, C.A.; Shield with St. George's Cross. The President's cup is very large—5½ inches high. Four inscribed ones are 4¼ inches high. The one inscribed H. Wilkens 3¼ inches high. Three small ones, 3 inches high.

Dr. Tate, thanking me for the Douai paper I sent him, thus writes :—"The account of the Douai 'diggings' is most interesting. Surely the cup of Mr. Daniel, the last President of Douai, and the first President of Crook, will be restored to Ushaw ; and when we have the pleasure of seeing you I hope to drink your health with the *spumans patera* duly charged :—"

——" *Impiger hausit*
Spumantem pateram et pleno se proluit auro."

As will be seen above the President's cup found its way to Ushaw.

THE VERY REV. DR. WILKINSON.

In succession to the Right Rev. Mgr. Tate, D.D., the Very Rev. Francis Wilkinson, D.D., was installed in the important office of President (the seventh) of St. Cuthbert's College, and his name claims to be mentioned with especial honour.

Francis Wilkinson was born on the 10th of October, in the year 1820. At a very early age he was placed at a Catholic school in Darlington, kept by Mr. Kirkley, and there commenced a friendship with several boys about his own age, with whom he remained on terms of affectionate intimacy during life. In July, 1832, in his twelfth year, he was removed to St. Cuthbert's College, Ushaw, and was placed in the second Class of Rudiments. Here he gave early promise of brilliant talents, and was remarkable for that diligent application to study which enabled him to take the lead in his class during the six years of his Humanity studies. But though distinguished for his great ability and earnest attention to classical studies, he was still more so for that amiability of disposition, and that fervent piety and devotion which so eminently characterised his whole life. The years 1838 and 1839 were spent in the study of Physics and Metaphysics, and in these subjects again we find him at the head of his class. On February 18th, 1840, a Decree of the Senate of the University of London, admitting students from the Catholic colleges as candidates for degrees in Arts, &c., received the Royal sanction. Mr. Wilkinson at once threw himself with all his usual energy and earnestness into the preparation for taking the degree of B.A. He and his fellow-student, Mr. Richard Wilson, went up to London for the examination which took place in May of that same year, and although the time for preparation had been so short, their efforts were crowned with complete success by obtaining a First Class Degree. They were the first Catholic students who took a degree at the University of London. They were both complimented by the examiners on being found quite equal, and in some points superior to the students of University College and King's College, though they had but a few weeks to prepare for the examination. On June 5th, 1840, he received the Tonsure and four Minor Orders. In 1841 he commenced his Theological studies; on September 24th, 1842, he was ordained sub-deacon; on September 23rd, 1843, deacon; and on December 23rd, of the same year, he received the order of priesthood, at York. On the day following he was appointed Prefect of Studies, and this post he continued to fill with eminent success until the year 1858. From 1849 to 1856 he occupied the chair of Moral Philosophy, until, owing to the untimely death of the Very Rev. Michael Gibson, D.D., he was called upon to take the office of Vice-President of the college, and to fill the chair of Moral Theology. About this time a large extension of the College buildings was in progress, which under the name of the "Seminary" was intended for young boys between the ages of eight and fourteen. The name of the "Seminary" has since been changed to that of "Junior College." In 1858, after the celebration of the Jubilee of the College, a portion of the new buildings was entered, and the "Seminary" was commenced under the immediate care and direction of Mr. Wilkinson. Here it was in an especial manner that his warm heart found room for the display of that fatherly love and solicitude for the welfare of those under his charge which no words can describe, but which must have been seen to be understood. In 1860 he resigned the Vice-Presidency, and was succceeded in that office by the much lamented Dr. Gillow. He now devoted himself to his new duties with undivided and untiring energy. These duties he continued to perform until the death of the Right Rev. Mgr. Tate, D.D., in August, 1876, when by the unanimous election of the Bishops interested in the College, and by the universal wish and desire of the professors and clergy, and with the heartiest congratulations of the laity, he was chosen the seventh President of St. Cuthbert's. In the Jan.

after his election, at the President's Feast, in answer to the toast of his health, Dr. Wilkinson, as a proof of the way in which he realised his position as a Father of boys, told how a priest, a particular friend of his, had in sending him his congratulations on his elevation to the office of President, added these words of Holy Scripture which by coincidence occurred in the office of the very day. "Have they made thee ruler? Be not lifted up: be among them as one of them. Have care of them: and when thou hast acquitted thyself of all thy charge, take thy place and receive a crown as an ornament of grace."—Eccles. xxxii. Two months after his appointment as President he received from the hands of the Holy Father the degree of Doctor of Divinity. During the year of his Presidency, his health, which was before not strong, became very much worse, and in accordance with the wishes of his friends he, on one or two occasions, for a short time tried the effect of change of air, but without much benefit. To satisfy the desire of his friends, rather than with much hope of permanent improvement, he went, during the midsummer vacation, to Spa, in Belgium. Here he remained for about four weeks, and would seem to have reaped considerable benefit from the mineral waters. On the 6th of September he started on his journey back to the college, but began to feel ill after reaching Brussels, and, with some difficulty, got to London on the 8th. Here he had accepted an invitation to spend a day or two with his intimate friend, the Count de Torre Diaz, but, on arriving at his house, he soon became so ill that medical advice had to be taken. For some time it was not quite clear what the disease was from which he was suffering, but as it developed, it became more and more evident that it was typhoid fever. As soon as he became aware of his danger, all his thoughts were given to prepare himself for death. During his short illness he communicated several times, and on the Friday evening (Sept. 21) immediately preceding his death, he received the Viaticum and Extreme Unction with the greatest devotion. Until Saturday evening hopes of his recovery had been entertained, but during the night a great change for the worse came over him, and a little after three o'clock on Sunday morning he calmly expired, after receiving absolution and the last blessing. During the whole of his illness he was in full possession of his faculties; his earnest preparation for death was most touching, and his entire resignation and patience were most edifying to those around him. He died at the comparatively early age of fifty-six, but his days were matured with virtues and merits. His remains were removed to Ushaw, September 25th (Tuesday), where the funeral took place on the following day. A solemn Requiem was sung by Dr. Chadwick, Bishop of Hexham and Newcastle, at which were present Dr. Cornthwaite, Bishop of Leeds, Dr. Vaughan, Bishop of Salford, Dr. O'Reilly, Bishop of Liverpool. The sermon was preached by the Right Rev. Mgr. Consitt. His body was placed side by side with that of his predecessor, the Right Rev. Mgr. Tate, in the cloister of the college cemetery. Years have passed, but he is not forgotten. He is still mourned both by many priests in whose training for their sacred office he had so large a share, and by others who have either themselves experienced in their youth his kind, tender, and fatherly care, or on whose children he had so long bestowed the love and affection of his warm heart. To such as these this short account of his useful and meritorious life, so prematurely closed, will be, I am sure, not unacceptable. Though he was President but for one year, yet it was a year full of promise and activity. Not one of his least monuments is the series of dramas he composed, or adapted during the leisure hours of his duties as professor and head of the Seminary.

On the mural tablet near his grave is inscribed —

R. D. FRANCISCUS WILKINSON, S.T.D.,

Præses Septimus, 1876-1877,

Præf. Stud., Phil. et Theol. Prof., Vice-Præses.,

Seminarii Rector,

Per totam vitam in laboribus assiduis in hoc Collegio

Pro Dei gloria occupatus,

Pie obiit 23 Sept., 1877,

Ætat 56;

Vir ingenii præclarissimi, prudentia, humilitate, devotione ergo B.V.M. conspicuus, benignitate semper parata ac vere paterna omnibus carus.

F.   Pater mitissime vivas cum Jesu.   W.

The vacancy occasioned by the lamented and premature death of Dr. Wilkinson was supplied by Bishop Chadwick, who, in compliance with the wishes of the other Bishops interested in the college, and of the Professors, accepted the Presidency, and was installed in the office on the 30th of October, 1877. To every inmate of the house it was an inexpressible delight and satisfaction to have the Bishop for their President; and by the Bishop himself, to whom Ushaw was the joy of his heart, the focus of his affections, the scene, in the days of his youth, of tranquil and innocent enjoyments,

—— " The spot of earth supremely blest,
A dearer sweeter spot than all the rest,—"

his residence as President at his dear *Alma Mater* was looked forward to with unfeigned pleasure. But, though he could say in regard to Ushaw—

" *Ille terrarum mihi præter omnes
Angulus ridet,*"

finding that he was unable to discharge satisfactorily the dual duties of a large diocese, and of President of an important college, he retired from the office which he had filled for a year, on October 26th, 1878, and again went to reside at Newcastle. Bishop Chadwick, on his resignation, was succeeded by

RIGHT REV. MGR. WRENNALL, D.D.

Mgr. William Wrennall, Ushaw's ninth President, was born in Lancashire, at Lea, in the Fylde, on the 5th of July, 1819, of respectable parents, who lived after the good old Catholic fashion, were diligent frequenters of all holy duties, "sworn liegemen" of the faith which had been transmitted to them from their forefathers, and which was valued by them more than treasures of gold and silver. William was the eldest of the four brothers who became priests, and devoted their lives to the service of the Church, to the education of youth, and the labours of the mission. The Rev. Joseph Wrennall was for many years the energetic Prefect of Studies at Ushaw; subsequently, towards the close of the year 1869, he went on the mission to Birchley, and his remains, at his death, July 14th, 1872, at Harrogate, were interred in the hallowed ground of Birchley cemetery. The Very Rev. Mgr. Thomas Canon Wrennall is Rector of St. Bede's College, Manchester; the Very Rev. Henry Canon Wrennall is Missionary Rector of Stella-on-Tyne. The Right Rev. Dr. Newsham was their great uncle. Their uncle, Rev. James Wrennall was among those students who came from Crook Hall to Ushaw in 1808; in 1809 he was in his first year's Theology; in the following year, sub-deacon; and on being ordained priest in 1812, he was made General Prefect, October 27th, of that year. On leaving Ushaw, March 13th, 1814, he went on the mission to Houghton Hall, Yorkshire. After a few years there, he removed to Linton-on-Ouse, from which mission he retired in 1850 or 1851. The last fourteen years of his life were spent with his relatives in Lancashire: he died near Clayton Green, 30th of December, 1865, aged eighty years. His nephew, William Wrennall, left his home at Bellfold, in Woodplumpton, to commence his studies at Ushaw, in the autumn of 1834, and having, with exemplary diligence, application, and piety, gone through the college course, he was raised to the priesthood, February 15th, 1845. Being appointed Prefect of Discipline he held that office nine years, till September, 1854, when he resigned the fasces to teach Natural Philosophy. Early in August, 1877, Dr. Gillow, the Vice-President, died, and the Rev. William Wrennall succeeded him as Vice-President. In 1879 he was created Doctor of Divinity, and in the following year, on January 27th, 1880, he was raised by His Holiness, Leo XIII., to the dignity of Domestic Prelate, and a Monsignore. During Mgr. Wrennall's Presidency, the foundation stone of the new Collegiate Chapel of St. Cuthbert was laid, on July 27th, 1882; on October 4th, 1884, the Chapel was solemnly blessed, and on the day following was entered by the students and priests of the college. It was not till July 29th, 1885, that the solemn opening took place. The author (Rev. Henry Gillow) of the "Chapels at Ushaw" remarks—"The untiring energy with which Mgr. Wrennall pushed forward the building of the New Chapel to its completion, and the great and successful efforts made by him to relieve it of debt, will be a lasting memorial of his usefulness and zeal for the welfare of the college."

In the last week of November, 1885, he resigned the Presidency. In announcing his resignation the *Tablet* in its "Notes" of December 5th, says—"A wide circle of the old students and friends of Ushaw College will learn with unmixed regret that Mgr. Wrennall is about to close his long career of service to the college as Professor and Superior, by resigning the office of President, which he has held since the death of Dr. Wilkinson. We are informed that he has had this step in contemplation some time, and that he took the occasion of the Bishops' annual business visit to the college last week to beg of them to relieve him of this burden of responsibility. The resignation was finally accepted by their Lordships, not without the expression of the deep sense of their appreciation of his high character and great merits, and of the long and valuable services which will connect his name inseparably with the history of the college."

Shortly after his resignation, Mgr. Wrennall was appointed by the Bishop of Liverpool, Right Rev. Dr. O'Reilly, to the mission of Wesham Cross, near Kirkham, where a new church was being erected, and which was consecrated and dedicated to St. Joseph, March 18th, 1886, and was solemnly opened the Sunday following. Here Mgr. Wrennall is doing good work, and has erected new schools in connection with the church. The same regularity, punctuality, and exactitude, the same conscientious discharge of his duties, as when he was a student, a Professor, and President at Ushaw, characterise him as a missionary priest at Wesham Cross. Rarely is he absent from his post; seldom goes abroad, keeps at home, and when duty calls, is sure to be found—so sure—that as the man, who was asked if Mr. Wrennall was at home, replied—"at hooam, aye; yore shoor to foind him abaat sumweear." Like a tranquil, noiseless, ceaseless stream flows on, at Wesham Cross, the every day life of Mgr. William Wrennall, D.D.

As soon as it became known that Mgr. Wrennall had resigned the office of President of the college, many friends desired to testify their esteem and respect for the worthy prelate. Accordingly, at a large gathering of his friends among the clergy and laity, at the Palace Hotel, Birkdale, an address and a purse containing £400 was presented to him. Mgr. Wrennall warmly acknowledged their kindness.

WILLIAM CANON DUNDERDALE.

"The choice of a successor to Dr. Wrennall," as the *Tablet* thus announced at the time, "has fallen upon Canon Dunderdale, of Great Harwood, in the Diocese of Salford, and the choice has been received with applause. Canon Dunderdale has long enjoyed the confidence of the clergy of Lancashire, of whose fund he has been for many years the indefatigable Secretary. He has also been for some time an active member of the Poor School Committee. His excellent business habits, punctuality, and considerate kindness to all are no doubt strong recommendations; and his intimate acquaintance with the practical work of a priest's life on the mission, and his knowledge of what is required in the education of the clergy to fit them for their arduous duties, are no less important qualifications for one who is to preside over a college with some two hundred ecclesiastical students."

William Canon Dunderdale, son of Richard and Ellen Dunderdale, was born at Bolton, October 1st, 1827. He went to college February 10th, 1840, and commenced his studies in the first class of Underlow. He had for schoolfellows among others of the clergy, Revs. G. Coulston, D.D., George Flint, and Gerald O'Reilly. At the close of his Philosophy in July, 1848, he was appointed Minor Professor, and taught mathematics, arithmetic, writing, and drawing for three years; the drawing he continued to teach till the close of his college course in 1854. He was ordained priest, September 23rd, 1854, and went on the mission, October 3rd, in the same year, as assistant priest to the Very Rev. Canon Toole, D.D., at St. Wilfrid's, Hulme, Manchester. On June 24th, 1857, he commenced a new mission at Great Harwood, with 78 Catholics for a congregation. Of this mission James Lomax, Esq., was a liberal patron and benefactor. In April, 1858, the new church of our Lady and St. Hubert was begun, and on November 3rd, 1859, was opened. In July, 1860, he was elected Secretary of the Lancashire Infirm Secular Clergy Fund, succeeding the Very Rev. Canon Worthy, then made Treasurer; at the close of 1885 he had held the office for 25½ years. On the 12th of March, 1875, he was elected by concursus Canon Theologian of the Diocese of Salford. On January 5th, 1886, he left his mission at Great Harwood, with its 1300 Catholics, and entered on the discharge of the responsible duties of President of St. Cuthbert's College, Ushaw, to which he had been appointed by the co-interested Bishops, on the resignation of the Right Rev. Mgr. Wrennall, D.D., on November 26th, 1885. On New Year's Day, 1886, the members of our Lady and St. Hubert's, Great Harwood, in testimony of the high esteem, love, and gratitude, which they entertained for him, presented Canon Dunderdale with an illuminated address and purse of gold containing £110. The address expressed the deep regret which they felt at his loss from amongst them as their pastor, friend, father, and guide, for more than eight and twenty years, heartily congratulating him at the same time on the important position which he had been elected to fill, of President of St. Cuthbert's College, Ushaw.

It was not on the 5th, as above stated, but on the 7th of January, 1886, that Canon Dunderdale was able to leave Great Harwood, and assume the duties of his new and important appointment. Though he had lived for many years so far from Ushaw, he was intimately and affectionately known by all the professors, and was no stranger to the students. On his arrival, the heartiness of the welcome he received showed in a way not to be mistaken how he was regarded by those over whose interests he had come to preside. As soon as he entered the college, he was received with enthusiastic cheers, again and again renewed. When silence was obtained, Dr. Lennon, the Vice-President, read the following address from the professors and students :—

TO THE VERY REV. WILLIAM DUNDERDALE, PRESIDENT OF ST. CUTHBERT'S COLLEGE, USHAW, CANON OF SALFORD.

VERY REV. AND DEAR SIR,—With sincere respect and dutiful affection we venture on this your first appearance amongst us as our President to bid you a hearty and respectful welcome. The loyal and unhesitating obedience of the sons of Ushaw to their President is one of the proudest of our traditions. But in your case the delight with which we have heard of your appointment, and the joy with which we have looked forward to your coming, are more ardent and more enthusiastic than any sense of duty of itself could have evoked. Your great and various gifts and the alacrity with which you have devoted them to the service of Ushaw in the past, whilst they have earned our lively and lasting gratitude, have led us to hope for a splendid future for the College, when these gifts are employed exclusively in its service. We know, too, the sacrifices you are making in coming to us, we know the sacrifice your friends are making in consenting to your coming, and we are grateful—most grateful for it. The only return that it is in our power to make will be found in the hearty co-operation and sympathetic support which we shall give to your every effort to increase the usefulness and add to the reputation of the college. And whilst we promise you our affectionate and unceasing submission, we assure you our constant and earnest prayer shall be that your tenure of the office you are entering upon may be long and illustrious, and unclouded by anxiety or sorrow.—We are, Very Rev. and dear Sir, your obedient servants. (Signed) JAMES LENNON (on behalf of the Professors), THOMAS REILLY (on behalf of the Students).

The President, who seemed unprepared for such an outbreak of irrepressible and spontaneous sympathy and was much moved by it, said that though he had parted with pain from friends most dear to him, it was with sincere joy and gladness that after an absence of thirty years on the mission he found himself once more an inmate of *Alma Mater*. He was glad of the opportunity of returning thanks to the superiors to whom he looked for help in the arduous task that had been imposed upon him ; he thanked the students too, in whom he knew he should find true followers of their predecessors in their love for the college and their desire to be an honour to it. He had come to make their interests his interests, their sorrows his sorrows, their joys his joys, and he hoped that each one of them would find him a sincere friend. He trusted that if sacrifices had been made, not only on his part, but also on the part of others whom he had left behind, they would draw down a blessing on each one of them, that united they might be able to complete the good work they had in hand to the glory of God and the honour of *Alma Mater*.

As soon as he had concluded his reply, all repaired to the College Chapel where the *Te Deum* was sung. Nothing could have been more enthusiastic or more universal than the joy at Ushaw that day.

Canon Dunderdale's tenure of the office of President was however of short duration. Not many weeks after his installation, his health, which was not the strongest, began to give way under the onerous duties and responsibilities which had devolved upon him. Moreover, after an active missionary life, the seclusion of a college was far from being compatible with, or beneficial to his health's improvement. Hence for these and other reasons he found himself compelled to resign the dignity to which he had been raised. From Ushaw he retired to his former mission at Great Harwood, where he laboured with renewed zeal, enjoying the affection, gratitude, and respect of a faithful people.

The Canon's brothers, John and Richard Dunderdale, both received their education at Ushaw. The health of the former, after ten years' zealous and successful labours at Barnard Castle, failed him, and he died at his father's house at Bolton, January 4th, 1870, at the age of thirty-seven years. He was buried at our Lady and St. Hubert's, Great Harwood. The latter named brother, Father Richard Dunderdale, having been ordained priest, September 6th, 1856, commenced his missionary labours at St. Ann's, Manchester. He was next sent by Bishop Turner to found a new mission at Blackburn, where he first erected an iron church ; he then built St. Mary's beautiful church, which from time to time has been embellished by the gifts of friends and the liberality of others. Father Dunderdale was twenty-seven years at Blackburn : he went there October 15th, 1860. Previous to his death, he had been for some time in weak and delicate health. On the morning of the 9th of August, he calmly passed away at the age of fifty-eight years. The funeral obsequies took place at St. Mary's, Blackburn, at which the Bishop of Salford, and upwards of eighty of the deceased's fellow priests assisted. The Bishop preached; the Very Rev. Canon Dunderdale sang the Requiem Mass. His remains were then conveyed to Great Harwood, and interred in a vault by the side of his younger brother, the Rev. John Dunderdale, at Our Lady and St. Hubert's. The Rev. Richard Dunderdale was a priest of blameless life and manners—"*placuit Deo, et inventus est justus*"— devoted to his duties and the spiritual welfare of his flock, to whom he was much endeared, and five hundred of whom, the Sunday but one after his funeral, paid a visit to his grave, at Great Harwood.

The grave had scarcely closed over his deceased brother when Canon Dunderdale, whose state of health for some time past had not been very satisfactory, was overtaken by sickness, which terminated fatally, and cut short his useful life. Having borne with exemplary patience and resignation his protracted illness, and fortified with the Sacraments of holy Church, the Canon breathed forth his soul in peace on the morning of Sunday, October 2nd, the Feast of the Most Holy Rosary. On the day previous he attained the age of sixty years, thirty of which he had passed at Great Harwood, labouring with tireless zeal for the salvation of souls, and the advancement of religion. God be gracious to him! His flock, his friends, and fellow priests lament his departure; but let them take comfort—"*Beati mortui qui in Domino moriuntur.*" He has departed from their midst, and gone to

"Where fret and fear, and toil and troubling cease,
And knows at last what joy it is to live,
Where life is love, love immortality,
And perfect peace God's last best gift to give."

As the Bishop of Salford observed in his discourse at the funeral of the Canon, Canon Dunderdale had proved himself a model parish priest, and no greater meed of praise could be given to a priest; he was also in every way a model of order, regularity, and attention to duty. Indeed he (the Bishop) knew not where to turn to replace him. During his last illness, a crucifix, blessed by the Pope, with a plenary indulgence attached for the hour of death, along with his Rosary, was his constant companion. The body of the deceased was laid to rest by the side of his two brothers, Revs. John and Richard Dunderdale, in the cemetery attached to the beautiful church of Our Lady and St. Hubert. There was a very numerous attendance of the Salford diocesan clergy at the funeral. The Right Rev. Mgr. Wrennall, D.D., the Right Rev. Mgr. Gillow, Ushaw College, and the Very Rev. Canon Carr, V.G., of Liverpool, were also present on the mournful occasion.

VERY REV. JAMES LENNON, D.D.

For a short time after Canon Dunderdale's departure, the government of Ushaw by a President was in abeyance. The direction and management of its affairs became vested in a kind of Pro-Consul, or Pro-President: the Very Rev. Dr. Lennon, the Vice-President, held that office until May, 1886, when he was elected President of the College. His election was received with general approval and satisfaction, for Dr.

Lennon was held in deserved esteem and favour, and was a learned, pious, and prudent priest—"*justum et tenacem propositi virum,*" who from boyhood to manhood had been connected with St. Cuthbert's, who would strive to carry on its memorable traditions, safeguard its religious and historical associations, cherish its glorious memories, and preserve intact the time-honoured usages and customs transmitted from Douai to Crook, and from Crook to Ushaw. Inquiring of an Ushaw student how they liked their new President, the reply I received was—"We like him *immensely.*" I rejoiced to hear him thus testify to the love and esteem which they all entertained for their worthy President. *Diu lætus intersit Sti. Cuthberti Collegio, eumque Deus sospitem servet.*

Dr. Lennon is a native of Liverpool. He went a boy of thirteen to Ushaw, September 9th, 1842, and commenced his studies in "the royal school of Underlow." It is gratifying to notice this circumstance, because, as no one was considered a veritable college lad unless he had been three times subjected to the discipline of the birch, so no student was regarded as *regulariter doctus*, who had not passed through Underlow. Among his schoolfellows was comprised a goodly contingent of priests, viz., Canons Liptrott, Rogerson, *Scruton, and *Thos. Bennett; *Very Rev. Thomas Roskell, D.D. ; *Revs. William Walton, *Peter Holmes, *John Dunderdale, *Thomas Billington, Joseph Gibson, Alnwick ; and Very Rev. Dean Cooke, Southport. Those to whose names an asterisk is prefixed are now numbered among the dead :—

" Oh, Father give them rest—
Thy faithful ones, whose day of toil is o'er,
Whose weary feet shall wander never more
O'er earth's unquiet breast !"

Dr. Lennon having gone through his course studiously and commendably ; having as minor Professor taught Syntax for five years, and defended theses in Moral Philosophy, and twice in Theology, was ordained priest, September 24th, 1859. After his ordination, he taught, as a senior Professor, Rhetoric for one year ; and from September, 1861, to 1866, was General Prefect. Again, September, 1866, to 1869, he was Professor of Rhetoric ; in September, 1869, he began to teach Moral Theology and Ritual, and had charge of the large Library, assisted by Dr. Fellen. On the 1st of November, 1878, he succeeded Mgr. Wrennall as Vice-President ; on the 25th of December he was created Doctor of Divinity.

On the occasion of the inauguration of a Memorial Window erected in the College Chapel by the students, the following address was presented to the Very Rev. President, Dr. Lennon :—

VERY REVEREND AND DEAR PRESIDENT,—Now that the Memorial Window to our late venerated Bishop and President, Dr. Chadwick, is in its place, we, the students of St. Cuthbert's College, desiring to emulate the noble example of those friends of Ushaw, the members of St. Cuthbert's Society, who in 1881 presented to our new and splendid chapel the first of a series of windows illustrating the lives of our glorious northern saints, venture to ask your acceptance of this second window as a token of our lasting affection for him whose chief delight it always was to be amongst us and to advance our interests, and as a monument of our zeal for the adornment and enrichment of our college. Still adhering to the plan adopted by the members of St. Cuthbert's Society, who selected the saintly Archbishops of York and Metropolitans of the north to occupy the first place in our series of choir windows, we have chosen for the second place the Bishops of Lindisfarne and Hexham, who ruled and adorned this diocese, and found in Bishop Chadwick so worthy a successor. May he continue to watch over us now that he has passed to his reward, and may the sight of this memorial of him ever animate us to imitate his virtues, and to perservere in that love of our ALMA MATER and zeal for the advancement of religion, which tend, we fondly hope, to the recovery by our dear country of her once proud title "The Island of Saints."

Signed on behalf of the students,
EDWARD BEECH, Phil. Censor.
Feast of St. Edmund, the Martyr, November 20th, 1886.

The PRESIDENT returned his warm thanks to the students for their very acceptable and munificent present to the college, and noticed with pride and pleasure the generous spirit of self-sacrifice which had enabled them out of their slender means to set aside so large an amount as over £200 for this good object. As a beautiful and devotional work of art, he felt that the window was an acquisition to the College Chapel; and he was, moreover, pleased to think that each one of the students who had contributed towards its erection would find in this fact an additional link for binding his affections to the college.

The cost of the stained glass was £210, and almost the entire amount was colleeted amongst the students in the college during the time of the building of the new church.

The festive celebration of Queen Victoria's Golden Jubilee was kept with enthuslastic jubilation at St. Cuthbert's, Ushaw; and as the joyful event occured in the second year of Dr. Lennon's Presidency, a record of it may not here be considered out of place. The *Tablet* from which I quote says—" Ushaw has been keeping high festival in honour of the Queen's Golden Jubilee. On Sunday, June 19th, the usual solemn High Mass was made more solemn still by special prayers for her Majesty the Queen. The Antiphon, *Domine salvam fac*, sung on all Sundays after the High Mass, was, in honour of the occasion, sung to an adaptation of the beautiful air of the Austrian national hymn. As the last notes died away the organ pealed forth the opening notes of the *Te Deum*, which was then sung in thanksgiving for the many blessings showered down on our Queen and country during her fifty golden years of a golden reign. In the evening service too the *Te Deum* was again sung with the additional Versicles, Responses, and Prayers ordered for occasions of solemn thanksgiving. On Monday morning, the ringing of the "big bell" announced a whole "play-day" for the students; with its iron tongue it sang out, "Jubilee, Jubilee," if ever a bell sang or spoke. So thought the students at any rate, who in their scores had gathered round the Bell turret, cheering so lustily for the Queen that the loud and ceaseless song of the bell "Jubilee, Jubilee," was drowned by the deafening chorus that greeted the "Censor's" appeal to young warm hearts: " Nine times nine for her Majesty, our noble Queen, Victoria." Tuesday morning—Jubilee day itself—came, and at an early hour the Very Rev. President (Dr. Lennon), Professors and students, mustering close on 300, assembled on the terrace facing the college; and there, with the college band in their midst, they reverently and solemnly sang "God save the Queen." As the swelling notes rose and were borne along over the still morning air, blackbird, thrush, and linnet, which a minute before had been singing as for dear life, stayed their orisons, and hushed, listened to the "Jubilee" hymn,

And when the oft-repeated "God save the Queen" had died away for the last time, these Ushaw birds, that haunt that "shaw" of "yew," once more took up their morning song in notes sweeter than usual; they too had caught the key-note "Jubilee," and for the rest of the day warbled song after song of triumphant joy and gladsomeness. This day too did the students, at the welcome bidding of the Very Rev. President, lay aside book and pen, and hastened some to the tennis courts, others to the cricket field, where at stated times the college band played in excellent style a choice selection of "Jubilee" music. On Wednesday morning again the "big bell" sang out "Jubilee, Jubilee," announcing another whole "play-day." All honour to our noble Queen! Long may Victoria reign! God bless the Queen!"

It was with supreme delight I read this account of the celebration of the Royal Golden Jubilee:—

" The ancient spirit is not dead,
Old times thought I are breathing here."

The narrative was to me like an echo of the past; it recalled the days of old, when the iron-tongued bell under the old stairs rang out with delirious clang a play-day, and when the shouts of the joyous youths congregated around were so vociferous that they might have been heard even to Russell's wood, alarming the hawks and owlets, and startling the squirrels in their aerial nests.

In the same year, on Sunday, March 20th, 1887, the twelve hundredth anniversary of St. Cuthbert, the Patron Saint of the College, was celebrated at Ushaw with special solemnity and devotion. "At ten o'clock High Mass was sung in the college chapel dedicated to St. Cuthbert. The high altar was tastefully adorned with a profusion of plants and flowers interpersed with candles, and the magnificent chapel, as a long procession of professors and students passed up its centre, seemed to assume even grander proportions to do honour to the great Saint whose name it bears. After the Gospel, a brief but eloquent sketch of the life of St. Cuthbert, by the Right Rev. Mgr. Consitt, Vicar-Capitular, was read. St. Cuthbert's College is possessed of one of the very few relics of St. Cuthbert now in Catholic hands, St. Cuthbert's ring. Perhaps the most striking ceremony of the day was the veneration of this holy relic. It was presented by the celebrant to each of the community to kiss, and from the oldest to the youngest of that large body there was not one whose heart was not inflamed with increased love and devotion as his lips pressed upon that sacred souvenir of God's honoured and chosen servant. At the conclusion of the Mass the Blessed Sacrament was carried in solemn procession through the College ambulacra, previous to being exposed in St. Cuthbert's for the rest of the day. Exposition was inaugurated by a choral *Te Deum*, sung by the united voices of the whole college. The Second Vespers of the feast were sung in the afternoon. At the conclusion of the Exposition the *Te Deum* was again sung. Monday, in spite of the somewhat unpropitious state of the weather, was observed as a whole play-day."

DEATH OF BISHOP BEWICK.

Dr. Lennon had not been President long before the death of Bishop Bewick took place. His days on earth were alas! short, and the years of his episcopacy few :—"*Præcisa est quasi a texente vita ejus.*" Four years and a few days after his consecration as Bishop he passed to his rest, October 29th, 1886, at his residence the Martyr's Peace, Tynemouth. May that rest, that *in cœlo quies* which he sighed after and hoped for, be fully enjoyed by him in company with his predecessors, the Celtic and Saxon Saints and Bishops of Northumbria. To Ushaw the Bishop's death might be considered a misfortune, for whatever difficulties and discouragements it might have to encounter, it would rely mainly on him for counsel, guidance, and support, as being of the Bishops the most interested in its welfare, and because his attachment to Ushaw— "our glorious college," as he called it, was most sincere, unfailing, and friendly. The shortness of the period of his episcopacy, and his precarious state of health prevented him from accomplishing many projected works, but many remain to testify to his zeal, earnestness, and ability. For the Catholics of Newcastle he provided the cemetery of the Holy Sepulchre, at Gosforth, where it was his wish to be buried, and where his remains repose. During his short episcopal rule he was able to place the missions of his diocese on a securer and sounder basis, and by a careful and prudent administration of the diocesan funds to reduce the debt upon them by many thousands of pounds. Several new churches, schools, temporary chapels, and charitable institutions were also opened during his episcopate. No man is given to see his work through— "Man goeth forth to his work and his labour until the evening." The death of Bishop Bewick was much regretted, and was felt to be a severe loss to the diocese. It took place on the Feast of St. Bede, the Venerable, of whom he had written a Life, and a copy of which, just issued from the press, was placed in his hands shortly before he died. Nearly a year elapsed before Dr. Bewick's successor in the See of Hexham and Newcastle was appointed. After the Bishop's funeral the Chapter elected the Right Rev. Mgr. Provost Consitt Vicar-Capitular.

DEATH OF PROVOST CONSITT,

VICAR-CAPITULAR.

*Quis desiderio sit pudor aut modus
Tam cari capitis?*—Hor.

Unexpectedly and prematurely was this eminent and esteemed ecclesiastic, this pious, prudent, and venerated priest surprised by death and removed from the midst of men. Mighty monarchs, princes, and prelates have all to succumb to death : it is the final end of every earthly destiny. God be merciful to the soul of Edward Provost Consitt, Vicar-Capitular of the diocese of Hexham and Newcastle, and

Missionary Rector of St. Cuthbert's, Durham. He has been gathered to his fathers, and now rests from his labours—the labours of "wearied humanity," and has gone to receive the reward of them—gone from this land of exile, to take his place among the dead who die in the Lord—

" To summer with them high in bliss upon the hills of God"—
the everlasting hills, unto which in doubt, uncertainty, and solicitude, he raised his eyes and prayed to God for help.

Provost Consitt was unquestionably a man of mark and merit ; an ornament of the church, and the model of a priest ; leading a blameless life—"*sobriam duxit sine labe vitam ;*" revered and beloved by all who were acquainted or associated with him ; most courteous and affable in his manners and deportment ; and in his relations and intercourse with his fellow priests most kind and friendly. " Provost Consitt," a friend writes, informing me of his death, " is no more ; he breathed his last yesterday evening (July 21) at Durham ; a true gentleman and a true priest. *Requiescat in pace.*"

From this world of sin and sorrow,
His departure he has taen ;
Him each of us soon must follow,
Hence life's griefs and cares how vain !

The Provost was descended from a race of heroic and gallant seamen, who had manfully " braved the battle and the breeze." The family of Consitt—originally spelt Consett, whose estates were situated in Cleveland, Yorkshire, had kept the faith—the ancient faith of England, for centuries. The father of Provost Consitt was Thomas Consitt, who entered the Royal Navy, in 1793, as midshipman on board the " Defence," and took part in Lord How's famous victory in the Bay of Biscay. He was also present at the battle of Cape St. Vincent, and at the battle of the Nile. He afterwards went out to Canada, and during his stay there Provost Consitt was born in 1819, at Clifton, in Upper Canada. The father subsequently went to reside at Bruges, where his son commenced his early education, and was also for a short time at the English Benedictine College of Douai. From Douai he was transferred to St. Cuthbert's College, Ushaw, which he entered April 10th, 1833, and went through his course there studiously and commendably. In the year 1842 he was ordained priest, and in the following year he was made Prefect of Discipline, which office he retained till February, 1845, when he went as chaplain to Haggerston Castle, extending his missionary labours to the villages and hamlets of the neighbourhood. In 1855 a small community of priests was established at St. Ninian's, Wooler, in Northumberland, with the object of enabling a few zealous and learned men to devote themselves to study, and, having their feet shod with the Gospel of peace, to go from mission to mission preaching and giving retreats. In this work the Rev. Edward Consitt was usefully and zealously employed, together with the Rev. James Chadwick, afterwards Bishop. The house at Wooler having been unfortunately destroyed by fire, Fr. Consitt removed from thence to Gateshead, in 1858, where he founded the Gateshead mission, and built St. Joseph's church. In 1862 he left this mission, being recalled therefrom to teach

Moral Theology, at Ushaw, in which important duty he was engaged seven years, lecturing during the same term on Elocution, and giving frequent readings in those years, and subsequently also, to the students, of favourite passages from Shakespeare and other poets, and prose authors. As a ready, fluent, and eloquent preacher he pre-eminently excelled, and there were few important public occasions, sad or joyful, at which Provost Consitt was not invited to preach; and his discourses were invariably listened to with the deepest interest and attention, for "*ex ore ejus melle dulcior fluebat oratio.*" In 1868 he succeeded Provost Platt, at the church of St. Cuthbert, Old Elvet, Durham, of which he was nineteen years Missionary Rector. On the death of Provost Platt, in 1874, he was elected Provost of the Cathedral Chapter of the Diocese, and two years later the Pope conferred on him the dignity of Domestic Prelate. In Durham he was universally esteemed and respected. He was Catholic chaplain of Durham gaol, member of the Durham Board of Guardians, and had been chairman of the Durham School Board, since its formation. On the death of Bishop Chadwick, he, along with Dr. Bewick, was one of the three who were submitted to Rome as being eminently worthy to succeed to the vacant mitre. After Bishop Bewick's death, the clergy of the diocese petitioned for his appointment to the vacant See of Hexham and Newcastle, so appreciative were they of his excellent qualities and virtues, and in such loving esteem and veneration was he held by them. *Sed superis aliter visum est.*

Provost Consitt had been staying a few weeks at Lindisfarne or Holy Island for the benefit of his health, and for the purpose of making preparations for the forthcoming pilgrimage, in honour of the twelfth centenary of St. Cuthbert, to the hallowed spot where he had dwelt, to the ground made holy by his footsteps, to the remote island where the Saint had knelt and prayed, and where, as Venerable Bede narrates, he spent the nights in singing the praises of God. "It is impossible," writes the Provost, in his interesting and beautiful Life of St. Cuthbert, published a short time before his lamented death, "for any Catholic to visit this spot without being deeply moved, for here was the cradle of northern Christianity; here stood the first church of the whole district between York and Edinburgh; here for well nigh 900 years a body of holy religious served God in solitude and prayer; and from here went forth the saintly Bishops and zealous missionaries, who preached the faith to our wild and barbarous ancestors, and subdued the fierce northmen to the sweet yoke of the gospel of Jesus Christ." "The place," adds Provost Consitt, "was most dear to me from past recollections, and most intimately associated with the whole of my priestly life." While last sojourning in the Island, he was attacked on Sunday, July 17th, with illness; next day he left Lindisfarne and went to Newcastle, where he attended a meeting of the Chapter, and received medical treatment. Thence he proceeded home to Durham, where, on the following Thursday evening, after much suffering, he calmly and peaceably rendered up his soul to God, strengthened with the Sacraments of Holy Church, which he received with great devotion and resignation. The deceased Provost had hoped to conduct the northern tribes on pilgrimage to the "promised land" of Lindisfarne. But,

O fallaces hominum spes! he was not permitted to do so. God had ordained a more glorious pilgrimage for His servant, eke the pilgrimage on which his patron the sainted and wonder-working Cuthbert, 1200 years previously, had gone before him—a pilgrimage other than to Holy Island. Having traversed the storm-beaten shore of life's perilous sea, and passed across the furrowed expanse of its tide-washed sands, he has joined the pilgrim throng on their journey to the Lindisfarne of heaven—to the Jerusalem, city of the vision of peace, beatitude, and blessedness—

"*Cœlestis urbs Jerusalem,
Beata pacis visio.*"

The *Tablet*, July 30th, thus briefly and graphically describes the funeral of the deceased:—"Lovingly and tenderly he was carried to his last resting place in the little Catholic cemetery" on the Red Hills, near Neville's Cross. "There he was laid beside the cross he had erected in life, under the shadow of the great cathedral where repose the bodies of St. Cuthbert and Venerable Bede, and near the college that was the home of his youth and earlier life, and which he had always loved as his *Alma Mater*. He had chosen to lie among his own people, in the city of the seven hills. Durham had not witnessed such a sight for more than 300 years. There passed a vision of lights and a crucifix, and about fifty priests in surplices with burning tapers, and the Canons in their mozettas and rochets, as pall bearers. Slowly and solemnly the procession wended its way on foot through the narrow streets, the clergy chanting the psalms of the ritual. Every shop was closed and the blinds of the windows drawn, and the inhabitants crowded the pavement in silent and respectful sympathy. All had known and respected the good Provost, and many eyes were wet with tears, even of those who were not of the household of faith. It was as if the shadow on the dial of time had gone back three hundred years, and the clergy were carrying to the grave one of their Prince Bishops. No horse or hearse was allowed to take part in that *cortège*. All walked on foot, and the corpse was lovingly borne by the Catholic young men of the parish. The school children walked in the procession, and all was according to the Provost's last wishes."

The Dean of Durham (Dr. Lake), and Canon Body, of Durham Cathedral, both attended the funeral. The former thus writes to the newspapers:—"May I venture to express the deep feeling of regret which pervades all classes, and I may add, all communions in this city, at the sudden death of Provost Consitt, as well as the affectionate respect with which many of us hope to attend his funeral. . . . . The union of firmness and consistency in his character, with unvarying courtesy and kindness, had won for him universal respect and regard."

In his sermon at Durham Cathedral, Canon Body makes graceful and respectful reference to the deceased. "The name of Provost Consitt," he said, "would be remembered, and his memory treasured for many and many a year in the northern counties."

Lord Herschell, who formerly represented Durham, in a letter to a personal friend of the Provost, expresses great grief and sincere sympathy at the news of his death. He thus writes:—

"It is now thirteen or fourteen years since I first made his acquaintance, and during all that time I have found him a kind and hearty friend, and my respect and indeed affection for him have grown year by year.

His noble qualities were known and thoroughly appreciated by the whole of Durham, even by those least in sympathy with his views. What higher testimony can be borne to any one than this? Had it been at all possible, I should certainly have made a point of being present at his funeral.—Believe me, yours sincerely,

HERSCHELL."

The Mayor of Durham was among those present at the funeral, together with a numerous attendance of clergy and friends. The Right Rev. Bishop Hedley was celebrant of the mass, the priests who assisted being mostly Ushaw Professors. The reverence and regard entertained by his fellow priests and others for Provost Consitt are a proof that "in all hearts," remarks Bishop Spalding, "there is a deep and abiding yearning for great and noble men, and therefore an imperishable interest in the power by which they are moulded, *viz.*, the gracious power of education and culture. The presence of such men invigorates like mountain air, and their speech is as refreshing as clear flowing fountains. To know them is to be for ever their debtor. The company of a saint is the school of saints; a strong character develops strength in others, and a noble mind makes all around him luminous."

RIGHT REV. MGR. O'CALLAGHAN, D.D.,

APPOINTED BISHOP OF HEXHAM AND NEWCASTLE.

At length, between ten and eleven months having elapsed since the death of Bishop Bewick, the Right Rev. Mgr. O'Callaghan, D.D., Rector of the English College, Rome, was nominated to the vacant See of Hexham and Newcastle. The Right Rev. Prelate was born in London, and educated at St. Edmund's College, Old Hall Green. For upwards of twenty years he had been Rector of the Venerable English College; and after this long residence in the Eternal City, he quits the sunny south, the blue skies of Italy, and repairs to the bleaker and colder clime of the north, where not unfrequently "winter lingering chills the lap of May." He comes from the banks of the yellow Tiber, from the land through which flow the Po—*fluviorum rex Eridanus*, the Arno, and the Adige, to the country watered by the Tyne, the Wear, the Tees, and the Derwent; from the city on the seven hills—imperial Rome— *princeps urbium, domina gentium*—proclaimed happy in having been purpled by the blood of its two glorious Apostles—

" *O Roma felix, quæ duorum Principum
Es consecrata glorioso sanguine.*"

From this classic region he has come to dwell and exercise authority in places hallowed by the footsteps of SS. Cuthbert, Aidan, Acca, Eata, Wilfrid, John of Beverley, and Bede, the Venerable. He has retired from the Rectorship of the College of St. Thomas de Urbe, the duties of which he so ably discharged, to occupy the vacant See of Hexham and

Newcastle, previously filled most worthily by Bishops Hogarth, Chadwick, and Bewick. Subject to his immediate episcopal sway is St. Cuthbert's College, Ushaw. Several of his Lordship's predecessors, Rectors of the English College, and other eminent ecclesiastics, who have been elevated to the dignity of Bishops, were in great part educated at Ushaw, completing their studies at the "*Venerabile.*" Ushaw cannot claim Bishop O'Callaghan as an alumnus; it would however always be prepared to give him a cordial welcome, and do him becoming reverence, whenever it was his pleasure to pay it a visit, or to make there a temporary sojourn. By Bishop Bewick Ushaw was designated "our glorious College;" and Bishop O'Callaghan will doubtless regard it as such, when he becomes acquainted with it, and identifies himself with its traditions, its past and present history, its educational advantages, and religious associations. These and other considerations cannot fail to enlist his sympathies in its behalf, induce him, when occasion offers, to uphold its claims, and support its cause; to watch over its interests, and take care "*ne quid detrimenti respublica capiat.*" Then will St. Cuthbert's continue to be established in peace and honour; its influence and prestige become more and more extended; the number of its students largely increased; and priests, churches, and missions multiplied throughout the diocese. Nor can it be doubted that eventually the Bishop will with reason consider Ushaw as his joy and his crown, and the brightest jewel in his mitre. He will discover that "all its ways are beautiful ways, and all its paths are peaceable." He will attach to him professors, masters, and students, and be "a good odour of Christ unto all." "*Tu sis eis honor, tu gaudium, tu voluntas; tu in mœrore solatium; tu in ambiguitate consilium.*" Remove not however, we pray, the ancient landmarks of Ushaw's history; change not, nor do away with its time-honoured customs and privileges; and usages consecrated by antiquity religiously preserve. "*Obsecro te per gloriam Dei et merita Sanctorum Martyrum, nil minuito, nil demito, nil mutato, antiquitatem pie restitutam servato, et sic te Deus adjuvet per orationes Sanctorum.*" Then will Ushaw's friends and alumni unite in extolling Bishop O'Callaghan as the protector, guardian, and friend of St. Cuthbert's, and each one's prayer will be "*Dominus conservet eum, et vivificet eum, et beatum faciat eum in terra.*"

Although, as stated, Bishop O'Calllaghan was born in London, it might be inferred from the name he bears that he was of Irish extraction—"a true O'Callaghan," descended from the Eugenian races, and from the same stock as the M'Carthys and O'Sullivans—"*ambos claros genere factisque.*" They (the O'Callaghans) took their name from their ancestor, Ceallachan Cashel, the celebrated King of Munster, in the tenth century. The O'Callaghans, Lords of Clonmeen, were in former times very powerful chiefs, and had their principal residence at the castle of Clonmeen, the ruins of which remain on a rock near the Blackwater. There are several highly respectable families of the O'Callaghans in the County Cork. The Catholic Bishop of Cork, the Right Rev. Dr. O'Callaghan, O.P., is a member of this princely Irish family.—*Vide Franciscan Annals, December, 1887.* "*Among the Tombs in Muckross Abbey.*"

Four months expired, after his nomination to the See of Hexham and Newcastle, before Dr. O'Callaghan received episcopal consecration. The ceremony took place on the Feast of St. Peter's Chair, January 18th, 1888, in the new church of St. Thomas of Canterbury attached to the English College, at Rome, the consecrating Prelate being his Eminence Cardinal Parocchi, Vicar-General of his Holiness, assisted by the Bishops of Clifton and Portsmouth. The occasion will long be memorable as occurring immediately after the celebration of the Holy Father's Sacerdotal Jubilee, while the echoes of the glorious solemnity still lingered on the shores of the Tiber, in the marble halls of the Vatican, and underneath "the vast and wondrous dome" of that sublime temple in which

—"Majesty,
Power, Glory, Strength, and Beauty, all are aisled
In an eternal ark of worship undefiled;"

ere the immense concourse of strangers and pilgrims, who had resorted to Rome from the uttermost ends of the earth, to tender their congratulations and homage to his Holiness, to lay at his feet their offerings of filial devotion, to behold him and to be blessed by him, had all taken their departure from the Eternal City, wherein they had found

—"In his Vicar, Christ
Himself a captive, and his mockery
Acted again. Lo! to his holy lip
The vinegar and gall once more applied,
And he 'twixt living robbers doomed to bleed."

Dante Purg., xix.

Having concluded the historical notices of Ushaw's successive Presidents, I must not omit to include in my narrative the names of others who have been in power and place at St. Cuthbert's. Who are these and I will praise them?—*Viri optimi, et summa laude dignissimi.*

Subjoined is a list of the

VICE-PRESIDENTS.

Rev.	John Lingard.		Rev.	James Chadwick.	1849
,,	Rich. Albot.	1811	,,	Mich. Gibson.	1849
,,	Geo. Brown.	1814	,,	Fras. Wilkinson.	1856
,,	Thos. Youens.	1819	,,	John Gillow.	1860
,,	Robt. Tate.	1828	,,	Wm. Wrennall.	1877
,,	Chas. Newsham.	1831	,,	Jas. Lennon.	1878
,,	Thos. Cookson.	1837	,,	Thos. Tatlock.	1886
,,	Robt. Tate.	1840			

Rev. Richard Albot, who, in 1809 and 1810, was Professor of Rhetoric and Poetry, succeeded Dr. Lingard as Vice-President. In 1814 he left the college; was on the mission at Blackburn, and for eleven years was priest at Lea, near Preston, where he died April 3rd, 1837. On a brass plate, in front of the Sanctuary rails in the little rustic chapel of Lea, are inscribed the words—"Here lies the body of the

Rev. R. Albot, R.I.P. ;" and on a marble tablet in the same chapel you read—" Of your charity pray for the soul of the Rev. Richard Albot, for 11 years priest of this mission, who died April 3rd, 1837. R.I.P."

Of succeeding Vice-Presidents, as Vice-Presidents or otherwise, honourable mention has already been made, and a record of their lives been given. The names of Thomas Cookson and John Gillow must not however be cursorily passed over. Both were devoted priests, abounding in wisdom and godliness, and edifying all by the example of their saintly lives.

RIGHT REV. MGR. PROVOST COOKSON.—Provost Cookson was a most exemplary priest, grave, prudent, and discreet. He was a native of the Fylde, born in 1804, near Layton Hawes, an extensive farm situated between Lytham and Blackpool, subsequently occupied by his father, and afterwards by his brother. In the year 1816 he was sent to Ushaw to study for the priesthood, and, having diligently and unostentatiously pursued his studies, he was ordained Priest in 1828; on November 16th, of that year, he was appointed General Prefect of the college. This office he continued to hold till June 25th, 1834. He then commenced teaching Natural Philosophy; in 1837 he was elected Vice-President, and Professor of Dogmatic Theology. In 1840 Bishop Briggs selected him to take charge of the new mission and church of St. Augustine, Preston. The congregation of St. Augustine's soon learnt to appreciate Father Cookson's good qualities, his self-sacrificing zeal and labours, and became deeply attached to him; and in course of time he won the respect and esteem of others. He was the first priest, together with the Rev. Thomas Kiernan, who was placed, after its erection, at St. Augustine's; here, between fifteen and sixteen years, he laboured assiduously and unceasingly. Leaving Preston, he went to the Pro-Cathedral, Liverpool, and was made Vicar-General to Bishop Goss, and Provost of the Diocesan Chapter. His fellow priests placed the greatest confidence in him, and entertained for him especial respect and reverence. Towards junior priests he was kind, considerate, and indulgent; and, in regard to both old and young among the clergy, it may truly be said of him that he was

"*Notus in fratres animi paterni.*"

Among other offices he held successively those of Secretary, and Treasurer of the Lancashire Infirm Secular Clergy Fund. Previous to his departure from Preston the congregation of St. Augustine's and others of his friends, at a large and influential meeting held in the Corn Exchange, presented the Provost, in testimony of their affection and gratitude, with a farewell address, and a beautiful and costly chalice. Provost Cookson remained at the Pro-Cathedral till the year 1863, when, his health becoming impaired in that busy maritime city, in which so many devoted and useful priests have toiled and died, he was allowed to retire therefrom, and take charge of the less laborious and more peaceful mission of Fernyhalgh, where he pursued the noiseless tenour of his way, till, his days being numbered, and life's warfare over, he departed to his rest on the Feast of St. Joseph, March 19th, 1878, in the seventy-fifth year of his age, and the fiftieth of his priesthood. In the quiet and secluded "God's acre" of Fernyhalgh, in a grave fronting the entrance into the chapel, the mortal remains of the good Provost repose and sleep in peace. The Rev. William Gordon, now of St. Mary's, Chorley, educated at Ushaw and Rome, an estimable and much respected priest, became his successor in this ancient mission, whose history reaches into far off antiquity, and where the old religion, in spite of pains, penalties, and persecution, continued firmly and fixedly rooted among the people ; and "though doomed to death was fated not to die," for God was a protector and a house of refuge to it in time of peril.

A lovely, sylvan, Arcadian retreat is Fernyhalgh. Here, in the good old times of England, stood the venerable fane, erected, according to a traditional legend, many hundred years ago, by a wealthy and virtuous merchant, who, sailing on the Irish Sea and exposed to the peril of shipwreck, made a vow that, if he escaped, he would, in gratitude for his deliverance, and in fulfilment of his vow, perform some acceptable work of piety. Having landed in safety, a miraculous voice told him to look out for a place called Fernyhalgh, where he would find a spring, and a tree growing crabs without cores ; at this place he must build a chapel. After much search and inquiry, by good chance he discovered the spot unto which he was enjoined to go, and there he built and dedicated a chapel to the Blessed Virgin. When chantries, chapels, and shrines were suppressed *sacrilega manu* by irreligious and ruthless spoilers, the chapel of "Our Lady at the Well" was demolished. In 1685, after the lapse of nearly a century and a half, 1548-1689—an interval fraught with danger and disaster—another chapel was built near the site of the old one ; and in 1796 the present edifice was erected, a short distance from where the chapel last named stood. The beautiful spring called "Our Lady's Well" flows amidst trees, ferns, and mosses, as of yore, and around it lingers the glamour of many sacred traditions and memories :—

"Fount of the chapel ! with ages gray,
A voice that speaks of the past is thine."

But alas ! as in the "ages of faith," we hear of no pilgrimages being made to it, of no beads being recited, of no hymns chanted at the fountain by peasant, pilgrim, or herdsman :—

"Fount of the vale ! thou art sought no more
By the pilgrim's foot, as in time of yore ;
When he came from afar, his beads to tell,
And to chant the hymn at Our Lady's Well."

Flow on sweet, rustic, sacred fount ! The day may come (God hasten the time), when England, at present overrun with heresy, and the viperous progeny which heresy engenders ; an alien to the supernatural, central, and spiritual influences of Catholic unity, and in error's endless mazes lost, will return to the faith of its fathers, and once more rejoice in being called the dowry of Mary. Then shall Mary's devout clients of all ranks and conditions resort to thy waters, and utter at their brink their

Aves in honour of the Queen of the most Holy Rosary. Then shalt thou once more become a far-famed fountain "*fies nobilium tu quoque fontium*," and the place whence thou wellest forth—

"*unde loquaces
Lymphæ desiliunt tuæ*,"

shall again have a shrine placed there, consecrated to Mary.

Subjoined is the hymn to our Blessed Lady which was whilom sung by devout Catholics resorting to her "fountain of waters," and praying in "the chapel old and hoar," dedicated to her honour, at Fernyhalgh. It is a sweet, but quaint melody, redolent of mediæval times, and of the palmiest days of those ages, when

> "Faith in the wild wood's tangled bound,
> A blessed heritage had found ;
> When pilgrims in the forest brown,
> Slow wending on from town to town,
> Halting 'mid mosses green and dank,
> Breathed forth a prayer before they drank
> From waters, at the pathway side,
> Each day, at morn and eventide."

To Our Blessed Lady.

1

Of one that is so fair and bright,
　Velut maris stella,
Brighter than the day is light,
　Parens et puella,
I cry to thee, then see to me,
　Jam pia,
That I may come to thee,
　O Maria !

2

All this world was forlorn,
　Eva peccatrice,
Till our Lord was of thee born,
　De te genitrice ;
With Ave it went away,
Thus went night and cometh day
　Salutis,
The well springeth out of thee
　Virtutis.

3

Lady, flower of all things,
　Rosa sine spina,
Thou bore Jesus, heavenly King,
　Gratia divina,
Of all thou bearest the prize,
Lady Queen of paradise,
　Electa,
Maiden mild, Mother sweet,
　Effecta !

Provost Cookson must have left behind him a numerous collection of manuscript sermons. I remember how at Ushaw (and no doubt he continued to do so afterwards) he used to devote whatever time he could spare from his other duties to the composition of sermons—thus setting an example to young priests by no means ever, if possible, to omit the commendable practice of preparing and writing their sermons, before venturing to preach to a congregation. The Provost's discourses were instructive, solid, and serious. And he was an extremely serious character himself, rarely moved to laughter; grave and sedate, but gracious and urbane. One of the good priests who was associated with him at St. Augustine's, Preston, used to say that if once a week he could get a smile from Father Cookson, he considered himself abundantly repaid for his labour. I must not omit to state that Provost Cookson had the honour of being created by His Holiness the Pope one of his Domestic Prelates. The worthy old Provost had well merited this honour, having borne for many years "the heats of the day and the burden thereof." Now he sleeps in the dust; God's peace be with him! "*Ecce talis homo ingreditur fines pacis et quietis.*"

Provost Cookson, notwithstanding his removal to Liverpool and subsequently to Fernyhalgh, from St. Augustine's, Preston, remained to the time of his decease Missionary Rector of that church, and not till October A.D. 1887 was another Rector appointed, when the Rev. Lawrence Cosgrave received that honour, to the great joy of his flock and the congratulations of his friends. Father Cosgrave's education began at St. Edward's College, and was uninterruptedly, diligently, and piously pursued for seven years at St. Cuthbert's, Ushaw. In 1874, he received the sacred order of priesthood, being ordained at St. Augustine's, where he was placed as assistant priest. After three years he left Preston to become a Professor at St. Edward's College. As such he remained there for seven years. In 1883 he returned to Preston, was placed at the head of the mission of St. Augustine's, and finally made Missionary Rector of that church by his Lordship, Bishop O'Reilly, The congregation took occasion of Father Cosgrave's promotion to present him with a congratulatory address, most beautifully illuminated, in token of their gratitude and esteem, and in recognition of the distinction which had been conferred upon him.

Most of the priests, who have been connected with St. Augustine's, received their education at Ushaw; and depend upon it, in whatever diocese (be it said to the honour of St. Cuthbert's, and without wishing to depreciate the zeal, the learning, and the labours of the many good and estimable priests from other colleges) an Ushaw priest is found, work is quietly and successfully being done at the mission of which he has the charge. A truly apostolic spirit animates their lives and actions, flaming forth and running to and fro like sparks among reeds. "There is something in the atmosphere of Ushaw, that home of culture and Christianity," remarked a local journal "that brings out what is best in most of those trained there."

REV. JOHN GILLOW, D.D., was the youngest son of John Gillow, of Elswick Grange, and Salwick Hall, broad-acred farms, situated in the Fylde. He went as a student to Ushaw at the age of fourteen, and arrived at the college March 14th, 1828. He pursued his course of studies it the several classes, from Underlow to Philosophy, with assiduous and diligent application. In 1836 he was appointed Minor Professor, and taught consecutively Underlow, Low

Figures, and Grammar; was Professor also of Mathematics, and Writing Master. Ordained priest on the 23rd of September, 1842, he went on the mission the following day, but was recalled to Ushaw within two months to teach Natural Philosophy, of which school he was Professor, until he was appointed to teach Dogmatic Theology, in succession to Dr. Tate. For one year he was Professor of Moral Theology, having, in 1859, resigned the Professorship of Dogmatic Theology in favour of Dr. Reinerding. In 1857 he was made Canon Theologian of the Cathedral Chapter of Hexham. In the year 1859 he went to Rome on business connected with the college, and before departing from the Eternal City, he received from His Holiness Pius IX. the degree of D.D. Returning to *Alma Mater* he was chosen Vice-President, and again appointed to the chair of Dogmatic Theology, which he continued to teach till his death, for a period of twenty-three years. Dr. Gillow possessed a vigorous intellect, and an eminently philosophical mind—well ordered, trained, and cultivated. Despising and casting aside mere superficialities, he held firmly to first principles, and aimed not only at acquiring and imparting sound knowledge, but aspired "higher still and higher" until he was permitted "*integros accedere fontes atque haurire.*" His lectures, on whatever subject he treated, possessed breadth, depth, and solidity, and his replies to questions and objections were precise and decisive, and given with much clearness and readiness. Not only was he a profoundly learned and sound theologian, he was gifted with considerable scientific attainments, and was well skilled in architecture and experimental chemistry. But with Dr. Gillow it was "*Deus meus et omnia*," hence he regarded knowledge as "a barren tree, bereft of God." Dr. Gillow considered that the new order of studies introduced into Catholic colleges with a view of meeting the requirements of the London University was no improvement on the previously existing system, but in many respects the reverse; that the London philosophical examination in particular was a grievous hardship,

"Obtruding false rules prank'd in reason's garb."

Inquiring of a priest, who in his college course had excelled in, and obtained prizes for mathematics, what this kind of learning availed him in the work of the mission, he candidly avowed that he believed he could not now demonstrate or solve a problem in Euclid. The same avowal was made by another—"*ex uno disce omnes.*" Such is not the case with those whose tastes and studies have familiarised them with the classics—the "*exemplaria Græca et Latina*," which have an enduring interest, clinging to you like a well fitting vesture. Both of the above named, in assigning a reason why the classics were more neglected and made less account of than formerly, stated that they were crowded out by the new learning, and the new departure in the programme of studies, and by the introduction into the course of a wide range of other subjects, considered more in accord with the spirit of the age and more in touch with the progress of modern intellectual culture. Hence the study of the Greek and Latin authors was to some extent thrust aside, and studies of more ephemeral interest substituted, calculated, unless special care was taken, to unsettle, enervate, and poison the mind. "I had wandered about in all sorts of science," says Goethe, "and had early enough been led to see its vanity."

Dr. Gillow was a great sufferer, being cramped and crippled by chronic rheumatism, and had been so for many years. But under his sufferings he was patient and resigned, and most exact and punctual in the discharge of his various duties. It was at dear *Alma Mater*, where he had passed his life from boyhood to declining years, that death put an end to his suffering and infirmities, on the 9th day of August, 1877, of his age 63. He rests in the cloister of Ushaw's secluded cemetery among the sainted dead—Bishops, Priests, and Presidents, who have gone before him. Almighty God be gracious to him! On a mural tablet, placed opposite to where his ashes repose, may be read the following inscription :—

JOAN. GILLOW, VICE-PRÆSES. 1860-1877,

CONSTANS, HUMILIS, DOCTUS,

CATHEDRÆ PETRI MIRIFICE DEVOTUS,

PER OMNE VITÆ SPATIUM HUIC COLLEGIO INDEFESSA

DEVOTIONE INSERVIVIT.

OBIIT 9 AUG., 1877. ÆTATIS 63.

PATER VENERANDE VIVAS CUM JESU.

"It is sad to see such men passing away," a learned writer remarks,—"the last born of those generations which had a real love for learning." They held the chain of many generous and noble traditions which, it is to be lamented, pass away with them and in time are forgotten.

The Venerable Dean Gillow and Rev. Henry Gillow, were brothers of Dr. Gillow. They went to Ushaw, August 6th, 1812, and were ordained priests together, December 21st, 1821. The younger of the two brothers, Henry, died of fever, at St. Mary's, Mulberry Street, Manchester, February 25th, 1837, at the age of 41. The elder brother Richard, (Dean Gillow) was for 40 years priest at Fernyhalgh, having been there from the close of the year 1823. He died August 16th, 1864, having attained the age of 70 years. A small cross opposite the entrance to the chapel marks his place of sepulture.

REV. THOMAS TATLOCK.—The Vice-Presidents of Ushaw, numbering 15, are, it will be seen, brought down to the year 1886, the last named on the list being the Rev. Thomas Tatlock, a worthy and excellent priest. A native of the quaint old city of Chester, he was sent at the age of thirteen, on October 7th, 1840, to St. Cuthbert's College, and was a diligent, pains-taking scholar, steadily pursuing his studies, until he was advanced to the priesthood in Ember week, 23rd of September, 1854. From that date he held the appointment of General Prefect, in succession to the Rev. Wm. Wrennall, until the same month (September) in the year 1860. From 1860 to July 1876, he was part Professor of Mathematics ; and Vice-President and Procurator in the Junior College from July 1876 to March 22nd, 1886. He was then made House Procurator in the Senior College, and besides that appointment he was inducted October 9th to the office of Vice-President. During the erection of St. Cuthbert's Collegiate Chapel, Father Tatlock watched unceasingly the progress of the work, and scarcely a stone was placed upon a stone without passing the ordeal of his vigilant observation. A noticeable feature in Father Tatlock's character was his gentle, placid, and patient demeanour, and to all, who approached or consulted him, he was right courteous, condescending, and obliging. For punctuality, exactitude, and faithful discharge of his duties he might be regarded as a model.

PROCURATORS.

Ranking next to the Vice-Presidents may be classed the Procurators of the college. They fill an important post, involving much responsibility, mindfulness, and forethought. The Rev. Wm. Hogarth, afterwards Bishop of Hexham and Newcastle, combined the office of Prefect with that of Procurator in 1811-12, being the first whose name I find inscribed as Procurator in the College Register. We are afterwards introduced to the Rev. John Kirk, as Procurator. He was a native of Osmotherley, Yorkshire; commenced his studies at Crook Hall; in 1809 was at Ushaw, in Syntax, having as schoolfellows Joseph Curr, James Crook, and Francis Turville. Subsequently no trace appears of him till early in 1817, when he was appointed the College Procurator, and he was well fitted for the office. No one knew better than Father Kirk how to economise, even in matters that might be considered trifling and profitless. He was clever and ingenious in turning every thing to the best purpose and advantage. Over household and farm he exercised Argus-eyed supervision; and in points of good husbandry he was as great an authority as old Tusser. He could tell

" *Quid faciat lætas segetes ; quo sidere terram*
  Vertere, ——
  Conveniat ; quæ cura boum, qui cultus habendo
  Sit pecori."

So strict a rigorist was Father Kirk in regard to economy, and understood it so thoroughly, that the resources of the college, during the term of his Procuratorship, greatly improved, its stores increased, and its means grew more ample and abundant:—"*a fructu frumenti vini et olei sui multiplicati sunt.*"

For two years before going on the mission, the Rev. James Fisher was associated with Father Kirk in the Procuratorship, the former being nominated House Proc. *(Œconomus intus)*, the latter the Farm Proc. *(Œconomus foris)*, devoting his attention and experience to the agricultural department, the succession of crops, the breeding, feeding, and rearing of cattle and sheep, and other matters and pursuits connected with husbandry.

REV. JOHN GLOVER.—About the year 1823, John Glover, a tall, stalwart, large-hearted Lancashire man, born at St. Helens, came to Ushaw to study for the priesthood. Being a young man, aged twenty-one years, or thereabouts, he ranked among that respectable class of students yclept 'Patriarchs.' It was the age of corduroy and kerseymere 'shorts,' blue coats with brass buttons, and white cravats. Thus apparelled I just remember John Glover. In 1825 or 1826 he had reached the class of Rhetoric, and having completed his Philosophical and Theological studies, he was ordained priest July 11th, 1829. His missionary life commenced at Hexham; he was then sent to Houghton Hall, Yorkshire; and next to Bolton-le-Moors, whence in 1840 he came to Ushaw as House Procurator, which office he resigned in 1841, and returned to his former mission of Houghton Hall. From this place he removed to Whitby; was a year at Sheffield, and again at Whitby from 1867 to 1874, when he retired from missionary duty at the age of 72, and died full of days, May 18th, 1878, in his retirement at Whitby, the last scene of his labours.—*In Pace.*

VERY REV. LAURENCE CANON TOOLE, D.D.—Laurence Toole, another of the Patriarchal race, was admitted a student at Ushaw, July 11th, 1837, at the mature age of twenty-nine years; and from 1837-8, he took his place among the students in the school of Rhetoric. In 1841 he was promoted to the Priesthood, having for some time before his ordination taught mathematics in the college. He succeeded the Rev· John Glover as House Procurator, which post he retained about a year and a half, when in January 1843, he left Ushaw and went on the mission to Weld Bank. In 1847 he is found located at SS. Peter and Paul's, Bolton, and in the year 1848 he took charge of the mission of St. Wilfrid's, Hulme, Manchester, of which church he became Missionary Rector. In course of time he was made a Canon of the Salford Diocesan Chapter, Rural Dean, &c.; was created Doctor of Divinity, and elected Member of the Manchester School Board. The Very Rev. Canon Toole, D.D. is well learned, well read, and well informed; he possesses talents of no mean order, and his knowledge and erudition, ecclesiastical, historical, and theological, are varied, profound, and extensive. Though advanced in years his friends and fellow priests hope and pray that he may be spared to celebrate the golden jubilee of his priesthood.

RIGHT REV. MGR. GILLOW.—In succession to the Very Rev. Canon Toole, D.D., the Rev. Charles Gillow was installed Domestic Procurator *(Œconomus intus)*. He belonged to the honoured and respectable family of the Gillows, of Leighton Hall, Lancashire. His two older brothers, Robert and George Gillow, were priests of holy church: the former died in Liverpool during the fatal fever year; the latter, Father George Gillow, was well known as an eloquent and effective preacher, and was greatly beloved and respected. For many years he was resident in Preston, and its suburbs. The eldest brother, R. T. Gillow, Esq., inherited the Leighton Hall estate; his son, Rev. Francis Gillow, was missionary priest at St. Andrew's, Cottam. He as well as his father and uncles was educated at Ushaw.

The date of Mgr. Gillow's going to Ushaw was the year 1831, August 25th. Then a little boy, he grew up a pious, peaceful, docile youth; obedient to rule, submissive to superiors, kind and obliging to equals and inferiors. Having finished his course of studies, he was ordained Priest, January 20th, 1843, and was appointed House Procurator, the duties of which he faithfully discharged till 1850 On the decease of Father Kirk in that year, the transactions, manage‑

ment, and superintendence of the farming department devolved upon him. To Ushaw, his *Alma Mater*, Mgr. Gillow was a generous and liberal benefactor. On December 14th, 1880, he was raised by the Holy Father to the dignity of a Domestic Prelate. His portrait has been placed in the college refectory, among other celebrities who have been connected with, or interested in the welfare of St. Cuthbert's. There was one trait in Mgr. Gillow's character which deserves notice, *viz.*, his singular patience and resignation under all vicissitudes and difficulties, and the apparent great mental composure exhibited by him :

" *Æquam memento rebus in arduis
Servare mentem*"

was an admonition with which he studiously complied and acted upon.

REV. THOMAS CROSKELL.—My list of Ushaw's Procurators concludes with the Rev. Thomas Croskell. He was placed in that responsible post, September 21st, 1850, and occupied it until March, 1886, a period of thirty-six years. Father Croskell, brother of the Venerable and Right Rev. Mgr. Robert Provost Croskell, D,D., Vicar-General of the Diocese of Salford, and an Alumnus of Ushaw, was born September 5th, 1820, near Hurst Green, and baptised at the college church, Stonyhurst. On the 2nd of November, 1835, he went from Well House, Lancaster, to St. Cuthbert's College; was school-fellow of John Canon Walker, Major Myles O'Reilly, &c. ; was ordained priest in September, 1850, and appointed House Procurator. His was a long tenure of the office—thirty-six years—fully half the allotted space of man's life. During that term his urbanity, hospitality, and kindness to the visitors and guests of the college, earned for him no small share of respect and favour, and the grateful recollection of many friends. A straightforward, matter of fact man, but few more generous-hearted than the Rev. Thomas Croskell. On his retirement from the post of Procurator, a testimonial consisting of a richly illuminated address and £395 was presented to him by a number of friends and well wishers. In a feeling reply Father Croskell gratefully acknowledged the testimonial with which he had been honoured, stating that to whatever field of labour he might be appointed, he was prepared to work with renewed energy, and would continue to wish success to dear *Alma Mater*, trusting that its well-earned prestige might be maintained, and even go on increasing. The mission of St. Bonaventure, Bentham, Yorkshire, was assigned to Father Croskell, by the Bishop of Leeds ; and here as a good shepherd, he tended his flock, and laboured with pious zeal for the salvation of souls.

GENERAL PREFECTS OF CROOK & USHAW.

CROOK.

1794.—Rev. J. Bell, Pref. Gen. and Prof. of Rhet., Poet., Synt., Grammar and the Rudiments.

John Bell, born at Snaith, Yorkshire; left Douai, November 8th, 1792; tutor to the young Silvertops, at Minsteracres; then General Prefect at Crook Hall, where he was ordained priest, December 23rd, 1794; was Professor of Rhetoric and Poetry there till 1807; missionary at Samlesbury, near Preston till 1828; then at Kippax Park, Yorkshire, whence he retired and died at Selby, May 31st, 1854, aged 87.

1795.—Rev. Chas. Saul, Pref. Gen. and Prof. of Rud.
1796.   do.   do.   do.   and Grammar.
1797.   do.   do.   do.   do.
    Left August 20th.

Charles Saul was a native of Yorkshire; escaped from Douai, October 12th, 1793; pursued his studies at Old Hall Green and Crook Hall; ordained priest at Crook Hall, where he was General Prefect, and master of the several schools under Poetry; missioner at Carlisle from 1798 till Christmas, 1800, and at Bishop Thornton till his death, June 5th, 1813, aged 46.

1797.—August 20th.—Rev. G. L. Haydock, Pref. Gen. and Prof. of Gram. and Rud.
1798.   do.   do.   do.
1799.   do.   do. & Prof. of Syntax
1800.   do.   do.
1801.   do.   do.
1802.   do.   do.
    Left January 20th, 1803.

George Leo Haydock, born April 11th, 1774; escaped from Douai August 5th, 1793; went through his course of studies at Old Hall Green and Crook Hall; ordained priest at Crook Hall, September 22nd, 1798, and was there General Prefect, and Professor of all the schools under Poetry for four years and a half; went on the mission at Ugthorpe in 1803, Whitby in 1816, Westby in 1830: retired to the Tagg, Cottam, for eight years and a quarter; missioner at Penrith from 1839 till his death, November 29th, 1849, of his age 75 years.

1803.—Rev. John Bradley, Pref. Gen. and Prof. of Gram. and Rud.
1804.   do.   do.   do.   do.
1805.   do.   do.   do.   do.
1806.   do.   do.   do.   do.
1807.   do.   do.   and Prof. of Rud. only.

USHAW.

1808.—Rev. John Bradley, Pref. Gen. and Prof. of Rud. only,
1809.   do.   do.   do.
1810.   do.   do.   do.
    Left September 9th, 1811.

John Bradley was born on Lune side, at Heaton, near Lancaster; went to Douai to study for the priesthood in the latter part of the eighteenth century; escaped from France during the frenzy of the Revolution, January 16th, 1794; completed his studies at Tudhoe and Crook Hall; was ordained priest at the latter, December 4th, 1802; was General Prefect, and a Professor, both at Crook and Ushaw; went on the mission in 1811 to Yarm, where he continued to reside till his death, A.D. 1853. At his particular request he was interred in the cemetery cloister, at Ushaw, and his remains repose next to his friend, Dr. Lingard. The brass tablet to his memory bears the following inscription :—

R. D. JOANNES BRADLEY,

IN HOC COLLEGIO

LITTER. HUMAN. PROF., PRÆF. GENERALIS,

MISSIONAR. APOST. APUD YARM,

1811—1853.

OB. OCT. 24, 1853.

ROGATU SUO HIC REQUIESCIT.

During the occupation of Crook Hall by the Douai colonists, the four persons above named were in authority as Prefects of Discipline. That their memory may not become extinct, I have appended after their respective names a short biographical notice of each of them. Father Bradley, it will be seen, was General Prefect also at Ushaw for three years or more after the students were transferred from Crook to St. Cuthbert's. Since that date to October 27th, 1887, Ushaw counts 27 General Prefects, 16 of whom, life's fitful fever over, have gone to their last homes, and sleep in the dust.

1811.—Rev. Wm. Hogarth, Pref. Gen. and Proc.
1812.　　　do.　　　do.　　do.
　　Resigned Oct. 27th.
1812.—Rev. J. Wrennall, Pref. Gen., Oct. 27th.
1813.　　　do.　　　do.
1814.　　　do.　　　do.
　　Resigned March 5th, 1815.
　　Left March 13th.
1815.—Rev. J. Anderton, Pref. Gen., March 5th.
1816.　　　do.　　　do.
1817.　　　do.　　　do.
1818.　　　do.　　　do.
　　Went on the mission, March 2nd, 1819.
1819.—Rev. Jas. Crook, Pref. Gen., Feb. 25th.
1820.　　　do.　　　do.
1821.　　　do.　　　do.
1822.　　　do.　　　do.
1823.　　　do.　　　do.
　　Left May 9th, 1824.

The Very Rev. Provost Crook.—Whittle-le-Woods, near Chorley, was the birthplace of the Very Rev. James Provost Crook. He was the son of James Crook and Jane Cottam; was born April 23rd, the Feast of St. George, A.D. 1792, and was baptised at St. Chad's, South Hill. He commenced his ecclesiastical studies at Crook Hall, and completed them at the new college of Ushaw, where in the year 1809 he ranked as a Syntaxian, having for schoolfellows, Joseph Curr, Wm. Eyre, John Kirk, Frank and Henry Turville, and Thos. Strickland. When in Deacon's orders, he taught the school of High Figures, and on being ordained priest at the end of the year 1818, or early in 1819, he was appointed General Prefect, February 25th of the latter year. His tenure of this office lasted until the 9th of May, 1824, a period of upwards six years. I remember how in days of old he was spoken of as having been a strict disciplinarian, and a terror to wrong doers. The missions enumerated below were subsequently served by Fr. Crook; and a most zealous, useful, and laborious missionary priest he was:—Rochdale, 1824, Granby Row, Manchester, 1825-1842, St. Wilfrid's, Hulme, 1842, Blackburn, 1843, Aughton, 1845, St. Patrick's, Liverpool, 1847, St. Nicholas's, Liverpool, 1851. Fr. Crook was Vicar of West Derby and Cheshire in 1850; in 1851 he was appointed Vicar-General to Bishop Brown, and the first Provost of the Cathedral Chapter of Liverpool. The Very Rev. Provost Crook, D.D., (this latter distinction had been conferred upon him,) finished his earthly pilgrimage, June 17th, 1856. He died at Eaton House, West Derby, and was buried with honour and solemnity, at St. Oswald's, Old Swan.

1824.—Rev. John Pratt, Pref. Gen., May 9th.
    Resigned Dec 23, 1824.
1825.—Rev. Wm. Brown, Pref. Gen., Dec. 23rd, 1824.
    Left Dec. 29th, 1825.
1826.—Rev. Jos. Render, Pref. Gen., Dec., 1825.
    Left Oct. 2nd, 1826.
1826.—Rev. Wm. Carter, Pref. Gen., Oct. 1826.
1827.   do.   do.
    Left Nov. 16th, 1828.
1828.—Rev. T. Cookson, Pref. Gen., Nov. 16th, and continued till June 25th, 1834; afterwards Prof. Phil. Nat., and V.P.
1834.—Rev. Jas. Pemberton, Pref. Gen., June 25th.
    Resigned Dec. 30th, 1836.
1837.—Rev. Jas. Chadwick, Pref. Gen.
1838.   do.   do.   and Prof. Eccles. Hist.
1839.   do.   do.   do.
1839.—Rev. T. Kiernan, Pref. Gen., Oct.
    Left July 27th, 1840.
1840.—Rev. John Worthy, Pref. Gen., July 27th.
1841.   do.   do.   and Prof. of Chemistry.
1842.   do.   do.   do.
    Left Jan. 9th, 1843.

John Canon Worthy.—My records of notable and important characters would be incomplete, if I omitted to include, among those whose life and labours, virtues and attainments, have added lustre to "our glorious college," that energetic and self-denying priest, honest John Canon Worthy.

Canon Worthy went through his course of studies, and was ordained priest at Ushaw; and was placed in authority and taught in the schools at Ushaw. He was the son of William Henry Worthy, and Elizabeth A. Blundell, of Preston, and was born Nov. 7th, 1815, at Halifax, Nova Scotia. His father's uncle, William Henry Worthy, was agent at Durham for St. Cuthbert's, Ushaw. His (the Canon's) primary education began at Sedgley Park School, in 1825; from that noted school he was removed to Ushaw, in November, 1828. His school fellows formed a numerous class : from among them 18 became priests, all of whom, excepting about four, have paid the debt of nature. Bishop Grant was one of the Canon's school fellows ; Bishop Goss was one school higher. Ordained priest July 25th, 1840, he was instituted General Prefect, and continued such until January 9th, 1843. He was also part of that time Professor of Chemistry. In that year, 1843, he was placed at St. Chad's, Rook Street, Manchester ; in 1845 at St. Mary's, Burnley ; in 1849 at St. Nicholas's, Liverpool ; and in 1851 at St. Mary's, Euxton, where he built the present church, presbytery, and schools. In 1856 he was elected secretary of the Lancashire Infirm Secular Clergy Fund, in succession to Provost Cookson ; and at the decease of the Very Rev. Henry Gradwell, he was, in 1860, chosen Treasurer of the same fund—a trust which he administered uprightly and efficiently, and to the entire satisfaction of the brethern. "A true good man," to quote from old Chaucer, was John Canon Worthy :—

"And rich he was in holy thought and work ;
And thereto a right learned man ;—
Benign he was, and wondrous diligent,
And in adversity full patient."

Hence he bore not only a worthy name, but a most worthy character also; was a man of varied knowledge, practical experience, and unflinching firmness ; skilful, ingenious, and methodical, and able to impart information on all manner of subjects—from the mechanism of a watch to the construction of a steam engine ; from the erection of a church, a presbytery, or a college, to the building of a school or a school house. Some might consider Canon Worthy blunt and off-handed in his manner ; but he was kind-hearted and generous, charitable and compassionate, and ever ready to succour the distressed. "*Miseris succurrere disco*," was a text extremely applicable to him.

In penning these Records the Canon has placed me under no small obligation to him, by supplying me with many dates, and details of events, of which I was doubtful or ignorant.

1843.—Rev. Ed. Consitt, Pref. Gen., Jan. 9th.
1844.   do.   do.
1845.   do.   do.
   Left Feb. 3rd, 1845.
1845.—Rev. Wm. Wrennall, Pref. Gen., Feb. 15th.
to
1851.   do.   do.
1852.   do.   do.   and Prof. Nat. Phil.
1853.   do.   do.   do.
1854.   do.   Vacated the office, Sep. 25th, to teach
   Nat. Phil. only.

1854.—Rev. Thos. Tatlock, Pref. Gen., Sept. 25th.
to
1860.   do.   do.   Resigned Sept.
1860.—Rev. Jas. Lennon, Pref. Gen., Sept.
to
1865.   do.   do.   Resigned Aug. 14th.
1865.—Rev. Ed. Walmsley, Pref. Gen., Aug. 14th.
1866.   do.   do.
1867.   do.   do.
1868.—Rev. John Nolan, Pref. Gen.
1869.   do.   do.
       Left May 5th.
1869.—Rev. Henry Berry, Pref. Gen., May 5th.
1870.   do.   do.
1871.   do.   do.   Resigned July 31st.
1871.—Rev. Austin Collingwood, Pref. Gen., July 31st.
to
1875.   do.   do.
1875.—Rev. Wm. Wickwar, Pref. Gen., August.
to
1881.   do.   do.   Resigned July 30th.
1881.—Rev. Robt. Thornton, Pref. Gen., July 30th.
to
1886.   do.   do.   Resigned Aug. 9th.
1886.—Rev. Chas. Rothwell, Pref. Gen., Sept. 16th.
1887.   do.   do.   Resigned Oct. 27th.
1887.—Rev. Jos. Preston, Pref. Gen., Oct. 27th.

REV. RICHARD GILLOW.

Although not on the roll of Ushaw's Vice-Presidents, Procurators, and Prefects, the Rev. Richard Gillow was for a number of years one of the college Professors, and has many claims why, among other men of note, of whom Ushaw may be proud, his name should not be omitted from these " Records and Recollections."

The branches of the Gillow family have given to the church several excellent and exemplary ecclesiastics, among them the Rev. Richard Gillow, cousin to Dr. Gillow, the Vice-President. He was a priest of sterling worth, whose memory I deeply revere and cherish. *" Virtutem illius viri amavi, quæ extincta non est."*

Dear Father Gillow, or as he was familiarly known among his *confrères* and contemporaries, as " Uncle Gillow," was a priest of the good old school, one of a generation that has passed away—who, born at the close of the last, and educated at the commencement of the present century, went forth into the vineyard to repair its broken fences, and to gather together the thinned and scattered tribes of their Catholic fellow-countrymen. Their mission was toilsome and onerous ; they had to sow in tears, but had at length the satisfaction of reaping in joy. They were a race of heroic men who on the age in which they lived have left an indelible impress,—self-denying, self-sacrificing priests, whose names, when lesser men of later times are forgotten, will be held in lasting remembrance, and the odour of whose virtues " is as the smell of a plentiful field, which the Lord hath blessed." " *Testantur adhuc vestigia derelicta quod vere viri sancti et perfecti fuerunt.*" Religion revived beneath their fostering care, and the old faith flourished and spread throughout the land. The Rev. Richard Gillow was one of the number of this venerable race of priests, who, " when they went up to the holy altar, they honoured the vesture of holiness." No one who knew " Uncle Gillow," could fail to love him, on account of his simplicity and kind-heartedness, and to esteem him by reason of his virtue.

Father Gillow was born at Newton, in the Fylde, on the 18th of July, 1794, and was the eldest of three brothers, his second brother being the Rev. Henry Gillow, who died at Appleton, May 6th, 1849. At the age of twelve years he was placed under the care and tuition of the Rev. Ralph Platt, of Puddington, in Cheshire, and after remaining with Mr. Platt about four years, he went on July 12th, 1810, to the then recently founded college of St. Cuthbert, Ushaw, to commence his course of studies for the ecclesiastical state. It imports not here to record with what zeal, ardour and assiduity he devoted himself to learning ; how fervent he grew in piety ; how meek and gentle he became in mood and manners. In 1818, the name of Richard Gillow is put down in the college diary as Professor of Poetry. At the end of that year, the English College at Rome had been restored and re-opened under the Pontificate of Pius VII., " after it had been desolate and uninhabited during almost the period of a generation." Several youths from Ushaw were sent to colonise it ; one of the number was his late Eminence Cardinal Wiseman. The year following, the little band of ecclesiastical students was joined at Rome by Mr. Gillow, whom we now picture before us in the hey-day of youth, traversing the Alps and the sunny plains of Italy, nearing Eternal Rome, and saluting it as the "city of his soul," and the centre of his hopes and aspirations. Having passed through his course of Theology, he was ordained priest, together with his brother Henry, who had gone to Rome with him, on Ember Saturday, June 16th, 1821, in the Church of St. John Lateran, by Archbishop Frattini. To the testimonial of his ordination is affixed the signature of "H. Card. Consalvi," protector of the English College; as also that of the Rev. Robert Gradwell (afterwards Bishop Gradwell), the Rector. The Vice-Rectorship of the college soon afterwards becoming vacant, Mr. Gillow was appointed to the office, and was Vice-Rector until the autumn of 1825. In that year, on the 7th of September, he left Rome—Rome whose memories and associations he kept enshrined, as in a casket, all life long—to proceed to England, and return to Ushaw, his *Alma Mater*, in order to become one of the Professors. He arrived at Ushaw on the 6th of December, and here, for about twelve years, he was engaged in teaching the classes of Poetry, Rhetoric, Philosophy, and Theology, and was for some time the Prefect of Studies in the same college.* Those whom he taught, and whose Professor he was, can best attest in what affection, reverence, and esteem, he was held by them. In 1837, Mr. Gillow's connection with Ushaw ceased, but his love for his college and his college friends contined to the last. In the above-named year he left Ushaw to take charge of the mission of Puddington, near Chester, vacant by the death of his former old master, the Rev. Ralph Platt. In the early part of 1846 the pastoral charge of the congregation of Euxton devolved upon him. Here he remained until near the end of 1851, when the more important mission of Chorley was entrusted to him. In this portion of the vineyard he laboured zealously for four years, when unto him was assigned, in 1855, on the Feast of the Purification, the pastorate of St. Mary's, Newsham, in succession to the Rev. J. B. Marsh, who had retired, and who died in July, 1857, aged seventy-three years. Fr. Marsh was educated at Crook Hall, and Ushaw, and was thirty-six years at Newhouse. Newhouse was the last scene of Fr. Gillow's labours—of those labours which he performed so assiduously, cheerfully, and lovingly,—having ever before his eyes the honour and glory of his Divine Master, and being always most solicitous for the salvation of the souls with which he was entrusted. He was by nature of a strong and vigorous constitution, but within two years and a half previous to his death his health began to fail. Nevertheless, he continued to discharge his duties without intermission till the spring of the year 1867, celebrating Holy Mass when he was scarcely able to stand at the altar, and reciting his daily office until eventually he found himself obliged to take to his bed. He could proceed no further; he closed his book at Sext. From that day for seven or eight weeks, he gave up all thoughts and concerns of this world, and resigned himself entirely

---

*The Rev. R. Gillow was a Professor at Ushaw twelve years, but not that length of time, as I have seen it stated, of Theology, which he taught for three years only. In the Divines' class room may be seen his portrait, subscribed for and presented to him by the Divines, whom he taught.

into the hands of that God whom from his tender youth he had loved and served so well, calmly awaiting His summons and the approach of death with the greatest tranquillity and composure ; for he could look on duties well performed and days well spent ; and to such, death has no terrors, and comes not as a thief in the night—

———" He died
As one who had been studied in his death,
To throw away the dearest thing he owed,
As 'twere a careless trifle."

Sweetly, peaceably, and tranquilly did this good man render up his soul, his departure taking place on Sunday, November 3rd, shortly before Mass, and while his congregation were assembling to assist at it. To that congregation he was much endeared, and on his death being announced to them they wept for him as a father. He had a kind, affable, jocular word for all, and towards all he was gentle, benignant, meek, and peaceful. Nor was he less loved and reverenced by his fellow-priests and other dear friends, who looked upon him as one ripe for heaven, and striving daily to attain it. A man of few wants, frugal, and self-denying, he was kind, generous, and indulgent to others, and had a heart and hand "open as day to melting charity." Meek and humble of heart, he had long learnt to possess his soul in patience. No troubles, no vexations, appeared to ruffle or perturb him, but

" Sic vultu semper placidus, sic mente serenus,
Pectore sincero frons sine nube fuit."

Almost the sole recreation which he sought was in books and studies, to which he devoted the entire leisure of his life, his reading being most varied and extensive, and his desire of knowledge unbounded. Even a year or two before his death I heard him facetiously remark that he was reading, and able to read the Greek of St. Chrysostom without the aid of glasses. Nor was he less eager to impart instruction to others, and to promote education among his people. For this purpose he was always glad to lend them books, or to procure them for them, and to provide the missions to which he was attached with schools and efficient teachers—Newhouse among the number. This much concerning our dear departed friend, of whom I may truly say—
" He did much good to me, and I am bound to him by gratitude."

The deceased was buried with solemn obsequies in the cemetery attached to St. Mary's Chapel ; his resting place being next to that of his predecessor, the Rev. J. B. Marsh. His funeral was attended by a great number of fellow-priests, his two nephews, Rev. P. and R. Liptrott, of Manchester, being chief mourners. After the Requiem Mass, the Rev. William Walker ascended the pulpit and delivered a short and touching discourse, selecting for his text, " Blessed are the meek, for they shall possess the land," St. Matt. c. 5, and showing how this Beatitude was especially exemplified in the life and character of the deceased, who "did all his works in meekness, and was therefore beloved above the glory of men ;" and who, in order to attain this virtue, must have been constantly mindful of the presence of God, joining great humility to fervent prayer and vigilance. Thus closed the grave over the mortal remains of the Rev. Richard Gillow. A serene autumn day saw him committed to the earth, to enjoy, all will pray, in heaven, a serener and more effulgent day, and that blessedness promised to those who are meek and humble of heart. The deceased at one time was Canon of the Diocesan Chapter of Liverpool, but he subsequently resigned that dignity. Among his successors at Newhouse may be named the Rev. Austin Powell, and the Very Rev. Canon Bilsborrow, both educated at Ushaw. The Rev. Thomas Carroll, educated at Ushaw also, was the next resident priest at Newhouse.

ATTACHMENT OF USHAW STUDENTS TO THEIR ALMA MATER,

"The noble College of St. Cuthbert."*

"*Movemur nescio quo pacto locis ipsis, in quibus eorum quos diligimus aut admiramur, adsunt vestigia.*"—CICERO.

Who among the students educated at Ushaw is not warmly attached to his college—to the *domus antiqua* of his boyhood and youth; to the aged yew tree from which Ushaw derives its name—*clarum et venerabile nomen*, to the spreading beeches and other trees which ornament the playgrounds and lend shelter to the walks; to the ineffaceable cat ring, ball place, and racket courts; to the football field and cricket ground; to the pond, its islands, and the swans upon its waters. Nay, even for the old clock that tells and strikes the hours, and is inscribed with the name of the maker, "Joannes Bolton, fecit 1812," refaced however within recent years by the renowned Tom Shaw, artificer in brass and iron, is felt a quasi reverential regard :—

> "What transport to recall our boyish days,
> Our early bliss, when each thing joy supplied !
> The woods, the mountains, and the warbling maze
> Of the wild brooks !"

But what sincere and enduring attachment is cherished, even after long years, for the very class rooms, study place, library and reading rooms,— and most of all for the dear old pedagogue's room, to which each of his pupils had at all times "leave" or access; where we were assisted by

---

*The new Bishop of Hexham and Newcastle, Dr. O'Callaghan, in his first Pastoral Letter, dated from the English College, Monte Porzio, near Rome, writes—"For the development and extension of all these good works of our diocese, we shall rely on the noble College of St. Cuthbert, which has been the cherished ALMA MATER, the home wherein so many of our clergy have been trained to the duties of the apostolic ministry."

Bishop O'Reilly, in his Pastoral on behalf of the Ecclesiastical Education Fund for the diocese of Liverpool (Feb. 14th, 1888) speaks of Ushaw as "the glorious old seminary for the whole of the North of England."

him in preparing our lessons for class, and received from him valuable and wholesome instruction. I regret exceedingly to learn that the pedagogue or tutorial system has been abolished, after having been adopted, tested, and approved of since the foundation of the college. I may almost say with certainty that the system was part and parcel of the Douai code, and was thence brought and ingrafted on the Crook and Ushaw course.

But to resume :—the cloisters, the corridors, the chapels, the oratories, the enshrined relics, and other devotional objects—statues, pictures, paintings, &c.—to these the mind recurs with transport ; to Thy Altars especially, O Lord of hosts—" *Altaria tua, Domine virtutum, rex meus et Deus meus ;*" and to those sweet images of piety representing that gentle, chaste, and spotless maid, whom all generations call blessed, and who at Ushaw is venerated by her clients as the " *beata mater, auxiliatrix nostra.*" Nor is there any one who from time to time will not in serious and contemplative mood revert to those happy, peaceful days of retreat, when in silence and solitude God spoke to his heart ; or to the holy communions and devotional exercises with which, together with his fellow students, he celebrated the Church's recurring festivals. With freedom of heart they applied their mind to prayer and contemplation ; and " the mind of man," says St. Bonaventure, " is a paradise while he meditates celestial things." How sweet are these retrospects which the memory of our college days supplies !

PLAY-DAYS—GREEK & FRENCH.—Next doubtless remembered— "*forsan et hæc olim meminisse juvabit*"—will be the exultation and delight with which a play-day was hailed ; how the bell was rung ; how noisy voices proclaimed "leave out," and "studies off," or announced in its season a party game at cat between Yorkists and Lancastrians, or in winter the glad and welcome news that the pond would bear.

On the subject of certain play-days (Greek and French), and a few other matters, a correspondent thus writes :—" We still enjoy our two Greek play-days per annum ; they are kept as of yore on Jan. 27th, and May 9th, the respective Feasts of those two illustrious Doctors, masters of the Greek tongue, to wit, St. John of the golden mouth, and St. Gregory Nazianzen, Archbishops of Constantinople both. The custom is for the first in Greek in Rhetoric, for Jan. 27th, and the first in Greek in Poetry, for May 9th, to get leave for them the night before from the President, and then to 'cry' it in the ambulacra just after breakfast on the day itself. On these two days the Rhetoricians and Poets are in 'high feather,' and consider themselves as most important personages, looking upon the play-day as having been secured by their own individual deserts and exertions."

" The monthly half play-days for French are no longer in existence. They have died out a long time ago, in consequence, I suppose, of the cessation of the obligation to speak French on certain days."

"The boys are not confined to their play rooms or 'fire schools' after supper ; in winter they go in and out *ad libitum*, and pace the ambulacra, whilst in summer they range 'the bounds.' Of course in 'olden times,' when the ambulacra were only lit up by an occasional 'tallow dip' dotted here and there, there was good reason for keeping the sportive youths confined to their fire schools ; but as they are now well lit with gas, there is no longer any reason for preventing them (the boys) from using them as cloisters to walk in, even as their very name of ambulacra betokens."

Old Ushaw students will notice, in the account of the Greek play-days, a deviation from the obstreperous manner in which they were proclaimed in days of yore : in the morning a rush was made, with skates or catsticks, into the study place, and the play-day there being given out, *oriebatur clamor ingens, et strepitus Graiorum*.

CHRISTMAS NIGHT.—"*O nox purpureo splendidior die ; O nox deliciis omnibus affluens*" exclaims Cardinal Bona. This night and its solemnities at Ushaw have already been described in my introductory poem ; my readers will find the description at pp. 29-34. "Regarding Christmas Eve at Ushaw," writes a much respected friend, "the rules and hours are the same as they were fifty years ago. But the Christmas night of that time would appear very poor and tame to the present generation of students. Yet I believe the boys then enjoyed their Christmas night exceedingly. You will remember how they decked themselves out at 9 p.m. or earlier in their smartest habiliments from head to foot. Grand and 'foppish' waistcoats that seldom appeared in the college on other occasions were brought out on Christmas night. There is no such opportunity now. Since 1847, when we entered the new chapel, cassocks have been worn by all the students, and surplices by all in the stalls, on Christmas night, and whenever we have solemn services. The *Venite exultemus*, Hymns, Psalms, Responsoria *(Collaudantes, &c.)* are sung now as then ; High Mass, and Holy Communion, then *Lauds* as formerly. At the breakfast about 2 a.m., the large buns ('fasting cakes') are continued ; but instead of the spiced beer, or 'Tom Long,' there is now tea or coffee. Now also there is a *second* breakfast at 10, before the second High Mass."

The Christmas vacation commenced, dating from Christmas Day to the Epiphany or twelfth day,—all the more enjoyable, if there were frost and snow. Shortly afterwards the President's feast was held, and who does not remember how gladly it was welcomed, and with what *gout* hashed veal, roast goose, and "Sunday" pudding, supplied for the occasion, were relished ? Such are some, among others, of the historic memories, venerable traditions, and cherished associations which like so many tendrils, cling to the heart, and twine around the affections of the sons and alumni of *Alma Mater*. A good, venerable, old priest, one of Ushaw's worthies, used to amuse himself and others by singing—

> "Green grow the rushes, O,
> Green grow the rushes, O,
> The happiest days that e'er I spent,
> Were spent at Ushaw College, O,—"

a parody of the first stanza of one of the poet Burns's Scotch songs. My own feelings and affections in regard to Ushaw I have, in humble way and measure, embodied and set forth in verse as follows :—

USHAW.

Simple memories of the past! Sitting in my chair, I forget the by-gone years, the wrinkles on my brow, and the silver threads in my hair, as my boyhood's visions crowd upon my brain, and I cannot find in my heart to banish them, to drive them away by the sterner realities of the present.—LIGHT AND SHADE, BY THE REV. T. J. POTTER.

I've loved thee, dear old Ushaw,
    Through all life's chequered ways ;—
I loved thee in my manhood's prime,
    And in my boyhood's days.

Oh ! those were happy, blithesome days,
    The days at Ushaw spent ;
Our hearts were light, our spirits gay,
    Free from all discontent.

Our ways were ways of pleasantness,
    No worldy care was ours ;
Religion hallowed all our joys,
    And strewed our path with flowers.

Our schoolmates and companions
    Were trusty, kind, and free,—
We dwelt, as brothers and as friends,
    In peace and unity.

Alas ! of those how few remain,
    Who, neath the Ushaw yew,
Together with us studied, played,
    And unto manhood grew !—

How few are left to tell the tale
    Of those good olden times !—
Some to their last account have gone,
    Some dwell in distant climes.

And years on me are stealing fast,
    Like mists at close of day,
But while, dear Ushaw, life does last,
    With fervent heart I'll pray

That thou may'st prosper ; that thy sons,
    Unto each other true,
May all that's noble, good, and pure,
    Devotedly pursue.

Like to a stately forest tree,
 That from a sapling sprung,
Thy fame has grown, and eke by bards
 Thy praises have been sung.

Thy chapels, library, and halls,
 In stately grandeur stand,
And youths thy schools and cloisters pace,
 A studious happy band,

Within whose breasts a glow of zeal
 And piety shines forth,
Directing all their aims and ends
 To deeds of noble worth.

VISIT OF CARDINAL MANNING TO USHAW:

Address presented to him; the Cardinal's reply.

Let us now hear the sentiments of a distinguished authority, His Eminence Cardinal Manning, Archbishop of Westminster, as expressed by him, respecting Ushaw, when, in the month of September, 1885, he honoured the college by a visit. On that occasion he received an address from the President, Professors, and Students, in replying to which His Eminence thanked them for the kind and unexpected words with which he had been greeted; they had taken him by surprise. His absence at the opening of their new church had been a grief to him, but circumstances over which he had no control had compelled it, or otherwise nothing would have prevented his presence with them on that occasion. The happiness of the present visit was really a condonation and a compensation for the pleasure he was then obliged to forego. His Eminence could never visit Ushaw without many and deep feelings of thankfulness. The President had reminded him that it was ten years since his last coming amongst them, and his thoughts went back to that time. He remembered the old church was standing then; but, not content with it, beautiful as it was, they had rebuilt it on a larger scale. St. Cuthbert's College was a reproduction of the old mediæval colleges at Oxford—it equalled them in its material beauty, which exists to this day, but here there was the same faith animating it which had animated them in days of old. He felt a profound sympathy with the place, for it stood as a measure and a witness—a measure of what the church can do, and a witness that what it has done, it can do again. Another great reason which he would give for his feelings towards the college might be put in the words of St. Cyprian, writing of the church, for he would call it the "*radix et matrix sacerdotii.*" For well nigh a hundred years had Ushaw stood, and some eight hundred priests had gone forth from its walls, and many Bishops too; indeed he would say that the Church in the North of

England was the offspring of St. Cuthbert's College. This gave it a paramount claim on his affections. He had always used the name of Ushaw College to rebut the pernicious desire which some Catholics had to send their sons to Harrow, Eton, and the Universities. If any man had ever felt the influence of such places, assuredly it was himself. His early days had been spent at Harrow, and later on Oxford had been his home at that time of life when young men begin to educate themselves. Even now that University possessed a wonderful power over him. He had spent, he would not say the happiest days of his life, but at all events very happy days at Oxford, and its memories had a fascination for him. Surely, they might think, he at all events would be tolerant in his view of this desire for university life. But a double reason—his thorough knowledge and experience of what Oxford was, and, thank God, his knowledge of the Catholic Church, made it inconceivable to him how any Catholic could in conscience go there, or send his son to any university out of the Catholic unity. Continually for twenty years had this question been discussed, three or four times representations on it had been made to the Holy See, and three times decisions had been given there, but yet these decisions had been attenuated and evaded by some Catholics in this country. This might be the last time he should speak to his audience, but he would say to those he saw before him, who hereafter would guide the consciences of many, never let anything induce them to countenance by silence or toleration, much less to counsel, the sending of Catholic young men to any seats of learning where the character cannot be moulded by Catholic truth. Let them be sent to none but Catholic universities. Let them go to no universities which had not the Faith and the tradition of Catholic philosophy, and in this country he would point out to them St. Cuthbert's College at Ushaw. He would give the reasons why, in his opinion, there was this craving for university life. The leading motive was, he believed, not higher culture, but supposed worldly advantages; it was to form acquaintances in a high social position. Moreover Catholics were taught to believe that the comparison between the culture and scholarship of the Catholic colleges, and those of the public schools and universities of England, told vastly in favour of the latter. His Eminence bade them look at St. Cuthbert's College at Ushaw, and see what great success it had gained at the London University. The examinations of this latter body were not merely equal in exactness to those of the other universities, but were more severe. He had learned from the President of Ushaw and had thus had the opportunity of mentioning at Rome, that within the last fifteen years, St. Cuthbert's College had twice gained the gold medal of the University of London, in the classical M.A. examination. Surely this was a high proof of Catholic culture! A hundred years ago, there were no Catholic colleges in this land; and yet despite the penal laws, despite of poverty, despite the slender means of the Bishop who had laid the first stone of Ushaw, he could now point in proof of the Church's fertility to Ushaw, St. Edmund's, Downside, Ampleforth, Stonyhurst, and other lesser colleges numbering perhaps between sixteen and twenty. If so much could be done in a hundred years, what might not be expected in the course of a few generations? Nay more, he would say that the average Catholic students went forth better educated men than those of Oxford or Cambridge. One of the heads of the colleges at Oxford had written a book in which he stated that seventy per cent. of the undergraduates left that university in his judgment uneducated men, not fit to take a degree. Catholic students, ages being equal, were more even, more equal all round than Oxford or Cambridge men, and he attributed that fact to the more conscientious and diligent care of the teachers, and to diligent and conscientious study on the part of the students. Many men left Oxford and Cambridge much in the position of the man who when talking of his education said "My Greek was drowned long ago, and my Latin is swimming for its life." His Eminence would confess to them that in these holidays he had been reading once more Cæsar's Commentaries, and the Odes of Horace—reading them too with greater understanding and pleasure than in his youth. He hoped that those before him, when they had attained his age, would go back to their old studies in the classics, and find in them the same sweetness and delight. Let them study hard and conscientiously, not merely, however, to gain knowledge, but because it was a high moral duty to use aright the gifts which God had given them. He did not believe that Greek or Latin or science was beyond the reach of the ordinary faculties of a man who would only resolutely apply himself. Boys thought Greek grammar a mystery, known well enough to their masters, but beyond their reach, but there was in reality no mystery about it. With ordinary faculties and a resolute will they could master any language. Perseverance must be theirs, for it would be cowardice in them not to do what is done even at Oxford and Cambridge. In these days there was great talk about science, about the mud beneath their feet, the stars above their heads, the laws of Nature, and the powers of chemistry. He would compare science to a pyramid, the lowest part of which might represent the world—that is, the physical sciences; the middle part the science of man and of morals, and at the apex rests the science of God, *i.e.*, Theology. Modern science would have people busy themselves mainly at the base of the pyramid, but at St. Cuthbert's it was not so, for there men were taught that the first science is the science of God, and all other sciences were dependent on Him. No person, his Eminence said, could be a successful student unless he were a conscientious student, for study is not only intellectual, but also a moral effort of the will. Referring again to the dangers of non-Catholic teaching for Catholic youth, he said that the peril lay in the men being there put out of the unity of the intellectual tradition of mankind. The existence of God, His attributes, the immortality of the soul, the freedom of the will, the office of conscience, were all clear to men by the lights of nature, but in these days there was every form of doubt, agnosticism and scepticism undermining the foundations of all certainty, both supernatural and natural alike. But now he found he had said more than he intended; however, he wished them to look well at what had already been done by the Church in England, and at what she could do hereafter. He trusted that a succession of priests would in the future continue to go forth from Ushaw, and that the laymen who were trained side by side with them there in brotherhood would still continue to maintain in after life the friendship which they had there formed in youth. His last words should be, *Aspirante Deo, floreat Sancti Cuthberti Collegium in ævum.*

Dr. Müller, a German Catholic priest, in an essay on English intermediate education observes : " Tradition is a mighty factor in all schools in England, Protestant and Catholic. The eye meets everywhere the portraits of famous past students, in corridors, refectories, libraries ; their names and deeds are ever on the lips of masters and pupils. How often have I heard at Ushaw College the names of Drs. Newsham, Lingard, Wiseman, formerly students of this excellent establishment in the North of England."

SIXTY YEARS AGO.

Sixty years, and four added to that number, is no brief period in man's life. Those years—upwards of three score—have passed over my head, since, not yet twelve years old, I was set my first lesson in Latin at Ushaw, in the old "Douay Figures." How few remain who remember or who learnt that time-honoured Latin Grammar ! " Is not the school," remarked Bishop Spalding, in a discourse on University Education, at the Cathedral, Baltimore, " for all men a shrine to which their pilgrim thoughts return to catch again the glow and gladness of a world wherein they live by faith and hope and love, when round the morning sun of life the golden purple clouds were hanging, and earth lay hidden in mist, beneath which the soul created a new paradise ? To the opening mind all things are young and fair, and to remember the delight that accompanied the gradual dawn of knowledge upon our mental vision, sweet and beautiful as the upglowing of day from the bosom of night, is to be for ever thankful for the gracious power of education."

Educated in youth at Ushaw, the shrine to which my pilgrim thoughts are apt frequently to return ; the sanctuary of religion and learning—*sacrarium religionis ac bonarum artium* ; a visitor, once a year at least, to *Alma Mater ;* holding friendly relations and correspondence with most of those, both young and old, who have there pursued their studies ; having my memory stored with the unnumbered traditions and associations, that are engraven as it were on its hallowed walls—

" Long, long be my mind with such memories fill'd,
Like vases where roses have once been distill'd,
You may break, you may shatter the vase, if you will,
But the scent of the roses will hang round it still,—"

it has afforded me considerable pleasure to note how from year to year the college has grown, increased, and expanded ; how it has diffused religion, and learning, and helped to propagate the faith by sending labourers into the vineyard, who *" in omnibus sumentes scutum fidei,"* went forth to preach the Gospel, and to distribute the bread of life in places and among peoples, where there was a spiritual famine.

The late lamented Bishop Bewick, in a pastoral, dated " The Martyr's Place in Tynemouth, the 9th day of November, 1883," ordering collections throughout his diocese towards building the new Collegiate Chapel of St. Cuthbert, speaks in these terms of Ushaw. " It (the College) is not exclusively Ours, though situate within the boundaries of the Bishopric, and within the limits of Our jurisdiction. Five other Bishops jointly with Ourselves have a stake in it, and an interest in its welfare. We however have the largest number of students located there and the greatest interest at stake." .... "It is known only in heaven how many and what benedictions and graces and spiritual influences we owe to its edifying example, its discipline, its fidelity to rubrics, its solemn functions and minor services, its prestige of name, its architecture, its buildings, and eminently above all, its church. What Lindisfarne and Durham were of old time to the North of England, that now is Ushaw College. It is a beacon, a pharos of light and learning and virtue for miles and miles around."

Ushaw is withal a house of peace, piety, and order, a house where you find true liberty, equality, and fraternity; and the peace of God that surpasseth all understanding :—

"And I said, if there's peace in this world to be found,
The heart that is humble may hope for it here."

O quanta devotio orationis! quanta æmulatio virtutis! quanta disciplina viguit! quanta reverentia et obedientia, sub regula magistri in omnibus effloruit! Testantur adhuc vestigia derelicta, quod vere viri sancti et perfecti fuerunt, qui tam strenue militantes, mundum suppetitaverunt"—words which we read in the "Following of Christ," than which words it would be difficult to find words more applicable to Ushaw and Ushaw's virtuous students. "*Beatus quem tu erudieris, Domine, et de lege tua docueris eum, ut mitiges ei a diebus malis, et non desoletur in terra.*"

GREAT MEN AND DISTINGUISHED ECCLESIASTICS.

Ushaw has produced great men, and distinguished ecclesiastics ;—Cardinals, Archbishops, and Bishops; Provosts, Canons, Deans, Vicar-Generals, and Doctors of Divinity ; sages, senators, judges, physicians, architects, soldiers, &c., &c.

"Great men have been among us, hands that penned,
 And tongues that uttered wisdom,"—

the story of whose lives—the lives of noble intelligences and men of renown, I have told, and exhibited historical portraits of them :

"Great men grow rarer daily ; great were these."

The eldest daughter of venerable Douai, its projectors laid its foundations wide and deep ; and though established in a part of the country which at that time was remote and unfrequented, wild and sterile, it not only in course of time subjugated the soil, made the wilderness blossom, and the country around productive and fruitful, but what is more, it has subjugated and improved by learning and culture the hearts, the minds, and the intellects of innumerable Catholic youths, and by the graceful and dignified discipline of collegiate life has trained them for the fitting and able discharge of ecclesiastical and secular duties. Under the patronage of St. Cuthbert, whose 12th centenary was celebrated at the college with sacred and solemn observance, Ushaw has become a great and flourishing college :

"*Exstat ut in mediis terris aprica oasis.*"

Since the date of its foundation it has done a great work in promoting religion and education among the Catholics of this country. And this work proceeds—the work of educating and training youths, of informing their minds, ordering aright their hearts, and qualifying them for their several duties, occupations, and positions in life. At Ushaw Dr. Lingard, the renowned historian, taught in the chairs of Philosophy and Theology. It was at Ushaw that Nicholas Cardinal Wiseman, and Ferdinand Cardinal De la Puente imbibed their love of learning, and acquired that ecclesiastical spirit, which in their future lives was so notably developed, that they not only advanced *de virtute ad virtutem*, but attained the highest pinnacle of honour and preferment. At Ushaw also were educated the late Mr. Sergeant Murphy, and Mr. Justice Shee, the first Catholic raised to the Bench since the Revolution. The Catholic Relief Act had been passed forty years, and he had been more than thirty-five years at the Bar, when he was selected as a Judge of the Court of Queen's Bench, in 1864. William Shee, with his brother, Joseph Shee, entered St. Cuthbert's College in the year 1817. Both were intelligent, diligent, and talented students. William Shee, the eldest son of Joseph Shee, of Thomastown, Co. Kilkenny, was born in 1804. He was called to the Bar, and admitted a member of Lincoln's Inn, June 19th, 1828. He began his forensic labours by travelling Home Circuit, and attending Surrey Sessions. Both at sessions and at the courts in London his advocacy received great encouragement, and in 1840 he had gained such a position as justified him in accepting the Sergeant's coif. His reputation increased by his publishing an edition of Lord Tenderden's great work on shipping, and the extensive knowledge displayed by Shee in that branch. He had long been head of his Circuit, and in London one of the most popular leaders. From 1852-57 he sat as M.P. for Co. Kilkenny. The family was originally from Kerry, but migrated to Kilkenny. While member for his native County of Kilkenny, Mr. Shee published "Proposal for Religious Equality in Ireland and for a Charitable Settlement of the Irish Church Question. Addressed to his Constituents, by William Shee, Sergeant at Law, M.P. for the County of Kilkenny."

To Scotland Ushaw has given a venerated and learned Archbishop (His Grace the Archbishop of Glasgow), decorated by the Queen Regent of Spain with the Grand Cross of Isabel la Catolica, the membership of which order carries with it personal nobility; a Bishop of Argyll and the Isles; and Bishops no less worthy to the Sees of Hexham and Newcastle, Liverpool, Salford, Beverley, Leeds, Middlesbrough, Nottingham, Northampton, and Southwark. Dear old Ushaw, who, among thy alumni and students does not honour and love thee, and delight to visit thy bowers, where learning and piety flourish, and where religion has raised an august and enduring monument which shall outlive all time? I know the place well; I know it almost by heart like the lessons which I learnt there, like the great truths and the grave duties, the high thoughts and amiable words—

"And love of truth and all that makes a man,"

which were there taught and inculcated. Through lapse of years and the flight of more than half a century, changes and transformations have been wrought; one generation has succeeded another, and few are left with whom I entered on a student's life, and with them climbed the hill of learning; howbeit I remember and know the place well, and experience much pleasure in greeting it as follows:—

Salve pulchra domus, salve gratissima sedes;
Sit semper felix, æterno floreat ævo;
Illustres salvete viri, necnon venerandi,
Quorum semper honos, virtus, laudesque manebunt;
Salvete O flores juvenum, spes nostra futura,
Salvete irriguæ valles, silvæque virentes;
Precibus et Sancti Cuthberti pace fruatur
Æterna, atque etiam durando sæcula vincat.

USHAW DESERVING OF A VISIT.

Ushaw is well deserving of a visit. Any one going there with a respectable introduction will be sure to meet with a cordial and hospitable welcome. From one and all—President, Vice-President, Procurator, and Professors, he will receive marked attention and kindness. In the summer of 1885, sixteen priests educated at the English College, Lisbon, paid a visit to Ushaw. They were delighted with the college, and highly gratified with the courtesy and hospitality with which they were received. One of them declared to me that, as a collegiate establishment, he had seen nothing equal to it in England. Near and around the college, its park, plantations, gardens, walks, parterres, shrubberies dense with yew, holly, laurel, and arbutus; the pond with its swans and islands, the play grounds, &c.; the noble pile of buildings forming the college; its adjuncts and environments, are objects of considerable interest and attraction; and to those who pride themselves on having Ushaw for their *Alma Mater* are "a joy for ever—"

"And up beyond them yellow fields of corn,
  And still ascending countless firry spires,
  Dry slopes of hills, uncultured, bare, forlorn,
  And green in rocky clefts with whins and briars;"

add to these verdant meadows and pastures; groups of grazing cattle and nibbling flocks of sheep; distant villages, rustic cottages, and homely farmsteads—all which outward shows of sky and earth, of hill and valley, combine to diversify the landscape, and lend enchantment to the view.

On entering the college, the visitor having saluted the image of our Lady, and hailed her as full of grace, as "the mother of fair love, of fear, of knowledge, and holy hope;" having besought her, in the words of a celebrated poetess, as the mother of sorrows and the refuge of the weary—

"O thou the Mother of all sorrows,
Aid, oh, aid, to pray and weep!"
"O sweet Mother! may the weary
Turn from this cold world to thee—"

he wends his way, or is conducted round the ambulacra profusely adorned with pictures, sees numerous suites of class rooms and other apartments, stops to look at the public reading room, and the study place; admires the splendid library and the magnificent collection of books contained in it; admires also the noble exhibition hall, and the grand refectory, with its floor of marble, and walls hung round with the portraits of renowned ecclesiastical dignitaries.

To the portraits which adorn the refectory at Ushaw—among them that of his late Holiness, Pius IX., has been added the portrait of the present illustrious Pontiff, Pope Leo XIII., painted in Rome, and obtained through the kindness of Monsignor Stonor for the college. By all who have seen it, it is considered an excellent likeness of his Holiness. The holy Father is represented seated in his chair, in the act of bestowing his blessing. Enaureoled with grace and dignity, firmness and gentleness are depicted on the features of this great Pontiff, a Pontiff universally recognised as pacificator and mediator in international disputes; foretold by ancient seers as the *lumen in cælo*; reverenced as the apostle of peace and justice, and as the promoter of theological and philosophical learning; honoured moreover and venerated as the guardian and defender of the rights and liberties of the Church and the Holy See.

Apropos of portraits. On December 10th, 1883, his Holiness raised the Rev. Charles Gillow, of Ushaw, to the dignity of a Domestic Prelate; and his (Right Rev. Mgr. Gillow's) portrait has been placed among the *veterum effigies* in the refectory. The portrait is nearly life size, and is on the same side of the refectory as those of the Right Rev. Mgr. Tate, D.D., the former President, and the Very Rev. Dr. Gillow, Vice-President.

Among the collection of portraits round the refectory walls, few or none surpass in excellence that of the venerable and saintly Bishop Smith (Thomas, Bishop of Bolina, and Vicar-Apostolic of the Northern District). It is an admirable likeness, and cannot fail at the first glance being recognised by those who remember *(eheu, quam pauci relicti!)* the good old Bishop. It was painted by Ramsay, and after sixty years is as fresh and fair as when it left the hands of the artist. I recollect, at the time of its being painted, some of us used to steal up to the Bishop's room at the college, to get a sight of it.

From the refectory, and the smaller elegant adjoining dining room, our visitor will probably proceed to the church, where the beautiful altars, chapels, and oratories, the richly painted and storied windows, the decorated walls and ceilings, the statues in purest marble of the Blessed Virgin and Child, with lights and flowers, and perhaps some pious, gentle youth telling his beads before them;—these, and "the rapture and repose that's there," will tend to inspire him with reverence and devotion, and love for the beauty of the house of God. Leaving the church, a person might next have a wish to see the Junior College, infirmary, &c. These buildings, though of more recent erection, are connected with, and form part of St. Cuthbert's College. Pursuing your way through a long spacious hall—wide, lofty, and well lighted, which has been fitted up as a museum, and lingering occasionally to examine the various objects and curiosities there exhibited, you at length find yourself in cloisters leading in one direction to the infirmary, a building admirably arranged and adapted for the purpose which it serves, in another to the seminary. In the seminary or Junior College younger and smaller boys are placed ; and after a certain curriculum pass into the college. During their course they are well taught, and well cared for in regard to both health and comfort, much consideration being had for their tender years, and kind, indulgent masters placed over them. Indeed, no one, observing the light-heartedness and cheerfulness of the youngsters who are here, can help feeling assured that they are " happy as the day is long."

" Gay hope is theirs by fancy fed,
Less pleasing when possessed,
The tear forgot as soon as shed,
The sunshine of the breast :

Theirs buxom health of rosy hue,
Wild wit, invention, ever new,
And lively cheer, of vigour born ;
The thoughtless day, the easy night,
The spirits pure, the slumbers light
That fly th' approach of morn."

Few will be disposed to leave the Junior College, after having gone the round of the class and study rooms, and through the fine, large, and well-aired dormitory, with sleeping accommodation for 106 persons, without paying a visit to the chapel, the beautiful chapel of St. Aloysius, of youth the angelic patron, and admiring its elaborately carved altar and reredos, their elegant garniture and adornments, and the lovely marble statue of the Virgin Mother and her Child divine. If a parent, and he has a son here pursuing his studies, devotion will excite him to kneel before the altar, our Lady's statue, or the statue of St. Aloysius in the same chapel, and offer up a prayer for a blessing on his boy. At the extreme limit of the seminary playground, encircled for protection with an iron palisade, the venerable old yew tree—venerable in decay and green even amid the snows of winter—spreads its sable scanty boughs ;

as yet
Unplumed by time, its hollowed trunk there stands,
And gives to Ushaw name.

From the seminary you may proceed through one of the corridors, and stroll to

THE CEMETERY.

> ———*Salut, champ funéraire,*
> *Des tombeaux du collège humble dépositaire !*
> *Je bénis en passant les simples monumens—*
> *Malheur à qui des morts profane la poussière.*
>
> DE LAMARTINE.

This abode of the dead is situated on the north side of the college, immediately behind the Junior College. Peace to the sleepers therein ! It is a sacred and solemn enclosure, planted round with cypress, yew, and holly, and is cleanly and neatly kept. Here repose, expecting the resurrection of the dead, and the life of the world to come—*resurrectionem mortuorum et vitam venturi sæculi* —youths, young ecclesiastics, missionary Priests, Bishops, Presidents, and Vice-Presidents of the college, of each of whom it may now be said " *Per diem sol non uret te, neque luna per noctem.*" " *Dominus custodit omnia ossa eorum.*"

" There is a voice from the tomb," writes the author of the Sketch Book, "sweeter than song. There is a remembrance of the dead to which we turn even from the charms of the living. Oh, the grave ! the grave ! It buries every error, covers every defect, extinguishes every resentment ! From its peaceful bosom spring none but fond regrets and tender recollections."

Roses were abloom in this God's acre when I last wandered alone among the green graves of the cemetery. A solitary one was blooming on the grave of John Kerr, son of the Marchioness of Lothian. He died January 24th, 1855, aged fourteen years. A plain wood cross marks the resting place of this youthful scion of a noble house. The elder brother, who died in 1811, of the late Thomas Fitzherbert Brockholes, Esq., of Claughton Hall, has over his place of interment a neat stone cross, with the following inscription upon it :—
" Orate pro anima Jacobi Fitzherbert Brockholes, filii Gulielmi Fitzherbert Brockholes, Armigeri de Claughton. Obiit die XXI. Martii A.D. MDCCCXI. Ætatis XII. R.I.P." Early in the year 1809, shortly after the college was opened, five youths died of fever. They are buried in close proximity to one another, and their respective graves are indicated by a wooden cross, inscribed with the name of the deceased and the date of his death. Considering the length of time that has elapsed since the college was founded, the " graves of the household" in the cemetery are far from being numerous, a circumstance which it is satisfactory to note, and which speaks favourably for the general health and healthy situation of the college. The last interment was that of a young student, Joseph Patrick Mc.Glone, who had just passed his matriculation with success, and whose death occurred on the 24th of of July, 1887. The solemn and sweetly sung Requiem in the college chapel, the procession to the cemetery round the ambulacra and the corridors, and the mournful chant swelling and dying away, sung by

innocent voices, was exquisitely touching. The happiness and simplicity of their early days recurred to many of the visitors, and the unbidden tear filled many an eye. Strew his grave with flowers—"*manibus date lilia plenis*"—he died young; and those, whom Jesus, Mary, and Joseph love, are taken away in the flower of their age and innocence; and may be classed among the blessed—the *innocentes et mundo corde*—who die in the Lord—"*Beati mortui qui in Domino moriuntur.*"

The cemetery cross is of elegant and elaborate design. The upper part is metal work, on a stone base, from which it rises to a considerable elevation. The Rev. Thomas Crowe, an alumnus and benefactor of the college, is buried underneath this cross, at the foot of which is the following inscription :—"*Pie Jesu Domine, propitiare animæ famuli tui Thomæ, et animabus omnium hic sub umbra crucis quiescentium ;*" and near the cross the late Bishop Chadwick, some time before his death, selected his place of sepulture; and the good Bishop reposes there. *Placide quiescat.* On the north and west sides of the cemetery there is a covered cloister, within which are deposited in peace the remains of Bishop Gibson, the founder of the college; and those of Bishops Smith, Mostyn, and Hogarth. The Presidents, Rev. Thomas Eyre, Dr. Gillow, Mgr. Tate, D.D., and Dr. Wilkinson; Dr. Lingard, Rev. Thomas Wilkinson, of Kendal, who retired to and died at Ushaw, at the advanced age of 94, Rev. John Bradley, of Yarm, Dean Trappes, and Rev. A. Macartney, are interred here also. God's peace be with them. An elegant black marble tablet, inlaid with brass, and inscribed with the name of the deceased, date of death, &c., is affixed against the cloister walls, opposite the grave of each.

In the open burial ground are several priests of the diocese, whose remains were brought there for interment; amongst them old Father Yates, of Esh, deceased June 11th, 1826; and in the same hallowed ground you find, and stop to offer a *De Profundis* at the tomb of the Rev. John Kirk, who had filled the office of Procurator from the year 1817 until near the time of his death, April 20th, 1850. Who does not remember old Mr. Kirk, so shrewd and so knowing, and who attached such importance to being thrifty and careful, that with Cicero he could say—"*Non intelligunt homines quam magnum vectigal sit parsimonia.*" The inscription on his tombstone reads as follows :—"*Rvd. Dns. Joannes Kirk, obiit die 20 Aprilis, 1850, ætatis 63. R.I.P. Fidelis servus et prudens quem constituit Dominus super familiam suam.*"

"I doubt," as Longfellow remarked on his visiting a certain beautiful cemetery, "whether any one can enter this enclosure without feeling the religion of the place steal over him, and seeing something of the dark and gloomy expression pass off from the stern countenance of death."

Monks were enjoined, when travelling, on passing a church or chapel, to incline devoutly, and invoke their holy patrons, and on no account to pass a cemetery without prayer for the dead—"*Cœmeteria absque oratione pro defunctis mullatenus decet pertransire.*"

"We are made acquainted with the form of collegiate burial," says Digby, in *Mores Catholici*, "through the account which is given of the customs that used to be observed in the English College at Douai." "At the burial of any of our members, the whole community attended in a very solemn procession from the college church to that of the parish, where high mass was sung. The corpse was carried by the schoolfellows and companions of the deceased ; a priest was borne on the shoulders of his fellow-priests, and a dozen or twenty scholars surrounded the bier with lighted flambeaux. At the head of the procession went the priest, deacon, and sub-deacon vested for mass, with acolyths, thurifers, and our own choir in surplices. The students followed two and two, in the order of classes, wearing cassocks."

Dismissing this grave subject, and quitting the tombs and the habitation of the dead, I return to the home of the living, premising that when at the cemetery, any one so disposed, may take a walk to the college garden, which is well stocked with fruit trees and vegetables, and covers an extent of more than four acres. It is enclosed with a high wall on all sides.

EXHIBITION WEEK.

It is the Exhibition week at St. Cuthbert's. The great week that brings to a termination the year's course of studies, the week in which take place the examinations for classical honours, the defensions of theses in natural and moral philosophy, and theology, the distribution of honours, medals, prizes, &c. All is life and joy, all are full of hope and expectation. St. Cuthbert's flag flutters aloft in the play-ground ; clergy and laity, friends and priests, are welcomed to *Alma Mater*, where they assemble and enjoy themselves in happy and social re-union. To how many does not a meeting like this make amends for long absence from the scenes and home of their youth, brightening life's dreary pathway, cheering its wearisome hours, recalling to remembrance old friends and companions, and replenishing the mind with joyful memories and bright dreams of past times. To me a visit to Ushaw on this occasion was a source of considerable pleasure. "*Innocuas amo delicias doctamque quietem ;*" and these peaceful pleasures, this literary repose, I rarely failed to experience, when I attended during the "Grand Week" the academical exhibition. "*In scholam redeo ; illam dulcissimam ætatem quasi resumo : sedeo inter juvenes ut solebam.*" On the first day especially, I used never to omit being present at the examination of the candidates for honours in the Greek and Latin classics, for I have grown old in these studies, and they continue to be to me a solace and delight. "*O homo ! si scires quantum doctrina valeret, non dormires, sed nocte dieque studeres.*" Homer, Virgil, Tacitus, Cicero, Xenophon, and Thucydides were, on one occasion when I was present, the authors from which selections were made for translation by the students, and these passages were rendered with wonderful correctness, acquirement, and culture. Their knowledge of the language of these authors was not mechanical and technical merely. They had evidently learnt "to feel the language, to think in it, to catch its genius and spirit, to become partakers of the mind of their authors, and to enjoy communion with them."

"*O dulces comitum valete cœtus;*" you have laboured hard and long; you have toiled through winter, and spring, and summer; go now and enjoy an autumn of repose; go from the flowery fields of literature *(e florigeris literarum arvis)* to inhale the breezes of the hills and mountains, and the health-inspiring freshness of the sea; seek the covert of the leafy woods, the valleys verdant with grass and flowers, and the dells "with wild thyme, and the gadding vine overgrown." Relegate Virgil to "smooth sliding Mincius, crowned with vocal reeds;" Horace to his Sabine farm—he will be happy there—*Satis beatus unicis Sabinis*, and Cicero to the beech groves of Tusculum. Homer, Herodotus, and Thucydides, let the old Greeks quietly take their repose. Do you eat your bread with joy, and drink your wine with a merry heart. For my part,

———"Where'er I go,
Thy genuine image, Ushaw,
Will dwell with me, to heighten joy,
And cheer my mind in sorrow."

USHAW COLLEGE AND THE LONDON UNIVERSITY.

I might here enlarge, but it is not my present purpose to do so, on the superior educational organism of Ushaw; the literary contentions, the competitive examinations, and the approved and successful course of studies there pursued. "By their fruits you shall know them," and these fruits have year after year manifested themselves in the triumphs and successes achieved by Ushaw students at the London University. The statement adduced below is suggestive and encouraging evidence of the triumphal march of intellect, the progress of knowledge, and the development of talent at "our glorious college."

"For five-and-twenty years Ushaw has sent up a continuous stream of students to the examinations held by the London University, and now proudly claims a greater number of achieved successes than any other Catholic institution can point to in the same period."—*The Tablet*, November 19th, 1887.

The B.A. Examination, anno 1887, completed the twenty-fifth year of the unbroken connection, which began in 1863, between St. Cuthbert's College, Ushaw, and the London University. For more than twenty years before this time Ushaw had been affiliated to the University, and students had occasionally been presented at its examinations. Indeed Ushaw was the first of the Catholic colleges in England to take advantage of the opportunities offered by the foundation of the new University; for in 1840, two years after its first examination was held, two students from Ushaw, Mr. Francis Wilkinson (afterwards President of the college) and Mr. Richard Wilson, took the degree of Bachelor of Arts. In 1863 preparation for the Degree in Arts was made a part of the regular course of studies, and since then the London examinations have been held regularly at Ushaw. The students in the class of Poetry are prepared for Matriculation, those in Rhetoric for the Intermediate Examination in Arts, and those in the first year of Philosophy for the final B.A. Examination. It may be interesting to sum up the results of the examinations during this quarter of a century.

I. At the Matriculation Examination, 281 students have passed, and it is worthy of note that this is a larger total than can be claimed by any other educational institution in England during the same period. Of this number fifty-nine have obtained Honours. Three prizes of £5 each have been gained for fifth, sixth, and seventh places, though in one case the winner of the prize was disqualified by age from receiving it. Eighteen candidates have obtained the number of marks qualifying for a prize, and nearly all the places from the fifth to the twenty-fifth have been gained at different times. Of the remaining candidates, one hundred and eighty-seven have been placed in the first division, and thirty-five in the second. During the last seven years only one student has been placed in the second division.

II. The Intermediate Arts Examination has been held at Ushaw nineteen times since 1863. Ninety-one candidates have passed, sixty-four in the first, and twenty-seven in the second division. Of these, sixteen have obtained Honours in Latin. The exhibition in Latin of £40 per annum for two years has been gained four times.

III. The B.A. examination has been held eighteen times. Fifty candidates have passed, thirty in the first, and twenty in the second division. Eight have obtained Honours, six in classics and two in animal physiology. Of the six who obtained Honours in classics, three held the first place on the list, and three the second. Of the former, one was awarded the University Scholarship of £50 per annum for three years, and another, though deserving the scholarship, was disqualified by being three days over the limit of age at the commencement of the examination. Of those who held the second place, two obtained marks qualifying for the scholarship. The prize of £30 was also gained by one of the two successful candidates in animal physiology.

IV. Seven students have taken the degree of M.A., two in mental and moral science, and five in classics. The gold medal in classics, which has been awarded only fourteen times since the foundation of the University in 1837, has been twice gained by a candidate from Ushaw.

DEVOTION TO THE CHAIR OF PETER.

On visiting Ushaw, one Exhibition week, A.D. 1871, I could not help being struck with the devotion cherished by the students to his late Holiness, Pope Pius IX. It manifested itself repeatedly during the week. It found a voice in the Pope's hymn, and in the Jubilee Ode to

Pio Nono; in the speeches and addresses, and a few weeks previously in the more tangible form of £177 subscribed by them to the Papal Jubilee Fund.

In the year of the Sacerdotal Jubilee of his Holiness, Pope Leo XIII., the Very Rev. Dr. Giles, Rector of the English College, presented, at an audience given, March 21st, 1888, an offering of £42 from the college, together with an album, magnificently bound and illustrated with views of the college and its surroundings, having as a frontispiece an excellent photograph of the square of the Duomo, in Perugia, a delicate attention which delighted the Pope, who examined the volume with great interest, making numerous inquiries relative to St. Cuthbert's College, and sent acknowledgments and a special Apostolic Benediction to the Faculty, the Alumni, and their respective families. His Holiness then asked for news of the Bishop of Hexham and Newcastle, on whom he pronounced an affectionate eulogy, listened with evident satisfaction to the accounts of the recent installation of the new prelate, and desired Dr. Giles to convey, by letter, to Bishop O'Callaghan, the assurance of his paternal sentiments, together with a heartfelt Apostolic benediction.

UNDER A PASSING CLOUD.

"Hope not sunshine every hour,
Fear not clouds will always lower."

Ushaw, like the sky, has had its clouds; its adverse and prosperous times; its reverses, mischances, and changes, but it has borne up manfully under them, and comforted itself with the assurance that

—"the darkest day,
Live till to-morrow will have passed away."

"*Post hiemem sequitur æstas; post noctem redit dies; et post tempestatem magna serenitas.*"

"And twinkles, through the cloudiest night, some solitary star."

Be it remembered, moreover, that all things on earth are subject to change and mutability, the Catholic Church being alone unchangeable—"*una est, quæ reparet, seque ipsa reseminet;*" and, as Horace reminds us,

"*Non semper idem floribus est honos
Vernis; neque uno luna rubens nitet vultu.*"

"Earth changes momently, each visible thing
Hath its fresh livery for every hour:
O'er human genius in its brightest power
The fever of a day may madness fling!
The elements unite and disunite,
The waters are absorb'd, then flood anew,—
The flower that flourisheth in vernal dew,
Fadeth beneath the winter's burthen white."

Having passed from under the cloud, and surmounted, let us hope, whatever difficulties and obscurities obstructed its path and progress, all friends of Ushaw will unite in praying for its peace and prosperity; that it may resume its beauty and comeliness; proceed on its course with renovated vigour; and continue to reign with untarnished fame and honour. So peace to the house and to all who dwell therein.

RELICS OF JOY.

Although, it is to be regretted,

——" Years are hastening to efface
Each record of the grand and fair old times,"

there are still left "relics of joy," that "clothe with golden clouds the desert of our life," and assuage the cares and sorrows which mortals are heirs to. Every spot in the neighbourhood of the college had, and many no doubt still have interesting and happy associations for Ushaw boys. Hill Top, the Crag, the old mill and mill dam, and the bridge near to it over the Browney, with its inscription "*hic pons publico sumptu conditus est,*" Witton Gilbert, the Cuts, the Bog, Bearpark, King David's Bridge, Aldin Grange, Cockpit Lane, Flass, Waterhouses, Russell's Wood, Brancepeth, Brandon, Stonebridge, Butterby, Croxdale, Pensher Hill, on which stands the first Lord Durham's monument, Chester-le-Street, Finchale and its ruins, Lanchester and its Roman encampment, High and Low Esh, Hydromoss and Hagwood, Harholm[*]; and though last not least, Biggen and Cornsay—all these places—

" Sites which are old with memories older still,
Whereon a new and coarser world intrudes—"

must necessarily conjure up in the minds and memories of past and present Ushaw students, a multitude of remembrances more sweet than "precious balm and spikenard of Arabian farms." They knew also every dingle, glen, and glade, every burn, beck, and stream, and pool wherein a trout was likely to lurk; every wood and wild ravine where a squirrel was to be found; where the stockdove, the raven, the hawk, and the owl build their nests, where in hazel thickets, in the nutting season, nuts grew in greatest abundance; and in what tangled brakes and underwood the blackberry and wild rasp could be gathered most plenteously.

---

[*] "There is a tradition," says Bishop Chadwick, in a note at the end of 'Verses on the Ushaw old Yew Tree,' "that one or two of the murderers of St. Thomas a Becket fled from Canterbury to what was then a hamlet, called Harholm, near Ushaw, and were there said to have concealed themselves, and to have done penance and died. There used to be, at Harholm, the ruins of what was supposed to have been a chapel, and a stone slab with a sword or cross carved upon it. Beneath it was supposed to have been the grave of the penitent murderer or murderers, and some of the students from the college used to amuse themselves, at times, by digging for their bones." A more probable account which I remember reading is that "the four miserable knights who murdered St. Thomas at Canterbury, after long wanderings, were enjoined to make a pilgrimage to Jerusalem, and there to live as penitential converts on the black mountain."

CORNSAY AND CORNSAY DAYS.

But what regarding Cornsay, it may be asked, which undeniably is among "the greenest spots on memory's waste?" To those pursuing their studies at Ushaw, wearied, no doubt, at times with books, themes, and compositions, it was a perfect Elysium, a place for mental and physical relaxation, a resort for an afternoon or a day's enjoyment, where dinners and tea were served in homely style but with plentiful supply, and where the appetite seemed to grow with what it fed upon. Then, a Cornsay Day afforded opportunities for long walks, and excursions to distant scenes and places—to Crook, to the Brooms, to the Ford, to Blanchland Abbey; to breezy hills and heath-clad moors. The verses which follow have probably no longer a place in the memory of the present generation. Formerly, though unclassical and doggerel, they were well remembered and oft repeated :—

> Witton for gooseberries,
> Kendal for snuff,
> When you go to Cornsay,
> You've generally enough.
> Heigh down, oh down, derry, derry down.
>
> Durham for mustard,
> Darlington for cheese,
> When you go to Stockton,
> You stand upon the Tees.
> Heigh down, &c.

These verses are reproduced that they may not be blotted from memory, but may go down to posterity among other recollections and records of the past.

Who did not enjoy a Cornsay day; the recreation attending it; and "the feast of reason and the flow of soul" inseparable from it? The Professors had their Cornsay days; the Divines had their Cornsay days; the Philosophers, Rhetoricians, and Poets had theirs also; so had each class down to Underlow. Before the introduction of books and medals as rewards and prizes given to those who, during the academic year, had distinguished themselves in their respective classes, in my time the students who had obtained most "pops," or marks of excellence, were rewarded with "a good lad's Cornsay day," a list of their names and classes being publicly posted up on the door leading out of the east ambulacrum into the play-ground. And these days, like "green islets in life's stormy ocean," were hailed with delight; they were anticipated, enjoyed, and calendared as red letter days. Tales and legends, snatches of old songs, jokes, anecdotes, and a variety of amusements, &c., are connected with Cornsay days. Some time previous to his death, the good President, Dr. Tate, took occasion in one of his letters to state that on such and such a day the Professors were going to have a Cornsay day, which he said he looked forward to with as much pleasure as he would have done fifty years thence. Our writing master, when we were taking special pains in writing our compositions, rubbing his hands would exclaim—"Well done," so and so, "you're on the road to Cornsay."

Cornsay house and domain lay to the west of Ushaw, some four miles distant from it, and were held in tenure by the college. The resident occupants of the house in times past were old George and Betty Farrow. George's features were as brown as a Rockingham tea-pot ; his hair coal-black ; and for his pipe of tobacco he was ready at all times ; it never came amiss. George was an old sailor, having been pressed in the time of the French war. He used to boast of having been one of the gallant seamen who fought at Trafalgar ; and of being on board the " Bullyruffin" (Bellerophon) when "Bony" surrendered to the British admiral. Betty Farrow was George's wife : she looked after the house ; George after the grounds and the farm. A certain school-fellow of mine, who long since has joined the majority, was reading and poring over Rollin's Ancient History. Not satisfied as to whether the Romans or the Carthaginians were the better soldiers, he asked old Betty's opinion. "Betty, what think *you*—were the Romans or the Carthaginians the better soldiers?" The question was a poser for Betty ; it settled her completely. We remember going down to " the old hermit's," who dwelt in a cottage below Cornsay ; it was milking time ; the old hermit's cow became frightened whilst we were there, and would not give her milk, so he ordered us away, his injunction being—" Arrah awa, th' coo winna milk."

Though we are told not to remove the ancient landmarks, but "*stare viis antiquis*," it is no violation of truth to assert that

" Old times are changed, old manners gone ;"

that ancient rites and customs are disappearing, and a new departure taking place. So as regards Cornsay days, and such enjoyable institutions, co-eval almost with the college, they are becoming things of the past, the sole record left of them being—"*ea quondam fuisse*"—such things were.

O, give us back our Cornsay days,
Days of the olden time,
And we will sing dear Ushaw's praise,
In strains of homely rhyme.

Bright sunny days they were indeed,
When from all tasks set free,
We of to-morrow took no heed,
But feasted merrily ;

And roamed the fields and woods among,
Or in some sylvan nook,
Far from the toiling busy throng,
Our ease recumbent took.

In Hutchinson's History of Durham we are told that "the first evidence we have of Cornsey is in the Bolden Buke, where they are noted to be the estates of Simon, the chamberlain (beginning of 13th century). Cornsey, under the distinction of Cornsey-row, in the 14th century gave a local name to its possessors, among whom we find Will-o-the-Raw and his wife, Dionesia-o-the-Raw, who held a moiety of the manor of Cornsey by homage and fealty, and the twentieth part of a knight's fee, paying 2s. yearly at the bishop's exchequer. The family of De Eshe had lands here, and Allan de Esh, then the Bishop's forester. In 1480 the family of Taillior or Taiclure became purchasers here, and Thomas Taylor, Esq., of the city of Durham, their immediate descendant, in 1794 held the lands, where he built a handsome mansion house." He was the lineal representative of the first purchaser, in the reign of Edward IV.; married a daughter of Sir Thomas Tancred, of Borough-Bridge, Bart., and had issue several sons, of whom the last survivor, the Rev. Thomas Taylor, priest, died December 1818. The family estate then became invested in his sisters. The estate, with the chief mansion house, according to Surtees, has been for above three centuries, the property of the Taylor family.

To revert to Cornsay days and Cornsay's joyful re-unions. Ambrose Lennon, a man of sterling worth, seriousness, and gravity of deportment, was educated at Ushaw, became Canon of the Chapter of Shrewsbury, and Vicar-General of the diocese; and being placed at St. Alban's, Liscard, he laboured with edifying zeal and piety. He was much attached to Ushaw, his *Alma Mater*, revered its time-honoured customs, and cherished the memory of its consecrated traditions. He forgot not the days when we used to trudge to Cornsay, feasted there, and made merry. In order to preserve and keep alive the memory of these festive gatherings, Ambrose, while priest at Liscard, instituted what became known as Lennon's Cornsay day, an annual festal institution to which all educated at Ushaw, young and old, were right welcome; and were most hospitably and bountifully entertained. I had the pleasure of attending one or two of these social Cornsay meetings, at which were assembled round the worthy Canon a number of his Ushaw contemporaries and friends. The health of the generous host, on an occasion when I was present, was proposed by one of his old friends and college associates, who said—" Twelve months have elapsed since we celebrated our last Cornsay day. It was to us all a joyful occasion, and I am delighted again to meet you, and to be associated with you in the generous and large-hearted sympathies with which our friend, Canon Lennon, receives and welcomes all those whom Ushaw, our *Alma Mater*, has trained and educated. I am delighted to be present with you at this annual entertainment, and to join with you in expressing to our venerable friend, the Vicar-General of the diocese of Shrewsbury, our sincerest respect and most grateful acknowledgments, recognising in him a true and devoted son of Ushaw, who there had his course in its entirety, and there was "*regulariter doctus,*" from Underlow to Divinity. Yes, I rejoice in this social re-union, this friendly gathering. It unites in a bond of fraternity and friendship the old and the young generations—the past and the present alumni of St. Cuthbert's. While it inspires the young with bright and ardent hopes, and makes them eager and earnest to complete their seed time, to reap their harvest, and to garner their sheaves; those more mature of age, and the more advanced in life, it surrounds with pleasant memories and joyful associations. It speaks to them of their boyhood and youth spent at Ushaw; it reminds them of their ardour in the pursuit of learning, when they treasured up knowledge like honey in the hive; of the palms they have gained and the victories they have won—aye, and of the defeats they have sustained ; it babbles in a language intelligible only to those who have been to Ushaw of play-days, of Cornsay days, of leave out, and pleasant rambles, of visits to gooseberry and strawberry gardens, of treats of pies, nutting, bathing, bird nesting, and squirrel hunting ; it recalls to their recollections the friends of their youth— "friends of my youth, where are they ? and echo answers, where are they?" It conjures up before them old associates—old familiar faces— "all, all are gone—the old familiar faces." Few remain, but among those few one kind and genial spirit is left ; he presides amongst us ; he prepares for us this annual feast, this "good lad's Cornsay day." Blessings upon him ! He cleaves and clings to Ushaw, and while Ushaw stands the name of Canon Lennon and his Cornsay days will go down to posterity. I have been somewhat prolix, but we love to dwell on these scenes and subjects ; on our college days, and on our college friends. The mind clings to them like a vine tendril round the elm ; they haunt us through all the vicissitudes of life. Time may write its wrinkles on the brow, may colour our locks, and impair the agility of our limbs, but the heart preserves its freshness and its verdure, and cherishes early friends and early associations, and kindly recollections even to extreme old age ; till the silver cord is broken, and the golden fillet shrinks back."

PRIESTS FROM LANCASHIRE AND THE FYLDE DISTRICT.

Lancashire not only contributed liberally from its pecuniary resources to the erection and foundation of St. Cuthbert's College, "the glorious old seminary for the whole of the North of England," but for many subsequent years numerous ecclesiastical students from Lancashire were there educated and raised to the priesthood. All honour therefore to Lancashire—to that western corner of the county especially, known as the Fylde, fertile not only in corn and cattle, and agricultural products, but pre-eminent as having given so many priests to the Church— priests learned and holy, who were born in the Fylde, reared in the Fylde, taught their religion and instructed in its precepts in the Fylde, and sent from the Fylde to study for the priesthood, and afterwards by their edifying lives and labours to win souls to righteousness and truth. What a goodly and heroic race of priests from the time of Cardinal Allen, born at Rossall, and founder of the English College of Douai— a college enhaloed by so many noble memories, and round which the hopes of the afflicted and persecuted Catholics of England centred, when the days were evil, has sprung from Lancashire ! And the good old Fylde priests, how I venerate them ! and at the same time lament that so few with priestly vocations now-a-days go from the Fylde to follow in their footsteps. Has faith in that land grown cold and languid—the *prisca fides* of those hardy sons of the soil, born in the farmhouse of rustic parents, as were popes, and bishops, and monks innumerable ; and has the old Catholic discipline relaxed, and ancient Catholic manners departed before the approach of modern civilization ?—

"God is lost, if faith be overthrown."

In what honour and respect do I hold those priests from the Fylde—the Billingtons, the Balls, the Carters, the Cooksons, the Gradwells, the Gillows, the Gillets, the Holdens, the Newshams, the Taylors, the Walkers; the Walmsleys of Flakefleet, Wrennalls of Bell Fold, Smiths of Clock House, Swarbricks of Nateby; Lund, Latham, Fayer, and Adamson; Bilsborrow of Breadkirk; Rogerson, Stirzaker, and Nixon, of Kirkham; and, though last not least, the pastor of Alston Lane, Rev. Thomas Walton, if, as hailing from Myerscough, he may be classed among Fylde worthies. Father Walton, the first priest whom Bishop Goss ordained, his ordination taking place at St. Edward's College, on Lady Day, 1855, was educated at St. Cuthbert's College, and retains many genial recollections of his college days. All the other Fylde priests above named received their education at the same college, and all became "the builders and architects of blessed life," and an honour to holy church. Many of the forefathers of these here named suffered persecution for conscience sake, but they were comforted in having sons and descendants who became *quasi sagittæ in manu potentis.*

THE REV. JOHN CARTER.

There are many noted men—*Alumni Ushavienses*—natives not of Lancashire only, but of other counties, who, on account of their blameless lives, and reproachless manners, their sacerdotal and apostolic spirit, might be recorded among the celebrities of St. Cuthbert's. Though not distinguished for brilliant talents and literary attainments, they were men of prayer and simplicity, who in their days pleased God, and were faithful in His service; labouring with devotedness for holy Church, and with zeal for the flocks of which they had charge; keeping themselves unstained and unspotted from the world, and in their actions, habits, and conversation exhibiting themselves models of every virtue. And the lessons of their lives how instructive and edifying! Those lives were not unfrequently characterised by much self-denial and privation, and by a great love of solitude and retirement. They were good, peaceable men, they seldom went abroad, they led a retired and concealed life, hidden from the world, and therefore, according to Tacitus, *eo ipso præfulgebant quod non visebantur.* The Rev. John Carter, of Woolston, was one of this class of venerable priests; was of very quiet and retiring habits, humble and detached from the world; seldom going from home, and scarcely known beyond the precints of his own little mission. It might be said of the Rev. John Carter, as the Gospel relates of our Blessed Lord, *abscondit se in templo—*

"The world forgetting, and by the world forgot."

In fact, like a tree in an obscure forest, he grew and decayed, but in his season he was adorned with leaves, and produced flowers and fruit—the fruit of many virtues.

It is most probable this aged priest was born at Preston. He was certainly baptised there, August 26th, 1801. The Register does not give the date of his birth. Till the age of twenty-four or twenty-five years he was engaged in business pursuits, but about the year 1825 he forsook his worldly calling, and repaired to Ushaw, to study for the priesthood. *Ecce reliquimus omnia et secuti te*, might he have truly said, for he quitted the world, its vanities, cares, and entanglements, and like a second St. Ignatius, commenced in the prime of manhood to learn the rudiments of Latin, and the lessons of smaller boys. While I, with the rest of my school-fellows—*studiosa caterva juvenum*—was writing Latin themes and translating Cæsar's Commentaries, John Carter was striving to master the conjugation of Latin verbs at the age of twenty-five, classed at college as a "Patriarch," and enjoying patriarchal privileges. Latin Grammar, Latin themes, and other literary exercises, must have been a tiresome and difficult task to the young man of twenty-five years, but he kept the goal in view, persevered, and supplemented mediocre talents by hard study and industry. If the *Selectæ e Profanis* were one of his class books, the sentence therein—*labor omnia vincit improbus*—would, no doubt, have stimulated and encouraged him in his studious labour. Years went on, and John Carter read, and wrote, and studied. In 1834 he was raised to the priesthood, and on the 17th of July in that year he went to Puddington, sent by his Bishop to assist the Ven. and Rev. Ralph Platt in the charge of that mission. He was, on the death of Fr. Platt, appointed, Oct. 1st, 1837, to the small mission of Woolston, near Warrington, which mission he served for thirty-seven years, and died there on March 16th, 1875, in the 74th year of his age. In his last illness he was attended with pious care by his friend, the Very Rev. Dean Fisher, of Appleton. His interment took place at Woolston, his Lordship the Bishop of Liverpool singing the Requiem Mass, assisted by twenty priests. The deceased had a particular devotion to the suffering souls in Purgatory, as his well-thumbed "Garden of the Soul" evidenced at the "Litany of the Dead." He would often remain three or four hours with those who were in their agony. God grant him rest and life eternal.

THE NEW COLLEGE CHAPEL OF ST. CUTHBERT.

We have already had evidence sufficient to show that the renovations and improvements, effected by Dr. Newsham, marked the term of his Presidency, as a period at Ushaw of evolution and development; hence it may be implied that the Doctor gave implicit credence to the maxim that to stand still was to retrograde. He became aware, as time went on, that the collegiate Chapel of St. Cuthbert, which was built from designs of the elder Pugin, and opened in the early years of his Presidency, had become too small, and its capacity too limited to afford to the increasing number of students requisite accommodation. Dr. Newsham's venerated successor, Mgr. Tate, was likewise quite cognizant that a church of ampler dimensions was needed, but to neither of these Presidents was the opportunity, or the means afforded of erecting such a church, for, "their days upon earth were as a shadow, and there was no stay" for them. For others was reserved the glory of building this second temple—to be a monument to future ages of Catholic faith and piety, and of the generosity and devotion of the friends, students, and alumni of St. Cuthbert's. Dr. Wilkinson succeeded Mgr. Tate as President, and a few months after his installation in the office, the project of erecting a new church was brought prominently forward by him in a letter soliciting subscriptions and sympathy in aid of the undertaking :—" Since the death of our late venerated President," Dr. Wilkinson wrote, "many of his friends have expressed an earnest wish to aid in some work which might be both a tribute to his memory and a permanent benefit to the college over which he presided. The form of memorial proposed was to carry out, if possible, an object which both he and his immediate predecessor had so much at heart, the erection of a church of sufficient size to accommodate the students. Moreover it has been urged upon me by many warm and influential friends that there could be no more suitable inauguration of the office, to which it has pleased God to appoint me, than an endeavour to supply at last so great a need. But above all, I have been encouraged to make the attempt by the cordial and unanimous approval of the five Bishops who are directly interested in the college. As the success of so large an undertaking must depend on the hearty co-operation of our friends, permit me to lay before you the following statement, that you may see how urgent are the motives that have induced us to attempt it. The present chapel was built at a time when the college contained less than half the present number of students; hence, even with the addition of an inconvenient and disfiguring gallery, more than a third of the students, with their masters and superiors, are now unable to attend the public services of the church in the College Chapel. I need not add that no accommodation can be found, without excluding the students, for the many friends, both clerical and lay, who at certain seasons of the year are accustomed to honour us with their company. In so small a chapel it is clearly impossible to carry out the church services with due splendour and solemnity; and yet in a church of sufficient dimensions, with so large a number of clerics and such a choir as the college could command, these services might and would be carried out in a manner that would recall the ancient glories of religion in this country. To witness from boyhood and to take part in such a ceremonial, could not fail to have a lifelong influence on the minds and hearts of the students, and would be a most powerful element in the training of those who are destined for the ecclesiastical state. To the alumni of St. Cuthbert's I know that I need say nothing to secure their interest in such a work. For years past this one great want of their *Alma Mater* has been their regret. But I may perhaps be permitted to remind our other friends that St. Cuthbert's is not without a strong claim to their sympathy and assistance, since the college at present holds a large portion of those who are preparing for the labours of the mission in the Northern Counties of England, and for nearly a century the preservation and propagation of the faith in the north has been in great part due, under God, to the zeal of the many hundreds of devoted priests who have gone forth from St. Cuthbert's to labour and die in the work of saving souls. The names of all benefactors will be added to those already inscribed in the *Liber Vitæ*, of whom a daily remembrance is made in the Holy Sacrifice of the Mass."

The Bishop of Hexham and Newcastle (Bishop Chadwick), and their Lordships the Bishops of Shrewsbury, Beverley, Salford, and Liverpool, co-interested in the college, expressed a cordial approval of this appeal.

Various schemes having been propounded, and considerable delay incurred in discussing them ; in considering also whether the old chapel, one of the elder Pugin's best works, could be so altered, adapted, and enlarged as to provide more than double the accommodation for which it was planned, it was ultimately decided to take down the old church, and on its site to erect an entirely new one.

In a circular announcing that the work of reconstruction had commenced, and containing a list of subscriptions to the building fund, the Right Rev. Mgr. Wrennall, D.D., who had succeeded to the office of President, wrote as follows :—"I am happy to be able to inform you that the church, which the late Dr. Wilkinson projected as a memorial to his predecessor, and for which he solicited subscriptions as long ago as the beginning of 1877, has at last been begun. The new church will be in most respects a reproduction of the one it is intended to replace. The general form of the old church, the screen, the Lady chapel, the altars, all the stained glass and all the stone-work of the windows will reappear in the new church. The gifts of former benefactors will be preserved with affectionate care. Apart from every feeling of duty in not sacrificing the memorials of many that are now no more, those who have day by day attended the services in the old church from its opening until now, are not likely to be insensible to the influence of associations, so sacred and enduring. It is our hope that the new church will be not unlike what the old one would have been, if forty years ago the students had been three times as numerous as they were, and the builders then employed had done their work more effectively. In size certainly the difference will be great. The choir of the old church was fifty feet in length by twenty-seven in width, and the sanctuary extended twenty feet beyond the choir. In the new church the choir will be ninty-three feet long by thirty-five feet wide, and the sanctuary will stretch thirty-six feet further. The old church was designed for about one hundred and forty students, the new one has been designed for about four hundred. One event, I am sorry to say, has occurred to sadden us at this moment. At the very commencement of the work and before he had seen a single stone touched, he, who took so warm an interest in it, has peacefully passed away. Whether, if we had lost our beloved Bishop sooner, we should now be beginning the church is very doubtful. His share in the labour will never be fully known. Just before his last illness came upon him, he wrote to congratulate and encourage us and to add another £100 to the £100 he had already subscribed. At this time too, it is touching to recall his own words, when, on becoming President after Dr. Wikinson's death, he issued a circular on the subject of the church, and, after referring to the fact that it was intended as a memorial to Dr. Tate, added : ' And now does not Dr. Wilkinson's own unlooked-for and deeply lamented death afford an additional motive why the work should be at once completed, that it may serve as a memorial of the two Presidents of whom *Alma Mater* has been, within so short an interval, bereaved ?" Now his own unlooked-for and deeply lamented death, following upon those of Dr. Tate and Dr. Wilkinson, has left us desolate indeed. I trust our church when completed may be a memorial not unworthy of those three venerated names."

The process of taking down the sacred edifice commenced early in spring, May 1st, 1882, and in the course of a short time not a stone was left upon a stone of the venerated structure, which had stood for forty years. It was not without considerable regret that the demolition of the original church was regarded, for its walls were consecrated by many solemn and sacred memories, and the very stones were cherished with affection—"*quoniam placuerunt servis tuis lapides ejus.*" Within those hallowed walls had been chanted the matin hymn and vesper song; therein had been offered daily prayer and praise and sacrifice; therein had stood the altar before which had knelt devout and ardent Levites, preparing and eager "*ad currendam viam,*" and to pay their vows to God, by whom their youth was, as it were, renewed and made glad :—

"And near this altar stood
A dame in sculpture, sweetly seeming to express
A mother's love."

Buttress and pinnacle, niche and arch, screen and gable, corbel and canopy, were all displaced, and having been taken down and removed, were carefully stored away, in order that they might be made available and replaced in the projected new edifice, of which on the 27th of July, 1882, the foundation stone was laid by the Most Rev. Charles Eyre, Archbishop of Glasgow. There were present on the occasion the Right Revs. Angus Macdonald, Bishop of Argyll and the Isles, Herbert Vaughan, Bishop of Salford, Richard Lacy, Bishop of Middlesbrough, Arthur Riddell, Bishop of Northampton; and a number of clergy and laity. Before that venerable and respectable assembly Provost Consitt discoursed learnedly and eloquently on the symbolism of the various parts of a church—its form, its position; its tower and bells; its spire pointing up to heaven, and the cross—"placed as a luminous beacon on the church top;" the west portal, aisles, nave, and transepts; the shapely arches, the pictured walls, and storied windows; the altar itself with its relics of Saints; its garniture of flowers and fragrance of incense; and burning before it the flickering lamp, which, during the garish day, and in the silent watches of the night, while the rest of the world is buried in sleep, shines like a solitary star, its diffusive, unextinguished light emblematical of the unwearied watch which our divine Lord, in the silence of the tabernacle, and hidden *sub umbra Sacramenti,* keeps over us, ever ready to receive the sighs and prayers of poor frail mortals. They with reason therefore might exclaim—"*Domine, dilexi decorem domus tuæ et locum habitationis gloriæ tuæ.*" ... "*In ecclesiis benedicam te, Domine.*" The Provost at the same time took occasion to express regret at the loss of a gem of the older Pugin, but joy that the expansion of Ushaw necessitated a larger and more spacious church. No wonder that the Provost especially should entertain a secret regret at the removal of the old church which for many long years had been to him a thing of beauty, and whose reverence and admiration for the ancient fanes of our Catholic forefathers was so notable, that he could say with truth—

"*Templa Dei saxo venerabar structa vetusto.*"

The old college chapel was a structure of goodly form and fair aspect, consisting of an ante-chapel, a choir, and sanctuary, and was approached from the college by a cloister, which also communicated with the sacristies. The building, its several belongings and appointments—altars, screens, stalls, stained glass and metal work, were designed by A. Welby Pugin, Esq. Solomon, about to build the temple, said to Hiram, "send me a skilful man that knoweth how to work in gold and silver, in brass and in iron, in purple, in scarlet, and in blue, and that hath skill in carving." Such a man, Dr. Newsham, of happy memory, was desirous to employ in the erection of the college chapel, and the renowned architect, Pugin, was engaged for the work.

BISHOP BEWICK APPEALS FOR CONTRIBUTIONS TOWARDS THE NEW CHURCH.

In November, 1883, Bishop Bewick issued a pastoral to the several missions and congregations of the Diocese of Hexham and Newcastle, soliciting help and subscriptions towards the fund for erecting the new College Chapel. "There is," his Lordship stated, "one fair and chosen spot in our Diocese, where a church is at this moment being erected—a spot which has peculiar, pre-eminent and pressing claims upon us and upon you. Next to our Cathedral Church it claims our best affection, our warmest support. Next to your own mission church it merits a large share in your good will and charity. It is in a sense the common property of all of us. We allude to St. Cuthbert's College at Ushaw. At the mention of Ushaw and its church—though it may not be the *Alma Mater* of all of us—some, as of old time, may weep for sorrow, some for joy—for *sorrow* that the exquisite gem of a collegiate chapel, erected there by the illustrious Pugin in 1846, should have had to be taken down—for *joy* that another on the old site, on the same plan, of the same outline and features, out of the old materials, yet larger and more worthy of the place and its requirements, is being erected in its stead. The church of St. Cuthbert at Ushaw is and will be instinct with Catholic life, learning, and sanctity. It is and will be the home and abiding place—if not of St. Cuthbert's relics—of Jesus Christ in the Blessed Eucharist. Thence goes forth perpetually a virtue on every side—a leaven leavening the whole mass. While other dioceses have had to encounter a heavy outlay of thousands of pounds in the founding of diocesan seminaries, and there have been collections and subscriptions for the purpose, we have been spared the cost by having Ushaw College in our midst. At Ushaw the Bishop has his students ever under his eye. For him it serves the purposes of a diocesan seminary. On the present occasion, therefore, we can afford, and we ought in common equity, to contribute more bountifully to its church building fund. At such a place—with such sacred interests at stake—with such vital objects in view—where the Levites are trained for the sanctuary—where the blossoming Martyrs—the "*flores Martyrum*" as St. Philip Neri christened the English students for the church—are nursed and tended; where the Priesthood for the north of England is mainly to be reared—it is imperative to have a church—large, capacious, well-equipped and tastefully furnished,—wherein the ceremonies of the Catholic ritual and the pontifical functions can be carried out with edification and in all their completeness—wherein the clerical students can be befittingly trained and imbued with a lofty and adequate sense of what "the house of God" ought to be in every parish or mission—in every corner of the vineyard, to which they may be sent. Some of you, sons of *Alma Mater*, and others, who though not nursed at her breast, have yet learnt to love her with a truly filial love, have already contributed towards the erection of the new church. All due honour and thanks to each of you! We now appeal with all fervour to each and every one of our flock, in each and every mission within our jurisdiction—to the poor widow, the servant, the working man, the tradesman, the professional classes, the landed gentry, the nobility, and the clergy—to contribute something, each according to his and her ability. Be it much or be it little, let it be something—something worthy of the object—something worthy of yourselves."

The work of building this second temple proceeded vigorously and uninterruptedly. The Right Rev. President, Mgr. Wrennall, in his solicitude for the speedy and successful completion of the church; anxious also that, when completed and opened, no debt should encumber it, made earnest appeals to friends for assistance, and had the gratification before the day of opening of receiving in answer to his appeals increased donations and subscriptions.

It is not my intention, nor will it be necessary for me, to give a description either of the old or of the new College Chapel of St. Cuthbert. They have already been elaborately described by abler pens than mine, by persons who during their erection were constantly on the spot, who daily saw the progress of the work, and who were familiar with the various structural and ornamental details of both churches. The old one, "a desirable house, formed of living stones," was ably and fully described, on occasion of its opening in 1848, by Bishop Chadwick, at that time a Professor in the college. For a description of the new church we are indebted to the pen of another of Ushaw's learned Professors, the Rev. Henry Gillow. As however, remarks Mr. Gillow, the windows, altars, and other details and features of the former are reproduced in the latter structure, Dr. Chadwick's description of them needed little more than to be re-arranged, and adapted to the present edifice. For the stones of the original building—a church of exceeding beauty, designed by an architect of world-wide renown—were skilfully replaced and refitted in the new one:—

"*Aptisque juncta nexibus*
Locantur in fastigio."

But for the sake of completeness it was thought advisable to extend the description to the smaller chapels, not in existence when Dr. Chadwick wrote, *viz.* the chapels of St. Joseph, the Holy Family, St. Charles Borromeo, St. Michael; and in the Junior College that of St. Aloysius.

On my part therefore it will suffice to state that the honour of designing the new church, and of superintending and directing the building operations, belongs to Messrs. Dunn and Hansom, Architects, and their work was performed most skilfully, efficiently, and satisfactorily. The church is a noble structure, destined to promote the glory of God, and devotion to His blessed servant, St. Cuthbert; for ages it will remain a monument of the energy, zeal, and perseverance of the Right Rev. President, Mgr. Wrennall, who had the satisfaction of seeing the edifice completed and opened, and of the bountiful benefactions of the alumni, and other kind friends of Ushaw. "By God's assistance," to quote an old chronicler, "a new church is begun from the foundations, and by the gifts of good men, the fabric rises; and thanks be to God, we now behold it raised on a stronger foundation, and to a loftier height than ever." The erection of the church occupied three years only—a short period compared with twenty years employed by St. Hugh, the sixth Abbot of Cluni, in building the church of his monastery. The cost of the building was £15,000, and in this sum are included all charges except those for objects specially given by individual benefactors, and the cost of enlarging and reconstructing the organ.

The organ, reconstructed by Bevington and Sons, of Soho, London, who built the small organ erected in St. Aloysius' Chapel of the same college some years since, was completely reerected by this firm in its new position. It contains 1,663 pipes. The old organ, which was a very fine instrument of its date, was erected about forty-five years ago. It was then a "GG" organ by Bishop, of London, with two and half rows of keys, and one stop (bourdon) on the pedal, the swell only extending to tenor C. When the church was enlarged and converted into the present beautiful building, it was decided by the authorities to remove the organ from the Rood-screen where it stood in halves, showing a painted window between them, to its present position in a chamber specially constructed to receive it opposite the cantors' lectern, where it is both heard and seen to advantage.

OPENING OF THE NEW CHURCH.

"Hail! sacred tabernacles, where Thou, O Lord, dost descend at the voice of a mortal. Hail! mysterious altar, where faith comes to receive its immortal food."

Having heard St. Cuthbert's new church spoken of in terms of the highest praise—"*gloriosa dicta sunt de te*"—I was most anxious to see it and to attend the opening. My wish was gratified. I travelled from Lancashire, and was present, among other friends of Ushaw and old Ushaw students, on the occasion. It was a great and memorable occasion; it occurred in the summer season, when roses were blooming, when the corn was ripening, and the heather in full flower was purpling moorlands and mountain sides. The ceremony was fixed for, and took place on Wednesday, July 29th, 1885, but the church had been solemnly blessed by Bishop Bewick, and the Blessed Sacrament carried in solemn procession to it from the temporary chapel, on the 4th of October, in the previous year.

The morning of the opening solemnity dawned brightly and hopefully—"*aurora cœlum purpurat*"—giving promise of a cloudless sunny day. For the celebration of feasts and festivals fine weather is an important factor; it cheers and exhilarates all those who take part in them. The preparations for the event were made with unceasing activity, and on a magnificent scale, for no efforts were spared to give *éclat* and effect to the celebration. Flowers were arranged within the recesses of each window in the cloister leading to the church; were placed before altar and statue; were conspicuous in the ante-chapel; adorned choir and sanctuary; and bloomed in choice profusion around and on the high altar :—

> "Bring flowers to the shrine, where you kneel in prayer—
> They are nature's offering, their place is *there!*
> They speak of hope to the fainting heart,
> With a voice of promise they come and part,
> They sleep in dust through the wintry hours,
> They break forth in glory. Bring flowers, bright flowers."

His Eminence Cardinal Manning had promised, and was expected to grace the ceremony by his presence, and to preach, but he was unavoidably, much to his own and others' regret, prevented, a few days only before the opening, from fulfilling his promise. Cardinal Howard, who chanced to be in London at this time, was then applied to to attend in place of Cardinal Manning, but anterior engagements rendered it impossible for him to be present. He expressed however the kindest sympathy with the work, and for the welfare of the college. Numerous invitations had been issued by the President, Right Rev. Mgr. Wrennall, and they were numerously responded to, and accepted. Venerable Bishops, Priests, young and old; laymen from remote and distant parts, friends and guests, well wishers and benefactors to the college, assembled in goodly concourse—"*Illuc enim ascenderunt tribus, tribus Domini, ad confitendum nomini Domini,*" as well as to testify their devotion to Ushaw, and their admiration of its second temple, its noble architecture, its carven imagery, and deep dyed windows, ablaze

"With forms of Saints and holy men who died,
Here martyred, and thereafter glorified."

I enter the sacred edifice, this house of peace and prayer :—

"*Pax æterna ab Æterno huic domui!*"

"And as a pilgrim, when he rests
Within the temple of his vow, looks round
In breathless awe, and hopes some time to tell
Of all its goodly state;" e'en so my eyes
Cours'd up and down,

and were filled with amaze and admiration on beholding

"The beauty that ornaments the sacred pile;
The gold and crimson dyes
Shot on the pavement from the storied glass;
The net-like screens, the delicate canopies
O'er wings angelic spread and martyrs' diadems."

Another sight next attracts my wondering gaze : I see, as it advances into the church, a gorgeous and imposing procession, such as we can picture taking place, before England revolted from Catholic unity, in our ancient cathedrals, and other old churches of the land. They come with measured step and slow—an array of mitred prelates, attended by their chaplains, assistant priests and deacons, preceded by Canons in furred and purple attire, by surpliced priests, clerics and acolytes, torch bearers, and thurifer; and the uplifted cross—"*fulget crucis mysterium*"—the emblem of man's salvation, leads the way.

Sacred and solemn temple, house of prayer—"*domus mea domus orationis vocabitur*"—where devout supplication is made, and grace in copious stream descends—house of prayer, open wide thy portals, for the desired of all nations shall come to sanctify this house dedicated to eternal peace, and to fill it with His presence; and the glory of this last house shall be greater than of the first. Though cedars and fir trees were not sent from the forests of Libanus to form its beams and rafters, nor gold to adorn its walls from Ophir, nor spices and costly stones to enrich it from Saba, this temple contains a treasure infinitely more exquisite, more precious, and more desirable—even "the good thing, the beautiful thing, the corn of the elect, the wine from which virgins spring forth like flowers among thorns." "*Desiderabilia super aurum et lapidem pretiosum multum, et dulciora super mel et favum.*" With Jacob, awakening out of sleep after his vision at Bethel, we may exclaim—"*Quam metuendus est locus iste!*" or, in the words of a French poet, it may be said concerning it—

"*C'est un lieu saint, c'est une auguste temple,
De quelque part que mon œil le contemple,
Temple vraiment, vrai séjour d'oraison,
Fait pour prier en chacun saison,*"—

an august and stately temple, dedicated to the worship of Him whose temple is all space, and whose majesty filleth heaven and earth. Hence, "*Domum tuam decet sanctitudo, Domine, in longitudinem dierum.*"
"Who," cries St. Bernard, "would fear to call the walls of the church

holy, which the hands of consecrated priests have sanctified with so many mysteries, within which the sacred lessons are read, and the devout whisper of holy prayer ascends—walls which are honoured by the blessed presence of the sacred relics, and where flights of angels are known to keep watch."

Onward, onward moves the procession of Bishops and Priests,

"A glorious pageant more magnificent
Than conqueror's return:"—

no sound of trumpets, nor noise of cymbals heralds the procession; it enters the church and passes into the choir to the pealing and triumphant strains of the majestic organ—"*Introite in conspectu ejus in exultatione, atria ejus in hymnis.*" Then the inspiring and thrilling music of the choirs burst forth; then there seemed to be heard

———"a voice which sang,
Behold the House where God will dwell with men."

The holy and adorable sacrifice ended, the glorious and world wide hymn, "*Te Deum laudamus,*" entoned for countless years in every church, cathedral, and minster in Christendom, was sung by a multitude of voices in jubilant and joyful tones of thanksgiving:—

"Be ours to sing thanksgiving to our God;"

to pray for the good estate, the temporal and eternal welfare of all those who in any way aided or contributed to the erection of this noble church, beseeching the Giver of all good gifts to grant them health and peace, and so to order their lives that after their earthly course is run, they may arrive at life and bliss eternal :

———"And may rest
And place of pardon granted be to all
That reared these glorious shrines and sacred towers."

The Pontifical High Mass, celebrated in the presence of the Bishop of the Diocese (Dr. Bewick), was sung by the Right Rev. Robert Cornthwaite, Bishop of Leeds. The Bishop of Hexham and Newcastle was assisted by the undermentioned :—

Assistant Priest, Right Rev. Monsignore Gillow.
Assistant Deacons, Revs. T. Murphy and G. Bradley.
Mitre Bearer, Mr. W. Leeming.
Crozier Bearer, Mr. D. O'Donoghue.
Book Bearer, Mr. W. Drysdale.
Bugia Bearer, Mr. E. Pyke.
Train Bearer, Master Glennie Greig.

The following attended the Celebrant :—

Assistant Priest, Rev. G. Coulston, D.D.
Deacon, Rev. O. Dolan.
Sub-deacon, Rev. P. Lonsdale.
Mitre Bearer, Mr. J. Blackoe.
Book Bearer, Mr. J. Milburn.

Gremial Bearer, Mr. Merry del Val.*
Train Bearer, Master Gerard Morgan.
Cross Bearer, Rev. H. Mann.
Masters of Ceremonies, Rev. R. C. Laing and Mr. B. Mc.Cabe.
Acolyths, Messrs. J. Newsham and J. Rogers.
Thurifer, Mr. A. Malempré.

BISHOPS PRESENT.

Bishop of Liverpool, Chaplain, Rev. C. V. Green.
Bishop of Middlesbrough, Chaplain, Rev. G. Phillips.
Bishop of Northampton, Chaplain, Rev. H. Newton.
Bishop of Portsmouth, Chaplain, Rev. A. Bennett.

CANONS OF HEXHAM AND NEWCASTLE.

Right Rev. Monsignore Provost Consitt.
Canon Joseph Browne.
Canon Joseph Watson.
Canon Henry Wrennall.
Canon R. J. Franklin.
Canon John A. Cooke.

MUSIC.

"*ECCE SACERDOS,*" by Glover, sung by the choir, when the procession of the Bishops and clergy entered the church.

Kyrie.
Gloria.
Credo.   } Gounod's Messe Solennelle.
Sanctus.
Benedictus.
Agnus Dei, Haydn's No. 2.
Offertory Piece, Emmerig's Magnificat.

The Cathedral Chapter occupied the stalls, namely, Provost Consitt, Canons Watson, Wrennall, Franklin, Browne, and Cooke. There were also present Mgr. Gadd, from Manchester; Canons Carr, V.G., Bennett, and Taylor, from Liverpool; Canons Toole, Beesley, and Liptrott, from Salford; Canons Carroll, V.G., and Rogerson, from Shrewsbury; Canons Pearson and Riddell, Middlesbrough; Canons Gordon, D.D., and J. Gordon, Leeds.

THE SERMON.

The Bishop of Portsmouth preached the sermon, taking for his text: "And David said to Solomon, his son, act like a man, and take courage and do: fear not, and be not dismayed: for the Lord my God will be with thee, and will not leave thee, till thou hast finished all the work for the service of the house of the Lord."—*I. Paralip., xxviii., 20.*

---

*Son of the Spanish Minister at Vienna, and Supernumerary Privy Chamberlain to the Pope; he made part of his studies at Ushaw. He then entered the Noble Academia Ecclesiastica at Rome, and accompanied to England Mgr. Ruffo-Scilla, the Special Envoy sent by His Holiness to present his felicitations and Jubilee offering—a magnificent mosaic—to the Queen, on the fiftieth anniversary of her accession to the throne. He also accompanied Mgr. Galimberti, Envoy Extraordinary from the Pope to the Court of Berlin, and was decorated by the Emperor, Frederick III., with the Order of the Crown.

This building was in one sense, he stated, a new temple of God, and yet it was not altogether new. It must have cost many an anxious thought to those who determined—he would not say to destroy—to arrest the continuity of order in this building, or to extend its cords and stakes because it had grown too small for the requirements of the community. It must have been a grief to seem to undo that beautiful work which had been begun by the Right Rev. Mgr. Newsham. He was in Rome just at the time this chapel was first built, and he saw Mgr. Newsham there. He was gathering at that time some of those beautiful works of art which now adorned that chapel and other chapels that surrounded it, and he knew that his love for that chapel was one of the strongest passions of his heart. And so it had always been with those who were associated with St. Cuthbert's College. Therefore, in any way to seem to destroy it, or to alter it, must indeed have been a great pang. And yet it was a work necessary to be done from a supernatural motive. There was still wanting a good deal before the chapel could be considered complete. The high altar at present was but temporary. Many munificent gifts had been made to the chapel. Great generosity had been shown by those who took an interest in the college, but still there was more to do to complete the beauty of this stately edifice. He believed the generous sons of St. Cuthbert would come forward and not rest until everything had been done to make the place complete and beautiful. It was a holy place. In that place, especially, holy memories clustered round it. Within those walls the stones that built the old church had been carefully and reverently preserved. He heard that morning that the foundation stone which was laid with the rites of the Catholic Church many years ago, had not been discovered when the walls were disturbed, so that the chapel was but the enlargement and continuity of what existed before. The incense and prayers that had been offered within its walls had left their fragrance behind ; and so, please God, it would go on for many years to come. Wherever the eye turned there was something beautiful to rest upon, something which showed them that the best of men's possessions had been given to God. That was the true Catholic spirit, the spirit that animated our country in its old days, and the spirit which he was sure every one of them desired to revive.

In the afternoon the college entertained the guests at dinner, when the usual loyal and other toasts were honoured.

The prizes awarded at the close of the year's curriculum of studies were on the day previous to the opening of the church, distributed in the Exhibition Hall by Dr. Bewick, amidst repeated cheers. His Lordship expressed to the students the greatest satisfaction at the results of their year's course of studies. They had not all won prizes ; they had all given satisfaction. After the solemn function of the following day they would enter on their holidays ; they would depart from the college, some of them never to enter again as students. It was to be hoped, however, that they would, as ex-students, return to the old *Alma Mater* from time to time, and keep up a fond affection for her. She had been a good mother to them in their youth, and he trusted that they would all be to her good, affectionate, dutiful sons, no matter where they might be placed. No matter in what part of the world their lot might hereafter be cast, let them remember that spot among the hills of Durham. He hoped they would enjoy themselves, but at the same time he had a word of warning to utter to them. Let them unbend the bow, but let it be always in innocence, and as became good Catholic youths. They must remember that they had duties to perform as well as pleasures to enjoy during their holidays. They would go forth and they would bear, as it were, in their hands the fair name and the honour of their college. Therefore, in whatever society they mixed, and with whomsoever they came in contact, let them bear in mind that they were Ushaw students; let them bear in mind that they were to exhibit themselves worthy of that great college; let them bear in mind that they must spread, as it were, the fame and the reputation, and uphold the honour of that institution, where they were to spend some years, where they had received so many advantages, and from which they carried away with them so much learning. He asked them, therefore, to bear themselves as well conducted, edifying youths, when far from the college bounds, spreading abroad the good odour of their *Alma Mater's* reputation and honour.

The Right Rev. Dr. Virtue, Bishop of Portsmouth, who was received with the most cordial applause, also delivered an address. It was, he said, with great pleasure he found himself amongst them that day. He looked upon them all as his first cousins, for he was a son of St. Edmund's College, Old Hall, which he regarded as a brother or sister of Ushaw. That was not the first visit which he had had the happiness to pay to Ushaw, and he could assure them that for Ushaw he had a very warm corner in his heart. Some of his greatest and most revered friends in life had belonged to Ushaw; but whilst he himself had for many years known of the merits of that venerable college, he had not had until now the pleasure and honour of being present on such an interesting occasion as that. He would tell them one thing which had given him the very highest opinion of Ushaw and its training. It was an experience of twenty-seven years as an army chaplain. In this capacity he had been brought into contact, in various climes and in many countries, with young men who were officers in the army and had been brought up in our colleges; and this he had to say in favour of Ushaw that he had seldom, if ever, met an officer in the army educated at Ushaw who was forgetful of his duties as a Catholic. He would be sorry to say a word in disparagement of any of the other colleges, but he could not give the same testimony of any of them that he could give of Ushaw. For that reason Ushaw, as he had said, had a very warm corner in his heart, and he should always look to Ushaw as one of the best—as the best—of our colleges in England. As a proof of what he thought about Ushaw, he might say that, when some two or three years ago, he had a young student from Malta whom he wished to place for some time in a Catholic college, under English ecclesiastical discipline, it was to Ushaw he addressed a petition for his reception; and he was sorry to say that he was not successful. He would, however, return good for evil. In conclusion, with their Bishop, he would express the hope that they would have a pleasant vacation, make a good use of it, and return at the proper time.

The annual athletic sports were held in the afternoon, and were a great source of attraction to the students and the visitors. The various items were well contested, those who competed for them proving that whilst Ushaw maintains its high standard as a seat of learning, it can likewise boast of students who can well hold their own as athletes.

FEAST OF THE ENGLISH MARTYRS.

Ushaw was not unmindful of the task that devolved upon her, as descendant and representative of old Douai College, of paying to our Beatified Martyrs an especial tribute of gratitude and honour. For it was at Douai College and its substitute at Rheims that by far the larger body of those who suffered during the reign of Queen Elizabeth—one third in fact of the fifty-four beatified—received ecclesiastical training. The triduum in preparation for the festival coinciding with the opening days of the month of Mary, the nightly benediction and devotions in her honour were marked with additional solemnity. The Litany of the English Martyrs was also recited, particular fervour on each occasion being noticeable at the invocation "Blessed Cuthbert Maine, Protomartyr of our Seminarists, pray for us." On the Feast itself great numbers of the students received Holy Communion, and at 9-30 solemn High Mass was celebrated, Dr. Crookall's *Justorum Animæ* being sung as an offertory piece. At the end of Mass the Gregorian *Te Deum* was chanted. The rest of the day was kept as a play day, under a genuine May sky. In the evening Solemn Benediction, preceded by the hymn, "Faith of Our Fathers," brought the celebration to a close.

Such is the account which at the time appeared in one or more of the Catholic newspapers. To this record of the solemnisation of the Feast I may be permitted to add as follows :—

"*Filiæ Jerusalem, venite et videte Martyres cum coronis quibus Deus coronavit eos in die solemnitatis et lætitiæ.*"

Ushaw had special cause to rejoice, and celebrate with praise and thanksgiving, great joy and gladness, the Feast of the Blessed English Martyrs, being lineally descended and closely allied to the college at Douai, which upwards of two hundred years, during the merciless and cruel days of persecution, till its seizure and suppression, and the dispersion of its inmates in 1793, was the home of religion and learning, the seminary of glorious martyrs and confessors, who went forth to gather together those among their fellow countrymen, who, wandering from the fold and left without shepherds, were dispersed through the desert places of heresy and schism. With this object in view, and in order to console and minister to the spiritual wants of their afflicted Catholic brethren, clad in the armour of God, they courageously undertook their mission, in spite of the cruel edicts of the rulers in high places, and were ready even to suffer death and to undergo the severest tortures and torments.

"*Cæduntur gladiis more bidentium ;*"

and on the rack, the gibbet, and the scaffold, they offered up their lives without murmur or complaint, for the sake of faith and fatherland. Like the grain of wheat cast into the earth and left to decay, the blood of the martyrs had a principle of vitality, a germinating power which fructified and produced a harvest of saints, and which, in course of revolving years, will, it is to be hoped, attach England to the centre of Catholic truth and unity, and cause her once more to become the joyful mother of children—"*matrem filiorum lætantem.*" Then will England be truly glorious—*tunc habitabit gloria in terra nostra ;*—then will those nations and peoples who have kept the faith, and maintained their allegiance to the mother and mistress of churches—"of all nations and all times that wonderful church of Rome"—rejoice in the blossoming of her second spring, and welcome her return to the religion of her forefathers.

Among the pictures that adorn the walls of the college ambulacra, there hangs in the west ambulacrum an old engraving of the venerable college of Douai. Often have I stood looking at this picture, recalling and pondering over the scenes, events, and incidents which, from the date of its foundation 1568 by our illustrious countryman, to its confiscation and downfall on the 12th day of October, 1793, during the presidentship of the Rev. John Daniel, I represented to myself as having taken place in that renowned and hallowed domicile, where the English youths—the *flores martyrum*—were trained and taught to suffer all things even death itself, for the sake of Christ—*omnia pati pro Christo.* As above stated, I have frequently stood gazing at this picture, and on one occasion there stood with me the late Major Myles O'Reilly, an old Ushaw student, looking as intently as myself at the engraving which revived so many reverent memories of Douai, and of its saintly heroes—the confessors and martyrs, who having trod the wine press of sorrow and suffering, and endured patiently unto the end, received as their reward a crown of glory and honour—*gloria et honore coronasti eos, Domine.* At the bottom of the picture is the inscription *Alma Mater Duacena.* Between the words *Alma Mater* and *Duacena* is an escutcheon or shield, charged with a St. George's cross ; and at the top of the shield is represented the device of an escalop shell. On each side of the same shield is a palm-branch, and on a ribbon border at its foot the legend "*Perenne quæ fert gaudium.*" One end of the border has the figures 15, the other 68, the date of Douai's foundation. The object which this engraving purposes to have is laudably set forth in the inscription underneath it—*Ne pereunte aliquando Domus fabrica, intereat etiam ipsius memoria majorumque religionis insigne monumentum.*

To the pilgrim journeying to the Holy Land the cross which he assumed was the mainspring of his hope—*ave crux spes unica*, and a source to him of endless joy —*perenne quæ fert gaudium.* The escalop shell, when placed on the top of a shield, is not a part of the coat of arms: used in christian art, it signifies pilgrimage. It was the usual badge or emblem of pilgrims, and was taken to serve all purposes, of cup, dish, and spoon ; and attached to the flap of the wide-brimmed shadowing hat, was adopted by pilgrims as part of their costume, and was a natural and obvious convenience. The palm-branch which the pilgrim brought back was significative of the toils, dangers, and hardships he had encountered and overcome, and the deeds of high emprise he had performed :—

> The faded palm-branch in his hand
> Show'd pilgrim from the Holy Land. —*Scott.*

Among the "Miscellaneous Poems" of Mrs. Hemans is one entitled "The Palmer," who, being asked what he had brought from Palestine, makes this reply :—

> I have brought but the palm-branch in my hand,
>   Yet I call not my bright youth lost ;
> I have won but high thought in the Holy Land,
>   Yet I count not too dear the cost !
>
> I look on the leaves of the deathless tree—
>   These records of my track ;
> And better than youth in its flush of glee,
>   Are the memories they give back.
>
> They speak of toil and high emprise,
>   As in words of solemn cheer ;
> They speak of lonely victories
>   O'er pain, and doubt, and fear.
>
> A rich light thence o'er my life's decline,
>   An inborn light is cast ;
> For the sake of the palm from the holy shrine,
>   I bewail not my bright days past.

In another of her poems, "The Crusader's Return," occurs the following passage :—

> Rest, pilgrim, rest ! thou'rt from the Syrian land,
>   Thou'rt from the wild and wond'rous east, I know
> By the long wither'd palm-branch in thy hand,
>   And by the darkness of thy sunburnt brow.

BISHOP O'CALLAGHAN VISITS USHAW:

Receives a Cordial and Affectionate Welcome.

The *Tablet*, April 7, 1888, informs its readers that "The ceremonies of Holy Week at Ushaw derived in the year 1888 additional interest and splendour from the fact that the Right Rev. Dr. O'Callaghan paid his first visit to the college in order to take part in them, and sang Pontifical High Mass for the first time in his new diocese. The Bishop, accompanied by his Vicar-General, the Very Rev. Canon Wilkinson, arrived at the college on the Wednesday afternoon, but as the students were in retreat, there was no formal reception. The retreat ended on the Thursday morning with the General Communion, and at nine o'clock the Bishop sang High Mass and consecrated the holy oils. Those who have seen this solemn ceremony carried out as it is at Ushaw, with all the splendour with which the Church invests it, and with the strict attention to rubrical details for which Ushaw is famous, will easily understand the impression it must have made both upon the Bishop who performed it for the first time, and upon the students who then saw the throne that had been so long vacant filled at length by a worthy successor to their own St. Cuthbert. The Bishop wore upon his finger St. Cuthbert's ring which is preserved at the college as a priceless treasure, and which, though used as a rule only at ordinations, was worn on this occasion as a token of his rightful succession to St. Cuthbert's throne. In the evening the Bishop was informed of the earnest desire of the students to give him a true Ushaw welcome, and he at once complied with their request. The front ambulacrum was filled with an excited throng, and as soon as his Lordship appeared upon the stairs all knelt to receive his blessing, and then round after round of hearty cheers testified that though till that moment he had been a stranger to them, he was to be so no longer, but was to be received into their hearts, and to take his place there along with his venerated predecessors whose names are so dear to every Ushaw man. When silence had been restored, the Bishop addressed the students. Thanking them for the warm welcome they had given him, he said that he regarded it as a happy omen that the day upon which he performed his first episcopal ceremony at St. Cuthbert's College was the anniversary of the very day on which he came into the world. He spoke of the regard in which he had ever held the college, and his desire to do everything in his power to promote its welfare. He exhorted the students to practise the virtues which ought to distinguish a student's life, and to take advantage of the opportunities which were then before them. In conclusion, he asked their prayers for himself and the arduous work which had been laid upon him. An allusion to a play-day in his honour, for which he asked the President to make arrangements, raised another storm of cheering, in the midst of which he withdrew. On Friday the Bishop assisted on the throne at the Mass of the pre-sanctified, and in the afternoon at *Tenebræ*."

This declaration on the part of the good Bishop was received with warm-hearted and sympathetic applause, and was most encouraging to the Superiors, learned Professors, and Students of St. Cuthbert's. It was a pronouncement that rejoiced all hearts, and was hailed as a happy augury for *Alma Mater*. Hence to all, who had become acquainted with the learned and amiable Prelate, it was a source of extreme regret that in consequence of delicate health, and the responsibilities of so extensive and important a diocese as that of Hexham and Newcastle, Bishop O'Callaghan was compelled to repair to Rome, shortly before the "lovely feast" of Whitsuntide, and ask, if not permitted to resign the episcopal office, to have a' Bishop Auxiliary appointed, to aid him in the administration of the diocese. The northern climate, with its cold piercing east winds and "eager nipping air," could not, as was apprehended, be otherwise than most trying to a person, who for twenty years and upwards had resided in fair sunny Italy,

" *Ver ubi longum, tepidasque præbet*
Jupiter brumas ;—"

that land of beauty, of vineyards and olive groves, the classic land of poets and artists, of Dante and Petrarch, of Michael Angelo and Raphael. It is the sincere wish and earnest prayer of all, that, after a season of quiet and repose, his Lordship's health may be so far improved as to enable him to take up his abode in the patrimony of St. Cuthbert, there to be helped by the prayers of that blessed Saint and Bishop, and by those of the other great prelates and Saints of Northumbria.

PROVOST WILKINSON; HIS APPOINTMENT AND CONSECRATION AS BISHOP AUXILIARY.

Not long after Bishop O'Callaghan's arrival at Rome, it was announced that a Bishop Auxiliary, the Very Rev. Provost Wilkinson, had been appointed to assist in the government of the diocese, with the territorial title of Bishop of Cisamus *in partibus infidelium* (the island of Crete). The new Prelate, on the death of Provost Consitt, was elected Vicar-Capitular by the Chapter, and when Dr. O'Callaghan succeeded to the vacant See of Hexham and Newcastle, he was appointed Vicar-General of the diocese, and Provost of the Cathedral Chapter. Bishop Wilkinson, who belonged to an influential Durham family, was brought up in the Church of England. In or about the year 1847 he became a Catholic, and went to St. Mary's College, Oscott, to pursue his studies in theology, where, on December 23rd, 1848, he was ordained priest by the late Cardinal Wiseman. After his ordination he was appointed to a mission at Wolsingham; there he built a church, not far from his father's residence, Harperley Park, Co. Durham. He was subsequently transferred to the neighbouring mission of Crook, and, as a virtuous and godly priest, he laboured indefatigably and successfully, until his health became impaired, and he was obliged to retire from missionary work. St. Cuthbert's College was well known to the Bishop Auxiliary; he was a frequent visitor there; and enjoyed the esteem and friendship of the late Right Rev. Dr. Newsham. It is not necessary therefore to commend the interests of " our glorious college" to his protectorate and patronage.

Inured to the climate, and born in the Bishoprick, where a great part of his life had been passed, he is thoroughly acquainted with the ways, and manners, and habits of the people committed to his care, and they, on their part, will the more, on that account, esteem him, and confide in him.

"Bishop Wilkinson," says the Newcastle *Daily Chronicle*, "is a North countryman of the best type, and no stranger hereabouts. He is the scion of a Durham county family, well known and much esteemed by rich and poor. Amiable, accomplished, and good, his Lordship is worthy to be a helper to Dr. O'Callaghan, and to succeed the men eminent for their wisdom and virtues who have preceded him in the See of Hexham and Newcastle." All his friends and all priests in the diocese cordially unite in wishing that the good Bishop's life and episcopacy may be prolonged *ad multos annos*.

The impressive and imposing ceremony of his consecration took place on the Feast of St. James, the Apostle, July 25th. His Lordship elected to be consecrated, and meet it was that he should do so, at St. Cuthbert's College, Ushaw, in which the Bishops of Hexham and Newcastle have a great and paramount interest. "There never was a time," observed Bishop Hedley, who preached on the occasion, "when the unction of the Holy One was poured out more solemnly than at the consecration of a bishop." The rites, ceremonies, and sacred functions of the church are in few places carried out with greater rubrical exactness, solemnity, and magnificence, than at this noble college; and the splendour and completeness, with which the ceremonial of the new Bishop's consecration was invested, was no exception to the manner in which at Ushaw the solemn ceremonies of the ritual are accustomed to be performed. Besides the officiating Bishops and Priests, and the Canons of the Cathedral Chapter, most of the clergy of the diocese attended; and several of the relatives and friends of the Bishop Auxiliary were present at the ceremony. The undernamed Archbishops and Bishops assisted at the sacred function :—The Hon. and Right Rev. W. Clifford, D.D., Bishop of Clifton, Consecrating Bishop; the Most Rev. Charles Eyre, D.D., Archbishop of Glasgow, and the Right Rev. A. Riddell, D.D., Bishop of Northampton, Assistant Bishops; the Most Rev. W. Smith, D.D., Archbishop of St. Andrews and Edinburgh, with chaplain; the Right Rev. J. C. Hedley, D.D., Bishop of Newport and Menevia, with chaplain. The Right Rev. Mgr. Charles Gillow, was Assistant Priest, and the Rev. R. C. Laing, one of the College Professors, officiated as Master of Ceremonies, which under his direction were most effectively conducted.

This is the seventh episcopal consecration which has taken place at Ushaw; the first on June 29th, 1824, when Bishop Penswick was raised to the episcopate, as co-adjutor to Bishop Smith, Vicar-Apostolic of the Northern District; Bishops Briggs, Mostyn, Riddell, Hogarth, and Chadwick were also there consecrated.

The presence of one or more Bishops at Ushaw used in past times to guarantee a series of play-days in honour of as many of them as, on any particular occasion, were assembled at the college. Has the good old custom lapsed into desuetude? I hope not.

At the conclusion of the ceremony the two archbishops, the newly consecrated bishop, and the three bishops, the clergy, and a number of the friends and guests to whom invitations had been addressed, sat down to luncheon in the spacious dining hall. Dr. Lennon, the president of the college, in the chair. The entertainment was provided with that bounteous hospitality for which Ushaw is noted.

Bishop CLIFFORD proposed the health of the newly consecrated Bishop. Every one must feel that it was an advantage to the diocese that Bishop Wilkinson, who was held in high esteem, had been raised to the episcopate.

Bishop WILKINSON in response proposed the health of their Lordships, the Bishops, who had come to assist on that occasion. It was a matter of special satisfaction to him that the heads of the Roman Catholic Church in Scotland were there. The Archbishops of Glasgow and St. Andrews and Edinburgh had crossed the Border—formerly they used to cross the Border for other purposes—but now they crossed it with a message of peace. He had known Archbishop Eyre intimately during the forty years of his priesthood, and he had come there that day to his great joy. It was a great joy to have an Ushaw man amongst them—an Ushaw man that they might be proud of. Ushaw was proud of him. He coupled with the toast the names of Dr. Clifford and Archbishop Eyre.

Dr. CLIFFORD having briefly replied,

Archbishop EYRE said that in the name of the Bishops of Scotland he expressed their exceeding indebtedness for the kind way in which the toast had been received. He was sure when the Bishops of Scotland read the papers and saw that on a festive occasion like that they had been so kindly remembered it would warm their hearts more than ever, if it was possible, towards this side of the Border. The Border at one time was an impenetrable barrier between them, but at present it was reduced to those insignificant streams, the Tweed and the Eden. They (the Archbishop and Dr. Wilkinson) had worked together for a long time. He might say they had "lived and loved together." He would like to express his devoted attachment to the College of Ushaw. He went there, a very little boy, in the year 1826, and remained there thirteen years, so that they could imagine how deeply rooted his affection for the college was. He would also like to express his undying love for the Diocese of Hexham and Newcastle. He commenced work there in the year 1843, and remained there for thirty years. He had since been twenty years in Scotland, and he thought many of them would consider it was high time he retired altogether. He was very sensible of the kind feeling which prompted Bishop Wilkinson to ask him to be an assistant in the ceremony that day, but he felt there was another tie, and that the man who hailed from Thistleflat House had done well in asking one who came from that country where the national emblem was the thistle.

Dr. WILKINSON then gave "Success and every blessing of the good God and St. Cuthbert on that great college." He paid a high compliment to the richness of the adornments of the chapel, and the exquisite taste displayed in their arrangement, and to the wonderful hospitality with which they had been received. They all, whatever their religious belief, loved the college, and wished it success.

Dr. LENNON expressed, on behalf of himself and the other professors, the great satisfaction they felt in seeing Dr. Wilkinson in the position he occupied that day. He had long been connected with them, and though living without its walls, he was really and truly one of them, and was always at their gatherings. The professors had desired to do all in their power to make his consecration a success in every possible way. They in the college, with one voice, wished him many happy days. They wished from the depths of their hearts that he might have strength and power to accomplish the work set before him. He had to propose another toast in the health of the visitors, who had honoured Bishop Wilkinson and the college with their presence that day. The toast having been drunk with due honour, the proceedings terminated.

NORTHUMBERLAND AS DESCRIBED BY FROISSART.

Bishop Wilkinson, I doubt not, is well read in the topographical history both of Durham and Northumberland, and, in the course of his reading, may have met with the short graphic description which Froissart gives of what Northumberland was like at the end of the 14th century. He describes the country as being "a savage and wylde countrey, full of desarts and mountaignes, and a right pore countrey of everything, saving of beestis, and through the whiche there runneth a ryver, full of flynt and great stones, called the ryver of Tyne." But since the days of old Froissart a wonderful and unmistakeable transformation has been wrought through the whole length and breadth of Northumberland. From Tweed to Tyne the desert places have been brought into cultivation—looking fair with crops of golden corn; while the hill sides and irriguous valleys abound in grass and herbage, and afford ample pasturage for the flocks and herds there grazing. A peaceful, law-abiding, and industrious population—unused to the feuds and frays, so common among them in times past, inhabit the country; and the Tyne, converted into a magnificent estuary, on whose banks might be counted twelve or fourteen miles of valuable factories, and on its waters rich freights of merchandise, flows with abounding stream through a busy populous city, the centre of industry and commerce, of scientific skill, engineering and mining activity.

I quote from Akenside, the poet, who was born at Newcastle-on-Tyne, and wrote the "Pleasures of Imagination," the following passage:—

        O ye dales
Of Tyne, and ye most ancient woodlands; where
Oft as the giant flood obliquely strides,
And his banks open and his lawns extend,

Stops short the pleaséd traveller to view,
Presiding o'er the scene, some rustic tower
Founded by Norman or by Saxon hands:
O ye Northumbrian shades, which overlook
The rocky pavement and the mossy falls
Of solitary Wansbeck's limpid stream!
How gladly I recall your well-known seats,
Beloved of old, and that delightful time
When all alone, for many a summer's day
I wandered through your calm recesses.

MINOR INCIDENTS, EVENTS, AND USAGES.

No one, I apprehend, will hesitate to acknowledge that Ushaw has a history, and is not without numerous venerable and cherished traditions. An institution—school or college—which has no traditions, no monuments of historic interest, has few claims to recommend it. Having, however, already traversed a large extent of ground—

"*Jam nos immensum spatiis confecimus æquor.*"

I must be permitted to pass over many minor incidents, events, and usages connected with college life at Ushaw, and the associations and reminiscences interwoven with them. I omit any detailed account of religious and secular celebrations occurring at stated periods; of festive gatherings, and the good old songs and lays of Ushaw minstrels—

——" Sing aloud
Old songs, the precious music of the heart."

I pass over likewise the dramatical and musical entertainments; the Shakspearian and other readings; dialogues, debates, and recitations; the various sports, games, and pastimes; rival football, cat, and cricket matches, and the surprising prowess, skill, and dexterity displayed at them. Nor are the feats and performances of Ushaw skaters less remarkable. There are few Ushaw boys who have not learnt to skate, and all take delight in that healthful recreation. Seldom also is a skating play-day refused, when applied for in the season.

LONDON UNIVERSITY MATRICULATION EXAMINATIONS:

USHAW PRE-EMINENTLY SUCCESSFUL.

Having brought down to the most recent date the *memorabilia* of Ushaw's interesting history, I would, before concluding my narration, respectfully beg to offer most hearty congratulations to those studious youths—"heroes," said Bishop Wilkinson, "should he call them, who had so bravely upheld the character of their *Alma Mater*, in those very difficult and trying examinations of the London University." Fifteen of these "heroes" contended in the Matriculation Examination of 1888, and fifteen were pre-eminently successful, deserving to be saluted with an "*Io triumphe!*" One of the students obtained the third place in the Honours List, with an exhibition; another a tenth place and the third prize; and in the same list the fourteenth and sixty-fourth places respectively were assigned to Ushaw, which thus passed four in Honours, nine in the First, and two in the Second Division; total 15.

Having done signal credit to yourselves, and honour to the noble college where you are being educated, permit me, ingenuous youths, to exhort you to persevere, and to apply with renewed diligence to the course of studies which is each year marked out for you, in order that Ushaw's prestige may be maintained, and your own well earned success be an example and encouragement to others among your fellow students. Pursue your career therefore manfully and courageously, remembering that in whatever sphere of life your lines may be cast, there will be giants to encounter, foes to conquer, dangers to face, enticements to shun, and the blandishments of the world and its votaries to guard against. *Viriliter ergo agite, vosque Deus juvet, instruat, et custodiat.*

See under the head "Ushaw College and the London University," page 296, account of Ushaw's successes at previous compctitive Examinations.

CONCLUSION.

On one side of the road leading from Ushaw to Durham stands an ancient boundary stone, having the words " Here ends Ash Chapelry" inscribed upon it; and here end my " Records and Recollections" of St. Cuthbert's College, Ushaw.

Nunc perventum est ad finem metamque laborum ;

"so I will here make an end of my narration; which, if I have done well and as it becometh the history, it is what I desired ; but if not so perfectly, it must be pardoned me." My task, though performed less ably than I could have wished, was undertaken for the sake of gathering together, preserving and perpetuating the scattered traditions and lingering memories of "our glorious college." In compiling this history, I have questioned the visions of the past, have ransacked the archives of former generations, and searched diligently whatever historical fragments and memorials relating to bygone times had been preserved and handed down to us. I applied, moreover, to, and sought information and assistance from those friends and acquaintances who, I considered, might be able to supply it. To quote from St. Basil—" *Velut apes non omnibus floribus insidunt, neque ex eis, ad quos accedunt, omnia auferre conantur ; sed quantum ipsis ad opus suum necessarium fuerit, comprehendentes, reliquum dimittunt, ita nos sobrii, sapientesque, quidquid est utile carpentes, noxium vitemus.*"—St. Basil.

To this counsel I have endeavoured to adhere, omitting from these records whatever might be deemed prejudicial, frivolous, or hurtful. Therefore, " *Jam faustis eat auspiciis libellus, et plurimos, si fieri potest, patronos et fautores sibi quærat ;*" and having howbeit unskilfully done our part, and made an end of our narration, "*quid cælum petimus ultra ?*"

ADIEU.

Dear Ushaw, with years and life's burden oppress'd,
'Neath thy yew tree how peaceful and calm could I rest ;
There, there I could wish, at my life's final close,
'Mong the friends of my youth in the grave to repose.

Asylum of virtue and learning, adieu !
To thee may thy sons remain constant and true ;
And whatever their lot and their fortune may be,
May they turn with endearing affection to thee.

Nor let those who taught them in boyhood and youth,
Who guided their steps unto wisdom and truth,
Be ever effaced from their heart and their mind,
But in grateful remembrance be kept there enshrined.

FINIS.

ADDENDA.

ADDENDA.

AN ODE ON PATIENCE:

TO SISTER CLARA DALTON, CARMELITE NUN AT COCKEN.

By the Rev. John Lingard, D.D.

On Carmel's sacred summit grows
   A flower of beauteous form :
'Mid summer heats and winter snows
   It still braves every storm.

Its colour vies with those that shine
   On seraph's radiant wings,
Its odours every sweet combine,
   That Saba's zephyr brings.

Yet know ; to pluck this beauteous rose
   Requires a timid hand :
To guard it thorns, in thick'ning rows,
   Around luxuriant stand.

It's name is *Patience*—heaven-born flower ;
   Affliction's choicest guest !
Let Clara pierce the thorny bower,
   And plant it in her breast.

And then, should care, disease, and pain,
   Attempt to shake her peace,
Patience will view them with disdain,
   And bid each murmur cease.

By Patience to the sorrowing heart
   The martyr's crown is given—
Patience assuages every smart,
   And lifts the soul to heaven.

   The above was copied from the original preserved among a number of letters addressed by Dr. Lingard to the late Rev. Richard Gillow, who died at Newhouse, November 3rd, 1867.

   Sister Clara Dalton, to whom the Ode is addressed, belonged to the old Catholic family of the Daltons of Thurnham, and was a Carmelite nun at the Convent, Cocken Hall, Co. Durham, occupied, previous to their removal to Carmel House, Darlington, by the Carmelites or Teresians. Dr. Lingard's connection with and affection for Ushaw, together with his renowned literary and historical attainments, cannot fail, in the eyes of the alumni of St. Cuthbert's and others, to stamp with especial interest any production of his learned pen. Hence I insert among "Addenda" this hitherto unpublished "Ode to Patience."

COURSE OF STUDIES AT USHAW.

The Studies are arranged in three Courses, the Lower, the Higher, and the University Course.

The Lower Course provides elementary instruction for those who enter at an early age. It embraces the study of the English Language so far as to enable a pupil to acquire accuracy and facility in Composition, a complete course of Arithmetic, the outlines of Bible History, of English History, and Modern Geography, the study of French and Latin Grammar, and of easy authors in those Languages. The students in this course occupy a separate portion of the college buildings, where the hours of study and other arrangements are adapted to their age.

The Higher Course embraces the study of the Greek Language, of Algebra and Geometry, and of the Histories of Greece and Rome, in addition to the further study of the English, French, and Latin Languages, of the History of England, and Modern Geography, with continued practice in English Composition.

The University Course by which these studies are followed and completed is arranged for a period of four years. In it is embodied the curriculum of the London University for a Degree in Arts. In the first year the whole class is prepared for Matriculation. The second and third years are spent in the preparation of the subjects required for the Intermediate Examination in Arts and the B.A. Examination. The fourth year is devoted to the study of Metaphysics and Moral Philosophy.

These general studies are succeeded in the case of those who are studying for the Church by a course of Theology.

Quid majus, quam animis moderari, quam adolescentulorum fingere mores? Omni certe pictore, omni certe statuario, cæterisque hujusmodi omnibus, excellentiorem hunc duco, qui juvenum animos fingere non ignoret.—S. Joan. Chrysost.

ODE.

"OUR COLLEGE HOME & HOLIDAYS."

A STRAIN WHICH USHAW HEARTS AND USHAW VOICES JOYFULLY RE-ECHO.

Chorus. Once more we gladly meet,
  To proclaim with song and cheer,—
 A hundred hearts will beat
  With rapture when they hear
 " The days of toil are past"
 " And the goal is won at last :"
  " These are our Holidays !"

Solo—Tenore. Yet ere we bid a short farewell
 To *Alma Mater*, let the swell
 Of our united voices tell
  The love we bear our College Home.

Chorus. Yes ! *Alma Mater* claims our love,
 Whate'er our lot may be,
 By word and deed we'll ever prove
  We love her faithfully.

Solo—Basso. Our hearts indeed are not less true
 To that dear home our childhood knew,
 Where friends and parents dwell,
 Yet is not our affection due
 To this our *Alma Mater* too ?
Chorus. She cherished us as well.

Chorus. What name will best our love declare ?
Solo. List ! echo says " our Home,"
Chorus. What name should *Alma Mater* bear,
 But this " our College Home ?"

Solo—Soprano. She kept us safe from every ill
 In boyhood's days, and guards us still
  With all a mother's care ;
 She guided us in all our ways,
 Taught us our minds and hearts to raise
  To Heaven, and fix them there.

Chorus. She guided us in all our ways,
 Taught us our minds and hearts to raise
  To Heaven, and fix them there.

Chorus. Yet *Alma Mater* will not blame,
 If joyfully we raise
 Our voices in loud chorus to proclaim
  Our Holidays,
 These are our Holidays !

CORRIGENDA.

Page 41, line 7, *for* universe *read* unwise.

Page 41, line 21, *for* Anglo-Saxon monastery *read* Celtic monastery.

Page 58, line 39, *for* 4,500 *read* 40,000.

Page 61, line 11, *for* last summer *read* a few summers ago.

Page 137, line 16, *for* revered *read* reverend.

Page 149, line 2, *for* Bedford *read* Shefford.

Page 222, line 26, *for* Jerome Æmillan *read* Jerome Æmilian.

Page 237, line 35, *add after* names, how delightful the occupation.

Page 271, line 37, *for* Bonaventure *read* Boniface.

The Rev. John Glover was never, as stated at page 270, on the mission at Sheffield. In 1860 he removed from Houghton Hall to Whitby, from which mission he retired in 1874, and died in 1878. It was his nephew, the Very Rev. Canon Glover, of Carlton, who was at Sheffield, which he left in 1867.

I had hoped that with the preceding *Addenda* and *Corrigenda* these "Records" would have been completed, and I was preparing to place the book in the hands of the binder. Let me explain how it has otherwise happened. Having sent to Carmel House, Darlington, a copy of Dr. Lingard's "Ode on Patience," a misprint in the third stanza was pointed out to me, viz., "*a* timid," instead of "*no* timid hand." The good Religious in calling my attention to the misprint, says: "I enclose another Ode composed by the same learned and holy Priest for our Community, whose great friend he was in the first portion of this century. *This* is a copy, written by the Mother Mary Clare (Dalton), for whom he composed that 'On Patience,' for she was a great sufferer.

Wishing every success to a work which must be highly prized by not only St. Cuthbert's Alumni, but all its friends,

I remain,
Yours faithfully in Christ,"

The Ode which is as follows, and which I have much pleasure in bringing under the notice of my readers, will be esteemed and treasured by all unto whom the memories of Ushaw are endeared, and by whom the name of Lingard, who was so closely identified with that college, is revered and cherished.

ODE
FOR THE FEAST OF THE GLORIOUS MOTHER, ST. TERESA.

Carmel rejoice, and hail the day,
   When closing to this world her eyes,
Teresa winged her spotless way
   To realms of never ending joys.

Ah! mark the path your Mother trod,
   Ye daughters of the sainted maid;
That path will lead you to your God,
   And to those joys which never fade.

Mark well her heart, that heart which glows
   With raptures of ecstatic love,
Nor yet its own perfections knows,
   Nor thinks of ought but God above.

See how around each virtue twines,
   Ambitious to adorn it best;
There hope, there resignation shines,
   Sweet calmer of the troubled breast.

Obedience too, the sure defence
   Against the wily tempter's aim;
And sweetly smiling innocence
   That thinks no harm and knows no shame.

With charity which bleeds to see
   That man can dare to offend his God;
And wills to bear, on bended knee,
   For others' sins the chast'ning rod.

Loved parent of the virgin train,
   Enrich'd with each celestial grace,
Give us through life t'avoid each stain,
   And faithfully thy footsteps trace.

Leaning from thy throne above,
   Grant us the blessing we implore;
With thee to suffer and to love,
   Is all we wish, we ask *no more*.

www.ingramcontent.com/pod-product-compliance
Lightning Source LLC
Chambersburg PA
CBHW032049220426
43664CB00008B/921